The Road to Number 10

The Road to Number 10
From Bonar Law to Tony Blair

ALAN WATKINS

> Why, damn it all, such a position was never held by
> any Greek or Roman: and if it only lasts three
> months, it will be worthwhile to have been Prime
> Minister of England.
>
> Tom Young to Lord Melbourne, quoted
> in David Cecil, *Lord M*

Duckworth

To the memory of
three of my former editors
Richard Crossman, John Junor and Iain Macleod

Second impression May 1998
First published in March 1998 by
Gerald Duckworth & Co. Ltd.
The Old Piano Factory
48 Hoxton Square, London N1 6PB
Tel: 0171 729 5986
Fax: 0171 729 0015

A catalogue record for this book
is available from the British Library

ISBN 0 7156 2815 1 (hbk)
ISBN 0 7156 2883 6 (pbk)

Typeset by Ray Davies
Printed in Great Britain by
Redwood Books Ltd, Trowbridge

Contents

Acknowledgments

My principal debt is to Julia Mount, who put my handwritten manuscript on to a word processor speedily and accurately. Ferdinand Mount read the text and made several valuable suggestions. Robert Blake did the same and made even more equally valuable comments. John Griffith, John Grigg, Robert Harris and Geoffrey Wheatcroft helped me by answering various questions. Anthony Howard both answered my questions and lent me some of his books. The staff of the Library of Lincoln's Inn were unfailingly helpful. Clare Bartley of the *Independent on Sunday* retrieved Harold Macmillan's 1963 memorandum to the Queen which first appeared in that newspaper and is reproduced as Appendix B. Deborah Blake of Duckworth and my agent Giles Gordon were as encouraging as ever. To all of these I am grateful. I am solely responsible for any mistakes.

Alan Watkins

Introduction

How matter presses on me!
What stubborn things are facts
William Hazlitt, *Table-Talk*

This book is about how politicians become Prime Minister or leader of their party, from Bonar Law to Tony Blair. Its theme is the rise of party democracy during this period and the consequential diminution in the royal prerogative to choose the Prime Minister – a change welcomed at the Palace.

Conservative leaders have, in this century, tended to become Prime Ministers; Labour leaders have tended not to. Of the 13 Labour leaders since the end of the First World War, five – Ramsay MacDonald, C.R. Attlee, Harold Wilson, James Callaghan and Tony Blair – have been made Prime Minister. Of the 12 Conservative leaders in the same period, only Austen Chamberlain and, so far, William Hague have failed to reach 10 Downing Street. Of these 12, two, Neville Chamberlain in 1937-40 and Alec Douglas-Home in 1963-4, found themselves in the same position as James Callaghan in 1976-9 and occupied No. 10 without having been put there by the voters. The choice by the Crown of Chamberlain to succeed Stanley Baldwin was uncontroversial. The choice of Douglas-Home (rather than R.A. Butler) to succeed Harold Macmillan aroused and still arouses a good deal of dispute. Callaghan, by contrast, was elected by the Parliamentary Labour Party after Wilson had resigned in 1976.

The Conservatives did not introduce a system of election until 1965. Before then the party leader was effectively chosen by the Crown because the Crown appointed the Prime Minister. Despite the party's reputation for ruthlessness over its leaders, not one of the party's leaders in 1918-65 was chosen while it was in opposition (for in 1922 the Conservatives had been part of the Lloyd George coalition from which they withdrew). The only leaders to have been chosen in these circumstances were Edward Heath, Margaret Thatcher and William Hague. Though Baldwin, Winston Churchill, Anthony Eden and Harold Macmillan all (unlike Chamberlain and Douglas-Home) won general elections, they owed their pre-eminence to an antecedent decision by the Sovereign.

Thus George V preferred Baldwin to Lord Curzon in 1923. George VI did not exactly prefer Churchill either to Chamberlain or to Lord Halifax

in 1940. Ideally he would have liked Chamberlain to continue, as head of
a coalition government rather than of a nominally national government
which was for all practical purposes Conservative. But he was forced to
take Churchill. Though Chamberlain remained formally leader of the
Conservative Party till autumn 1940, Churchill became the real leader by
becoming Prime Minister. Elizabeth II appointed Eden, the expected
choice, in 1955, as her grandfather had appointed Chamberlain, the
expected choice, in 1937 – though the former appointment was a longer
drawn out affair. She appointed Macmillan rather than Butler in 1957.

The one exception, perhaps more apparent than real, was provided by
Bonar Law in 1922. When George V asked him to be Prime Minister after
the fall of David Lloyd George, he insisted, rather to the King's irritation,
on being first elected by his party. The four disputed successions since
then – Baldwin in 1923, Churchill in 1940, Macmillan in 1957 and
Douglas-Home in 1963 – all involved the Conservatives. In 1931 a Labour
Prime Minister, MacDonald, succeeded himself as Prime Minister of an
ostensibly national government.

Part I of this book deals with the old system, when the Monarch could
exercise some choice. Part II gives an account of the various forms of
democracy which have always existed in the Labour Party: the exhaustive
ballot of MPs until 1981, the electoral college of 1981-93 which produced
Neil Kinnock and John Smith, and the new electoral college (only partially
based on one member, one vote) which produced Tony Blair. Part III is
about the new system which started with the Conservative Party's democratisation of 1963-5. The book ends with a chapter on the dissolution of
Parliament.

There have been no disputed successions since the Conservative Party
democratised itself. This is not to ignore episodes such as the resignation
of Harold Wilson in 1976 and the removal of Margaret Thatcher in 1990.
But on each occasion the transmission of office to James Callaghan and
John Major respectively proved constitutionally uncontroversial and free
of trouble. The power of the Crown has been superseded by – has, indeed,
been willingly surrendered to – the power of the party.

The nature of the parties is, however, changing. For 15 years after 1965,
both operated a system where their members of Parliament did the
choosing. The period produced Michael Foot as party leader; Edward
Heath and Margaret Thatcher as party leader and subsequently Prime
Minister; James Callaghan and John Major as Prime Minister. But the
movement is now towards mass democracy both in the Labour Party
(where a true system of one member, one vote can be only a matter of time)
and among the Conservatives as well. Inevitably this will place greater
power in the hands of the press and television. A candidate will be better
placed if he or she receives favourable publicity and is or, anyway, is
thought to be 'good on television'. Both conditions were satisfied when
Blair succeeded Smith as leader of the Labour Party in 1994.

Clearly, one danger is that the party's MPs will have imposed on them a politician who is not their first or perhaps even their second choice. The Labour Party managed to avoid this not only when Blair was chosen but when Kinnock and Smith were elected under a different franchise. The party was in this respect lucky. It may not be so lucky in future. Nor may the Conservatives, if they change their system, as they seem almost certain to do. If John Major's successor had been chosen by the whole party, it would almost certainly have been Kenneth Clarke (contrary to the expectations of most commentators) rather than William Hague, who was preferred to Clarke by his parliamentary colleagues. There may be trouble in store all round.

Part I

The Old System

1

Customary Processes

It is not a principle of the Conservative Party to stab its leaders in the back, but I must confess that it often appears to be a practice.

A.J. Balfour, after the Carlton Club meeting, 1922

This chapter is concerned with an era in our constitutional life which now seems as remote as that of the Exclusion Crisis in the 17th century, when the Whigs tried to keep James II from the Throne. It is the period when the Monarch could exercise the royal prerogative and use a discretion in appointing a Prime Minister. It lasted until 1964, when Harold Wilson succeeded Lord Home. As this book is concerned with modern politics, the appointment of Bonar Law in 1922 is taken as the start of the period. This is to some extent arbitrary: but the first peacetime Prime Minister, following the reign of the war leader David Lloyd George, seems as appropriate a person as any with whom to start.

Some constitutional authorities, notably Lord St John of Fawsley, would maintain that the period has not truly come to an end, even now. According to this view, the discretion which the Sovereign used to possess in the appointment of the Prime Minister still exists. Thus the process of election which the Conservative Party introduced in 1965, and which the Labour Party has always maintained, is advisory rather than binding. Election has so far produced two Prime Ministers, as distinct from party leaders in opposition: James Callaghan as successor to Harold Wilson in 1976, and John Major as successor to Margaret Thatcher in 1990.

By all accounts, the Queen was delighted to have the decision made on her behalf, and showed no desire to use her prerogative powers: certainly not to use them merely to provide a demonstration of Lord St John's views of constitutional propriety. Indeed, if Her Majesty had chosen aberrantly to disregard the wishes of the MPs of the ruling party, the politician whom she chose would have refused to accept her invitation or would have been unable to form a government. Had he succeeded, the majority party in the Commons would have fragmented. One of these would certainly have happened if, say, Michael Foot, the runner-up to Callaghan, had been invited to form a government in 1976, or Michael Heseltine, the runner-up to Major, had been invited to form one in 1990.

Nevertheless, the precedents before 1964 could still prove important, if we had a Parliament in which no party held an absolute majority. In 1922 the problem was different.

BONAR LAW AND STANLEY BALDWIN 1922-3

As Lord Beaverbrook wrote, David Lloyd George was a Prime Minister without a party.[1] As Prime Minister of the coalition government which had been elected in 1918, he was the prisoner of the Conservatives. That was the year of the 'coupon election'. Many persons, otherwise well-informed, but with their experience formed by the Second World War and its aftermath, have the vague idea that this election was to do with rationing, privation and the civilian conditions of war. In a sense, certainly, it was: Lloyd George's bestowal of the coupon – the imprimatur of his personal approval – on selected Liberal candidates closely followed the support which he had received in the Maurice debate of 1918. These Members are often referred to as National Liberals. To avoid confusion with the Liberal Nationals who formed a group after the 1931 crisis, it is perhaps better to call them Coalition Liberals. After the 1918 election the strength of the parties had been: Coalition Unionist 335, Coalition Liberal 133, Coalition Labour 10, Conservative 23, Irish Unionist 25, Liberal 28, Labour 63, Irish Nationalist 7, Sinn Fein 73, Others 10.

The Conservatives withdrew because they distrusted their own leaders and disliked Lloyd George. In particular, they were apprehensive that as a Graecophile – who equated Greece, as he tended to equate all such countries, with Wales – Lloyd George was intent on a war with Turkey, a country which had already given Britain a bloody nose, and was in the course of effectively frustrating all the endeavours of the Allied peacemakers to determine its borders as they thought best.[2] Efforts have been made to reconstitute the reputation of the 1918 Coalition Government, notably by Kenneth O. Morgan.[3] Alas, it remains the government of the hard-faced men who looked as if they had done well out of the war. The phrase was originally Stanley Baldwin's. He had used it in conversation with J.M. Keynes when he was Financial Secretary to the Treasury, Keynes was a Treasury adviser and Baldwin first glimpsed the 1918 intake. Keynes subsequently used it, with partial acknowledgment, in *The Economic Consequences of the Peace*.[4]

It was Baldwin, not Bonar Law, who made the crucial speech at the Carlton Club meeting. He said that Lloyd George was described as a dynamic force, but that a dynamic force was a terrible thing. In March 1921 Law had resigned the leadership of the Conservative Party owing to ill-health. His place was taken by Austen Chamberlain. F.E. Smith said of Austen that he always played the game, and always lost it. He was the half-brother of the dyspeptic Neville and the son of the authoritarian Joe, who was certainly a dynamic force. Joe nearly destroyed two parties: the Liberals over Irish Home Rule, and the Conservatives over Tariff Reform.

In the twentieth century his record was equalled, even exceeded, by one other politician, David Owen, who almost destroyed Labour, and certainly destroyed the Social Democrats. Austen was not as fierce as either of these. He comes down to us as a man with an eyeglass and an orchid, at once supercilious and ineffectual.

As soon as the result of the Carlton Club meeting was declared, Chamberlain announced that he would have to consult with his friends. At the meeting itself, he had spoken against withdrawal from the coalition. Even so, he could have said that he remained leader of the party and, as a good democrat, accepted the party's decision. But it is not the Conservative way to say that you are a good democrat and accept the majority view. It never has been. It is not the way today, despite the 'democratisation' of the party under Margaret Thatcher and John Major. Meetings, elections, votes, majorities: they play little part in Conservative culture, as anyone knows who has studied the perplexity of Conservative MPs when they are confronted by an election of any description within their own party.

At five o'clock in the afternoon of 19 October 1922 Lloyd George went to Buckingham Palace and tendered his resignation.[5] It would still have been possible constitutionally for King George V to send for Austen Chamberlain. He did not do so. On the contrary: at the very moment when Lloyd George was taking his leave, the King's private secretary, Lord Stamfordham, was in communication with Law at his house, 24 Onslow Gardens, Kensington. First, Stamfordham telephoned Law and asked him to come at once to the Palace. Law 'demurred'.[6] Accordingly Stamfordham called on Law.

Law was a Scotch Ulsterman who had lived in Canada and had worked and been educated in Glasgow. He was a man of integrity whose iron firm had, however, been in trouble during the war for breach of certain regulations. He was loved and assisted financially by Lord Beaverbrook. His chief recreations were playing chess and smoking a pipe, which may have contributed to his death from cancer of the throat.

On this occasion he was in no mood to be any more obliging than he usually was. According to Stamfordham, he explained that he was not the Leader of the Conservative Party. The party was, for the moment, 'broken up'.[7] Until he knew that he could count on the party's undivided support, he could not accept office. Therefore it was indispensable that he should be present at a meeting of the representatives of the 'whole Conservative Party' where he could satisfy this condition and others – including one limiting his period of office to one year.

The King's private secretary was not used to being addressed in this fashion, certainly not by Canadian Ulstermen. He 'ventured to suggest' to Law that the King was sending for him 'independently of these party considerations' into which he 'did not enter'. Having accepted Lloyd George's resignation, the King had a duty to form a new government as soon as possible. In pursuance of this obligation he had to send for whomever he considered to be the proper person to carry out this 'great responsibility'.[8] Stamfordham used an additional argument. Not for the first or the last time, Ireland played a part in British domestic politics. He pointed out that, unless a new government were constituted immediately and elections held, it would be impossible to ratify the Irish Treaty by 6 December 1922 and that the treaty would accordingly lapse.[9] It is difficult to see why a new Parliament, as distinct from a new government, should have been necessary for ratification of this treaty to be effective. It is equally hard to understand why the King's private secretary thought it proper to advise – or instruct – a potential Prime Minister about the calling of a general election.

Law remained unmoved. He refused to take office until the party had elected him leader. Much telephoning followed between Onslow Gardens and Buckingham Palace. Eventually George V accepted the position but requested that Law should at least come and talk to him. Law drove to the Palace, where he promised to call a party meeting as soon as possible. Meanwhile he would consult with those who might help him form a government. It was agreed that the Court Circular should state 'the bare facts' that Lloyd George had resigned and that the King had granted an audience to Law.[10]

Harold Nicolson stated that Law 'was with no unnecessary delay re-elected Leader of the Conservative Party'.[11] This was an attempt to place the King in as dignified a light as possible – understandable enough in an official royal biographer writing in more deferential times than today's. It would have been possible to hold the Conservative meeting on Friday 20 October 1922 or on Saturday the 21st (for Saturday was then a working day). It was Monday 23 October before a meeting of Conservative peers, MPs and parliamentary candidates was held at the Hotel Cecil. Proposed by Curzon and seconded by Baldwin, Law was unanimously elected leader of the party. He immediately went to Buckingham Palace, where at 5.30 p.m. he was formally appointed Prime Minister and First Lord of the Treasury.[12] On 24 October he announced the names of the Cabinet. On 26 October Parliament was dissolved, and a general election fixed for 15 November 1922.

It was this election rather than the Carlton Club meeting which was responsible for the formation of what came to be known as the 1922 Committee. Under the leadership of Sir Gervais Rentoul, it was formed for the guidance and encouragement of new Conservative Members.[13] In May 1923 Bonar Law was mortally ill with cancer of the throat. He was to die on 30 October. On 20 May he wrote to George V tendering his resignation. The succession was complicated by several factors.

Law was too ill to make any recommendation personally to the King, even if he had wished to do so (which is doubtful). He resigned on Whit Sunday. His son-in-law, Sir Frederick Sykes, and his private secretary, Colonel Ronald Waterhouse, took his letter of resignation to the King.

They also carried with them a letter from Law's parliamentary private secretary, the supple Scotsman John Davidson.[14] Davidson's letter or memorandum strongly favoured the claims of Stanley Baldwin, the Leader of the House of Commons, over those of Lord Curzon, the Foreign Secretary. Law had nothing to do with it. Indeed, it misrepresented his views.[15] Throughout this period the King and Queen were staying for a week's visit at the Royal Pavilion, Aldershot, 'an unpretentious though comfortable wooden bungalow'.[16] Lord Stamfordham, the King's private secretary, returned alone to Buckingham Palace to take soundings.

The King thought that the new Prime Minister ought to be a member of the House of Commons.[17] He nevertheless believed he should consult some Privy Councillors. Lord Salisbury, the Lord President of the Council, was summoned from Devon and travelled up on the milk train. He considered that the claims of Curzon should not 'lightly be ignored'.[18] Walter Bridgeman, the Home Secretary, and Leo Amery, the First Lord of the Admiralty, favoured Baldwin. So did the former Prime Minister A.J. Balfour, who was summoned from his sickbed, ill with phlebitis, at Sheringham in Norfolk.

Balfour had two meetings with Stamfordham on 21 May. At the first he told the private secretary that the King should follow 'the obvious though not the inevitable course' and, in the first instance, ask the Leader of the House of Commons, Baldwin, to form a government. The 'apparent difficulty' was that Curzon was 'a man of greater age, greater experience and greater position' than Baldwin who, as far as Balfour was aware, 'had no special capacity as a parliamentarian'.[19] This was Balfour's own account of the meeting. In Stamfordham's account, he was even more dismissive of Baldwin's capacities. He said that he was speaking regardless of 'the individual in question'. On the one hand, his opinion of Curzon was based on 'an intimate, lifelong friendship, and the recognition of his exceptional qualifications' while, on the other, his knowledge of Baldwin was 'slight'. So far, his public career had been 'more or less uneventful' and 'without any signs of special gifts or exceptional ability'.[20]

He went on to say that there were 'several difficulties at the present time' in having a Prime Minister in the Lords. First, important Cabinet posts were already held by peers 'in a quite unusual proportion'. Second, to add a Prime Minister to the existing Secretaries of State in the Upper House would 'certainly be resented' by a 'a number of people' and might well render the position of the Leader of the Commons one of 'great difficulty'. And, third (Balfour made clear that he did not mention this objection, though it was in his mind), the present Opposition were the Labour Party, who had no representative at all in the Lords. He was told by Stamfordham that these views were 'probably in very close conformity' with the King's.[21]

Balfour believed and often said that even in Victorian times – under a more restricted franchise, and before the appearance of the Labour Party

– Lord Salisbury could hardly have kept in proper touch with the feeling of the country unless he himself had been leading the House of Commons.[22] Late that night he returned to Sheringham. The house party included Lady Desborough, the political hostess, and Mr and Mrs Edwin Montagu, of whom the former had been one of H.H. Asquith's Ministers, and the latter one of his confidantes. One of these asked:

> 'And will dear George be chosen?'
> 'No,' Balfour replied, 'dear George will not.'[23]

Kenneth Rose, the biographer of Curzon as well as of George V, calls this a 'mischievous story' whose implication was that Balfour had deliberately framed his arguments to exclude Curzon from the premiership.[24] Not at all. According to Churchill, Balfour expressed with conviction the view that in those days a Prime Minister must be in the House of Commons. He confined himself strictly to this point. He was careful to use no other argument.[25] Two days after Curzon's rejection, Stamfordham wrote to Balfour that it was 'a matter of satisfaction to the King' that he, with his 'exceptional experience of a long parliamentary career and of the office of Prime Minister', should have confirmed his opinion that, 'at all events in the present circumstances', the Prime Minister should be in the Commons.[26]

The King tried to ease Curzon's pain. He felt that, in view of the 'deep mortification' which would inevitably be caused to him, it would be kinder if he were warned in advance. Stamfordham sent him a telegram at his country house, Montacute: 'I will be at Carlton House Terrace [the Foreign Secretary's London residence] at 1.20.' Curzon was not better informed about what was going on in London because he refused to install that 'disastrous invention', a telephone, at Montacute.[27] Stamfordham visited him at Carlton House Terrace at 2.30 on Tuesday 22 May. He told him that within less than an hour Baldwin would be appointed Prime Minister. The news came as a 'bewildering shock'.[28]

Curzon still possessed enough spirit to be able to see the King face-to-face and to ask why he had not been made Prime Minister. Stamfordham, who was present at the meeting, recorded – or remembered – enough of it to communicate it to Neville Chamberlain two days afterwards, who then put it in his own diary:

> Curzon: Am I to understand then, Sir, that you consider that no peer can ever be Prime Minister?
> King: No, I didn't say that. What I said was that there were circumstances in which it was undesirable that a peer should be Prime Minister and in my view this was such a case.
> Curzon: But then, what about the Foreign Secretary? He is almost as important as the Prime Minister, particularly in these days. How is it that I can be a peer and Foreign Secretary at the same time without your objecting?
> King: Because the Prime Minister is responsible for everything you do.[29]

Maurice Cowling states that it is 'probable' that Law did not favour Curzon, with whom he had had 'difficult moments' during his premiership.[30] Oddly enough, Cowling supplies a supporting reference telling us that on 20 May Law told Baldwin that he did not see how Curzon could be avoided.[31] The only evidence that Law preferred Baldwin comes from that wily Welshman Thomas Jones: at tea on 20 May he told Jones that if the King asked for his advice about a successor, he 'would put Baldwin first'.[32] Though the King did not ask for Law's advice, he can hardly be blamed for the omission. Law had made it clear that, owing to his health, he was in no position to give counsel of any kind.[33] And, though one does not welcome an event by accepting its inevitability, there is little doubt that Law considered Curzon's accession to be certain.

On Sunday 20 May one of Law's earliest visitors at Onslow Gardens was Baldwin, who had hurriedly returned the night before from Worcestershire. Law told him that, though he was making no recommendation, he had no doubt that Curzon would be chosen. Baldwin's time would come in due course. Meanwhile he should try to serve loyally under Curzon. Baldwin replied that he would gladly serve under anyone who could hold the party together. When he left, Law felt easier in his mind, convinced that he had persuaded Baldwin to work amicably in a Curzon administration.[34] Lord Blake gives his source as Lord Beaverbrook, who was present at the meeting between Law and Baldwin. Beaverbrook encouraged him to write Law's biography and supplied him with much information. Leonard Mosley was a general author and a former film critic of the *Daily Express*. His life of Curzon was not only inspired by Lord Beaverbrook but, from internal evidence, largely dictated by him as well.

It remains to assess the significance of the Davidson Memorandum. It came to general notice with Lord Blake's biography of Law in 1955. Stamfordham noted: 'This is the Memorandum handed to the King on Sunday, May 20th, and which, Colonel Waterhouse stated, practically expressed the views of Mr Bonar Law.'[35] Law's family had insisted that his son-in-law, Sir Frederick Sykes, should accompany Waterhouse to Aldershot to ensure that the latter did not misrepresent Law's views.[36] This, in its overemphasis on the case for Baldwin, is what it did.[37] Sir Frederick Sykes does not seem to have done a very good job.

Nevertheless, it is doubtful whether the outcome would have been different if the memorandum had never been written at all – or if, having been written, it had been presented to the King as representing the views, not of Law, but of a group of Conservative politicians anxious to advance Baldwin's chances. Who exactly wrote it is still a matter of controversy, even of mystery. The circumstances surrounding its composition are clearer.

Stamfordham discussed with Davidson the politicians whom the King ought to consult about the succession. Davidson proposed Salisbury and Balfour. During these telephone conversations, Stamfordham suggested that, if he had time, Davidson might make a note of 'his own views'.[38] It was at Stamfordham's request that he proposed the memorandum. Davidson recounted to Robert Rhodes James that as Miss Watson, the secretary, took it from the typewriter he put it together. There was no time to read it then or even to sign it. The car was waiting and 'Sykes was impatient to be off'. Miss Watson clipped the sheets together and put them into a quarto envelope addressed to Lord Stamfordham. He sealed the envelope and 'may have added' his initials in a corner to indicate its source. Owing to his long association with Stamfordham, Davidson 'knew he would understand' why he had not signed it or sent a covering letter. He did not sign it because he 'did not wish it to be taken as Bonar's view', with whom he had had 'no opportunity or desire that weekend to discuss succession'.[39]

It may be noted that Davidson changed his story. He began by saying that he did not sign the memorandum because, owing to the importunity of Sir Frederick Sykes, he did not have time. He ended by saying that, if he did not sign, Stamfordham would 'understand' that it did not carry Law's imprimatur. But, as we have seen, Stamfordham did not understand, owing to the intervention of Waterhouse.*

The account Davidson gave Randolph Churchill is slightly different. When he 'dictated on to the typewriter that memorandum', he had 'no time to read it through'. Instead he took it from Miss Watson, folded it and returned it to her. She put it in an envelope addressed to Stamfordham and sealed. Davidson then handed it to Waterhouse, with the request that he should deliver it personally to Stamfordham at Aldershot. It was 'inconceivable', Davidson considered, that Waterhouse should have broken the seal; though it was always possible that Stamfordham would have divulged the contents to him after opening the envelope and reading the document himself.[40] Davidson thought that knowledge of the memorandum had come to light in Nicolson's *George V.* In fact it had become public in Blake's *Unknown Prime Minister,* which was published three years afterwards, in 1955. Lord Kilmuir found himself in a similar muddle in 1964. In his memoirs, *Political Adventure,* he said that his famous – and even then grievously inaccurate – phrase, 'loyalty is the Tories' secret weapon', had been uttered to and published by John Mackintosh. But the author that Kilmuir had in mind was Anthony Sampson.

The only substantial difference between these two accounts is that Randolph Churchill's implies that Davidson dictated the memorandum to Miss Watson, who typed it out directly. Rhodes James's implies that she was typing from a fair copy. It may be that Davidson was himself dictating either from a fair copy or from notes. In any event, it is highly unlikely that he was making it up as he went along. What were its origins? Davidson is coy.

Randolph Churchill did not purport to be telling Davidson's story: he

* See above, p. 13.

has merely a part in a play about Lord Derby. Rhodes James, however, was giving us the political life of John Davidson, in a book skilfully blending Davidson's diary and retrospective interviews with the author's own observations. He writes that Stamfordham's request to Davidson – which is undisputed – was a 'crucial point in understanding what subsequently occurred'.[41] Certainly the King, through his private secretary, asked for advice. He asked it not of Law but of Law's parliamentary private secretary. It seems clear that initially, before Waterhouse put a gloss on it, Stamfordham was asking for Davidson's advice not as Law's parliamentary private secretary but as a leading Conservative backbencher. Even then, Davidson was known to be close to Baldwin. Paradoxically, Waterhouse was known to be 'violently anti-Baldwin'.[42] That, according to Beaverbrook, was the reason why Law's relations insisted that his son-in-law, Sykes, should be joint-messenger to Aldershot with Waterhouse.[43] The Sovereign can ask for advice of anyone. Even so, it does not seem that Stamfordham's approach to Davidson, though it may have been constitutionally correct, was constitutionally wise.

From Rhodes James's account, one might think that the memorandum was Davidson's own work. Perhaps it was. Beaverbrook believed that, though Baldwin had 'inspired it', Davidson had written it. Blake says that the memorandum was 'in fact composed by Davidson after discussion with Baldwin on Friday night'.[44] As Baldwin was still in Worcestershire at this time, coming to London only on the Saturday, the discussion must have been on the telephone – which would have been perfectly possible, even though among politicians of those days it was used more to make an appointment than to have a discussion.

Cowling says that the memorandum was 'the work of Waterhouse, Davidson and perhaps Amery'.[45] He cites Blake as evidence for this. But Blake makes no relevant mention of Waterhouse or Amery on the page cited.[46] Cowling also cites Thomas Jones. Jones was shown the memorandum on 20 May after it had been dispatched by A.J. Sylvester, private secretary to Lloyd George. Jones said it had been written by Waterhouse, Davidson and Amery the night before.[47] Cowling concludes that it is not easy to accept Davidson's view that the real explanation of the 'mystery' of Baldwin's being preferred to Curzon arose out of the general political situation which, in the opinion of those the King consulted, precluded a peer from holding the office of Prime Minister. He adds that it is not 'easy to match the manner of the memorandum with Lord Davidson's epistolary style'.[48]

Leaving aside the question of the Davidson Memorandum, we may note that, on the succession to Law, Cowling defends a position which is attacked by Blake, Rhodes James and, most strongly of all, Nicolson and Rose. The last two were biographers not only of King George V but also of Lord Curzon. Their view, shared to a greater or lesser extent by Blake and

Rhodes James, is that Curzon was excluded from the premiership by his peerage.

Yet in 1940 Lord Halifax was well in the running to succeed Neville Chamberlain; was, indeed, the favourite among the political classes, in the sense of being the horse considered most likely to win.[*] In 1953, after Winston Churchill's stroke and during Anthony Eden's absence through illness in the United States, it was proposed by John Colville and others that Lord Salisbury should act as Prime Minister till Eden was well enough to take up the office himself.[†] True, Lord Home renounced his peerage and fought a by-election in 1963 to become Leader of the Conservative Party and, briefly, Prime Minister as Sir Alec Douglas-Home. But during the 1950s and before, it was generally believed that, in the modern world, no peer could be Foreign Secretary. In 1960 Harold Macmillan bestowed the office on Lord Home with surprisingly little fuss: the objection was not that he was a peer but that no one had ever heard of him. In 1970-4 he was Foreign Secretary again, having acquired a life peerage as Lord Home of the Hirsel. In 1979-82 Lord Carrington, a hereditary peer of 18th-century creation, was Foreign Secretary. Till his resignation over the Falklands, he was regarded as highly successful and was talked of (by, for example, Harold Wilson) as a successor to – or, rather, as a replacement for – Margaret Thatcher.

Is it not possible that the Conservatives in the House of Commons simply would not put up with Curzon? Certainly he would not have been the last politician to be regarded in this way. R.A. Butler – a less flamboyant, equally public-spirited but, perhaps, even more suspect character – was to suffer similarly.[‡] If the contest had been between Mr Stanley Baldwin and Mr George Nathaniel Curzon, can we be sure that Mr Curzon would have won? It is doubtful, to say the least.

RAMSAY MACDONALD IN 1924[49]

Maurice Cowling's principal thesis is that in 1920-4 the old parties, the Conservatives and the Liberals, continued to resist the establishment of Labour as one of the principal political parties. If this is so, one can only conclude that they made an extremely poor job of it. After the general election of 6 December 1923, the number of Conservative seats fell from 346 to 258. The Liberals rose from 117 to 159. So did Labour, from 144 to 191, making them the second largest party in a House where no party held an absolute majority.

Baldwin had called the election on the issue of tariffs. He was calling it, he said, because he was a new Prime Minister who wished to carry out a

---

* See below, p. 39.
† See below, p. 53.
‡ See below, pp. 66, 75.

policy which had not been put to the electorate by the Conservative Party at the previous general election. Such frankness, and such dedication to the (after all, most un-Conservative) doctrine of the mandate, caused indignation and, worse, alarm among not only his enemies but those who had previously been prepared to put up with him.

To his old friend Davidson, however, he confided that his motives had not been quite so pure. His intention was to scupper the chances of any return to pre-eminence by Lloyd George who, he had been reliably informed, was planning to come back to political life by espousing tariffs.[50] Whether deliberately or not, this is what Baldwin accomplished: Lloyd George never held office again after being toppled from the coalition in 1922. George V played a subsidiary part in the same enterprise. The exclusion of Lloyd George certainly benefited the Conservatives at the expense of the Liberals (though, after the hurried Liberal reunion of the 1920s, he would almost certainly have betrayed them again). But the principal beneficiary was Labour. There has been no Liberal government since 1915, when H.H. Asquith formed the first wartime coalition. There have been six periods of Labour rule since: in 1924, 1929-31, 1945-51, 1964-70 and 1974-9 and from 1997. This section is concerned with the manner in which the first of these came about.

The day before the result was announced, Lord Derby, in a letter to Lord Birkenhead, speculated about the outcome. Which, he asked, was to be the second party? If it was Labour, Baldwin, after resigning, would probably advise the King to send for Ramsay MacDonald. That, Derby believed, would be 'absolutely fatal'. The Conservative Party would 'cease to exist'. If, on the other hand – assuming the Conservatives were the largest party – Baldwin could be persuaded to resign, and to 'ask the King to send for somebody else in our party to see if he could form a government', why should Birkenhead or Austen Chamberlain not 'take it and see if you could not come to an agreement with Lloyd George for a coalition government?'[51] Similar suggestions were the small change of political conversation in the first half of December 1923. They had as their common factors the removal of Baldwin, the frustration of MacDonald and the continuation in office of either a Conservative or a coalition government. Baldwin's first response was to resign. He had, after all, led everyone and not just his own party into a messy situation.

Stamfordham saw Baldwin at 10 on Saturday morning. Baldwin asked that the King should postpone seeing him until Monday 10 December. He had returned to London only on the previous night, 7 December; had so far seen only a few of his colleagues; and had therefore come to no decision about his actions. His present view was that he should not meet Parliament but resign. He had asked the country for a mandate for Tariff Reform. This had been refused. The honourable course would be for him to resign at once. He thought Asquith might form a coalition with the Conservatives, though 'there again Mr Lloyd George might be a difficulty'.

Stamfordham asked Baldwin whether it would not be possible for someone else to form a coalition and mentioned Austen Chamberlain, 'but this did not seem to appeal to him much'.[52]

Later that morning Stamfordham saw Balfour. The former Prime Minister's view was that, as the Conservatives had the largest representation in the Commons, the King would 'naturally' turn to someone else in the party to form a new administration. But no 'lasting government' could be formed without coalition. Stamfordham referred to a proposal in *The Times* of that morning that a government might be formed with Balfour as Prime Minister. But they both recognised that the reason for the King's decision in May – not to appoint a peer Prime Minister because it was, in the King's opinion, 'essential' that he should be in the Commons – was even more urgent in December than it had been then. On the other hand (Stamfordham added in a strange reversal), it might 'possibly' be argued that the reasons favouring a peer as Prime Minister might be stronger now than they were.[53]

In the afternoon Geoffrey Dawson, the editor of *The Times*, had a 'long talk' with Stamfordham, in the days when editors of *The Times* could call at Buckingham Palace. Stamfordham was 'revolving possible Prime Ministers in his mind', with an 'obvious preference' for coalition under an elder statesman such as Asquith, Balfour, Derby or Grey. Dawson, however, suggested (and Stamfordham apparently agreed) that all the arguments used against Curzon were 'incomparably stronger' now. Dawson also said (again with Stamfordham's apparent agreement) that the King should be 'very careful' to give no ground for any impression that he was trying to form a government.[54]

Dawson reported that Lord Milner thought Baldwin's immediate resignation would 'stop intrigue'. He, on the other hand, was becoming more and more convinced that the intrigue had started anyway and would probably be successful – in the sense that Baldwin would be replaced by another Conservative or by a Liberal – if he was to 'disappear forthwith'. Clearly he had changed his mind or was harbouring an insubordinate leader-writer. He emphasised his views of 8 December by writing a letter to Stamfordham on the 9th and publishing a leader in *The Times* to the same effect on the 10th. On this day Stamfordham telephoned him 'early' to say that the King agreed with both the letter and the leader.[55]

On this weekend, 8-9 December, Baldwin invited his allies to Chequers. The gathering included John Davidson (who had been defeated at Hemel Hempstead), Walter Bridgeman, Leo Amery, Sir John Baird and Neville Chamberlain.[56] In Amery's frank words, these were Conservative politicians who would be 'thrown out on the street if Baldwin threw up [sic] the sponge' and left them 'without a leader at the mercy of all the intriguers'.[57] These included – at any rate in the eyes of those assembled at Chequers – Balfour, Austen Chamberlain, Derby, Worthington-Evans, Joynson-Hicks, Lloyd-Graeme (later Swinton), Beaverbrook, Birkenhead and

Rothermere. They might try to construct a coalition with the Liberals: in effect, restore the government from which Law and Baldwin had rescued the Conservative Party two years previously. Baldwin's friends were by no means certain that he would choose MacDonald. At that stage, who can say that they were wrong? They pressed their leader to stay in office until he was defeated in the House of Commons.

Oddly enough, Balfour had come round to agreeing with them. On 9 December he had a conversation with the King. He told him that, despite 'the fiasco of the election', Baldwin was 'more popular with his party than any possible substitute'. In these circumstances it was 'very important that he should not resign the leadership'.[58]

One of the principal intriguers against Baldwin was Lord Derby, 'King of Lancashire', a bluff, horse-racing peer who was popular in the country because he behaved as people felt a Lord should. On Monday 10 December he lunched with another Liverpool peer of more recent creation, Lord Birkenhead. Birkenhead told him – quite inaccurately as things were to turn out – that Baldwin was going to resign and that the King would ask Balfour for advice. Balfour was going to advise that Austen Chamberlain should be summoned, because it gave the King 'one other alternative' before sending for MacDonald.[59]

Derby also made his views known to Stamfordham, who was not greatly taken with them. According to him, Derby 'deprecated' any idea of sending for MacDonald. He wanted the Conservatives to remain in office under a Prime Minister other than Baldwin, against whom there was 'a very bitter feeling in the party'. He added that there was 'not one word of truth' in press reports that he was party to a movement to make himself Prime Minister. He thought Austen Chamberlain would be an 'acceptable' Prime Minister. He hoped the King would accept Baldwin's resignation and send for Chamberlain. Stamfordham said he did not think the King would approve of this course and felt that Baldwin should stay on and meet Parliament as Prime Minister.[60]

The King's private secretary was further importuned on the morning of 10 May by the Conservative MP Commander Oliver Locker-Lampson. He announced that he was speaking on behalf of Birkenhead, Austen Chamberlain 'and, he added, but rather parenthetically, Lord Balfour'. What Birkenhead had understood on 9 December (the Commander said) was that Baldwin had advised the King to send for MacDonald. At lunch on the same day, Birkenhead was to tell Derby that, though Baldwin was still going to resign, the King would ask Balfour for advice. Perhaps this change in Birkenhead's predictions – equally inaccurate as it also turned out to be – was the result of the splendid rebuke which Stamfordham administered to his emissary:

Here I interposed to remind Commander Locker-Lampson, and also Lord Birkenhead, that it was not the province of the outgoing Prime Minister to

advise the King what he was to do, unless that advice was sought by His
Majesty, with which Locker-Lampson concurred.[61]

It was noon on Monday before Baldwin saw the King. He said that, after
the election, his first thought had been to resign immediately. But he
thought on reflection that he should meet Parliament. Former precedents
did not apply here. (The decision about whether to resign or to meet
Parliament had much exercised politicians of the 19th century.[62]) The
issue concerned not two but three parties. The House of Commons was the
proper place for the choice of the electorate to be made known. Baldwin
said that he was 'not quite certain whether his resignation necessitated
that of his Cabinet, but the King held that the one involved the other'.
Baldwin added that he was 'absolutely opposed' to any coalition. He had
killed one and would never join another: though in 1931 he reluctantly did
so. The King suggested that, if Baldwin continued in office, he might be
able to approach Asquith with a view to ascertaining what, if any, co-
operation the government might receive from the Liberals.[63]

Derby, however, remained determined to defeat Baldwin's horse. Unfortunately, within a few days he tried to change jockeys: from
Chamberlain to Balfour. Alas, the sporting peer had once again been
misinformed. He went to see Balfour, and was disappointed to be told that
he was 'strongly of the opinion' that, though there were precedents for a
different course, constitutionally the right procedure was for the Prime
Minister to meet Parliament and to abide by the decision of a vote of
confidence. He 'strongly advised' Derby to 'support that point of view'.[64]
Derby also wrote to the King threatening resignation and then withdrew
his threat. Stamfordham was placatory. The withdrawal was a 'relief to
me' and 'what is far more important, I know it will be a relief to the King'.
Stamfordham concluded his, in the circumstances, highly polite letter by
urging Derby to accept that the 'really constitutional course' was to wait
until the decision of the electorate was 'made known through *its representatives in the House of Commons*' (italics in original). Stamfordham
added that 'this was the King's own view as made known to Baldwin'.[65]

Balfour continued to comfort Baldwin's enemies, while discouraging
them from doing anything that might dislodge him. He wrote to Birkenhead that the solution must be 'either something less than coalition, or
coalition called by some other name'. There would have to be an arrangement between the two parties. Otherwise the general feeling of insecurity
would be intolerable. He favoured 'not hastening a crisis'. This could best
be accomplished by the government's following 'the very sound constitutional practice of waiting for the decision of Parliament'. He added that if
it were left to him to settle who should be leader, he would 'not hesitate
for a moment. In personal claims, in political experience, in debating
power, Austen seems to me incomparably the superior.'[66]

Poor Austen Chamberlain: recommended by Balfour, his claim advanced likewise by Derby (until Derby advanced Balfour's instead), every Conservative's favourite, yet never to receive the highest position, becoming, indeed, the only Conservative leader – for such he was in the Law interregnum – never to have become Prime Minister, a fate which Lord Home, Edward Heath and John Major all escaped. Here again Austen's hopes were to be raised only to have the ropes swiftly cut. Balfour trusted that his friends would 'hesitate' before attempting 'to change horses while crossing the particular stream which threatens to overwhelm us'.[67]

Beatrice Webb agreed with Balfour. She had been in love with Austen's father Joe. She did not nominate Austen Prime Minister but had him in the Cabinet nevertheless.

> The honest way out of the *impasse* [she wrote in her diary], the one which would be approved by the majority of the British people, would be a Liberal-Conservative coalition – Asquith, Baldwin, Chamberlain, Lloyd George Cabinet, Free Trade and anti-socialist in home affairs and pacific in foreign policy.[68]

Whether such an arrangement came about depended on Asquith and the Liberals. There are those who consider that Asquith's greatest disservice to his party was his failure to abort the first Labour government.[69] Others maintain that both he and Lloyd George enjoyed less freedom of manoeuvre than seemed apparent at first sight. Each of them was – possibly for different reasons – prepared to chose MacDonald to form a minority Labour government. There is no doubt that Lloyd George approved Asquith's approach.[70]

On 18 December Asquith addressed a meeting of Liberal Members of the new House of Commons at the National Liberal Club. There had, he said, been 'no overtures of any kind' either from or to the leaders of the two other parties. As far as the Liberals were concerned, the other parties were free while, as far as the other parties were concerned, the Liberals were free also. That freedom he intended to preserve 'uncompromised and unfettered'. The days of Baldwin's government were 'of course, numbered'. It seemed to be 'generally assumed' that, as the second largest party in the House of Commons, Labour would 'be allowed to assume the responsibility of government'.

> Well, this may reassure some trembling minds outside: If a Labour government is ever to be tried in this country, as it will sooner or later, it could hardly be tried under safer conditions.[71]

Lloyd George and Sir John Simon gratifyingly 'expressed their hearty concurrence' with these sentiments.[72] Ten days later Asquith wrote to someone rather coyly denoted as 'my correspondent'. It is a graphic letter which deserves to be quoted fully:

You would be amused if you saw the contents of my daily post-bag: appeals, threats, prayers from all parts, and from all sorts and conditions of men, women, and lunatics, to step in and save the country from the horrors of Socialism and Confiscation. If I were to agree at this moment to enter into a compact with the Tories, I have little doubt that I could count on a majority in the House of Commons of more than two to one. As you may imagine, having seen so much in these latter days of the poisonous effect of coalition, I am not at all tempted.[73]

There were numerous Labour supporters who urged MacDonald to hold back; suspected a trap; could see nothing but trouble ahead (as, indeed, turned out to be the case). But MacDonald pointed out that if the Labour Party were to refuse office after defeating the government with the aid of the Liberals, and if Asquith were then to form a government instead, the Liberals would sit on the government benches. The opposition front bench – and most of the other opposition benches as well – would be occupied by Conservatives. The Labour Party would be relegated to the position of a group, and would probably sit below the gangway on the Liberal side of the House. (The 'gangway' is the passageway which divides each side of the House into halves. Smaller groups – such as the Liberals, the Nationalists and the Ulster Unionists in recent times – have always sat below the gangway, together with backbenchers who are distinguished or independent-minded or desire to be so regarded.) When the Liberals were defeated, as they would be 'in due course', it would be they, not Labour, who would take up the opposition front bench. By refusing office, the party would lose all the parliamentary advantages it had gained through being the official opposition in 1922. Its position in the country 'would be put back by a decade'.[74]

A week before the crucial vote, Asquith wrote that seemingly the immediate future was now settled. Baldwin was to resign, MacDonald to 'come in'. He doubted whether either of them was right. Baldwin could 'easily have snapped his fingers' at the no-confidence amendment and announced that, as leader of

much the largest section of the House, he had better moral authority than anyone else to carry on the King's government until he was absolutely blocked, and Ramsay might well have decided to start the first Labour government under impossible parliamentary conditions.[75]

But neither Baldwin nor MacDonald was inclined to embark on such a bold course. James Callaghan showed no disposition to follow the same path in March 1979 – when the government lost a vote of confidence at the end of a Parliament – though some of his followers urged him to do so. The vote duly took place. On 15 January 1924 the King opened Parliament with a Speech setting out a full legislative programme. On 17 January the Labour frontbencher J.R. Clynes moved an amendment to the address in the name of the Labour Party. On 21 January MacDonald recorded in his diary:

> Consultation w Thomas, Henderson, Clynes, Snowden, Spoor ... Speech at 9.47. Govt defeated and so I am to be P.M. The road will be heavy and I am so much alone.[76]

On 22 January Baldwin came to Buckingham Palace and handed in his resignation. The King did not consult him in any way about his successor. Stamfordham wrote in a letter to an un-named friend that, ever since the election, he had 'taken for granted that, on Baldwin's defeat in the House of Commons, the King would send for Ramsay MacDonald'.[77] He had 'deprecated any attempt to prevent his having the same facilities which would be accorded to any Minister entrusted by the Sovereign with the formation of a government'.[78] The King was 'not affected' by the Labour politician (and future leader) George Lansbury's attack on him at the Shoreditch Town Hall on 5 January but 'did take exception to Mr Lansbury's basing his remarks upon the idea of intrigue at Court'.[79] He made clear that it would not be right for him, in sending for the Leader of the Labour Party, to attach any conditions to his offer.[80] On 21 January Baldwin's friend Davidson had an audience with the King on relinquishing the Duchy of Lancaster. George V expressed the view that a Socialist government would have an opportunity of learning their administrative duties and responsibilities under favourable conditions and that it was essential that their rights under the constitution should in no way be impaired.[81]

It is not to depreciate the straight dealing of Stamfordham and the King to point out that their task was eased by Baldwin's decision not to resign. That decision was Baldwin's, not the King's: it was the result of the Chequers weekend of 8-9 December, and the pressure he came under on that occasion from his political friends, who depended on him to keep their careers afloat – or feared they would be swiftly sunk if Baldwin were to be replaced by another Conservative or by a coalition Prime Minister. The King was certainly capable of persuading a Prime Minister not to resign, as he was to demonstrate with MacDonald in 1931.[*] But this was not to be one of those occasions.

Derby and others came perilously close to urging the Sovereign to use his long-defunct prerogative to dismiss a Prime Minister. The King (in practice, Stamfordham) duly sent them packing. If Baldwin had resigned, the King could properly have sent for Austen Chamberlain, MacDonald or even Asquith – for whoever could form a government. In those circumstances, the arguable first course would have been for the King to send for Austen Chamberlain, so that he, as Baldwin's successor, could meet

---

* See below, p. 33.

Parliament. But, as we shall see, the doctrine of meeting Parliament was soon to fall into abeyance.

STANLEY BALDWIN IN 1924

This chapter is concerned not with the fall of governments or the loss of general elections but with the choice of Prime Ministers. It is nevertheless worth saying something about the collapse of MacDonald's first administration. It was brought about by an episode on one of those mist-enshrouded hills where law and politics meet and which surround the British constitution. The charge was that the Cabinet had improperly induced the Attorney-General, Sir Patrick Hastings, to withdraw a prosecution for sedition against the editor of the *Daily Worker*, J.R. Campbell.[82]

MacDonald had taken office on the understanding that he would resign only if defeated on a crucial issue of policy or on a vote of confidence. The Campbell case, he thought at first, was 'no more than a passing skirmish in the masquerade of party warfare'.[83] He told the King that it was 'all one of those malicious newspaper stunts which are becoming so common nowadays'.[84] But by the beginning of October he thought it had become a matter on which he must demand a vote of confidence.

At the Cabinet meeting on 6 October, it was decided that the Conservative censure motion and a Liberal amendment calling for the establishment of a select committee should *both* be treated as motions of censure. If either were carried, MacDonald would ask for a dissolution. At the same time it was decided to vote with the Conservatives to defeat the Liberals and then with the Liberals to defeat the Conservatives.[85] This was madness. Clearly, MacDonald was not going to gain a vote of confidence from the Conservatives. But there was no purpose either in opposing the Liberals' – in the circumstances, perfectly reasonable – call for a select committee or in voting with the Conservatives to defeat the Liberals. No doubt Asquith was using the select committee device to separate the Liberals from the Conservatives, and intended to turn MacDonald out as soon as he could. But that was no reason for MacDonald to fall in with Asquith's plans. He was like someone saying: 'Go on, then, hit me.' And knocked to the ground he duly was.

However, the outcome of the debate was not certain until Baldwin spoke towards the end. He announced that the Conservatives would vote for the Liberal amendment and against their own motion of censure. Labour voted in the Aye lobby to reject the Liberal amendment, while the Conservatives voted with the Liberals in the No lobby. The result was Ayes 198, Noes 359. When the amended motion calling for a select committee was put, it was carried 364-198. At 11.30 p.m. the Cabinet met in the Prime Minister's room and 'took note of the Prime Minister's intention to see the King at 10 a.m.' to ask for a dissolution.[86]

The election was held on Wednesday 29 October 1924. The result was

Conservatives 419, Labour 151 and Liberals 40. At 5.30 on 4 November MacDonald was received by the King, who accepted his resignation and assured him 'that he would always regard him as a friend'. Whether in or out of office, he 'trusted that he could always look to him to do his best' for the country and the Throne. 'I like him,' the King noted in his diary, 'and have always found him quite straight.'[87] At 7.00 on the same evening the King sent for Baldwin and asked him to form a government. He urged him to come to 'close and powerful grips with such questions as housing, unemployment, and the cost of food and education'[88] – a clear rebuke directed towards those who were over-concerned with the constitutional position of the Attorney-General.

RAMSAY MACDONALD IN 1929

The result of the 1929 election was Labour 288 seats, Conservatives 260 and Liberals 59. Labour was the largest single party, as it had not been in 1923. After what was described as 'careful thought', Baldwin decided it would be 'more honest' to resign immediately.[89] Though some constitutional experts felt that the right course would still be for him to face the new House of Commons and thereby oblige Lloyd George and the Liberals to declare their hand, Lord Stamfordham was having none of it:

> If I were Prime Minister I should not give a moment's consideration to what Lloyd George would or would not do; nor to any other of what might be called the 'expert parliamentarian' points of view. The fact is that you and I [he was writing to Sir George Murray], who naturally are inclined to look back to precedents, must remember that they are almost as little applicable to England today as they would be to China. Democracy is no longer a meaningless sort of shibboleth; and, with the enormous increase of voters by the women's franchise it is the actual voice, and for better or worse the *political* voice, of the State.[90]

Baldwin agreed, though he did not commit himself to Stamfordham's view that the women's vote had changed the British constitution. He informed the King that the public might regard it as 'unsporting' if he did not resign immediately. They might suspect that he intended to do 'some deal with the Liberals' to keep Labour out.[91] He came to Windsor on 4 June and handed the King 'the resignation of the government'. This, not 'his' or 'the Prime Minister's' resignation, is the form of words which Harold Nicolson uses.[92]

On the same afternoon, Stamfordham saw MacDonald. After inquiries about the King – who was suffering from the reopening of a surgical wound – he told Stamfordham that he wanted to go to sleep, for he had not slept for 'more than a fortnight'.[93] Stamfordham gathered that he had settled very little with his colleagues. Evidently 'things were not going easily'. Indeed, MacDonald said that he was by no means certain yet that he would tell the King that he was prepared to form a government. Stamfordham told him that he expected the King would speak to him about the National Executive Committee, which was 'popularly supposed to have much control' over a Labour government. MacDonald assured Stamfordham that this was not the case. However, two members of the Cabinet would act as 'sort of liaison officers' between the party and the government. He emphasised that the government was never influenced by and certainly never followed 'the dictates of the committee', unless the committee's views coincided with the government's.

On the evening of Wednesday 5 June MacDonald drove to Windsor. The King received him in his bedroom, wearing a Chinese dressing-gown.[94] He discussed several of the proposed appointments and suggested that J.H. Thomas, 'owing to his close intimacy with Mr MacDonald, might prove an excellent Foreign Secretary'.[95] MacDonald replied that, whoever was appointed Foreign Secretary, he would retain in his own hands the conduct of Anglo-American relations, to which he attached 'supreme importance'. The King asked him whether he was satisfied 'in his own conscience' that his party was justified in assuming the title 'Labour'. How many of the 'gentlemen whose names they had been discussing' had ever undertaken 'hard manual work'? MacDonald replied that 'he himself at least had actually gained that qualification'.[96] He then kissed hands and agreed to form an administration.

RAMSAY MACDONALD IN 1931

The formation of the national government in 1931 was almost entirely malign in its consequences. It destroyed for a decade the order for which Stanley Baldwin had been working.[97] It produced (or confirmed) the myth of betrayal in the Labour Party. It led to the pre-eminence in the Conservative Party not of Baldwin but of Neville Chamberlain. Indeed, Chamberlain himself was – with the King, the King's private secretary, Sir Clive Wigram, and the acting leader of the Liberal Party, Sir Herbert Samuel – one of the principal architects of the new government.

The origins of the 1931 crisis lay in Britain's return to the gold standard in 1925, when the Chancellor of the Exchequer, Winston Churchill, fixed the parity of the pound sterling to the price of gold. This was supported by the majority of Ministers after 1929 but not by J.M. Keynes. In February 1931 the Conservatives put down a motion censuring the government for constantly adding to public expenditure. The Liberals put down an amendment demanding an independent committee to advise the Chancellor on reductions in spending. The Cabinet decided – fatally, as things were to turn out – to accept the amendment. The debate began on 11 February. The Chancellor, Philip Snowden, warned the Commons about the disaster that would follow any hint that Britain's budgetary position was unsound. He called on the country 'to put its financial house in order'. The Liberal amendment was carried 468-21, and a committee under Sir George May duly established.

Another factor intervened. The German government announced that it was unable to meet its reparations obligations under the Treaty of Versailles. Germany suspended cash payments on 13 July and imposed currency controls. Speculation against sterling followed. Over the next three weeks the Bank of England lost about £60 million in gold and foreign exchange. On 23 July bank rate was put up to 3.5 per cent and a week later to 4.5 per cent. On that day, 30 July, the May report was also published. It forecast a budget deficit of £120 million and recommended cuts in expenditure of £97 million, including a £67 million cut in unemployment benefit. The government failed to issue any accompanying statement in which its attitude was expressed and which might have acted as a stabilising influence. On 31 July the House rose and MacDonald left for his home at Lossiemouth in the North East of Scotland.

MacDonald began by writing to Keynes, asking his opinion on the May report. Keynes replied that his views were not fit for publication. The report would, he said, result in a substantial increase in unemployment. He suggested a devaluation of the pound of not less than 25 per cent. MacDonald then asked the advice of another economist, Hubert Henderson. He replied that the time for devaluation had not yet been reached and advised MacDonald to accept a large proportion of the savings recommended by May. MacDonald took the advice of Henderson rather than of Keynes. On 11 August he arrived in London from Lossiemouth.[98]

On 6 July Chamberlain recorded in his diary that MacDonald 'thought a national government should be formed'. The Labour Party did not wish to be forced to vote against the 'two things they thought necessary' – reform of unemployment insurance and a tariff. He then saw Baldwin, 'and we agreed that our party "would not stand it for a moment"'.[99] Baldwin, for his part, was briefed by the Bank of England on the sterling crisis before he left for his holiday in France, and was furious about being recalled. Baldwin hated having his plans disturbed. He thought there was little more to be learnt or said and that Labour should be afforded no opportunity to dodge their duties.[100] This had originally been Chamberlain's view too. He could also see some advantage for the Conservatives in putting the blame on Labour. 'From the party point of view,' he asked a colleague, 'could any conceivable thing be more valuable ... than to get this terrible question of economy out of our way and tightly strapped to the back of a Socialist government?'[101]

John Davidson made contact with Baldwin in France towards the middle of August. Davidson now thought it 'almost certain' that there would be an attempt to form a 'Government of All the Talents' to rescue the Labour Party – a course to which his friend and master was opposed, though he was eventually to acquiesce in it. Baldwin told Davidson that he would be prepared to help in a national crisis, but that 'it was the

Labour government's mess' and 'they ought to clear it up'.[102] According to Davidson, neither Baldwin nor Chamberlain was unsympathetic towards MacDonald and the Chancellor of the Exchequer, Philip Snowden. The Conservatives were 'fully aware' of the difficulties which MacDonald and Snowden would have to face inside the Labour Party. Baldwin, though at that time 'quite unwilling' to envisage a coalition, went out of his way to indicate that the Conservative Party would take a 'helpful' line in Parliament.

He said this at a meeting with Chamberlain and others on 13 August. Davidson had gone to Normandy to fetch him back for this meeting. After it had finished, he decided to resume his holiday, while Chamberlain remained in charge in London.[103] Sir Clive Wigram took a less relaxed view of the situation. He told the King:

> We are sitting on the top of a volcano, and the curious thing is that the Press and the City have not really understood the critical situation. The Governor of the Bank of England is very pessimistic and depressed. If a crash comes in Germany ... a minority government will hardly be able to deal with the situation, and it is quite possible that Your Majesty might be asked to approve of a national government.[104]

Throughout the preliminary exchanges, the King had remained at Sandringham. Before leaving by train for his annual Scottish holiday on 21 August, he asked whether the Prime Minister wished him to change his plans. MacDonald thought it would further alarm the public if he cancelled his journey. As soon as the King reached Balmoral on Saturday 22 August, MacDonald sent a message that it might be necessary for him to return to London. Wigram 'at once spoke to His Majesty, who quite rightly said that there was no use shilly-shallying on an occasion like this, and he would proceed south that night'.[105]

On 20 August MacDonald wrote in his diary that for the Cabinet to 'evade responsibility' through resignation would involve 'great humiliation'.[106] Resignation would be 'the end of Labour government' for 25 years'.[107] On 21 August the opposition leaders arrived in Downing Street – Neville Chamberlain and Samuel Hoare for the Conservatives, Herbert Samuel and Donald Maclean for the Liberals. They had been led to believe that the Cabinet intended to make economies of £78 million and to cut unemployment insurance by £48 million. Now they were told that the respective valuations were £56 million and £22 million. They asked whether this was the government's last word and were told that it was. They then asked what would happen if these measures failed to restore confidence. Snowden said: 'The deluge.'[108] The opposition leaders then retired to MacDonald's room upstairs. They returned, to announce that the government's proposals were 'wholly unsatisfactory' and that they would join forces to defeat them as soon as Parliament reassembled.[109]

Chamberlain suspected that the Cabinet was divided. He expected

MacDonald either to submit to Cabinet opinion, propose inadequate cuts and precipitate a final collapse or to accept a Cabinet split and propose a national government. He did not expect a Conservative or a Conservative-Liberal government. He thought a national government under MacDonald could not be refused.[110] He also wrote gloatingly that if a Labour Cabinet cut unemployment benefit – which had taken over from any other economy as the banner under which Arthur Henderson and his allies marched – the party would be 'irrevocably split' and 'shaken to its foundations', have 'its sting drawn' and perhaps be 'unable to last long'.[111]

In any case, Chamberlain added, he and his colleagues expected the financial crash to come before they were able to turn out the government. It was the Prime Minister's 'bounden duty' to avoid that event. The Conservatives were prepared to give him any support in their power for that purpose, either with his present or with a 'reconstructed' government. Samuel, according to Chamberlain, 'followed on exactly the same lines'. MacDonald 'began by drawing a touching picture of his own position (a thing he loves to do)'. He did not think resignation would help. He would remain Prime Minister, invite his colleagues to support him and tell those who would not that they could go when they liked.[112]

The Cabinet decided against a cut in unemployment benefit. But 24 hours later it went through the argument all over again. On 22 August Sir Ernest Harvey of the Bank of England telephoned MacDonald and said that if the three parties all supported a scheme of economies proposed by the Bank 'they might get away with it'.[113] He telephoned MacDonald to say that the request for a loan had to be addressed to the government's United States banker, J.P. Morgan & Co., and not to the Federal Reserve Bank. He would not have the final answer till 23 August but was 'not unhopeful'.[114] Arthur Henderson and the other dissentients declared that if the Conservatives, the Liberals and the bankers persisted in regarding the Cabinet's proposals as inadequate, the Cabinet should resign and allow another government to be formed. The whole Cabinet accordingly agreed that – as the Conservative and Liberal leaders had already suggested – MacDonald should inform the King of its differences and advise him to consult the other party leaders.[115]

At this stage, 21-2 August, Chamberlain had already consulted those of his colleagues who were in London. They included Cunliffe-Lister (formerly Lloyd-Graeme, later Swinton), the first Lord Hailsham, Eyres-Monsell, Kingsley Wood and Davidson. They all agreed that the cuts proposed by the Cabinet would not effectively restore confidence abroad unless there was also a cut in unemployment benefit. After MacDonald had talked formally with Chamberlain and Samuel, he talked less formally with Chamberlain, Hoare and Davidson. He gave Hoare the clear impression that he was thinking about resignation.[116] Chamberlain, however, urged him to consider the possibility of the formation of a national government. 'Very reluctantly' Davidson agreed that each party should

temporarily jettison its own programme and combine to pursue an economic policy to save the nation from bankruptcy. The influence which he
had with Baldwin was, according to Davidson, thereafter used to persuade
him of the wisdom of this course.[117]

Davidson's first task was to follow Chamberlain's instructions and to
remove a cross Baldwin from France. He met him in Paris on Saturday 22
August and travelled back with him across the Channel. They reached
London shortly before 7.30 in the evening and were met at Victoria by 'a
large crowd', who seemed to share Davidson's view that Baldwin was 'the
man to save the country'. Baldwin was staying with the Davidsons at their
house in Great College Street, Westminster. After dinner, Chamberlain
and Hoare joined Baldwin and Davidson in the library. Chamberlain,
Davidson was sure, 'had his eye on the Chancellorship of the Exchequer',
while Hoare was 'a man of unlimited personal ambition'. Though they put
the national interest first, they – and some other leading Conservatives –
'had thought a good deal about what position they would have in a national
government'.[118] Baldwin was reluctant to envisage a new coalition. He had
destroyed one and did not wish to form another. (Compare his attitude in
1923-4.) Chamberlain became 'very impatient' with Baldwin's attitude,
making it clear that 'he could see no other way out of the situation'.
Baldwin 'agreed that if that was indeed the case it would be his duty to
take part in it'.[119] Davidson's recollection was, he claimed, 'very distinct'.
Baldwin said:

> Well, they've got into this mess, let them get out of it. As the situation
> develops I may or may not have to take some part in it, but that time hasn't
> arrived.[120]

MacDonald saw the King at 10.30 a.m. on Sunday 23 August. The King
was 'most friendly' and expressed his thanks and confidence. MacDonald
'repeated the situation' and told him that 'after tonight' he 'might be of no
further use'. He told him about the request put to New York. Even if the
Americans were prepared to offer credits on the basis of a £76 million
economy programme, Henderson, Graham and other Labour Ministers
might resign – in fact had already threatened to resign – rather than
accept the necessary cut in unemployment benefit. If they did so, the
government's resignation would be 'inevitable'.[121] He would resign together with the whole Cabinet. The King asked whether he would advise
him to send for Henderson. MacDonald said 'No', 'which he said relieved
him'. MacDonald advised the King to send for the leaders of the other two
parties and have them report the position from their points of view. The
King said he would do this and, further, advise them to support him.
MacDonald went on to explain his hopeless parliamentary position if there
were any number of resignations. The King replied that he was 'the only
person who could carry the country through'. MacDonald said that, if he

shared this belief, 'I should not contemplate what I do, but that I did not share it'. The King expressed horror at the prospect of an election. Mac-Donald replied that there would be no election until the crisis was over. As far as he could see, 'and on the assumption of resignations, no man could avoid it then'.[122]

MacDonald added that Henderson and others, of whom he named Alexander, Lees-Smith and Johnson, had met after Cabinet on Saturday 22 August and decided to resign on the 10 per cent cut in unemployment benefit. They would be in a good tactical position as an opposition if the crisis was avoided. MacDonald was preparing a statement likewise, 'to give to the press at once', if he resigned.

> I commit political suicide to save the crisis. If there is no other way I shall do it as cheerfully as an ancient Jap.[123]

These passages demonstrate that as early as Sunday morning, when MacDonald had his first audience with the King, the King was anxious either for a Labour government supported by the Conservatives and Liberals or, failing that, for a coalition government. Whatever happened, he wanted MacDonald to continue as Prime Minister. MacDonald, by contrast, was set on resignation.

The next visitor to the Palace was Samuel, for the Liberals. Lloyd George was ill and remained at his house at Churt in Surrey. MacDonald came there seeking that support, as did Samuel, the Liberal leader in the Commons, and Lord Reading, the leader in the Lords. Lloyd George refused to give his support. The effect of the 1931 crisis on the Liberal Party was to divide it not into two groups, as it had previously been before the somewhat factitious 'reunion', but into three: the followers of Sir Herbert Samuel; the followers of Sir John Simon, the Liberal National; and the followers of Lloyd George, who consisted mainly of his relations.[124] Samuel told the King that he would prefer MacDonald to stay in office to implement the necessary programme of economies. If, however, he failed to carry enough of his colleagues with him, the best course would be for MacDonald to head a national government comprising members of all three parties.[125] Samuel later recorded: 'The King listened attentively. He was a very good listener sometimes.'[126]

Earlier on the Sunday morning Wigram had telephoned Dawson, the editor of *The Times*. He said that the King was about to see MacDonald 'and was considering what line to take with him'. He proposed to see Baldwin and Samuel later in the day, 'so as to have the views of all parties at first hand'. Dawson 'suggested respectfully' that the King should impress upon MacDonald 'that it was his business to get the country out of the mess and to dwell, with any flattery he liked, upon the opportunity and the responsibility'.[127] Baldwin telephoned Dawson soon afterwards. He came round to his house in the middle of the morning and stayed talking until lunch time, when they both went together to the Travellers Club. Baldwin 'agreed entirely' with Dawson's views – that MacDonald should continue in office as head of a Labour government, committed (or forced) to carry out measures of economy. He hoped the crisis would be 'temporarily settled' on these lines by the next day, Monday 24 August.

> He then fell to discussing what should be the *personnel* of a new government if by any misfortune he was to be called upon to form one at once, saying that it was easier for him to talk these matters over with me than with any of his political colleagues.[128]

It has sometimes been said that Baldwin was late for his audience with the King – even that he 'could not be found'. In fact he had spent the previous evening at Davidson's house, passed part of the morning with Dawson and, then, lunched with Dawson at the Travellers, reaching the Palace at three in the afternoon. Evidently he saw no reason for rush. When he met the King they talked past each other, even drawing a different understanding of what had been said. To the King's question of whether, if the Cabinet resigned, Baldwin would serve under MacDonald in a national government, Baldwin replied that he was 'prepared to do anything to save the country'. He then added that if MacDonald resigned he would be ready to form a government himself with Liberal support. The King understood this to be a clear affirmative answer to his question.[129] Such were the perils of long lunches at the Travellers Club. The Cabinet met later that Sunday.

> The Prime Minister informed the Cabinet that a situation had now to be faced of a particularly difficult character because, if the Labour Party was not prepared to join with the Conservatives [sic] and Liberal Parties in accepting the proposals as a whole, the conditions mentioned in Mr Harrison's [of the Federal Reserve Bank] message regarding a national programme would not be fulfilled.[130]

Each member of the Cabinet then gave his or her opinion on the 10 per cent cut in unemployment benefit. Eleven were in favour: Ramsay MacDonald, Philip Snowden, Lord Sankey, Lord Amulree, Herbert Morrison, Lord Passfield, H. Lees-Smith, J.H. Thomas, Margaret Bondfield, Wedgwood Benn and T. Shaw. Nine were against: Arthur Henderson, William Graham, George Lansbury, Arthur Greenwood, T. Johnson, A.V. Alexander, Christopher Addison, W. Adamson and J.R. Clynes.[131] Though the majority of the Cabinet supported the cut, it was clear that some at least of the dissentients would resign rather than accept it, and that the government could not carry on. MacDonald said that he intended to see the King at once and that he would advise him to hold a conference between Baldwin, Samuel and himself on the following – the Monday – morning. The Cabinet agreed to this and authorised him to inform the

King that all the members of the Cabinet had placed their resignations in the Prime Minister's hands.[132]

MacDonald left Downing Street shortly after ten, telling Sir Ernest Harvey, whom he happened to pass on the way out: 'I'm off to the Palace to throw in my hand.'[133] He recorded in his diary that the Cabinet decided to resign but to meet at noon on 24 August to see whether 'any new situation would arise' as a result of the meeting with Baldwin, Samuel and the King.[134]

At the Palace, late on 23 August, the King assured MacDonald that he was the only man to lead the country through the crisis and again asked him to reconsider his resignation. The King added that MacDonald knew he could depend on Conservative and Liberal support, and agreed to preside over the meeting of the three party leaders on the following day.[135]

The three leaders then had a preliminary meeting, late on the Sunday, with Chamberlain present also. According to Chamberlain, MacDonald said that the United States credits 'could be raised' but that he 'could not keep the Cabinet'. While a majority supported him, eight or nine Ministers had refused to accept the 'dole cut'. He had told the King this, recommending him to see the three leaders. For himself, he would 'help us to get these proposals through', though it meant his 'death warrant'. But it would be of no use for him to join a government. This would 'bring odium to us as well as himself'. Chamberlain then intervened. He asked MacDonald whether he had considered that, though he did not command many votes in the House, he might have 'much support' in the country. Would not a government which included members of all parties have a much stronger position? And had he considered foreign opinion?[136]

According to Davidson's draft memoirs, Josiah Stamp was also at the meeting, which was held at Downing Street. It was 'quite clear' that MacDonald intended to resign and had 'no intention' of joining a coalition, even though the King had urged him to lead one. Chamberlain pressed on him the support in the country which he would bring to a coalition and the effect which his membership would have in restoring confidence. His arguments seemed to be unavailing. It appeared quite certain that MacDonald intended to resign. Baldwin returned from the meeting convinced he would have to form a government.[137]

On Monday morning, for the third time in 24 hours, the King told MacDonald that his resignation was out of the question. He said that by staying at his post with those colleagues who were still faithful to him, his position and reputation would be enhanced. He must come to an arrangement with Baldwin and Samuel to form a national emergency government which would restore British credit and the confidence of foreigners.[138] The discussion lasted two hours. Both Baldwin and Samuel agreed to serve under MacDonald. There was to be no coalition but, rather, a co-operation of individuals to cope with the emergency. Once the requisite measures had been passed, Parliament would be dissolved and the parties could go to the country independently. The King was then told what had been decided, while MacDonald set out for Downing Street to tell the Cabinet.[139]

The Cabinet expected to hear that he had tendered their collective resignations, including his own, to the King. Instead he announced that he was to lead a national government. The result was 'consternation'.[140] They agreed that MacDonald should – once again – place the government's resignation in the King's hands that afternoon. On the motion of Lord Sankey, they decided to record 'their warm appreciation of the great kindness, consideration and courtesy invariably shown by the Prime Minister when presiding over their meetings'.[141] Sankey came with him into the new government, together with Snowden and Thomas.

Looking, in Sir Clive Wigram's words, 'worn and weary', MacDonald returned to the Palace at four o'clock.[142] At last he was allowed to resign as Prime Minister of the Labour government – to kiss hands as the Prime Minister of what was intended at the time to be a short-lived national government:

> The Prime Minister this afternoon tendered to His Majesty the resignation of the Ministry, which was accepted by His Majesty, who entrusted Mr Ramsay MacDonald with the task of forming a national government on a comprehensive basis for the purpose of meeting the present financial emergency. Mr Ramsay MacDonald accepted the commission, and is now in conference with Mr Stanley Baldwin and Sir Herbert Samuel, who are co-operating with him in the formation of such an administration.[143]

When the members of the new administration were receiving their seals of office two days later, what was described as MacDonald's 'mournful countenance' was accentuated by his black frock coat and black tie. The King said:

> You look as if you were attending your own funeral. Put on a white tie and try to think it is your wedding.[144]

The historians are generally agreed about the role of both the King and Sir Clive Wigram in the formation of the national government. Thus Kenneth Rose: 'That the King personally strove to establish a national government is undeniable.'[145] David Marquand: 'Even before his discussion with Samuel, the King was anxious that, if the Labour government resigned, MacDonald should stay in office with Conservative and Liberal support.'[146] Philip Williamson writes that the King and Wigram were

> well-prepared in case the Labour government could not continue. They had been so since the previous October, and were now presented with an opportunity to make their views effective. Although during most interviews that day [23 August 1931] they observed the constitutional form of seeking advice, their real objective was to obtain agreement with the King's own view.[147]

The politician who used to be held chiefly responsible was Herbert Samuel. His role has been perhaps exaggerated. The strongest force on the Conservative side was Neville Chamberlain. His biographer Keith Feiling writes: 'For himself he returned to the Ministry of Housing, but the testimony of colleagues and the instinct of opponents alike make it clear that of this great political change he was the constructive engineer.'[148] Feiling's reference to the Ministry of Housing may well have been calculated to acquit Chamberlain of engineering the new government in pursuance of his ambition to be Chancellor. This is what Davidson was to allege.

Ramsay MacDonald was not treacherous, ambitious or calculating. He was not even, on this occasion, specially vain – the vice of which he is most frequently accused. He was simply weak. He gave in, but to the King rather than to Chamberlain: for most of the evidence is that, late on 23 August, after he had seen Chamberlain and others, he was unconvinced. It was the Labour Cabinet who gave him the opportunity to be convinced. Having resigned collectively on one day, they not only authorised MacDonald to meet the two party leaders and the King on the next but further instructed him to report back to them on what had happened. This was to ask for trouble, which duly came about.

The correct constitutional course would have been for MacDonald and the Cabinet to resign – which they tried to do, and which the Cabinet thought they had done – and for the King to send for Baldwin. This is what Baldwin thought would happen, though he would have preferred MacDonald and a Labour Cabinet to remain in office and pass the economy measures with the support of the Conservatives and the Liberals. It is often asserted that George V acted constitutionally because at all stages he took the formal advice of his Prime Minister.[149] Indeed, so far as his meetings both with the Prime Minister and with opposition leaders were concerned, he took, in a sense, the advice of all his Ministers assembled in a Labour Cabinet.

The question of advice much exercised Sir Ivor Jennings. He relied principally on Sir Harold Nicolson's account. Nicolson wrote that MacDonald warned the King that some of his most influential colleagues, notably Henderson and Graham, would not consent to the economy measures. If they were to resign, it would not be possible for him to carry on. The resignation of the Labour government as a whole would then become inevitable. The King, on hearing this information, decided that the correct constitutional course was to consult the leaders of the Conservative and Liberal oppositions.[150] Jennings wrote that there was a statement missing here but that it was supplied by the official notification:

On the Prime Minister's advice [Jennings's italics] the King has asked Mr

Baldwin and Sir Herbert Samuel to see him, because His Majesty wishes to
hear from them themselves what the position of their respective parties is.

The italics, Jennings thought, were important. If the King acted on
advice it was indeed the correct constitutional course. It would not have
been an incorrect course if the Prime Minister had resigned. For then the
King could consult whom he pleased. As there had been no defeat of the
government, the King was not bound to call on the Leader of the Opposition to form an administration. Jennings says that the question of advice
was important, and that it was Samuel 'who suggested, at his audience on
23 August that a national government might be formed'.[151]

As we know, this was incorrect. Not only had a national government
been in the King's (and Sir Clive Wigram's) mind for some days or even
months. He had also proposed it to MacDonald at the meeting preceding
the one with Samuel. It became evident too that the King was urged to
seek the advice of the other party leaders not only by MacDonald but by
the entire Labour Cabinet – though it is unclear what they thought they
were doing when they authorised MacDonald to hold a further conference
at the Palace, after he was supposed to have handed in their and his own
resignation.[152]

The case against George V is not that he neglected to seek advice from
the proper quarters – for here he did enough to satisfy the most exigent
constitutionalist. It is that he resolved there should be a national government. Moreover, MacDonald was the only politician to head it. He acted
unconstitutionally in refusing to accept MacDonald's resignation, not once
but three times: on the Sunday morning, late on the Sunday evening and
on the Monday morning. Kenneth Rose, his biographer, writes that 'persuasion is not unconstitutional; indeed, it is a royal prerogative. Had
MacDonald persisted in his wish to resign, the King could not have
prevented him.'[153] The line between persuasion and refusal is a fine one.
But George V crossed it. In the 1930s this view was put most vigorously
by Harold Laski, Professor of Political Science and Labour Party lumi-
nary, later regarded as a uniquely sinister figure:

> It appears certain that the impetus to the peculiar form of the new admini-
> stration came wholly from the King. Mr MacDonald was as much the
> personal choice of George V as Lord Bute was the personal choice of George
> III. He is the sole modern Prime Minister who has been unencumbered by
> party support in his period of office; he provided only a name, while Mr
> Baldwin supplied both the legions and the power that goes with the legions.
> We need not doubt that the King acted as he did wholly from a conception of
> patriotic obligation. But since it is known that a Baldwin premiership was
> confidently expected at least as late as the night before the break-up of the
> Labour government, it is not, I think, unreasonable to term Mr Ramsay
> MacDonald's emergence as Prime Minister of the national Government a
> Palace Revolution.[154]

Buckingham Palace took note of Laski's unease. Sir Clive Wigram requested an interview, of which Laski kept a record. It was, he observed, 'most cordial'. In other respects it was perhaps less satisfactory. Wigram said that Laski seemed 'to have a down on the King'. He added that he was less interested in rehearsing what had happened than in assuring Laski that the Crown exercised 'due care to keep itself above politics'. Laski replied that the formation of the national government had been a case of 'going into and not keeping above politics'. Wigram concluded by saying that the people would approve the King's actions because they 'trusted his motives'. And that was that.[155]

Arthur Henderson succeeded Ramsay MacDonald as Leader of the Labour Party but lost his seat at the 1931 election. George Lansbury became acting leader until he succeeded as leader in 1932. The deputy leaders were, jointly, J.R. Clynes and William Graham and, from 1931, C.R. Attlee, who was to form the next Labour government 14 years later.

STANLEY BALDWIN IN 1935

Baldwin succeeded MacDonald on the afternoon of Friday 7 June 1935, at the beginning of the Whitsun weekend. It would be wrong to conclude that MacDonald was forced out of the premiership against his will, or even that there was a concerted Conservative attempt to get rid of him. Baldwin had been a loyal colleague – in the view of his familiar, Davidson, too loyal – but he possessed no illusions about MacDonald's capacities in his declining years.[156] He had, however, promised MacDonald that the Conservatives would serve under him until the end of the Parliament.

Baldwin himself was contemplating resigning the Conservative leadership in favour of Chamberlain.[157] Indeed, Roy Jenkins states that MacDonald's assumption throughout the 1931 government and almost up to the last moment was that Baldwin and he would retire together and that Chamberlain would become Prime Minister.[158] Lord Jenkins suggests that the backbenchers were seeking a sharper style than Baldwin was able to provide, a style which Chamberlain displayed perhaps in over-abundance. But it did not happen. Chamberlain's biographer merely observes: 'King George V kept his silver jubilee that May, after which Baldwin took over the trappings of power whose substance he had long controlled.'[159]

In August 1934 MacDonald had recorded that he was 'still pursuing' thoughts of the future. A new party did not seem possible because 'the Labour element would not be strong enough'. However, he felt himself 'less and less at home with the Conservatives'.[160] At the beginning of October he was due to return to London after a long holiday at his Scottish home in Lossiemouth. During this time he had been 'thinking a good deal' about what to do. 'I should like to retire; my road is not a Tory one.'[161] In January 1935 he noted that he had discussed his state of health with the physician

Lord Horder and that Horder thought he 'should not let my brain tiredness go too far'.[162] Malcolm Muggeridge wrote:

> He slowly faded away, existing at last in a kind of twilight; there and not there, making an appearance in Parliament and at public functions, once collapsing at a Lord Mayor's Banquet in the Guildhall, sometimes speaking, certainly moving, smiling, shaking hands and otherwise indicating that he was alive and in possession of whatever faculties he had, yet difficult to believe in; in the House of Commons, often seated alone, as though none cared to take their place beside so ghostly a figure.[163]

MacDonald was still capable of indignation. He became angry at the indulgence shown to Randolph Churchill and his friends after Churchill had stood as an 'Independent Conservative' in the Wavertree (Liverpool) by-election of 6 February 1935, helping to turn a Conservative majority of 24,000 into a Labour majority of almost 2,000. What he wrote in his diary demonstrated that any loss of lucidity was not accompanied by a diminution in eloquence:

> I have steered the country past the Charybdis of unprincipled bribery through doles and public charity which are to ruin those who get them and wreck the nation, but my hand is not to remain at the wheel if officers and crew are bent upon smashing us up upon the Scylla of opposition to a principle (that is, Socialism) which offers a guiding inspiration for this generation.[164]

On 10 February 1935 he saw Baldwin and talked about the situation. He told him that he was dissatisfied with the Conservatives' defence of the government. Conservatives defended Conservatives: no one defended him. He was being 'left to the wolves'. Baldwin pleaded guilty. MacDonald told him that it was time to change if the union was to last. He was 'prepared to do my part and make my contribution as rich as I could but there must be more unity in the country'.[165]

Four days later, however, Sir John Simon recorded that MacDonald was contemplating changing places with Baldwin.[166] David Marquand, MacDonald's biographer, believes that, though the arrangements for Baldwin's succession were not fixed until well into May 1935, the 'critical decision' had been taken by the end of March.[167] The King simply acted on the assumption that Baldwin was to succeed and appointed him without consultation. Baldwin immediately asked for two months' rest.[168] According to Kenneth Rose, the King simply consented to a change of Prime Minister, but successfully insisted that MacDonald should remain in the Cabinet as Lord President of the Council.[169] MacDonald resigned on 7 June 1935. Dawson, the editor of *The Times*, recorded:

> A very smooth and swift affair, carried out with every detail of kissing hands, a Cabinet meeting, a Privy Council, etc.: between the rising of the House at

four and the departure of Ramsay MacDonald for Lossiemouth and Stanley Baldwin for Himley soon after seven. What a contrast with the unhappy French ...[170]

NEVILLE CHAMBERLAIN IN 1937

Baldwin's confidant Davidson recalled that in the spring of 1937 Baldwin and he came to the conclusion that Baldwin should hand over to his successor after the coronation in May, and that Davidson himself should sever his association with the government, principally because he did not have the confidence in Chamberlain as Prime Minister which he felt he ought to have if he were to remain a member of the administration.[171] It is possible, of course, that Chamberlain would not have wanted Davidson in his government. It was certain that Chamberlain would succeed Baldwin: there were no challengers.[172]

The only person who seemed to have doubts was Chamberlain himself. As Chancellor of the Exchequer he put 30 pennies on income tax, bringing it up to five shillings (in modern currency, 12.5p and 25p respectively). He also inaugurated the National Defence Contribution – a graduated tax on the profits of trade and business, whose purpose was to find a temporary device 'capable of growth in itself' and adjustable to an expenditure that would rise to a peak and thereafter decline. This 'brought a political tempest'.[173] Chamberlain described it as 'the bravest thing I have ever done since I have been in public life, for I have risked the premiership'.[174] In March 1937 his half-brother Austen died. Neville wrote to his sister:

> I am not a superstitious man, and indeed I should not greatly care if I were never to be Prime Minister. But when I think of Father and Austen, and reflect that less than three months of time, and no individual, stands between me and that office, I wonder whether Fate has some dark secret in store, to carry out her ironies to the end.[175]

On 2 May 1937 Baldwin held his last Cabinet, where Chamberlain paid tribute to him. On 28 May he kissed hands and became Prime Minister. Fate waited for three years.

WINSTON CHURCHILL IN 1940

There is still an element of mystery about Winston Churchill's emergence as Prime Minister in May 1940. If, as has been commonly supposed, Neville Chamberlain wanted Lord Halifax to succeed him, why did he not simply advise King George VI to send for Halifax – which, in default of Chamberlain's remaining, was the King's own preferred solution?[176] Why introduce Churchill at all into the discussions which took place at No. 10 Downing Street on 9 May 1940? Could it be that, secretly, Churchill was Chamberlain's choice? But Churchill, as First Lord of the Admiralty, was directly responsible for the disaster – the Norway campaign – for which Chamberlain was being impugned. It is best to take the matter chronologically.

In September 1939 the Conservative Member for Southend, Henry ('Chips') Channon, was parliamentary private secretary to the Under-Secretary of State for Foreign Affairs, R.A. Butler. Channon was vain (but not conceited), snobbish, homosexual, rich, in love with the surface of life. He was also a diarist of genius. He recorded that he had observed Churchill 'whispering' to Chamberlain in the House. Churchill was 'behaving well' but the 'deep mutual antagonism' between him and Chamberlain 'must sooner or later flare up and make co-operation impossible'.

Then, Channon added, 'we shall all be sacked' – for, though quite uninterested in politics in any conventional sense, he was extremely proud of his position under Butler, and hoped that it would lead to higher things. There would be a 'glamorous' centre-government (glamour being synonymous with Anthony Eden and perhaps with Duff Cooper also). It would be reinforced by 'extreme Left Conservatives' and by 'some Socialists' who were already saying that, while they had refused to serve under Chamberlain, they would agree to serve under Churchill. This indicates that by this time, 6 September 1939, Chamberlain had already tried unsuccessfully to form a national or coalition government. 'I see it coming,' Channon wrote. Three weeks later he noticed that the 'glamour boys' were beginning to intrigue again. 'We must watch out.'[177]

Harold Nicolson was National Labour Member for Leicester West. He had been one of the few Labour MPs to follow Ramsay MacDonald after 1931. Like Channon, he was a homosexual; had no real notion of serious politics; and was a great diarist. Perhaps he did not have quite Channon's touch, on account of his possession of those very qualities of intelligence, combined with historical and literary knowledge, which Channon lacked. In conventional prose he was certainly an immeasurably better writer. In the politics of war, he was on the opposite side to Channon.

In September Nicolson reported the effect of a speech by Churchill in the House. In those 20 minutes, he wrote, Churchill brought himself nearer to the premiership than he had ever been before. In the Lobbies afterwards even Chamberlainites were saying: 'We have found our new leader.' 'Old party hands' confessed that never in their experience had they seen a single speech to change the temper of the House.[178] A week later Nicolson attended an Eden Group dinner at the Carlton Club. Lord Astor was there. He felt it was 'essential' that Chamberlain should be removed and Churchill take his place.[179] Nor was Lord Halifax always enthused by the Prime Minister. Nicolson reported him as saying:

I wish the Prime Minister would give up these weekly statements [in the House]. It is as if one were in East Africa and read the *Times Weekly Edition* at regular intervals.[180]

In December 1939 the House held a secret session. The effect, Nicolson wrote, 'was to show the Whips what their supporters really felt'. The 'tremendous reception' given on the government benches to a speech by Sir Archibald Sinclair, the leader of the Liberals, attacking the conduct of the war, must in itself have shown the Whips how precarious was their hold on their own party. 'We have got them,' Nicolson concluded.[181] He was sure that Britain would not win the war with politicians like Sir John Simon, Sir Samuel Hoare and Leslie Hore-Belisha in important positions. He did not, however, want a coalition government at this stage: '*We* must keep our second wind for the moment when true disaster occurs.' Chamberlain should remain. But he and his 'satellites' should know that he was there 'on sufferance' and 'under the very sharpest observation'. He was bound to realise this by now.[182]

At the beginning of April 1940 Hitler decided that his Scandinavian campaign should precede his attack on France by a month. Denmark was overrun in a few hours, Copenhagen occupied by a single German battalion. The Norwegian ports of Narvik, Trondheim and Bergen were seized from the sea on 9 April. Oslo was captured from the air on 10 April. Quisling set up a pro-Nazi government there, while King Haakon fled with his cabinet to the northern mountains and appealed for British help. Britain and France responded with two successful naval actions on 10 and 13 April at the approaches to Narvik. Three small military forces were then dispatched to points outside the Narvik fjord. This operation failed. The advance on Narvik itself was impeded by deep snow and by the reluctance of the British military commander to land at the port itself.

In April Channon was reporting 'secret conversations and meetings' between Churchill and Sinclair, together with the Labour politicians C.R. Attlee and A.V. Alexander. They were, he thought, 'drawing up an alternative government, with the idea of succeeding at the first favourable moment'. Eden was 'on the fringe', where he was 'watching and waiting for his chums'.[183] On 25 April Harold Balfour and Kingsley Wood took the Chief Whip, David Margesson, to dinner at the Mirabelle in Mayfair (then one of the grander London restaurants). They warned him of what Channon called the 'glamorous development' of which he was 'already half aware'. It was decided to send word to No. 10 at 10 that evening to 'warn' Chamberlain and to 'consult with him'. Wood – as we shall see, a most ambiguous figure in these dealings – duly went. Chamberlain was 'shaken and indignant'. Channon predicted 'a first class political struggle between the Chamberlain men and the "glamour" group'. The Chamberlainites might 'weather the storm' but there was 'trouble ahead'.[184]

The Whips put it about that the unsuccessful campaign in Norway was all Churchill's fault as First Lord of the Admiralty.[185] This was not altogether successful. The blame for the Norway campaign was placed principally on Chamberlain. Halifax was angered by efforts which were being made 'to represent the Norwegian business as the result of timid colleagues restraining the bold, dashing and courageous Winston. As a matter of fact the exact opposite would be at least as near the truth.'[186] In the House there was 'more talk of a cabal against poor Neville'. A parallel was being drawn, according to Channon, with 1915 – though in that year Asquith was persuaded to form a coalition rather than forced to relinquish the premiership. The latter happened in 1916. It was this year that Channon had in mind, writing as he did of the talk 'that Winston should be Prime Minister as he has more vigour and the country behind him'.[187] By 2 May Channon was 'beginning reluctantly to accept that Neville's days are, after all, numbered'.[188] Next day Margesson was saying that they were 'on the eve of the greatest political crisis since August 1931'.[189]

From the two diarists there was no mention of the Foreign Secretary, Lord Halifax. Harold Nicolson wanted Churchill to succeed at some time of the Conservative rebels' own choosing; 'Chips' Channon feared the triumph of one of what he called 'the glamour boys'. Halifax could certainly not be so described. C.R. Attlee said of him: 'Queer bird, Halifax. Very humorous, all hunting and Holy Communion.'[190] When he was asked, over a quarter of a century later, whether he would have supported Halifax as successor to Chamberlain, he replied that he 'would have supported anybody who would get on with the war'.[191] Lord Home, however, states that Halifax 'was the personal choice of Mr Attlee'.[192]

Herbert Morrison wanted Halifax, as did Hugh Dalton. But Morrison's biographers oversimplify when they assert: 'The Labour leaders' choice for a successor to Chamberlain was Halifax.'[193] The Labour Party created a myth, which it exploited in general elections and on other occasions from 1945 onwards, that it had made Churchill Prime Minister and so helped win the war. This was not so. As we shall see, Labour refused to serve under Chamberlain. But by the time the party's official refusal came through, Churchill had already been selected though not appointed.*

Yet it is equally a myth that the party's leaders wanted Halifax. What is true is that it was Attlee who was chiefly responsible for the holding of the Norway debate which was to bring down Chamberlain. He demanded a two-day debate on the failure of the Narvik expedition, to open on 7 May 1940. He resisted the Liberal Clement Davies's urgings to make it an issue of confidence, in case dissident Conservatives rallied round Churchill.[194] The debate was held on the motion for the adjournment. The Parliamentary Labour Party decided to force a vote on this motion, which Morrison announced when he opened for Labour on 8 May.[195] Even before that, on 7 May, Lord Dunglass (later Sir Alec Douglas-Home and Lord Home) had told R.A. Butler that there was a danger of a vote. Chamberlain was talking of staying on if the vote was more than 60 in his favour. Dunglass pointed out to Butler that his survival would depend additionally 'on the

* See below, p. 49.

extent to which the Labour leaders were encouraged to enter the government'. He asked Butler 'to talk to Halifax and to persuade him to become Prime Minister'.[196]

Chamberlain saw the King on the evening of the first day of the debate. He said 'smilingly' that he had not come to offer his resignation and that he had not yet abandoned all hope of reconstructing his government as a national coalition which Labour would join. The King asked Chamberlain whether it would help if he spoke to Attlee about, in the King's words, 'the national standpoint of the Labour Party', saying that he hoped they would realise that they must 'pull their weight and join a national government'. Chamberlain replied that he thought an appeal should be postponed till after the party's annual conference, which was to be held at Bournemouth over the next weekend. The King told Chamberlain that he did not like the way in which – with all the worries and responsibilities he had to bear in the conduct of the war – 'he was always subject to a stab in the back from both the House of Commons and the Press'.[197]

At this stage the King's view was that Chamberlain should continue as Prime Minister of a coalition government. Chamberlain was by now prepared to make concessions to his Conservative critics. At seven on 8 May, while the debate was going on, Lord Dunglass saw the Conservative rebels Paul Evans and Derrick Gunston, indicating to them that, if they and their allies agreed to vote with the government, Chamberlain would see them on 9 May and that they would find him 'ready to meet' their demands. When he was asked what that meant, he indicated (though without committing Chamberlain) that, to save himself, Chamberlain was prepared to sacrifice Hoare and Simon. But 'we say things have gone too far'.[198]

Dalton and Morrison told Butler that Labour would come into the government under Halifax but not under Chamberlain or in the company of Simon. Dalton said there was 'no other choice' but Halifax. Churchill should 'stick to the war', while Sir John Anderson, the dour Home Secretary – an implausible choice under virtually any circumstances – had been insufficiently 'built up'. Dalton 'saw no objection' to the 'Lords difficulty'.[199] Leo Amery claimed that Attlee had dined with Brendan Bracken and told Bracken that Labour would never serve under Churchill owing to the Tonypandy episode before the First World War. (Churchill, as Home Secretary, had dispatched troops to confront the miners of Tonypandy and adjacent areas. The facts are undisputed but complicated.) Attlee said he had never dined with Bracken alone and had never had any such conversation with Amery or, indeed, with anybody else. Attlee preferred Churchill, though he would have been prepared to serve under Halifax.[200]

At the end of the Norway debate on 8 May, 33 Conservatives and 8 of their supporters voted with the Opposition. Sixty abstained. The vote was 281 for the Government, 200 against. A united Conservative Party would have given Chamberlain a majority of 214 rather than 81. Lord Beaverbrook saw Churchill on the morning of 9 May. He asked him whether he intended to serve under Halifax. Churchill replied that he would serve under any Minister capable of prosecuting the war. This was 'a disappointment' to Beaverbrook. He had hoped that Churchill would be Prime Minister. The country wanted him. Any other choice would be 'a shock'. The choice of Halifax 'would simply mean the continuance of the present administration'. Beaverbrook's account went on to say that Brendan Bracken intervened. He asked Churchill to remain silent and 'after much argument' Churchill agreed.[201]

Churchill saw Eden also on that morning. He telephoned him at 9.30, saying he wanted to see him as soon as possible. While shaving he rehearsed to Eden the events of the previous evening. He thought that Chamberlain would not be able to bring in Labour and that a national government must be formed. Later Eden lunched with Churchill and Kingsley Wood. Wood thought Churchill should succeed Chamberlain and urged him to make plain his willingness to do so.[202] That was Eden's account in his diary. In his memoirs he expanded – some might say modified – it. He wrote that he was surprised to find Wood giving a warning that Chamberlain would want Halifax to succeed him and want Churchill to agree to this. Wood advised: 'Don't agree, and don't say anything.'[203] He was 'shocked' that Kingsley Wood should talk in this way, because 'he had been so much Chamberlain's man', but it was 'good counsel, and I seconded it'.[204]

Meanwhile Butler had passed on Dalton's and Morrison's friendly messages to Halifax. On the morning of 9 May Butler waited in Halifax's room to hear an account of his conversations with Chamberlain. Halifax returned with, in his own words, 'a bad stomach ache' – his phrase, literal rather than metaphorical, for his condition when he was worried or disturbed. Chamberlain had pressed him strongly to accept the succession: Halifax had put all the arguments he could think of against himself. He told Butler that he felt he could do the job. He also felt that Churchill needed 'a restraining influence': himself. Could that restraint be better exercised as Prime Minister or as a Minister in Churchill's government? Even if he chose the former role, Churchill's qualities and experience would surely mean that he would be 'running the war anyway'. Halifax's own position in the House of Lords would rapidly turn him into a kind of 'honorary Prime Minister'. This would be 'an impossible situation'. Butler did not try to contradict Halifax's arguments:

> I saw their force. I also saw that, in truth, Edward did not really want the premiership, was indeed bent on self-abnegation.[205]

As early as January 1939 Halifax had taken account of the possibility of the premiership, only to dismiss it because of 'being in the Lords'.[206] On 9 May 1940 he put to Chamberlain all the arguments he could think of against himself, notably 'the difficult position of a Prime Minister unable to make contact with the centre of gravity in the House of Commons'.[207] On the same day he repeated to Chamberlain that, if 'the Labour people' said that they would serve only under him, he would tell them that he 'was not prepared to do it' and see 'whether a definite attitude could make them budge'.[208]

Chamberlain's first biographer Keith Feiling asserts that he decided to resign the premiership 'instantly' at the end of the Norway debate. He felt that a national government should be formed, 'knowing that he would not lead it'. 'Consultations' convinced him that his first preference, Halifax, 'was not the way out', and he agreed to put Churchill's name to the King.[209] This is nearer the truth than A.J.P. Taylor's version, which depicts Chamberlain as clinging to office.[210] Nevertheless, even after the crucial division, on 9 May Chamberlain apparently saw Amery – 'apparently' because Amery's testimony is not always of the best – and offered him the choice of the Exchequer or the Foreign Office. Amery refused. Only when it became clear that the rebels, or 'the malcontents' as *The Times* of the day called them, had refused all concessions did Margesson inform Chamberlain that he could not continue as Prime Minister.[211] Nevertheless, he reverted briefly to thinking that he himself could carry on. He was fortified in this view by the German invasion of Holland and Belgium. Kingsley Wood, who was to succeed Simon as Chancellor on 12 May, told Churchill on 10 May that Chamberlain was 'inclined to feel' that the battle in the Low Countries made it 'necessary for him to remain at his post'. Chamberlain had earlier put the same point of view to Hoare.

At 4.30 on 9 May Chamberlain met Churchill and Halifax at No. 10. Chamberlain said that the 'main thing' was national unity. Labour must come into the government. If they refused to come in under his leadership, he was 'quite ready' to resign. Attlee and Greenwood then arrived.[212] They sat on one side of the table while the Prime Minister and his two colleagues sat on the other. They were asked whether they would join a national government. Attlee said, quoting himself from memory:

> I have to be quite frank with you, Prime Minister, our party will not serve under you. They don't want you, and in my view the country doesn't want you.[213]

Attlee thought this was 'very rude', though 'true'.[214] Churchill, on the other hand, considered that 'the conversation was most polite'.[215] Attlee further recalled the meeting to his biographer, Kenneth Harris:

> He seemed to have no idea that he was finished. He seemed to think he could carry on. He said that it was now necessary to have a national government and he asked us if we would serve in it under him as leader. It was incredible. When he finished, Winston spoke up and said we should come in under Chamberlain. That was understandable; in any case Winston had Norway

on his back. And he cared more about getting a government that could win the war than about who was to be Prime Minister. Was quite sincere. Halifax said nothing.[216]

Attlee was then asked whether Labour would participate in a coalition of which someone else was the head. He said he thought it would but that, as the party was holding its annual conference at Bournemouth, he would 'go down and ask the delegates'.[217] It was agreed that he should ask two questions. First, would the Labour Party serve under Chamberlain? And, second, would it serve under someone else?[218] A.J.P. Taylor was wrong to write that Attlee and Greenwood 'shrank from responsibility'.[219] On the contrary: they behaved in a most responsible manner. As *The Times* accurately recorded:

> They gave a preliminary indication that they would accept office in a new government, but that they could not do so with Mr Chamberlain as Prime Minister. They undertook to give a formal reply after consulting their colleagues of the executive committee of the Labour Party.[220]

J.W. Wheeler-Bennett asserts that there were two meetings: the first, attended by Chamberlain, Halifax, Churchill and Margesson, at 4.15; the second, attended by Chamberlain, Halifax, Churchill, Attlee and Greenwood, at 6.30.[221] Robert Blake follows Wheeler-Bennett as to the number and the order of the meetings.[222] Martin Gilbert, Robert Rhodes James and Kenneth Harris say there were three meetings: the first attended by the three principal Conservatives; the second attended by them and the two Labour leaders; and the third attended by the three Conservatives again, with Margesson putting in spasmodic appearances at this meeting, at the first one or at both.[223] Andrew Roberts, however, implies that the most important meeting, at which Churchill effectively made himself Prime Minister – by keeping silent – occurred before the arrival of the Labour leaders.[224] A.J.P. Taylor implies that Chamberlain met the Labour leaders alone.[225] This is clearly wrong. Attlee and Churchill are in agreement that Churchill and Halifax were also present.[226] The best evidence about the chronological order of the meetings is to be found, not in Halifax's diary, but in the account he gave Alexander Cadogan immediately afterwards, reproduced in Cadogan's own diary. No. 10 Downing Street possesses no records of visitors there on the day in question.[227]

> After they [the Labour leaders] had gone, PM, Winston and I discussed possibilities. PM said I was the man mentioned as the most acceptable. I said it would be hopeless position. If I was not in charge of the war (operations) and if I didn't lead in the House, I should be a cipher. I thought Winston was a better choice. Winston did *not* demur. Was very kind and polite but showed that he thought this right solution. Chief Whip and others think feeling in the House has been veering towards him. If NC remains – as he is ready to do – his advice and judgment would steady Winston.[228]

There are two other pieces of persuasive evidence for the crucial meeting's having occurred after the departure of Attlee and Greenwood. First, Churchill urged them to join a coalition under Chamberlain. He would scarcely have done that if it had already been agreed that he would be Prime Minister. And, second, Churchill himself erroneously gave the date of the meeting as 10 May rather than the 9th.[229] He was at any rate clear that it had happened *after* the Labour leaders had gone.

According to Halifax, Chamberlain said he had made up his mind he must go: either he or Churchill should succeed him. He would serve under either. Margesson said unity was essential. He thought it would be 'impossible' to attain under Chamberlain. This was Halifax's impression. Margesson later gave a different account. Certainly he told Chamberlain that his own party could no longer be relied on to support him and that he should resign. Chamberlain asked who Margesson considered should succeed to the premiership. He answered that the House of Commons would prefer Halifax.[230] Halifax then said that he thought that 'for all the reasons given' Chamberlain must 'probably' go, but that he had no doubt in his own mind that for him to take the premiership would 'create a quite impossible position'. Apart from Churchill's qualities as compared to his own 'at this particular juncture', what in fact would be his situation? Churchill would be running Defence. In this connection one was forced to remember how rapidly the position between Asquith and Lloyd George had become 'impossible'. Moreover, he would have no access to the House of Commons.[231] In a famous passage, Churchill recalled, having erroneously cast the meeting from the evening of 9 May to 11 a.m. on the 10th:

> I was again summoned to Downing Street by the Prime Minister. There once more I found Lord Halifax. We took our seats on the table opposite Mr Chamberlain. He told us that he was satisfied that it was beyond his power to form a national government. The responses he had received from the Labour leaders left him in no doubt of this. The question therefore was whom he should advise the King to send for after his own resignation had been accepted. His demeanour was cool, unruffled and seemingly quite detached from the personal aspect of the affair. He looked at us both across the table. I have had many important interviews in my public life, and this was certainly the most important. Usually I talk a great deal, but on this occasion I was silent … As I remained silent a very long pause ensued. It certainly seemed longer than the two minutes which one observes in the commemorations of Armistice Day.[232]

In his life of Halifax, Andrew Roberts makes perhaps over-heavy weather of the length of this silence.[233] After all, Churchill did not say that it lasted for two minutes but that, to him, it felt like two minutes. Churchill then gives a brief account of Halifax's intervention, accurately summarising but not supplementing Halifax's own version. After Halifax had finished:

It was clear that the duty would fall upon me – had in fact fallen upon me.
Then for the first time I spoke. I said I would have no communication with
either of the opposition parties until I had the King's Commission to form a
government. On this the momentous conversation came to an end ....[234]

That night Churchill dined at Admiralty House with Sinclair, Eden,
Bracken and Lindemann. Churchill said he 'thought it plain' that Chamberlain would advise the King to send for him, as Halifax 'did not wish to
succeed'. Later that night he telephoned his son Randolph and said: 'I
think I shall be Prime Minister tomorrow.'[235]

On 9-10 May Hitler invaded Holland and Belgium. The attack made
Chamberlain waver. He contemplated remaining at his post. He told
Beaverbrook that he had made up his mind about the course he should
pursue and had agreed it with Churchill and Halifax. But, as he had
expected, Hitler had 'seized the occasion for our divisions to strike the
great blow and we cannot consider changes in the government while we
are in the throes of battle'.[236]

Kingsley Wood, who was to succeed Simon as Chancellor on 12 May,
told Churchill on the morning of the 10th that Chamberlain was 'inclined
to feel' that the battle in the Low Countries made it 'necessary for him to
remain at his post'. Chamberlain had earlier put the same point of view to
Sir Samuel Hoare. Hoare was Minister for Air, Wood Lord Privy Seal.
They had changed places on 3 April. Hoare was prepared to grant Chamberlain a new lease of life: Wood was not, and told Chamberlain that, on
the contrary, the turn of events made it all the more necessary to have a
national government. Wood claimed that Chamberlain 'accepted' this
view.[237]

Attlee and Greenwood had not gone immediately to Bournemouth to
consult their colleagues. On the morning of 10 May they consulted the
Parliamentary Committee of the Parliamentary Labour Party, that is, the
Shadow Cabinet. Afterwards the following statement was issued:

> The Labour Party, in view of the latest series of abominable aggressions by
> Hitler, while firmly convinced that a drastic reconstruction of the govern-
> ment is vital and urgent in order to win the war, reaffirms its determination
> to do its utmost to achieve victory. It calls upon all its members to devote all
> their energies to this end, and to stand firmly united through whatever trials
> and sacrifices may lie ahead.[238]

This declaration was presumably intended to acquit the Labour Party
of any lack of patriotic zeal if it refused to serve either under Chamberlain
(for at that stage it was not known for certain by the Labour leaders that
he would not continue as Prime Minister) or under anybody else. There
was no need to worry. Attlee, Greenwood and Dalton travelled to
Bournemouth later in the morning and met the National Executive in the
Highcliff Hotel. The Executive agreed unanimously to answer No to

Chamberlain's first question and Yes to his second. A resolution was passed stating that Labour should take its 'share of responsibility' as a full partner in a new government which, under a new Prime Minister, commanded 'the confidence of the nation'. The Executive agreed that this was a decision to be put to the conference not for discussion but for approval. As he was about to leave the hotel for the station, Attlee received a telephone call from the Prime Minister's Secretary: was he in a position to answer Chamberlain's two questions? Attlee said he was, did so and read out the Executive's resolution at dictation speed.[239]

The War Cabinet met in the afternoon. Chamberlain said he had now received the Labour Party's answer to his questions, which had been passed to him while the Cabinet was already in session. He read out the Executive's resolution. The minutes recorded:

> In the light of this answer, he [Chamberlain] had reached the conclusion that the right course was that he should at once tender his resignation to the King. He proposed to do so that evening. He thought it would be convenient that the new Prime Minister should be authorised to assume that all members of the War Cabinet placed their resignations at the disposal of the new Prime Minister, when sent for by the King, and that there was no necessity for this to be confirmed in writing. In the meantime, of course, Ministers remained in office and would continue to discharge their functions until a new administration had been formed ... The War Cabinet agreed to the course suggested.[240]

George VI thought it was 'most unfair' for Chamberlain to be treated in this way 'after all his good work'. He thought 'Conservative rebels like Duff Cooper ought to be ashamed of themselves for deserting him at this hour'. Chamberlain came to the Palace shortly after tea. He told the King what Attlee had said. He then said he wanted to resign to make it possible for a new Prime Minister to form a government. The King accepted his resignation and told him how 'grossly unfairly' he thought he had been treated. He was 'terribly sorry'. They then had an 'informal talk' about a successor.

> I, of course, suggested Halifax, but he told me that Halifax was not enthusiastic, as being in the Lords he could only act as a shadow or a ghost in the Commons, where all the real work took place. I was disappointed over this statement, as I thought Halifax was the obvious man, and that his peerage could be placed in abeyance for the time being. Then I knew that there was only one person whom I could send for to form a government who had the confidence of the country, and that was Winston. I asked Chamberlain [for] his advice, and he told me Winston was the man to send for.[241]

Had Chamberlain wanted Churchill all along? Beaverbrook asked Wood afterwards whether he had decided that Chamberlain ought to be supplanted by Churchill and, if so, when he had started working to that end. Wood replied that 'quite soon' after the start of the war Chamberlain told him that he would have to give way to Churchill. He had never intended that Halifax should be Prime Minister but always meant Churchill to be his successor. By the end of 1939 it had 'become obvious that the change was not far off'. He 'started negotiations' with Churchill which resulted in that change.[242] It is likely that Wood was both exaggerating his role vis-à-vis Churchill and explaining that disloyalty, real or apparent, to Chamberlain which had so shocked Eden. It is still possible, however, that Chamberlain wanted Churchill rather than Halifax to succeed him.

The Queen's Commission

It's a great thing, you know, to get the Queen's Commission. Yes,
that's what counts – the Queen's Commission.
Harold Macmillan to Henry Fairlie, 1959

C.R. ATTLEE IN 1945

The unexpected result of the 1945 election was that Labour won 393 seats
to the Conservatives' 213 and the Liberals' 12. Even before the result was
announced, Herbert Morrison and Harold Laski had been attempting to
dislodge C.R. Attlee, Deputy Prime Minister in the Coalition Government,
from the leadership of the party. As Attlee was later to write: 'Laski ... had
tried very hard to substitute Morrison for me as leader of the party in the
general election, but failed to get any response.'[1] Morrison's argument now
was that Attlee should not accept an invitation from the King to form a
government before the Parliamentary Labour Party had met and elected
a leader. He told his colleagues that he could not agree to serve under
Attlee there and then. Attlee and Bevin said it was out of the question for
the leader of the party, who had now been asked by the King to form a
government, to submit to a leadership election within the parliamentary
party. As Attlee put it:

> If the King asks you to form a government you say 'Yes' or 'No' not: 'I'll let
> you know later.' If you are asked, you try to form a government, and if you
> can't you go to the King and tell him so, and advise him to ask somebody
> else.[2]

On the afternoon of 26 July 1945 Attlee, Bevin, Morrison and the party's
general secretary, Morgan Phillips, gathered in Bevin's room at the party's
headquarters, Transport House, Westminster. Laski and other members
of the National Executive Committee were in Phillips's room. A message
arrived from Churchill conceding defeat and informing Attlee that he
would go to the Palace at seven that evening. Churchill added that he
would advise the King to send for Attlee.[3] Morrison, however, claimed to
have the support of Sir Stafford Cripps. While Morrison was out of the
room, Bevin asked Phillips about Attlee's prospects in a Parliamentary
Labour Party election. Phillips replied that, on a split vote, he thought

Bevin would win. Bevin turned to Attlee and said: 'Clem, you go to the Palace straightaway.'[4]

There things were quieter. George VI recorded that he saw Churchill at seven. It was 'a very sad meeting'. The King told him he thought 'the people were very ungrateful after the way they had been led in the war'. Churchill was 'very calm', saying that with the majority 'the Socialists' had over other parties and with 'careful management' they could be in power 'for years'. The King asked him whether he 'should send for Mr Attlee to form a government and he agreed'. At 7.30 Attlee followed Churchill to the Palace.[5] Throughout this change, the war outside Europe was continuing. Japan surrendered on 14 August 1945.

C.R. ATTLEE IN 1950

In 1950 Labour won 315 seats to the Conservatives' 298 and the Liberals' 9. As the House had been reduced to 625 Members from the 640 who had been elected in 1945, Labour had a clear absolute majority – 2 more Members, in fact, than the 313 who would have been required to produce that result. And yet the consequence was constitutional consternation. Four years later Attlee was to write, with a moderation characteristic of himself but untypical of the climate of the time:

> It was, of course, obvious that with so slender a majority our position in the House of Commons was going to be very difficult and that we could not embark on any major controversial measures, but the King's government had got to be carried on, whatever the difficulties.[6]

Late on Friday 24 February 1950 the Cabinet met and 'after discussion' decided to carry on in government.[7] Others were not so sure about whether Labour could – or, indeed, about whether it was right to try. A dissolution was thought to be imminent. There ensued a learned correspondence in *The Times* concerning the King's prerogative to grant or refuse a dissolution.[8] J.W. Wheeler-Bennett tells us in his life of George VI that there was 'some talk', presumably emanating from the Palace, of an all-party conference 'to consider the question of carrying on the King's government'.[9] This piece of royal meddling was rejected by both Attlee and Churchill. In a letter to the King's private secretary, Sir Alan Lascelles, Churchill reiterated his view, first expressed in 1923, that

> the principle that a new House of Commons has a right to live if it can and should not be destroyed until some fresh issue or situation has arisen to place before the electors is, I believe, sound.[10]

Attlee was received by the King on Monday 27 February and agreed to form a government.

WINSTON CHURCHILL IN 1951

In the general election of October 1951 the Conservatives won 321 seats to Labour's 295 and the Liberals' 6. On the afternoon of Friday 26 October Attlee – in a development that had begun with Benjamin Disraeli in 1868 – conceded defeat. At 5.00 p.m. he went to the Palace and resigned, receiving 'the thanks of his Sovereign for his great and important service during the arduous course of the past six and a half years'.[11] At 5.45 Churchill drove to the Palace and was asked by the King to form a new administration. As the Court Circular of 26 October 1951 put it, he 'accepted His Majesty's offer, and kissed hands upon his appointment as Prime Minister and First Lord of the Treasury'.[12]

ANTHONY EDEN IN 1955

After the 1951 election, Anthony Eden expected to succeed Winston Churchill within months.[13] It was not to be. The Conservative government of 1951-5 was dominated by medical matters: by Churchill's strokes and by Eden's botched gall-bladder operation, which necessitated a visit to the United States for remedial treatment that turned out to be only partially successful.

In January 1953 Harry Crookshank, the Lord Privy Seal, said to Eden that no one could tell when a general election might have to be held. Therefore Churchill should go at the coronation of Queen Elizabeth II on 2 June 1953. There was, Crookshank added – referring to the resignation of Baldwin and the succession of Chamberlain to coincide with George VI's coronation in 1937 – an historical precedent for this course. Eden replied that he did not think Churchill would much like the precedent. Crookshank said that some of them ought to consider how to make their views known to him but that he had not wished to 'make any move' without first consulting Eden.[14]

There the matter more or less rested until Churchill had his stroke. This was successfully concealed from the public by a conspiracy of newspaper proprietors organised by Churchill's private secretary, Sir John Colville. Robert Rhodes James states that the 'principal reason' for the concealment was Eden's absence owing to illness. Churchill did not consider Butler to be 'ready' for the premiership – which in any case added to his determination to hang on for as long as possible.[15] However this may be (for it is entirely possible that the concealment would still have taken place if Eden had been present in London, in rude health), the first Eden knew about the situation was contained in a personal letter of 26 June 1953 from Colville to Clarissa, Lady Eden. Colville said there was an agreement between Salisbury and Butler that if, as then appeared likely, Churchill had to resign, the advice to the Queen would be for a 'caretaker' government nominally headed by Salisbury, who would not take the title of Prime Minister and would relinquish his post once Eden was well again.[16] Colville recorded that Butler 'says he will serve loyally under Eden and that anyhow some of the Conservative Party might not want him (Rab) as PM because of Munich'.[17]

On 2 August Colville accompanied Churchill to the Royal Lodge, where he saw the Queen. He told her that his decision on whether or not to retire would be made in a month. He would then be able to see 'clearly' whether he was fit to face Parliament and to make a speech to the Conservative conference in October.[18] Colville's approach concerning the 'caretaker' government was made to the Queen's private secretary Sir Alan Lascelles.[19] The odd feature of this scheme was that Butler, the Chancellor of the Exchequer, had already been nominated both as chairman of the Cabinet and as acting Prime Minister in the absence of Churchill and Eden.[20] A quarter of a century later, Butler was to recall:

> At the time I was forbidden to mention it – forbidden. But, yes, it is fundamentally true. I kept quiet at the time because I felt there was something to do with the Crown being involved, in the very early days of the young Queen's accession. The point was that I was the only person who was active, fit and running everything – and I think they felt they should protect Anthony.[21]

Both Churchill and Eden duly returned to their tasks. Things were not going well between them. Their hostility derived from Churchill's conviction that he and he alone could save the world from nuclear incineration. He would accomplish this by means of a summit conference with the Russians. Following the death of Stalin in 1953 they would, he considered, prove more amenable. Eden was sceptical. He was so not because he was a more vigorous cold warrior than Churchill. In many respects, he was less of one. He demonstrated this in the Geneva Conference of 1954, which settled the pattern of Indochina until it was disrupted by the Vietnam war. But Churchill's way was not Eden's way of conducting diplomatic business.

On 2 July 1954 Churchill tentatively fixed 21 September as the day for handing over to Eden. At the same time he fixed early August as the time for a visit to Moscow of which, in the end, nothing was to come. He sent a telegram to the Russian Foreign Minister, proposing himself. His private secretary, Colville, remonstrated with him for not consulting the Cabinet first. If the Russians answered affirmatively it would be too late for his colleagues to give any contrary opinions. Churchill replied that he would make it a matter of confidence with them. If they opposed the visit, this would give him a good occasion to go.[22]

It was not only Eden who wanted Churchill to depart. Harold Macmillan, then Minister of Housing and Local Government, felt similarly. Churchill's coolness towards Macmillan increased as his wife Clemmie came to regard him as the leader of the Cabinet cabal pressing her husband to retire. In July 1954 Macmillan recorded that Churchill was 'quite incapable', mentally as well as physically, of remaining Prime Minister. His judgment was 'distorted'. He thought about one thing all the time, the Russian visit and his chance of saving the world. This had become an 'obsession'.[23] In the same month, Churchill confided to his personal physician, Lord Moran, that he would 'go soon', even though he did not 'want to go at all'. There was, in his judgment – he was probably wrong about this – no 'strong movement, either way' inside the Cabinet, though 'Anthony wants it awfully'. The day's Cabinet would be 'decisive. They must support me or I shall go.'[24]

Macmillan remained restive. He wrote in his diary that the Conservatives must have a completely new Cabinet, representative of the party. The present Cabinet was not so constituted. It was a 'Churchill creation', based on the practice not of peace but of war. All its members, who had 'loved as well as admired him', were being 'slowly driven into something like hatred'. They knew that illness had 'enormously altered and worsened his character'. He had always been an egoist, but a magnanimous one. Now he had become 'almost a monomaniac'. It 'breaks my heart' to see him 'begin to sink into a sort of Pétain'. Lady Churchill, according to Macmillan, longed for him to retire (which did not, however, prevent her from viewing Macmillan with suspicion). Lord Beaverbrook was, 'out of mischief' urging him to stay.[25] The Secretary of the Cabinet, Sir Norman Brook, agreed with Macmillan about the reality but interpreted it more favourably to Churchill. His conduct of business was

> really a *tour de force*. He picks it up as he goes along. He doesn't bother to master anything in advance. Plays bezique instead. It's really this business of meeting the Russians that keeps him from going. Anthony knows this. He ought to go before Parliament meets. There might be real trouble if he hangs on beyond that. He is trying Anthony and Rab very high.[26]

Four days later he was telling Colville that he had to make the most difficult decision of his life.[27] He told Moran that he did not know what to do. For half the day he was determined to stay on and 'see the business through'. Then, for the other half, his resignation seemed 'inevitable'. He thought Eden would be 'well advised' to become Leader of the House and Deputy Prime Minister. Churchill always considered Eden largely ignorant of home affairs, and thought he would be wise to remedy this deficiency. But he also wanted foreign affairs for himself, with Eden out of the way. Though Eden might want to be Prime Minister, 'I know my theme, and I don't want to give it up. I can do it better than anyone else.'[28]

In the middle of the month Churchill awoke in the morning at three and 'saw plainly outlined the most important and burdensome problem' which he had to solve: his relations with Eden. He did not see why Eden wanted to take over 'the dregs' at the fag end of a Parliament, with only one more session before the election, when nothing could be done. Churchill supposed Eden saw himself – this is Moran's account – as 'the brilliant young leader' who would 'change everything'. But there was 'no money' and 'without money, believe me, you cannot do anything'.[29] By 18 August Churchill had made up his mind that he would not go, at any rate until Christmas 1954. There might be 'a bloody row' but he did not care. He did not think the Cabinet would 'gain anything by knocking me about'.[30]

On the same day Butler wrote an emollient letter to Churchill. Whether it was intended to winkle him out through flattery or to fortify him in his resolve to stay is difficult to determine. Since summer 1953, Butler wrote, at the time of his 'severe illness', they had all accepted that Eden was to be his successor. Butler therefore had a loyalty to Eden which he had to be 'careful not to abuse'. How they would 'resolve all of this' he did not yet see. However, Churchill should know that 'I shall from now on expend a fund of understanding on your arguments and shall evaluate at its priceless worth the boon of your strength and experience in handling world events'.[31] It may be that Butler thought that, the longer Churchill stayed, the greater was his chance of the succession. At any rate, Churchill's will to hang on was strengthened. He said: 'I don't think I'm selfish, but it seems foolish to throw away all that I have to give, (though) I don't know why I am such a bloody fool as to want to go on.'[32]

Three days later Eden recorded that Macmillan and Butler came to see him. The latter said that he had been much embarrassed – that he had a dual loyalty both to Churchill and to him and had told Churchill so. Butler was convinced Churchill was determined to stay. Neither he nor Macmillan pretended this was desirable. The issue was what to do about it. Butler clearly wanted Eden to consider whether he could take over 'the home front' and the leadership of the House (a course which Churchill also favoured). This, Butler urged, would make Eden Prime Minister in everything but name. Macmillan did not conceal his concern at trying to carry on with Churchill. Nor did Eden. The reshuffle was 'merely a device to carry on longer while doing even less'. Churchill would then do nothing except interfere with the Foreign Office. This might have disastrous results. They all agreed that it was essential to have a meeting of a number of colleagues soon.[33]

Eden then walked over to see Churchill. He said that he had explained what he thought many times. If he was not fit to stand on his own two feet now and choose an administration, he would probably be less fit in a year's time. The government was not functioning well. This was putting a heavy strain on senior Ministers. They were able men but there was no co-ordination. Churchill 'didn't like this and said he had never missed a day since his illness'. Eden said that his was not the point. There was 'no co-ordination on the home front' and Cabinets 'dragged on far too long'.[34]

This courageous assault by Eden did not produce the desired effect. On 28 August 1954 Churchill said that he would 'resist and resent it' if they tried to push him out, though everybody had been 'very nice'. He would 'like to play the game' and wanted to be 'magnanimous and broad-minded'. He would go in a year's time.[35] Next day Churchill said that all the members of the Cabinet had accepted his staying on: 'there won't be any trouble, I think'.[36]

He had told Eden on the *Queen Elizabeth* (the purpose of the journey was to have discussions with President Eisenhower and his colleagues) that he intended to resign around 20 September. In August Colville recorded that he was showing 'new signs of irresolution'. The thought of abandoning office grew 'more abhorrent' as the time came nearer. Colville thought he did not realise what trouble was in store for him from his Cabinet colleagues if he stayed on but that at the same time he did realise how difficult it would be for them to turn him out 'without ruining their chances at the next election' – a questionable hypothesis, as Eden's victory in 1955, increasing the Conservatives' seats from 321 to 344, was to demonstrate.[37]

In early September Churchill wrote to Eden. His letter contained some sharp touches. He was sorry that Eden was not happy about taking over home affairs. He himself had experienced 'a rather trying time' during the past 15 months. In the first part of this period he had been much troubled by Eden's absence through illness and the 'uncertainty' about whether and when he would be able to return. Since this had 'happily occurred', he had been 'distracted by the continual pressure' of some of Eden's friends, who wanted him to resign in Eden's favour. But he had tried to discharge the duty to which he had been 'appointed by the Crown and Parliament'. He was glad to say that he had 'not missed a single day's control of affairs in spite of his temporary loss of physical mobility'. Now he had good reports from his doctor.[38]

Following this discouraging news, Eden had further talks with Harold Macmillan and the Chief Whip, Patrick Buchan-Hepburn. Unlike Colville, they were gloomy about the party's prospects if Churchill stayed and were 'a little inclined to complain, perhaps rightly' that Eden had made things too easy for Churchill. They were keen to press for Churchill's departure on his 80th birthday, 30 November 1954. Eden confided to his diary: 'I don't think we can succeed, but no harm in trying.'[39]

At the beginning of October Eden told Macmillan that he could not go on unless Churchill agreed to some definite date for the handover. He asked Macmillan to tell Churchill this, which Macmillan agreed to do.[40] Macmillan wrote to Churchill on the same day, saying he could quite see that there were 'difficulties about making more sweeping changes in the Government at this moment'. But he felt that the more important matter was Eden's position. This was 'vital'. After all that had happened, he hoped Churchill would find it possible to come to a clear and definite arrangement with Eden about the date of the handover. Eden should know this and have a fair run on his own before the election. Otherwise they might 'lose him now, as well as the election when it comes'.[41]

This was strong stuff: all the stronger for coming not from Eden himself, or Butler, the Chancellor of the Exchequer, or Lord Salisbury, the Lord President of the Council, but from Harold Macmillan, then the mere Minister of Housing and Local Government. Not only was he threatening the Foreign Secretary's resignation. Worse: he was also asserting that the continuing presence of Churchill as Prime Minister was imperilling the Conservatives' chances of re-election. Macmillan certainly deserves high marks for courage. But the only effect of the missive was to strengthen Churchill in his awkward resolve. Macmillan noted that he was to remain Prime Minister without any commitment 'written or verbal' about the date of his departure. He went on to acknowledge Churchill's 'skill and tenacity'. He had refused to see Ministers unless separately, playing off one against the other, and had emerged triumphant.[42] (When Margaret Thatcher, in very different circumstances, employed the same technique in November 1990 it was less successful.*)

In victory, however, Churchill was by no means serene. In October Moran found him in an 'explosive' mood, speaking bitterly of the folly of the Tories in rashly throwing away all he had to give. Moran suspected that his son-in-law, Christopher Soames – then Member for Bedford and Churchill's own Parliamentary Private Secretary – had told him of the feeling in the party that he ought to go. Moran claimed to have established that his 'guess was on the target'. However, though the colleagues might have made up their minds, Churchill had no intention of bowing to their wishes. 'If they try to get me out I will resist.'[43] The Conservatives, Moran concluded, had 'got it into their heads at last' that no one could turn Churchill out until he was willing and ready to go. The public, so the doctor – like Colville – believed, 'would not stand for it' and had given up speculating about the date of his retirement.[44]

On 10 December Churchill supplied his own date. He told Moran that he would 'clear out at the end of June'. He would do this not because he thought it would be good for the party or the country but because he was 'sorry for Anthony'. However, his expectations for Eden were not high. 'He may easily flop, though I shall protect him as far as I can.'[45] Eleven days later, Eden went to see Churchill at No. 10. His wife Clemmie was there with him. Eden found her charming, though worried about his colour. Churchill said he supposed Eden 'had been living too well in Paris', when he had been on official business. Following Clemmie's departure, Churchill, after a long pause, said 'in his most aggressive tone': 'What do you want to see me about?' Eden replied that Churchill had received his letter and agreed to discuss it. Slowly the argument began.

At first Churchill would concede nothing. All was 'as well as possible'.

* See below, pp. 229-31.

There was no hurry for an election or for him to hand over. The end of June or – extending slightly the period he had indicated to Moran – July would do very well. Eden explained 'laboriously' that the new administration should have the chance to establish itself with the public. The timetable favoured by Churchill gave it none. Furthermore, it would place him in a much stronger position if he could take over in a month when an election was possible. Then, if his 'authority or mandate' was challenged, he could either 'fight it out in Parliament' or say 'very well, let the country judge, and go to the country'. He could not do this in June. Churchill 'wasn't much interested' in this argument – not surprisingly. But when Eden

> made it quite clear that I was not interested either in taking over at the end of June he eventually agreed to meeting at 3.00 p.m. with the people I chose. But it was all most grudging. There was much rather cruel *divide et impera*.* For instance, he asked me how I got on with Harold. I said: 'Very well, why?' He replied: 'Oh, he is very ambitious.' I laughed.[46]

The meeting was held next day, 22 December, though Eden's diary suggests that it was to be held on the same day as his meeting with Churchill. Those present were Eden, Salisbury, Woolton, Butler, Crook-shank and Stuart. According to Eden's diary, it was 'not a pleasant business'. (Butler had told Eden on the evening of 21 December how 'unsatisfactory' the position was. The Cabinets which Eden had missed had taken no decision.) Butler annoyed Eden by coming out with a mass of technical arguments against the election in March 1955. Macmillan questioned this, saying that if there was an emergency Butler could presumably overcome these difficulties. Butler 'somewhat uncivilly' agreed. After a certain amount of further desultory conversation, Churchill 'rounded on' Eden and said it was clear they 'wanted him out. Nobody contradicted him.' At the end Churchill said 'menacingly' that he would think over what his colleagues had said and let them know his decision. Whatever it was, he hoped it would not affect their present relationship with him. 'Nobody quailed.' James Stuart, the Scottish Secretary and Churchill acolyte, said afterwards to Eden that the meeting had been 'painful but absolutely necessary'. Churchill had to be told that he could not pursue a course of 'such utter selfishness'.

Later, Salisbury, Macmillan and Eden met in the Foreign Secretary's room. They 'gloomily surveyed the scene'. It was clear to them that 'Rab would give no help'. Eden pointed out that he had had his say with Churchill. The others agreed that no more could be expected of him. Accordingly they would try to hold a meeting, without Churchill or Eden, of those colleagues who were still in London before Christmas 1954. Salisbury proposed himself for the task of organising it. Later, Butler assured him that he would attend 'and only wished to be helpful'. Eden

---

* cf. Macmillan above, p. 58.

could not tell what the result of all this activity would be, 'except that the
old man feels bitterly towards me'. But this 'I cannot help'.

> The colleagues are unanimous about drewling [sic] Cabinets, the failure to
> take decisions, the general atmosphere of '*après moi le déluge*' and someone
> had to give a heave.[47]

Nominally, the meeting was about the timing of the election. In reality
it was about how long Churchill should stay. He had now fixed July 1955
as his date of departure. According to Macmillan, Eden was 'in despair'.
Government business 'creaks along'. Stuart thought Churchill would
never again make any decision about anything, and would stay on until he
died or the Parliament ended in 1956.[48]

In the New Year Macmillan lunched with Moran. He told the doctor
that Churchill ought to resign. When he was at Housing, the Prime
Minister had left it all to him. Now he was at Defence (he had moved there
on 18 October 1954) he found Churchill could 'no longer handle these
complicated matters properly'. He could not do his job as Prime Minister
as it ought to be done. He did not direct. Of course he was still tough and
was not 'bothered with principles like Salisbury'. When the moment came,
he would have to decide how he went: 'he has missed so many curtains,
when he could have gone with everyone applauding'. It would not be so
easy now.[49] Later in January, however, there was a sign of a break in the
ice. Brendan Bracken wrote to Lord Beaverbrook that Churchill, under no
pressure from his wife, Eden or other Ministers – the last part of which
was patently untrue – intended to depart before July. He now said,
without any sign of regret, that it was now time he gave up. His only wish
was to find a 'small villa' in the South of France where he could spend the
winter months in the years remaining to him.[50]

Moran thought only Macmillan had shown the 'guts' to tell Churchill he
ought to go, which was unfair to Eden (though it may be that Moran was
thinking of Ministers apart from Eden).[51] However, both Butler and
Salisbury agreed with Macmillan and Eden that, in the latter's words, the
'situation must be chased up'. Accordingly Eden asked to see Churchill at
three on 1 February. 'All was quiet and smooth.' After a discussion of
Eden's plans, Eden asked for Churchill's. At Eden's suggestion, he sent for
a calendar. He admitted that he could not carry on after the dissolution
and said Eden could base his plans on his departure during the last week
of the session after Easter. Eden then told Butler, who confirmed later –
for Churchill would presumably have told Eden before Butler – that
Churchill had spoken to him in similar terms.[52]

On 3 February Christopher Soames telephoned Moran when Churchill
was out to inquire about his health. Moran asked a No. 10 colleague what
was in Soames's mind. She replied that he had one idea: he wanted the
Prime Minister to retire. It had taken a long time, but Soames had got his

way. The Prime Minister, she told Moran, would go in April. This is what happened. Moran wondered whether the credit should not go to Macmillan rather than to Soames.[53] A fortnight later Churchill confirmed his intentions to Moran:

> I'm earning my screw in these closing minutes. I work all day. I've made up my mind I shall go in April. But I'm not telling anyone. I want it to come as a surprise. So I'm spreading the gospel the other way that there is no reason why I should not carry on.[54]

On 26 February, at his country house, Chartwell in Kent, Churchill told Macmillan that he had fixed 5 April as the date of his resignation.[55] On 3 March he told Moran that there might be a coalition. If he had been a younger man he might have led it, but he would not go back on his decision. He was 'not thinking of a comeback. At least not yet.'[56] Macmillan, however, thought he was showing signs of backtracking. He was still contemplating the prospective summit. Eden was 'distraught' and said to Churchill: 'I have been Foreign Secretary for 10 years. Am I not to be trusted?' Macmillan described this as 'the most dramatic but harrowing discussion at which I have ever been present'.[57] Though Eden was a nervous man, his jumpiness was justified on this occasion. A fortnight before the planned date, Churchill was boasting to Moran that if he 'dug in' he did not think they could make him go.

> But I like Anthony so much and I have worked with him so long. And he wants to be Prime Minister terribly. Several times he has tried to bring on an election because he thought it would get me out.[58]

These last days were, according to Colville, 'painful'. Churchill began to form a 'cold hatred' of Eden who, he repeatedly said, had done more than anyone else to thwart him and prevent him from pursuing the policy he thought right. He also said that the prospect of giving everything up, after nearly 60 years in public life, was a 'terrible wrench'. He saw no reason why he should go. He was only doing it 'for Anthony'. But he could not possibly go at such a moment merely 'to satisfy Anthony's personal hunger for power'. If necessary he would call a party meeting and let the party decide. On the morning of 29 March he was determined not to go. He sent for Butler and dispatched him as an emissary to Eden to say that the proposed timetable must be revised. Colville advised Anthony Rumbold, then the Foreign Secretary's Principal Private Secretary, that for Eden 'amiability must be the watchword'.[59]

On 29 March the Churchills dined with the Edens. Next day Churchill told Colville that the occasion had been agreeable but that previously, at his audience with the Queen, he had said to her that he thought of putting off his resignation. He had asked her whether she minded and she had said No. However, he had enjoyed 'a very good night' and felt 'peacefully inclined'. He did not think there was much chance of a summit conference. That alone would be a valid reason for staying on.

At 6.30 on 30 March he saw Eden and Butler to confirm his decision to resign. Before the meeting he said to Colville: 'I have been altered and affected by Anthony's amiable manner.'[60] Even at this stage, matters did not move entirely smoothly. On 1 April the *Manchester Guardian* carried a report that Churchill would not retire until the end of the newspaper strike which was then going on. The paper claimed that he 'could not bear' to leave office in 'complete silence'. Churchill was angry:

> It is absurd. As if I would alter the date of the election because there are no papers; as if I cared a tinker's cuss what they say when I go ... I don't want to go, but Anthony wants it so much.[61]

On 4 April, his last night at No. 10, Churchill 'stared' at Colville and said 'with vehemence': 'I don't believe Anthony can do it.'[62] From his listening-posts at the Beefsteak and Travellers Clubs, Harold Nicolson reported on 5 April:

> At 4.30 Winston handed in his resignation to the Queen, who was graciously pleased to accept it. I suppose she will send for Anthony tomorrow.[63]

Three years previously, Butler had complained to Nicolson that his disability was that Eden was regarded as the heir-apparent.[64] As Lord Salisbury wrote afterwards to Eden: 'There was no question of who was to succeed Winston. The only problem was the timing.'[65]

Whatever hopes he may have entertained retrospectively, in his own memoir Butler was perfectly clear about the true position, showing no disposition to lament the past or to complain of unfair treatment:

> At the end of March Anthony and I were invited into the Cabinet room. Winston made a slip by asking me to sit on his right, but then corrected himself and beckoned to Anthony. We all gazed out over Horse Guards Parade. Then Winston said very shortly: 'I am going and Anthony will succeed me. We can discuss details later.' The ceremonial was over. We found ourselves in the passage where Anthony and I shook hands.[66]

In July 1955 Sir Norman Brook told Moran that the party – by which he evidently meant its senior figures – knew all about the date fixed for Churchill's departure. Eden could not have given way even if he had wanted to. President Eisenhower was told 'privately' that the Conservative Party had a general election in view. This forestalled any further talk of a summit conference. Then when all this was settled, Eden decided to take a chance and go to the country directly he took over from Churchill. Brook was certain that this was not just a trick to get Churchill out. The party had wanted to go to the country for some time. The 'real reason' why they wanted an election was that the economic situation was as good as it was likely to be. In autumn 1955 it might not be so good. The party refused to put the election off any longer. In this whole period, 1953-5, the crucial factor had been the correspondence of Eden's illness and Churchill's stroke:

> You know, [Brook said to Moran] if Anthony had not been ill when the P.M. had his stroke in 1953, Rab and Salisbury might have acted very differently. You see, the party had accepted Anthony as Winston's heir; he was ill, so there was nothing for it but to carry on with Winston, however incapacitated he might be.[67]

HAROLD MACMILLAN IN 1957

In January 1957 Anthony Eden resigned owing to ill-health. His doctors issued the following bulletin:

> The Prime Minister's health gives cause for anxiety. In spite of the improvement which followed his rest before Christmas there has been a recurrence of abdominal symptoms. This gives us much concern because of the serious operations in 1953 and some subsequent attacks of fever. In our opinion his health will no longer enable him to sustain the heavy burdens inseparable from the office of Prime Minister.[68]

Eden asked the Queen whether she could receive his wife and him at Sandringham. They drove there on 8 January.[69] The fraudulent official explanation was that Eden was visiting Sandringham to resume the practice of a weekly audience with the Queen. The Edens stayed overnight, returning to London on 9 December, as did the Queen. It was given out that a visit to her dressmaker required this visit to be made. It was a pretext. Just after six the Prime Minister's car drove into the forecourt of Buckingham Palace. Half an hour later, Eden was no longer Prime Minister.[70]

Previously, Eden had spoken about the succession to Sir Michael Adeane, the Queen's private secretary. He suggested to Adeane that a senior Minister who was not personally involved should be asked to take soundings in the Cabinet. The name of Salisbury came up immediately.[71] According to Eden's biographer, Robert Rhodes James, this did not mean that Eden wanted Salisbury to count heads, which is what he (with the Lord Chancellor, Lord Kilmuir) did.[72] The Queen's biographer, Ben Pimlott, tells us that Eden 'did not indicate any procedure'.[73] But it is difficult to see how Salisbury could have come up with a valid summary of the Cabinet's views – as distinct from a personal recommendation of his own – without going through the procedure which he and Kilmuir followed.

On the morning of 9 January Eden called Salisbury, Macmillan and Butler to No. 10 to tell them that he was going to resign and had called a special Cabinet later that afternoon to inform the other colleagues. According to Rhodes James, Salisbury had expected this: but both Macmillan and Butler were shocked.[74] Macmillan's biographer, Alistair Horne, agrees about Macmillan's condition.[75] However, Butler's biographer, Anthony Howard, tells us that Macmillan had warned Butler on the day after Eden's return to Downing Street, following his pre-Christmas break, that a number of the younger members of the Cabinet thought he could not possibly continue. This was a view which Butler rejected. He preferred the assessments of the Chief Whip, Edward Heath, and the chairman of the party, Oliver Poole. They both thought that Eden should at least be able to survive until the summer recess of 1957.[76] But Butler cannot have been wholly surprised if a somewhat mysterious letter from Sir Horace Evans to him is taken into account. He was Eden's doctor, and Butler's as well. After Macmillan had become Prime Minister, Evans wrote to Butler expressing his gratitude for 'your help and guidance over my difficult problems with AE ... Here we have made, I have no doubt, the right decision.'[77]

Salisbury went to see Kilmuir, whose advice was that the Queen was fully entitled to seek and receive advice from anyone she pleased to discover who would command the support of a majority in the House of Commons.[78] However, as in 1963, the Palace did not want to have to make a choice. The Queen's advisers wanted one name only. They 'took the view that it was for the Conservative Party to select its leader and that the Queen should not do anything until she was sure what the party had decided'.[79] If Eden had a preference, Rhodes James tells us, it was for Butler as a successor rather than for Macmillan. But he is firm that 'Eden played no part in the developments that led to the appointment of his successor'.[80]

James Stuart, later Lord Stuart of Findhorn, Secretary for Scotland and formerly Chief Whip, asserts that 'contrary to the usual practice, he left without tendering any advice to the throne as to his successor'.[81] Kilmuir is less sure but comes down in favour of the view that Eden did not offer any advice and was not asked to do so: 'I do not know for certain, but am fairly sure, that the advice of Sir Anthony Eden concerning his successor was not invited.'[82] Howard, however, states that Eden was 'certainly' asked, though whether he 'gave any specific recommendations as to his successor is still a matter of some dispute'.[83] Robert Blake is definite that Eden was not only asked to make a recommendation but did so, and that there was 'good evidence that he did not recommend Butler'.[84] Eden told Lord Blake that he was asked to make a recommendation. He did not say whether he agreed to do so. On the same evening he said: 'Rab was an arch-appeaser.' From this the historian concluded that his recommendation, if any, had not been Butler.[85] Keith Kyle asserts the opposite. He states that Eden volunteered that Butler had been both helpful and competent when he had deputised as Prime Minister during his periods of indisposition.[86] Kyle is right. Eden's account was:

> Her Majesty spoke of the future and of the difficult choice that lay before her. I agreed that it was certainly difficult. The Queen made no formal request for my advice but enabled me to signify that my own debt to Mr Butler while I have been Prime Minister was very real and that I thought he had discharged his difficult task during three weeks while I was away in Jamaica very well.[87]

Salisbury and Kilmuir then took it upon themselves to handle the succession. Kilmuir's role has perhaps been underemphasised, partly because, as a somewhat dreary and ill-favoured lawyer, he could not compete in glamour – or in the support which he lent to the theory of conspiracy – with the great Marquess of Salisbury, whose family had been involved in political intrigues of one kind or another since the days of Elizabeth I. It may have been depreciated too because it was Salisbury who, on the next day, saw the Queen to give her the Cabinet's and the party's advice. He meticulously reported the results of the soundings, and gave no views of his own.[88]

She also saw Churchill by her own request – or, rather, by that of Anthony Montague Browne, Churchill's private secretary. He took the view that it was important that Churchill should be seen publicly to have been consulted by the Queen. If his thoughts had not been heard, Browne considered, 'the omission might have been interpreted as indicating his disapproval' of her choice. He awaited a message from the Palace. None came. He telephoned Sir Michael Adeane and expressed his opinion. Adeane was 'somewhat brusque' and said: 'I really can't do business like this.' He suggested he might visit Chartwell to hear Churchill's views. Browne rejected this idea. He did not feel it would 'adequately indicate the thoroughness of consultation and satisify public opinion'. He also 'knew what a stimulant' a summons to the Palace would be for Churchill. Half an hour later Adeane telephoned Browne; apologised for having been 'rather shirty'; and made an appointment for Churchill to see the Queen next day.[89] On emerging Churchill was heard to remark: 'I said Macmillan. Is that right?'[90] He was personally fonder of Butler but doubted his decisiveness. He confided afterwards to Butler that 'I went for the older man'.[91]

Kilmuir and Salisbury agreed that they would consult all Cabinet Ministers, even though Selwyn Lloyd, the Foreign Secretary, took democratic objection to the Cabinet's being canvassed by a couple of peers.[92]

> Thereafter Bobbety [Salisbury] and I [Kilmuir] asked our colleagues to see us one by one in Bobbety's room in the Privy Council Offices, which could be reached without leaving the building. There were two light reliefs. Practi-

cally each one began by saying: 'This is like coming to the Headmaster's study.' To each Bobbety said: 'Well, which is it, Wab or Hawold?'[93]

Harold it was, by a large majority. To Rab, it was a spirit-breaking disappointment which led to his reluctance to fight again when the opportunity recurred six years later. The night before, he had been asking at a family supper at his home in Smith Square: 'What shall I say in my broadcast to the nation tomorrow?'[94] Butler's biographer writes that Macmillan's supporters had 'won the first round' when it was made clear that there would be no further announcement on the evening of Eden's resignation and that the Queen, following the precedent of the handover from Churchill to Eden in April 1955, would wait until the next day before asking a new Prime Minister to form a government.[95]

But there was nothing sinister about this. It was an *a fortiori* case. If the Queen had delayed a day without criticism before sending for Churchill's successor, she was certainly entitled to refuse to rush things before sending for Eden's. For Eden had been accepted as Churchill's successor (even if, in some quarters, with a reluctance which turned out to be only too well justified) as Butler was not accepted as Eden's. His only certain supporter in the Cabinet was Patrick Buchan-Hepburn, later Lord Hailes; though he later claimed the additional support of Walter Monckton and James Stuart.[96] All these were to leave the government when Macmillan became Prime Minister. In his memoirs Stuart says that he left voluntarily:

> It is always a help to an incoming Prime Minister to have a few vacant offices so that he can introduce new blood. Moreover, the new PM, knowing me well, as he had for 30 years, was aware that after nearly six years at the Scottish Office I was looking for something less arduous, or preferably retirement. Certainly at 60 I was not 'new blood' and, worse still, Harold was my brother-in-law by marriage. I suggested to him that if charges of nepotism ever came up he could refute the press by pointing out that at least he had sacked me![97]

It is not altogether correct to describe these events, as Alistair Horne does, as, in comparison with subsequent procedures, a 'cosy and domestic way' of selecting a new Prime Minister. Whereas in 1963 all Tory MPs would be canvassed by the Whips, the 1957 selection was 'essentially a straight Cabinet choice'.[98] Poole, the chairman of the party, was also seen by Salisbury and Kilmuir.[99] The Chairman of the 1922 Committee, John Morrison, later Lord Margadale, 'assessed back bench opinion with surprising confidence from the Isle of Islay'.[100] The Chief Whip, Edward Heath, was also consulted by the two peers. He told an early biographer that 'the outcome was "highly acceptable" to a "substantial" majority in the House, a majority to which he himself belonged'.[101] Harold Nicolson recorded: 'It is sad for the left wing of the Tory Party, since Butler was the leader of young Conservatives, but I dare say that in the circumstances it is right.'[102]

There was nevertheless a feeling that Butler had been done down by a conspiracy between St James's Street and Hatfield House. Eden's wife wrote to him:

Dear Rab,
Just a line to say what a beastly profession I think politics are – and how greatly I admire your dignity and good humour.
Yours ever,
Clarissa[103]

From the Bahamas, Lord Beaverbrook wrote in similar vein:

I am sorry you have been deprived of your Estate ... (1) If the House of Commons had been given the opportunity to decide the leadership, your selection was certain. (2) If the constituencies had been consulted, the result would have been in your favour – and very emphatically so.[104]

Beaverbrook was also to mention disapprovingly 'the "ambience" and connections of the present incumbent of the post at No. 10'.[105] However, the wily Canadian newspaper proprietor more than covered his bet by writing even more fulsomely to Macmillan, reminding him that he had always hoped for and prophesied his becoming Prime Minister.[106]

The Parliamentary Labour Party then took a hand. A press notice of 21 January 1957 stated that the Parliamentary Committee, or Shadow Cabinet, had given careful consideration to the relevant precedents. It had come to the conclusion that the one created by Bonar Law in 1922 offered the best guidance.* This, in the view of the Shadow Cabinet, was the precedent 'most in accord with the spirit of the Constitution'. It enabled the Crown to act in a manner 'free of all constitutional ambiguity'. Moreover, this course would be the only one which accorded with 'the democratic organisation of the Parliamentary Labour Party'.[107] Norman St John-Stevas, later Lord St John of Fawsley, criticised the Labour Party's statement as an unwarranted interference with the exercise of the royal prerogative. He was to do the same when Margaret Thatcher was challenged by Michael Heseltine in 1990.

LORD HOME IN 1963

Harold Macmillan was, in theory, as high for prerogative as any 17th-century Anglican prelate – or Lord St John of Fawsley himself. In 1963 R.A. Butler recorded that, in the course of musing about his departure

* See Appendix A, p. 273.

from 10 Downing Street, Macmillan's anxiety was 'to retain the discretion of the Crown so that the Crown could choose whomever she wished'.[108]

> He wants to preserve a proper degree of the Queen's choice and does not want a diktat from the 1922 Committee. However we cast our minds back on history, and agreed that almost no PM had chosen his own successor, and that this issue might have to be thrashed out, if he decided to go, without his having the final word. So much for the succession, or as far as we got with it.[109]

In September 1963 Macmillan explained to the Queen what was then his plan of announcing to the party conference on 12 October that there would not be an election in 1963 but that he would not head the party at the election which would have to be held in the following year. In the succeeding weeks Macmillan was to change his mind again. Oliver Poole (the joint party chairman with Iain Macleod) was doubtful, and Enoch Powell, possibly with another Cabinet Minister, was against. But his friends and relations, notably his son Maurice Macmillan and his son-in-law Julian Amery, were persuasive in urging him to continue in office. During the night of 7-8 October he reached a firm decision to fight the next election and intended to inform the Cabinet of it on the following morning.[110]

On 20 September, however, he had told the Queen that his plan would involve a change in January or February 1964. She expressed her 'full understanding'. Nevertheless he found her 'very distressed': partly, perhaps – Macmillan recorded with half-modesty – at the thought of losing a Prime Minister to whom she had become accustomed, but chiefly, no doubt, because of all the difficulties about a successor in which the Crown would be 'much involved'.

> We discussed at some length the various possibilities. She feels the great importance of maintaining the prerogative intact. After all, if she asked someone to form a government and he failed, what harm was done? It often, indeed at one time almost invariably, happened in the first half of the nineteenth century. Of course, it would be much better for everything to go smoothly, as in my case.[111]

Macmillan added that he 'was determined at all costs to preserve the prerogative, which had been so useful in the past and which might become so valuable in the future'.[112] He had something of an obsession with the procedure whereby the Queen asked a politician to try to form a government. This method was not calculated to favour Lord Home: if Butler, Maudling and Hailsham had adhered to their original agreement not to serve under him, he would have had to go back to the Queen saying he could not assemble an administration. As Macleod put it in his *Spectator* article: 'Maudling and Hailsham kept to their agreement with Butler and refused to serve unless Butler did.'[113]

At the same time Macmillan seemed, illogically, to equate his own conclusive recommendation with the Queen's unfettered discretion. Certainly the burden of Butler's quotation above (and, though the two men were hardly the best of friends, there is no suggestion that he misreported Macmillan) is that, while a recommendation or 'diktat' from the 1922 Committee would be unconstitutional or at any rate undesirable, an identical message from an outgoing Prime Minister would somehow preserve an unsullied prerogative. George V had possessed a choice in 1923 when he preferred Baldwin to Curzon; so had Elizabeth II in 1957 when she chose Macmillan before Butler. In one respect her choice had been more free than she might have expected. Two years previously, Eden had effectively been presented to the Queen as Churchill's successor. Macmillan resolved to follow this precedent rather than his own.

In June 1963 Home, as a figure then generally believed to be above the battle, was consulted by the Queen's private secretary, Sir Michael Adeane, for advice on the procedure to be adopted if the Prime Minister resigned. Home's opinion was that the Palace would inevitably become involved in the process. This, however, would not be a matter of political controversy if the Monarch took the advice of the outgoing Prime Minister.[114] Home's biographer, D.R. Thorpe, has called this approach 'You choose, we send for'. As Sir Edward Ford expressed it in 1963: 'You're the party, choose your undoubted leader and we will inform the Queen.'[115] This did not differ from the Palace's approach in 1957 as expressed by the same official.

Macmillan told Lord Hailsham in September 1963 that, if the Queen should ask for his advice, he 'would adopt the same kind of system that had followed Eden's resignation ..., although the range of consultations might be extended'.[116] Moreover, it was indicated to him 'quite clearly' from the Palace that the Queen would ask for advice.

> After all, I had served her for seven years and it was no surprise to me that she would wish for my help. It therefore became necessary for me to do what I would have preferred to avoid – become involved in the situation as it was after my colleagues had returned from the Blackpool conference ... [It] would have been much easier for me to follow Bonar Law's precedent and refuse to give any advice. I seriously thought of this way of avoiding a most tiresome duty. Yet it seemed to me, on reflection, a mean evasion, unfair both to the Queen and to the party.[117]

Oddly enough, on 15 October – a week after he had been stricken and taken into hospital, and when Lord Home's candidature was well under way – Macmillan could still admit that Butler was the choice of the Cabinet and the joint choice, with Maudling, of the parliamentary party.[118] Otherwise his references to Butler are uniformly disparaging. He did not feel that Butler could win an election (an extraordinary judgment) or 'receive the loyal support of the party as a whole'.[119] On 11 September he records that he was careful *not* (Macmillan's italics) to give Butler any idea about which of the several choices he would adopt when it came to his own resignation, for these were the days when Macmillan was contemplating departure in 1964. But he obtained

> a good idea of his own position. He would naturally (if I resign) accept the Premiership if there was a general consensus of opinion for him. But he doesn't want another unsuccessful bid.[120]

On 7 October, the day before his illness struck, he 'saw Butler – who would clearly prefer me to go on, for – in his heart – he does not expect the succession *and* [Macmillan's italics] fears it.'[121] This may have been a misunderstanding by Macmillan. It was Butler's intention to 'advise him in all sincerity that it would be wiser for him to go' and 'to offer my collaboration in joining in the choice of successor'.[122] On 12 October, in hospital, Macmillan recorded that he had handed over 'the conduct of the Government' to Butler 'but I shall take this back as soon as I am able to do so'.[123] On 15 October he showed Butler the minute of instructions about canvassing the party which he wished him to read to the Cabinet: 'he seemed to acquiesce willingly enough.'[124] On 4 October he had recorded his view that 'Butler would be fatal'.[125] Towards the end of 1962 the political scientist David Butler had met Butler at a party, who said:

> I don't think Macmillan is ever going to go. You know what he said to me last weekend? 'I don't see why I should make room for you, old cock.'[126]

Though Macmillan may have misunderstood Butler's view about the desirability of his carrying on, he was essentially correct about Butler's mental condition. After the disappointment of 1957, passion was spent.[127] He was decisive about only a few matters. At the Imperial Hotel, Blackpool, he moved in to occupy the suite reserved for the Prime Minister.[128] He persuaded the officers of the National Union to invite him to address the annual rally which was in those days held on the Saturday afternoon. Butler was very stubborn about being Macmillan's replacement on this occasion. The National Union would have been perfectly within its rights – though no doubt the course would have brought about adverse comment – if it had offered the engagement to Macleod, Hailsham or (by chance, its President in 1963) Home. As things turned out, he fluffed his chance: not unsurprisingly, for platform oratory had never been Butler's *forte*. But beforehand he had lost no opportunity of pointing out that he was to deliver what was at that time the most important speech of the week.[129] In his one other decisive move, Butler prohibited a proposed visit by Dilhorne to Macmillan's bedside on Sunday 13 October, saying he had 'checked with the hospital and found that Macmillan is not capable of more than three or four minutes of concentration'.[130]

It is curious that two successive Prime Ministers should have retired because of ill-health. Yet the first, Eden, lived for another 20 years and died at 79; while the second, Macmillan, lived for another 23 years and died at 92. The difference is that his physical health notwithstanding, Eden could probably not have carried on, owing to the political climate and his own mental condition. Macmillan could almost certainly have continued as Prime Minister and fought the 1964 election, when he would have been 70. In the couple of years before he resigned his plans had varied, almost, it seemed, from week to week. But immediately before he was struck down by his prostate condition he had decided to carry on. He had decided to announce this at the Cabinet meeting on 8 October. On the morning of that day he told the Queen's assistant private secretary Sir Edward Ford that (despite the reservations of Home and others) he had decided to continue. What he did not tell Ford was that during the night of 7-8 October he had awakened in great pain and been unable to urinate. His condition was alleviated by a doctor at 4 a.m. but it was clear that further specialist treatment was needed.[131] Before leaving the meeting in pain – he left twice – he said somewhat mysteriously: 'There has got to be a decision and I shall announce it at Blackpool.'[132]

The assembled colleagues, though knowing that Macmillan was ill, were mystified, puzzled about what was expected of them. Dilhorne said that, as he was not himself a candidate for the leadership, he would be available if anyone wished to have a talk with him. In the events of 1963, an unpopular Lord Chancellor was to play as crucial a role as his predecessor had in those of 1957. Home echoed Dilhorne: the same, he said, applied to him. Powell later cited this indication of Home's position as a kind of pledge from which, as events were to turn out, Home should have had the whole Cabinet's permission to withdraw. Home's view was that it was 'nothing so dramatic and pompous' and was 'merely a statement revealing that at that time the question of my succession to Macmillan had simply not crossed my mind'.[133] Powell's talk of pledges from which formal release had to be sought confused the issue. The point was that not only Powell but Macleod and several other Ministers thought that Home had excluded himself from the leadership.[134] Home's biographer D.R. Thorpe calls this 'a crucial tactical error' – though it was not an error of such dimensions as to deprive him of the prize.[135]

At about 1.30 Macmillan heard from Redmayne that the Cabinet, with one dissentient (in fact, Powell) had agreed to support him if he decided to continue until the election. He telephoned Poole at Blackpool. Butler came to see him. At 9.00 p.m. he went into hospital. David Badenoch, the son of the urological surgeon who operated on Macmillan, himself of the same profession, disputes the version of events which had previously been accepted: that Macmillan resigned because of an erroneously pessimistic prognosis. He says:

> [Alistair] Horne [Macmillan's biographer] suggests that there was a possible cancer of the prostate. This was not the case. The histology of the prostate showed benign hyperplasis and Macmillan was aware of this fact. At no time was he encouraged to resign by his medical attendants and indeed when he did resign he expressed great relief that he had reason to leave the political crises which he had faced. He termed this 'an act of God'.[136]

On the next day Home and Dilhorne paid a visit. It was settled that Home would take the chair at Blackpool as chairman of the National Union.[137] He also saw Home separately. Home told him of a message he had received from the Ambassador in Washington, Sir David Ormsby-Gore, about United States unease at the prospect of Hailsham as Prime Minister, on account of his performance during and after the negotiations for the Test Ban Treaty.[138] The question of the succession had not then, according to Home, crossed his mind. In one sense it clearly had, for on the previous day, at the Cabinet meeting, he had (with Dilhorne) excluded himself from it. But Macmillan pressed him to consider taking on the leadership. He replied that he was happy at the Foreign Office and in the House of Lords, which he had never contemplated leaving.

Macmillan 'seemed to accept that' and went on to say that he had concluded 'after much thought' that Hailsham might be the best choice. Home agreed, up to a point. During the Suez crisis he had watched Hailsham, who had 'displayed admirable calm at the Admiralty in testing circumstances'. While he had 'some misgivings about his famous "judgment"', he felt that Hailsham could nevertheless take on both the leadership and the premiership and make a success of it.[139] Even so, Macmillan was as early as 9 October having doubts about Hailsham's suitability. Why, otherwise, would he have asked Home to take on the job instead?

Lords Hailsham and Home found themselves in contention in the way they did owing to the efforts of Tony Benn (Anthony Wedgwood Benn, as he was in those days) to divest himself of the title Lord Stansgate, and his consequential disqualification to sit in the House of Commons. To start with, Benn contemplated legislation which would help only those in his position – commoners who had inherited peerages they did not want. Throughout the early 1960s the Conservatives were well aware of the effects which Benn's campaign, if successful, could have on the succession to Macmillan.

> I went to see Rab Butler. Butler was very cordial, and I was misled by this. He said: 'Very interesting case.' I told him what I had in mind (the right to renounce a peerage on inheritance) and he said: 'Well, we'll have to look at that. I'm sure Harold Macmillan would like these little points examined.' I

got the idea that he was vaguely on my side, which was clearly quite wrong. He went on: 'By the way, one thing: would your scheme permit Quintin to come back?' So I said: 'Well, no, it wouldn't really.' So he said: 'Ah well, that's all right.'[140]

But certain Conservative peers considered it unfair that the measure should apply only to Benn and to those who might find themselves in the same position. They wanted an element of retrospection, so that existing reluctant peers could avail themselves of the remedy which Benn was proposing for himself. Their amendment was not resisted by the government. When the Peerage Bill received the Royal Assent on 31 July 1963 it included the provision that any present peer could renounce his peerage straightaway or within 12 months. After the lapse of this period the option disappeared. Anthony Howard, in a political column in the *New Statesman* of 14 December 1962, was the first commentator to understand the full importance of the Benn legislation for both Hailsham and Home. The article made a 'deep impression' on Home, and Lady Home cut it out and pasted it in her husband's scrapbook.[141]

Macmillan tells us that, as a successor, he favoured either Hailsham or Macleod, preferably the former. He felt that these two were 'the men of real genius in the party' who were 'the true inheritors of the tradition of Tory Radicalism'.[142] In June 1963 he told Hailsham that he believed he was the right man to succeed him. Poole told Hailsham to expect to become the next Conservative leader when Macmillan retired before the election.[143] In September 1963 Macmillan, after many vicissitudes, was adhering to the same plan, and believed that Hailsham rather than Maudling was the right man to succeed him on account of his 'moral strength'.[144] He added that he had sent Hailsham to Moscow on purpose to oversee the Test Ban Treaty to test his powers of negotiation: 'he did *very* well.'[145] This was before Home brought him the information that the Americans did not consider Hailsham had done well at all.

As negotiations for this treaty began in May 1963, Macmillan cannot have known that Hailsham would have been enabled to renounce his peerage. *A fortiori* he could not have known it when Hailsham began to be a serious candidate in his mind, at the beginning of 1963.[146] It may be that Macmillan considered Hailsham could be both a Prime Minister and a peer. It is perhaps more likely that he thought the Benn legislation was bound to ease Hailsham's position in some way. What he wrote, however, was that if the Act had not become law on 31 July 1963

all our troubles would have been avoided. Neither Lord Hailsham nor Lord Home could in practice have ever been considered for the premiership. Butler must have succeeded, almost without challenge.[147]

Hailsham recalls that, when he saw Macmillan on 7 October, Macmillan told him 'formally' that he wished him to succeed (leading him to under-

stand, at this stage, that he expected to retire at about Christmas 1963).[148]
On 9 October, after Macmillan had been taken into hospital, he wrote in
his diary that 'if Hailsham is to be a competitor, he must at once give up
his peerage and find a constituency'.[149] On the morning of the same day he
told Amery, when he visited him, to go to Blackpool and 'make sure that
they get Quintin in'.[150]

Butler's biographer believes that the timing of the announcement by
Home of Macmillan's resignation was calculated to help Hailsham – the
more so as Macmillan specifically enjoined that the 'customary processes'
should be set in train without delay.[151] However, he regretted his action
virtually at once. Within two days of the announcement, he feared

> that all kinds of intrigues and battles are now going on about the leadership
> of the party. Perhaps those who were so anxious to get me out will now see
> the disadvantages ... What I do profoundly hope is that the *image* [Macmil-
> lan's italics] is not injured by all this public disputing.[152]

It would nevertheless have been possible to delay the resignation
statement until Sunday 13 October, when it would – from the constitutional point of view, more properly – have come from No. 10 Downing
Street rather than from that year's President of the National Union. But
if the announcement had been intended to help Hailsham, it had precisely
the opposite effect. As things turned out, Macmillan could not have done
his favoured candidate a greater disservice. Hailsham's fond public father-
hood of his baby was regarded as distasteful. He fed his one-year-old
daughter Catherine before the cameras at the Imperial Hotel. Sir Dennis
Walters, who was close to Hailsham in this period, has defended his
conduct. According to Walters, Hailsham brought his baby to Blackpool
out of domestic necessity rather than political calculation.[153] Hailsham
himself wrote to the same effect.[154] No matter: it was the impression that
counted, and the impression which Hailsham made in the upper reaches
of his party was not good. Nor did a notably decrepit Randolph Churchill
help his cause by arriving from the United States and handing out to all
and sundry lapel badges marked 'Q' (for Quintin). But it was the public
renunciation of his peerage after his Conservative Political Centre lecture
which did the greatest damage. What did the damage was not so much the
renunciation itself – distasteful though this may have been – as the
response which it drew from the audience, which led to the occasion's
being freely compared to a Nuremberg rally.[155]

After his announcement to the conference on 10 October, Home walked
back to the Imperial Hotel with Hailsham, who thought he was Macmillan's choice. He told Hailsham that he had his support also. Had he known
(Home tells us) that Hailsham 'intended to throw his claim to the leadership into the ring within a matter of hours' he would have tried to dissuade
him, 'for people never like being bounced, and least of all at a time of

emotional stress'. Others advised him to the same effect. Home himself had a cautionary word with him shortly before the CPC meeting. But by then it was 'too late', for Hailsham 'considered himself to be committed to his friends' – a reference which Home did not explain further but was presumably to Amery and Maurice Macmillan, among others. It was after what Home refers to as 'this débâcle' that numerous Conservatives came and told him that he ought to consider coming forward himself.[156]

Between 10 and 12 October the visitors to Home's hotel room, so he tells us – and there is no reason to disbelieve his account – became more insistent. They 'represented substantial and influential bodies of opinion in both Houses'. Among them were Lord Blakenham, Sir William Anstruther-Grey, Selwyn Lloyd and Dilhorne himself (who, as canvasser-in-chief and holder of the ring, ought more properly to have kept his views to himself). They argued that Hailsham would not be acceptable to the party 'and with that I was compelled by the recent events to agree', a rapid turnabout by Home. They asserted also that Butler would not have the support which was 'essential' if confidence was to be restored to the party in time for a general election, 'and that, too, I thought to be true'.[157]

He told Dilhorne that he would ask his doctor whether he could 'last the course' as Prime Minister.[158] On 12 October the Butlers lunched with the Homes, before the start of the rally at which Butler was to perform so wanly. Home said he thought it only right to let Butler know that he would be seeing his doctor in London during the following week.[159] He had told Hailsham the same on the afternoon of 10 October.[160] Home was seriously worried only about whether his eyes could stand the strain of the paperwork that would be involved, and had a separate examination from an eye specialist. He was reassured in both examinations, and on 15 October Martin Redmayne, the Chief Whip, was informed accordingly.[161]

Macleod took little part in the week's proceedings, except to make his usual fine speech. Maudling made a less good one, though he was to claim afterwards, as Butler was to claim likewise of his own effort, that it 'read well'. We tend to forget today that in the 1961-3 period, when Macmillan's position seemed increasingly vulnerable, it was Maudling rather than Butler who was regarded as the natural successor, certainly among Conservative backbenchers.[162] As Morrison, the Chairman of the 1922 Committee, said rather unhelpfully to Butler just before he had set out earlier for Rhodesia to unravel the Central African Federation: 'The chaps won't have you.'[163]

Morrison's role seems to have been larger than has been supposed. In July 1963 Edward Heath stayed with him in his house on the Isle of Islay. He told Heath that he had come to the conclusion with Sir Charles Mott-Radclyffe, the Vice-Chairman of the 1922 Committee, and Sir Harry Legge-Bourke, that Home should run for the leadership. Morrison was deputed to see Home, who told him on 31 July 1963, the day the Peerage

Act became law, that he would see his doctor.[164] If this is true, Mott-Rad-clyffe at any rate had changed his mind, for Sir Edward Ford told Ben Pimlott that on 17 October 'backbench MPs like Tony [Lord] Lambton and Charles Mott-Radclyffe were ringing up to express the view that Home or Rab would be disastrous choices'.[165]

Those who think most of the orderly conduct of government [Macmillan wrote in his memorandum to the Queen on 15 October]* tend to be for Mr Butler as he is likely to carry on the present policies, which he fully under-stands, and to give full freedom to the Treasury and to the Foreign Office in carrying out the policies which I initiated, approved and largely directed ... Obviously, members of the Cabinet and those likely to come into direct contact with the future Prime Minister will find it easier to work with Mr Butler.[166]

Hailsham's defects were altogether more spectacular:

They are afraid that Lord Hailsham would be impulsive, even arrogant, in his handling of their business. This applies to some younger members as well as to the older members of the administration, and is largely due to his habit, when he is not in the chair, of talking a great deal and sometimes without much reflection ... [However,] the people who dislike his behaviour will be in sympathy with Lord Hailsham's religious views, his churchmanship and so forth. They will merely be shocked at his rather boyish lack of manners. But they will not be shocked by his deviating from strict moral doctrines.[167]

Which other candidate or candidates might be guilty of these transgres-sions, Macmillan did not see fit to indicate; though, as for Home:

The only other political difference that may emerge is by the strong move-ment at the end of last week [Macmillan was writing on the Tuesday after the conference] to draft Lord Home unwillingly into the position of leader and Prime Minister ... the important fact is that Lord Home's candidature has not been set forward on his own merits but has been thought of as a last-minute method of keeping out Mr Butler now that Lord Hailsham has (according to the pundits) put himself out of court by his stupid behaviour in the foyer of the Imperial Hotel at Blackpool ... Apart from Home's actual lead, I am impressed by the general good will shown towards him, even by those who give reasons in favour of other candidates, and I cannot fail to come to the opinion that he would be the best able to secure united support.[168]

The question was whether Home really had received such firm support. Macmillan had directed – and on 15 October had endorsed his directions – that the views of the party should be ascertained in the following way: the Lord Chancellor, Dilhorne, would canvass the Cabinet. The Chief Whip, Redmayne, and his subordinate would see all other Ministers and Members of the House of Commons. The Chief Whip in the Lords, St

* See Appendix B, p. 274.

Aldwyn, would talk to members of the Lords who were 'regular supporters of the party'. The joint chairman of the party, Poole, would consult with Lord Chelmer and Mrs Peggy Shepherd, both of the National Union, to discover the views of the constituency parties 'as best they can'.[169] The opinion of many of those whose views had been solicited was that the official canvassers had weighted their question or questions in Home's direction.

Thus William Whitelaw was telephoned by one of the Whips asking him whom he wanted. With 'some misgivings', he wanted Butler. He was then asked: 'But if Alec Home was available, would you be prepared to support him?' Whitelaw thought this was 'a totally irregular second question'. Sir Reginald Bennett, Macleod's principal confidant during this period, was asked: 'If Home was nominated, would you vote against him?' According to the then backbencher, Humphry Berkeley, the question put to all those consulted, including himself, was: 'If there is a deadlock between Rab (Butler) and Quintin (Hailsham), would you accept Alec Home?' Berkeley refused to answer 'this hypothetical question' but was convinced that many other MPs had fallen 'into the trap' whereby Macmillan 'got the answer that he wanted'.[170]

Alistair Horne has tried to show that the various canvassers were not only honest in their conduct but correct in their conclusions. In particular, he has revealed that, as counted by Dilhorne, the first choice of 10 members of the Cabinet was Home – and that Macleod was one of those who had voted for him.[171] Responses have ranged from incredulity (Baroness Macleod of Borve and Powell, who voted for Butler) through accusations of error against Dilhorne (Lords Aldington and Gilmour) to posthumous allegations of deviousness in Macleod (Macmillan and Butler).[172] Macleod's most recent biographer, Robert Shepherd, has also challenged Horne's account.[173]

The news that Home was to be the man emerged several days before the date which Macmillan had set for his report to the Queen, 18 October.[174] Nor was this surprising, in view of the way in which Redmayne and his assistants had gone about their task. As we have seen, Home was a candidate from Saturday 12 October at the latest, when he told Butler and his wife that he was to be examined by his doctors in the following week. At some point between 9 October, when he urged Amery to go to Blackpool and 'get Quintin in', and 15 October, when he wrote disobligingly to the Queen about Hailsham, Macmillan transferred his allegiance to Home and saw to it, with his customary ruthlessness, that his man got the job.

The period 16-18 October witnessed several informal meetings of Ministers designed to frustrate Macmillan in his intentions – or, at any rate, to question them. The most famous of these occurred on 17 October at Powell's house. It may be that what was most crucial in Home's ability to form a government was not Butler's agreement to serve under him but Hailsham's. On 15 October Hailsham told Macmillan that Home's taking over would be 'absurd'.[175] But on Friday 18 October at No. 10, at a meeting attended by Home, Butler, Hailsham and Maudling, Hailsham was moving towards serving under Home. He had been warned by Selwyn Lloyd (a Home supporter from the start) that refusal would look like 'sour grapes'. Others, who had been Hailsham supporters – Amery, Poole and Thorneycroft – also advised him to serve. Hailsham decided he would if Butler and Maudling did the same, as they duly did.[176] Only Powell and Macleod held out.

As usual, Macmillan had been too quick for his colleagues. Throughout the 7-19 October period, from the onset of his illness to the appointment of Home as Prime Minister, he was roughly 12 hours ahead of everybody else. So it was on this day. For the advice had been given, the deed done. At the King Edward VII Hospital for Officers, Macmillan's working day had begun early, at 7.30. His private secretary, Timothy Bligh, telephoned to say that, in Macmillan's words, 'a critical situation' had developed. He and Redmayne would be round in an hour. The news that 'the general choice favoured Home' had got out. Meetings had been held, to organise a revolt by the 'unsuccessful candidates' against Home. In view of 'their inner rivalry with each other during recent weeks', there was, Macmillan recorded with every appearance of deep moral outrage, 'something rather 18th-century about this'. It was 'somewhat distasteful'.[177]

Feeling aggrieved, Home telephoned. He had been asked to come forward as a compromise candidate, to preserve unity. Now he felt like withdrawing. Macmillan urged him not to do so. If they gave in to this 'intrigue', there would be 'chaos'.[178] 'Look [said Macmillan], we can't change our view now. All the troops are on the starting line. Everything is arranged. It will just cause ghastly confusion if we delay.'[179] Nor did he. In 'this strange and somewhat unreal atmosphere', Macmillan decided to proceed with his plan unchanged or, rather, with Sir Michael Adeane's plan unchanged.

The Conservative peer Lord Swinton recalled that on 19 October Adeane had outlined to him 'the proposed drill' that when Macmillan was ready to advise the Queen on his successor she 'would visit him in hospital and accept his resignation and receive his advice'. Adeane had added that 'he thought it very important that he himself should not see the Prime Minister'. This 'would make it look as if the Palace was intervening'.[180] His letter of resignation was sent and delivered to the Palace at 9.30 a.m. He put on a white silk shirt under his dressing gown in her honour.[181] The Queen then visited him in hospital. She 'expressed her gratitude, and said that she did not need and did not intend to seek any other advice'. He then read her the memorandum favouring Home. She agreed he was 'the most likely choice to get general support, as well as really the best and strongest character'.[182] She then asked specifically about the 'revolt'.[183]

According to Macleod's most recent biographer, it was 'later claimed privately' by Adeane that he had been unaware both of the meeting at

Powell's house and of the force of opposition to Home.[184] Nevertheless, it is clear that she was apprised of the opposition to Home within the Cabinet. In these circumstances, Macmillan told her he 'thought speed was important and hoped she would send for Lord Home immediately – as soon as she got back to the Palace'. With these somewhat peremptory instructions the Queen obediently complied. Macmillan went on to advise her, both orally and in the memorandum which he handed to Adeane, not to appoint Home Prime Minister at the first audience, but to

> use the older procedure and entrust him with the task of forming an administration. He could then take his soundings and report to her. She followed this advice.[185]

'When they came back from the hospital,' Adeane's successor Martin Charteris confided later, 'the Queen wanted to send for Alec.'[186]

Though Macmillan despised Butler, he cannot have known for sure when this advice was given that he – together with Hailsham and Maudling – would agree to serve under Home. If these three, in addition to Macleod and Powell, had refused office, it is virtually certain that Home would have had to go back to the Queen to say that he was unable to form a government. 'We all understood,' Charteris said, 'that Alec could not form a government unless Rab agreed to serve and, if not, the Queen would have had to call for Rab.'[187] Whether intentionally nor not, Macmillan himself, through his advice to the Queen, handed Butler the loaded revolver which, as Powell said in a subsequent television interview, he fastidiously refused to discharge.[188]

On the evening of 18 October, however, Butler did say to Home that 'the thing had been rushed' and that there had not been 'sufficient consideration of the difficulties'.

> It was now up to him [Home] to make an effort to secure the necessary unity. He said he would do this by a series of interviews and possibly a meeting later. I [Butler] gave him the particulars of the Ministers who were unwilling to go on and he took down their names and said he would see them – One had to be as modest as possible. I was only trying to seek a solution, which would obtain the maximum unity. We decided to leave the matter until I met him again.[189]

Macmillan deprived the Queen, certainly to her relief, of any choice of Prime Minister. Macleod perhaps prudently – for attitudes towards the Monarchy were more circumspect in 1964 than they were to be 30 years later – declined to deal with this aspect of the prerogative in his article in the *Spectator* of 17 January 1964, which was written when he was the editor of the paper (he had been appointed by the proprietor, Ian Gilmour, after refusing to serve Home). The piece was ostensibly a review of Randolph Churchill's *The Fight for the Tory Leadership*, to which Macmillan had contributed heavily.

There is no criticism whatever [Macleod wrote] that can be made of the part played by the Crown. Presented with such a document, it was unthinkable even to consider asking for a second opinion.[190]

In all other respects Macleod could hardly have been more forthright. His case was that Butler was the choice of the majority, that he deserved to be that choice, that he was the best choice and that he was prevented from being recognised as such by a 'magic circle' of Etonians (with the exception of the Chief Whip, Redmayne, who had been at Radley). The phrase passed into the language of politics. But was it not a little unfair? Home's succession may or may not have been gerrymandered: but it had manifestly not been fixed in White's Club or at Hatfield House. Indeed, by his extensive consultations – and by his presentation of one candidate to the Queen – Macmillan laid the foundations for the new system. As Macleod put it:

The procedure which had been adopted opened up big issues for decisions in the future. That everything was done in good faith I do not doubt – indeed, it is the theme of this review to demonstrate it – but the result of the methods used was contradiction and misrepresentation. I do not think it is a precedent which will be followed.[191]

Ben Pimlott concluded:

The effect of the 1963 major confusion, on top of the 1957 minor one, was to end forever the Monarch's discretionary power over the mid-term appointment of a Prime Minister, except in the most exceptional of hypothetical circumstances. This was the opposite of the intention of the Queen – who, indeed, allowed herself to be duped by Macmillan ....[192]

The effect was certainly as Pimlott said it was. The Queen may also have been 'duped' by Macmillan. But not only did she have no choice in accepting what he advised: she had, after all, asked for that advice. She or, rather, her advisers – Adeane, Charteris and Ford – had made clear that they wanted only one name presented to her. They had done the same in 1957: except that the task of presenting it to Her Majesty had been left to Lord Salisbury rather than to the outgoing Prime Minister, Anthony Eden. The trouble was that, on both occasions, it was a name which left questions in the air and an unpleasant taste in the mouth.

HAROLD WILSON IN 1964

Shortly after a quarter to three on Friday 16 October 1964 Labour attained an absolute majority in the new House by winning 316 seats. The final figures were: Labour 317, Conservatives 304, Liberals 9. As soon as the figure of 316 seats was reached, Home, who had until then rightly refused to concede defeat, asked for an audience of the Queen and tendered the resignation of his government. This meeting took place at 3.30. There was some worry in the Labour camp that Home was going to try to carry on governing (as Edward Heath was later to do in February-March 1974).[193] He had no such intention. At 3.30 the Queen's private secretary, Adeane, telephoned Wilson and, according to Wilson, said: 'Would it be convenient for you to come round and see Her Majesty?'[194] He was told that a Palace car would be sent for him.[195]

No. 10 had already made arrangements for a change of government. Herbert Bowden, the Labour Chief Whip, had been told on the previous evening, before the polls closed, what Wilson should do. He would be asked to make Chequers available to the outgoing Prime Minister for a few days. On his arrival at No. 10 Wilson found an invitation to Home awaiting his signature.[196] Home thought this was generosity on Wilson's part – though there is no reason to suppose that Wilson either objected to the course which No. 10 had proposed or would not have proposed it himself.[197] Wilson was also told that he would need a morning coat and striped trousers. He preferred and duly wore a short black coat. No constitutional objections were raised.

On arrival at the Palace he was conducted to the Queen's private apartments. She asked him whether he could form an administration. A year earlier, in different circumstances, Home had been asked the same question, Macmillan having advised the Queen to ask it. Home had replied that he would have to engage in consultation. Despite the narrowness of the Labour majority, Wilson was in no doubt that a government could be formed. He was made Prime Minister 'on the spot'.[198]

Strangely to me and contrary to all I had understood about the procedures, there was no formal kissing of hands such as occurs with the appointment of all other senior Ministers. It was taken as read.[199]

Part II

Labour and Its Leaders

3

Ancestral Voices

The most conservative of all religions – ancestor worship.
Aneurin Bevan, *In Place of Fear*, 1952

We enter now a different world. It is a world, predominantly, of meetings, public and private, great and small. When Aneurin Bevan arrived at an unfamiliar place to undertake a speaking engagement, his first words were: 'When's the meeting?' But though these larger, public meetings will play their part in what follows, the chief role will be filled by those smaller, private gatherings whose operations Bevan himself so often despised and which, indeed, have been the subject of much satirical comment in the post-war years. 'I move the reference back ...', 'Card vote ...', 'Two-thirds majority ...', 'I must consult my Executive ...': there is here a whole political culture which, though it is not always antipathetic to the Westminster model, is separate from it: just as the books on old Labour's reading-list – not Marx's *Capital* but, rather, Kropotkin's *Mutual Aid,* Winwood Reade's *Martyrdom of Man*, Jack London's *Iron Heel* and Tressell's *Ragged Trousered Philanthropists* – were not recommended to those undertaking a course of study in history, politics or economics at our universities.

Until 1997, the Labour Party had supplied only four Prime Ministers, Ramsay MacDonald, C.R. Attlee, Harold Wilson and James Callaghan, of whom only the first three had been elected as the result of a general election.* All attained their positions on account, initially, of votes in the Parliamentary Labour Party; in Callaghan's case the difference in time between the final vote and his appointment as Prime Minister was of hours merely. Tony Blair attained his position on account of a vote by the entire party membership in 1994 following the death of John Smith, who, like Neil Kinnock (though not Michael Foot), had been chosen by different means.

All these developments will be considered in their place. But first we must go back to 1906, when there were returned to the House of Commons

---

* In this book Clement Richard, later Earl, Attlee is referred to as C.R. Attlee. He so signed himself. This is what appears on the title-page of his unjustly derided memoirs *As It Happened* (1954). Roy Jenkins has pointed out in the *Observer* that during his lifetime he was called 'Mr Attlee', 'Major Attlee' or 'Clem Attlee' but never 'Clement Attlee'.

400 Liberal Members, 157 Conservatives and 29 Members who called themselves Labour, together with one specifically Miners' MP.[1] As soon as the Parliament assembled, the Labour Representation Committee assumed the name the Labour Party. Its members proceeded to elect Officers and Whips. Ramsay MacDonald confided to his wife Margaret that he heard there was 'a great log-rolling' going on about the leadership of the party. He was 'rather afraid that personal jealousies combined with trade union exclusiveness' might 'produce nasty feelings and unfortunate results'. There would be 'a fearful amount of work adapting the machine' – MacDonald was secretary of the extra-parliamentary party – 'to the new circumstances'. But as soon as the new Members settled down and held their tongues, things would be 'all right I hope'.[2]

There were two candidates for the chairmanship: Keir Hardie of the Independent Labour Party and David Shackleton of the Cotton Weavers. The post which was being contested was the chairmanship: that of 'Chairman and Leader of the Parliamentary Party' was not created until 1922. However, in 1921 Hardie's hagiographical biographer, William Stewart, referred to his position in 1907 as 'chairman leader of the parliamentary party'.[3] Shackleton was a non-Socialist trade union leader. At that time it was perfectly respectable for Labour MPs not to be Socialists. For example, Arthur Henderson – arguably as important a figure in the early life of the Labour Party as Ramsay MacDonald – was an ex-Liberal and a former official of the Friendly Society of Ironfounders. When he became secretary of the external (as distinct from the Parliamentary) Labour Party in 1912, he judged it expedient to become a Socialist. This he accomplished by joining the Fabian Society.[4] Both Hardie and MacDonald were Socialists.

In the first, open vote, Hardie and Shackleton were equal. MacDonald, Henderson's predecessor as secretary of the external party, abstained. The second vote was by ballot, MacDonald again abstained and the result was the same. In the third ballot he voted, and Hardie was elected.[5] Stewart's hagiography of Hardie gives a somewhat imperfect account of the proceedings:

> Naturally, he was appointed chairman of the new party, which carried with it leadership in the House. There were other aspirants for the position, but a sense of the fitness of things prevailed, and the honour and duty of leading the first Parliamentary Labour Party fell, after a second ballot, to the man who, more than any other, had made such a party possible.[6]

MacDonald did not share these admiring sentiments. In July 1906 he wrote to Bruce Glasier that he had voted for Hardie with 'much reluctance' as he could not persuade himself that 'he could fill the place'.[7] Nor did Philip Snowden share them. In the same month he complained that Hardie's chairmanship was a 'hopeless failure' and that there was 'intense dissatisfaction' among members of the ILP.[8] Hardie had undertaken not to make the chairmanship permanent but to 'encourage a rotation of that office'.[9] He would have resigned at the end of the 1907 session even if ill-health had not forced the decision upon him.[10]

In 1908 he was succeeded by Henderson, who had yet to join the Fabian Society and was referred to as one of the 'old gang' of trade union leaders. Henderson was not, however, a success. Under his leadership the party seemed merely to offer encouragement from the touchline to the Liberal government. This position became more fixed after April 1908, when H.H. Asquith became Prime Minister and David Lloyd George Chancellor of the Exchequer.[11]

In 1910 Henderson was succeeded by George Barnes, the secretary of the engineers' union. In the first general election of that year the Conservatives won 273 seats, the Liberals 275 and Labour 40; in the second election the respective figures were 272, 272 and 42. In January 1910 MacDonald wrote to Hardie to say that everything was arranged. He was 'to be *put* [italics in original] into the chair of the party' and asked to resign the secretaryship, which was then to be filled by Henderson.[12] Next month Barnes wrote to MacDonald inquiring about his intentions. He offered to support MacDonald 'if required' but added that he was not prepared to stand down in favour of anyone else.[13] A week later Shackleton (who had only narrowly failed to become the first chairman of the parliamentary party) told MacDonald by letter that in his opinion MacDonald was the man for the post. If he agreed to accept, he would be glad to move him for the position. He had also given notice that at the party meeting he would move, first, that a vice-chairman should not be 'appointed' (this, not 'elected', was the word Shackleton used) but that the last preceding chairman should be vice-chairman by virtue of his former position and, secondly, that while the chairman should be eligible for re-election he had 'long felt that the position of chairman should be of a more permanent character than it is at present'.[14] MacDonald was to be chairman from 1911 to 1914, and chairman and leader from 1922 to 1931.

On 15 February 1910 Barnes was 'unanimously elected chairman'. In October Shackleton wrote saying he had done his best to persuade the MPs to 'appoint' MacDonald.[15] In June MacDonald confided to his diary that Barnes's chairmanship was 'a sad failure'. He had 'no energy and no grasp of policy'. Labour in the House was consequently 'feeble'. This had a 'v. bad effect outside'.[16] In August W.C. Anderson wrote to MacDonald earnestly hoping he would not finally make up his mind about the chairmanship. It should have been his 'before now'. Anderson knew 'something of what happened', which unfortunately he neglected to divulge. But, if MacDonald stood aside, 'then who?' It would be the party that would suffer, and he had 'given a big slice' of his life to the party.[17]

As chairman of the parliamentary party, Barnes had to submit a report to the party conference, which was to meet early in 1911. The first draft contained an attack on his colleagues' slackness, on their timidity and on their willingness to follow the Liberal government.[18] In January 1911 Henderson pointed out to MacDonald that, because his report would be public property before the meeting of the parliamentary party, it would be said 'by a section' that they had refused to re-elect him because he had spoken too plainly. But it was obvious that they could not re-elect him after this attack. At any rate, Henderson could not support him. He had not done so in 1910 because he 'was sincerely convinced he lacked those qualities necessary to the position'. He had 'proved a conspicuous failure' and now sought 'to blame the party for all the failures and blunders of leadership'.[19] Later in the month, T.D. Benson wrote to MacDonald saying that, if he could not 'pull the party round', no one could. He considered that the attempt was a 'duty' which he could not refuse to undertake, 'however distasteful' it might be to him. He would be 'exceedingly disappointed' unless MacDonald accepted.[20]

At the beginning of 1911, Barnes was ill. It was this, more than the professions of affection and esteem which his colleagues made to him, that enabled MacDonald to assume the chairmanship.[21] The parliamentary party met on 6 February 1911. A letter was received from Barnes announcing that he did not offer himself for re-election. According to Snowden, a bargain had been struck at the January party conference whereby MacDonald was to resign the secretaryship in Henderson's favour in return for becoming chairman.[22] In fact Henderson did not assume this position until 1912. Four days after MacDonald's elevation the *Labour Leader* wrote that 'the necessity of having a permanent chief for a fighting force' was 'becoming more and more obvious'.[23] MacDonald's local paper, the *Leicester Pioneer* (he was MP for Leicester 1906-18), thought his 'unanimous election' would 'mark a new epoch in the history of the party'.[24]

So it did: but any change in the nature of Labour leadership was not discussed openly at the time. Moreover, it was not at all obvious to contemporaries that it really had changed. Certainly, MacDonald – as his biographer, David Marquand, tells us – was not a party leader at all in the sense in which Conservatives or Liberals understood the term.[25] The office was still subject to annual election (a change which the Conservatives were to introduce 64 years later) and it did not even then carry with it a seat on the National Executive Committee. Two years after his election, in January 1913, the party was still as badly divided as it had been under any of his predecessors.[26] MacDonald resigned because of the United Kingdom's participation in the First World War. On 3 August 1914 he told the House of Commons:

> So far as we are concerned, whatever may happen, whatever may be said about us, whether attacks may be made upon us, we will take the action that we will take of saying that this country ought to have remained neutral, because in the deepest parts of our hearts we believed that that was right and that alone was consistent with the honour of the country and the traditions of the party [the Liberal Party] that are now in office.[27]

But on 5 August the Parliamentary Labour Party decided to support the Liberal government's request for war credits of £100 million. MacDonald resigned. Henderson, without election, was appointed in his place on a temporary basis. Soon the majority of the party under their temporary leader were supporting the government, participating in recruiting campaigns and accepting an electoral truce for the duration of the war.[28] MacDonald wrote in his diary that he 'saw it was no use remaining as the party was divided and nothing but futility could result'.[29]

Later in August 1914 MacDonald refused Henderson's invitation to return to the party chairmanship. In October he wrote to Henderson saying he thought 'on the whole' that Henderson 'had better just have your meeting and appoint our officers in the old way'. The party could not 'possibly go on with a temporary chairman'.[30] Next month he declined both to allow his name to be considered for the chairmanship and to make any promises about his future actions. He said that 'everything was so uncertain' and he 'did not know'. He made up his mind 'to say nothing during the sittings of Parliament' and 'to attend but little'.[31] In December 1914 he 'told them point blank' that he would not stand for the chairmanship. Henderson asked him to bind himself to return after the war. MacDonald refused. 'After some explanatory talk' it was agreed that Henderson would act as chairman, on condition that it was made known that this arrangement was to be temporary. This was confirmed at the party meeting, with Henderson saying that he wanted to retain not only his secretaryship of the party but also the right of reversion to Chief Whip: 'some did not agree'.[32] Henderson. however, retained the secretaryship till 1935, when he was succeeded by Jim Middleton.

In 1915 Asquith formed a coalition. Labour was invited to join along with the Conservatives. The Parliamentary Labour Party rejected the invitation. But the National Executive Committee voted 9-3 to accept it. A joint meeting of the PLP and the NEC then confirmed the latter's decision by 17 votes to 11. An attempt was made to insist that the government would not introduce any form of conscription. This was defeated and Henderson joined the Cabinet as President of the Board of Education, becoming Paymaster-General in August 1916. In December 1916 Asquith was ousted by Lloyd George. The official Liberal Party refused to join him in the new government. Labour was divided.

However, A.J.P. Taylor considered that in December 1916 the Labour Party 'came of age'. The moment, he wrote, could be 'precisely defined'. It was the meeting of Liberal Ministers on 4 December which advised Asquith not to co-operate with Lloyd George. Henderson attended the meeting, 'no doubt regarding himself and being regarded by others as one of Asquith's humbler followers'. Then, 'in a flash of blinding truth', he declared that Labour would support any Prime Minister who got on with the war. A few days later he was in the War Cabinet, 'no longer a Lib-Lab hanger-on, but spokesman of an independent Labour movement'.[33]

Beatrice Webb gives a slightly different account from Taylor's. She writes that the three office-holders in Asquith's administration, together with Barnes and J.R. Clynes, 'veered round'.[34] This was at a joint meeting of the Executive and the parliamentary party. The miners' representatives, 'true to their idiotic rule of never voting without instructions', expressed no opinion and took no part in the decision. After speeches against taking office from Sidney Webb and three others (none of these prominent), the meting decided by 18 votes to 12 in favour of it.[35]

MacDonald maintained that Asquith had at least been able to claim that he was leading a national government. No such claim could be made for the Lloyd George coalition, if only because the Liberal Party had refused to join it. In taking office in it, Henderson and his colleagues 'had called into question the very basis of the Labour Party'.[36] The Labour members of Lloyd George's government were Barnes, Brace, Clynes, Hodges and Roberts. Walsh and Wardle joined in 1917, the former having spoken against that course at the joint PLP-NEC meeting in December 1916.[37]

In May 1917 Henderson went to Petrograd on behalf of the War Cabinet. He returned convinced that Labour should support the call for an international socialist conference at Stockholm. It was made by neutral Scandinavia and by the Dutch parties and was supported by the new Russian government led by Kerensky. Labour was divided. Those Labour politicians who supported the war were unwilling to meet German or Austrian delegates or to encourage – or to seem to be encouraging – a negotiated peace. There was strong support for the meeting, as might be expected, from the pacifists and the left generally. The trade unions were divided. Henderson himself had led a section of the party into the Lloyd George coalition, having served previously in the Asquith coalition. But he had now come to fear the consequences if an exhausted Russia tried to continue fighting.

At first Lloyd George seemed to encourage the meeting. But under pressure from the Cabinet and from the French government, he declined to say whether he would issue the necessary passports. On 10 August a special Labour conference voted three-to-one in favour of the Stockholm meeting. Lloyd George described it as 'a fraternising conference with the enemy'. On 11 August Henderson resigned from the Cabinet. On 21 August the recalled Labour conference met again. The miners reversed their previous vote in favour of the Stockholm meeting, which gained only a narrow majority. Lloyd George duly witheld the passports.

Perhaps it was this episode – Henderson's leaving the Lloyd George coalition in 1917 rather than, as Taylor thought, joining it in 1916 – which was crucial in transforming Labour into an independent political party. Certainly Beatrice Webb thought so. In May 1918 she wrote that none of them had realised the enormous importance of Henderson's 'ejection' from the Cabinet. He had come out with a 'veritable hatred' of Lloyd George, who had insulted him at their last interview, immediately after the first Labour conference of August 1917. From that day 'Henderson determined to create an independent political party, capable of becoming His Majesty's Government, and he turned to Sidney to help him'.[38] In 1917 Henderson was succeeded by William Adamson (1863-1936), a Scottish miners' official. In January 1919 Beatrice Webb wrote:

> I have never seen Adamson, the chairman of the Parliamentary Labour Party before he lunched with us yesterday, except as a square figure on the platform of the Albert Hall mass meeting just prior to the [1918] election ... He is a middle-aged Scottish miner, typical British proletarian in body and mind, with an instinctive suspicion of all intellectuals or enthusiasts ... Adamson fumbles in political life as we should fumble with a pickaxe in the dark recesses of a mine, and gets about the same output as we should do. The thought of him as the leader of His Majesty's Opposition is even more strangely absurd than Barnes in the War Cabinet or at the peace conference.[39]

Nor was it only Adamson or Barnes who prospered during the war, despite Mrs Webb's severe and snobbish judgments. In June 1918 Clynes became Food Controller in place of Lord Rhondda, who had resigned. On 4 November the Labour Ministers, including Clynes, were pressing the National Executive Committee for a continuation of the coalition, on the ground that Labour could not survive the election. Clynes, so Sidney Webb reported to Beatrice, threatened that all candidates who 'did not get the Lloyd George letter' (what became known as the 'coupon') would be 'swept into oblivion' and that the Labour Party would be 'finally smashed'. By 12 votes to four, the Executive insisted on its former policy: that at the election they should be in opposition to the Lloyd George coalition, 'whatever fate were in store for them [as Beatrice Webb put it] at the ballot boxes'.[40]

The war ended on 11 November 1918. A majority of the parliamentary party favoured staying in office. But a special conference on 14 November decided by a large majority to withdraw from the coalition, with the miners, the railwaymen and the engineers carrying the motion against the cotton weavers and various smaller unions. Bernard Shaw was the Fabian delegate and intervened, 'brilliantly' according to Mrs Webb, to champion what was a 'foregone conclusion'. Clynes was the spokesman of the Labour Ministers – all of them, it appears – who wanted to stay in the coalition. Following the decision, however, Clynes and three of his colleagues resigned from the government, Clynes showing a marked reluctance to do so; while Barnes and Roberts left the Labour Party and 'futile Wardle is miserable in mid-air'.[41]

The general election was held on 14 December 1918 but the results were not known until 28 December. Coalition Conservatives (also called Unionists) won 335 seats, Coalition (also called National) Liberals 133, Labour

63, Liberals 28, Independent Conservatives 23 and Coalition Labour 10. Though few saw it at the time, this election was a triumph for Labour. Not only did it win more seats than ever before. It also, for the first time, won more seats than the Liberal Party, so setting the pattern for the rest of the 20th century in British politics. This was unclear in 1918, not only because it was impossible to foretell the future, but also because the parliamentary party had lost its outstanding performers. Henderson, MacDonald and Snowden all lost their seats, though Henderson returned at the Widnes by-election in 1919. Of the well-known leaders, only Clynes survived. When the parliamentary party met, they re-elected Adamson, whom Beatrice Webb also described as 'respectable but dull-witted'.[42]

In September 1919 she recorded that the spectacle of the syndicalist Oxford don G.D.H. Cole working through Henderson was 'almost as amusing as Sidney [Webb] working through Adamson'. In December, reporting a meeting of the International Congress at the House of Commons, she was even more severe with Adamson, who 'came in, invited as Chairman of the Parliamentary Labour Party, and sat himself down at the extreme corner of the long table, solitary and ignored, ugly, ineffective, almost mentally deficient relatively to his position as leader of His Majesty's Opposition'.[43] In 1920 the 'obviously incompetent' Adamson was succeeded by Clynes, 'an abler if not exactly dashing figure' – the words this time not of Mrs Webb but of the party's historian, Henry Pelling.[44]

In those days the Labour Party conference was held in the summer. At the conference of June 1921, according to Mrs Webb, Clynes brought the news (told him by Lord Robert Cecil) that Lloyd George was considering resignation, and that after the King had sent for other leaders and failed to get a government, he would advise the King to dissolve Parliament. Suppose he, Clynes, was sent for. Was he to accept office, form a government and go to the country? A sub-committee consisting of himself, Henderson, MacDonald and Sidney Webb decided that he should indeed do these things. Mrs Webb pronounced herself satisfied with the 'friendly partnership' between Clynes and Henderson.[45] Either might have led the Labour Party throughout the 1920s and beyond – though Henderson was always more interested in dominating the organisational side of the movement. Besides, he lost his Widnes seat at the 1922 general election, to return for Newcastle East in 1923. MacDonald, however, came back to the House as Member for Aberavon at the election itself.

The contest had other satisfactory features from MacDonald's point of view. Labour returned more Members, 142, than ever before. And those Members who were returned were more sympathetic to him than the intake of 1918. Then the ILP contingent had been reduced to four. Adamson, Beatrice Webb had complained, had been elected only because he was a miner, 'and such intellectuals as have survived the election are very inferior'.[46] The 1922 intake was not only larger but more promising intellectually. The result was: Conservatives 345, Labour 142, Coalition (or National) Liberals 62 and Liberals 54.

RAMSAY MACDONALD IN 1922

When Clynes opened the party meeting on 21 November 1922 (the election had been held on the 15th), he reported on what he had done to counter the Speaker's proposal that the Labour Party should share the opposition front bench with the Liberals. It was clear that he had done little. At the beginning of the meeting MacDonald was silent. After it had finished he made what Emanuel Shinwell, then a Clydesider aged 38, described as a 'fiery speech of protest'. The meeting proceeded to elect the officers for the coming session.

MacDonald's supporters proposed that the election should be by secret ballot. This was rejected. The ILP Members found themselves having to vote openly for MacDonald and against Clynes. MacDonald received 61 votes, Clynes 56. Accordingly 25 Members had omitted to vote. MacDonald's election was then put to the meeting and carried unanimously. Clynes said that the whole party was determined to support the new leader. This sentiment did not, however, prevent him from issuing a statement to the press deploring the activities of those new Members who had decided in favour of the change before the party meeting. He added, correctly, that this was the seventh occasion on which the party had changed its chairman. An official Labour Party statement said that MacDonald had been elected Chairman or Leader. This immediately became transformed in the general political consciousness into Chairman and Leader. This remained the designation until 1970, when Harold Wilson became Leader of the Labour Party. In 1922 the *New Leader* expressed the opinion that 'Mr MacDonald will infallibly become the symbol and personification which we have hitherto lacked'.[47]

Four days after his election, MacDonald wrote that the failure of the Party in the last Parliament had been that it had not been led as an opposition. It had never impressed itself on the country as an alternative government. It had won its 'great series of by-elections' mainly because of voters whom the coalition had 'thrown away'.

MacDonald then turned to the question of the opposition front bench, which (as we have seen) had played a part in his victory over Clynes. There were, MacDonald wrote, only two advantages in the front bench. The first was that you could put your feet up on the table. The second was that you had 'a box of nice convenient height whereon to lay your notes'. Nevertheless it was 'a symbol of authority'. When the Liberal Party had 'almost disappeared' in 1918, the Labour Party had 'lost its chance of occupying the whole bench'. If the party was 'to conduct the work of an opposition, it must have the facilities and recognition of an opposition'.[48]

Quite correctly, MacDonald was concerned to do down the Liberals and to establish Labour as the alternative party of government. He went into government in 1924 partly because he wanted to lay an indisputable claim to the opposition front bench. Henry Pelling writes:

> For nine years [1922-31] MacDonald had dominated the Labour Party, and for nine years he had held an authority which no single individual had ever possessed over its members before. He had received great loyalty from the parliamentary party, and not least from the trade unionists. But the final demands of the 1931 crisis were too great a strain on that loyalty.[49]

It has already been argued that George V behaved unconstitutionally during that crisis in refusing to accept his Prime Minister's resignation.* There were three constitutional solutions. First, MacDonald could have tried to continue as head of a Labour government: for it is often overlooked that the Labour Cabinet accepted, even though by a narrow majority, the cuts in benefit which were being demanded. Secondly – the most likely correct solution – Stanley Baldwin could have formed a Conservative administration. Or, thirdly, Baldwin could have tried to form a national government, which MacDonald and other Labour politicians could have joined, or not, as they thought fit. Almost certainly, they would have refused, and Baldwin would have been restricted to those Liberals who joined MacDonald's national government, the Liberal Nationals (as distinct from the National Liberals of 1918-22).

ARTHUR HENDERSON AND GEORGE LANSBURY 1931-2

As it was, the hurt was great. Raymond Postgate, George Lansbury's biographer, tells us that 'one eminent woman worker for the movement spent a fortnight in bed from shock when she learnt of MacDonald's defection'.[50] On 25 August 1931 the Trades Union Congress and the extra-parliamentary party took control of the parliamentary party and disavowed MacDonald's leadership. When the parliamentary party met it was at Transport House, Smith Square, London SW1, with members of the General Council present. Hugh Dalton wrote that this was an innovation, suggested by Henderson (whom he called 'Uncle', as others did, as in 'Uncle Arthur') to demonstrate party unity.[51] It also demonstrated the brute force of the trade unions. Henderson was overwhelmingly elected Chairman and Leader of the Parliamentary Party.

The general election took place on 27 October 1931. This was a fraudulent election. When the national government was formed, it was given out – by Baldwin and Buckingham Palace alike – that it was a temporary expedient to meet a current crisis, and that 'normal service would be resumed shortly'. After all, MacDonald's 1929 government had another

---

* See above, p. 36.

three years to run. Whether this was ever a realistic possibility must be doubtful: but the fact remains that a snap election formed no part of the arrangement which George V forced unconstitutionally on MacDonald. The result was: Conservatives 473, Labour 52, Liberal Nationals 35, Liberals 33, Others 5 and Independent Liberals 4.

Henderson lost his seat again, this time at Burnley. As his movements between constituencies tend to be confusing, it may be helpful to set them down: Barnard Castle, 1903-18; Widnes, 1919-22; Newcastle East, 1923; Burnley, 1924-31; and Clay Cross, 1933-5. For the first year of the new Parliament, Henderson continued as titular leader. But as he was not in the House, and was spending much of his time in Geneva as President of the Disarmament Conference, George Lansbury served as acting leader with C.R. Attlee as his deputy. In autumn 1932 Henderson resigned the leadership but remained secretary of the extra-parliamentary party. After the 1931 election the opposition front bench accommodated only one former Cabinet Minister, Lansbury, and only two of what Beatrice Webb called 'ex-Ministers of rank' in Stafford Cripps and Attlee.[52] Other casualties were J.R. Clynes, Hugh Dalton, Arthur Greenwood and Herbert Morrison, though Greenwood returned at a by-election in Wakefield in April 1932. Lansbury now became the titular as well as the actual leader.

He was a kindly, rubicund, mutton-chop-whiskered Londoner. He had made his name as a pioneer of municipal enterprise in Poplar, where he had often found himself and his councillor colleagues at odds with the government of the day. He was also a pacifist. When he told Henderson that he hoped Stafford Cripps (not a pacifist in those days but a virtual Communist) would succeed him as leader, Henderson said: 'If that happened, I would feel that all I have worked for had gone for nothing.'[53] But Lord Ponsonby, accepting the leadership of the Labour peers, said: 'Could I ask for anything more than to be rid of those people and to have Lansbury as my chief?'[54]

Nevertheless, after Hitler seized power in Germany in 1933 it was inconvenient, to say the least, to have a pacifist as Leader of the Labour Party. Beatrice Webb surveyed other possible leaders and concluded despondently that Hugh Dalton and Herbert Morrison had 'no success' as public speakers. Nor had C.R. Attlee, who 'though gifted with intellect and character and also with goodwill' had 'alas! no *personality!*' (italics supplied). He was not feared, disliked or admired but 'merely respected by Labour men and approved by the [national] government front bench'.[55]

C.R. ATTLEE IN 1935

The problem of Lansbury was resolved at the 1935 party conference, which was held at The Dome, Brighton, and opened on 1 October. Two days later Mussolini invaded Abyssinia. On 5 October a resolution was put by the National Council of Labour calling for sanctions against Italy and the use of 'all necessary measures' under the Covenant of the League of Nations. Lansbury made an emotional speech restating his Christian pacifism. He was given 'as great an ovation as a Labour Party conference has ever recorded'.[56] Ernest Bevin, the leader of the Transport and General Workers' Union, then went to the rostrum. He pointed out that Lansbury had supported sanctions in September and was against them in October. In a famous passage, he said:

> I hope this conference will not be influenced by either sentiment or personal attainment. It is placing the Executive and the Labour Movement in an absolutely wrong position to be taking your conscience round from body to body asking to be told what to do with it.

The resolution was carried by an overwhelming majority, Herbert Morrison having summed up for the Executive with a masterpiece of fudging designed to get the maximum vote and to please everyone.[57] Bevin resented what he thought was Morrison's half-hearted support. When the House reassembled on 8 October 1935, Lansbury resigned. On 23 October Baldwin announced a general election on 14 November. There was no substantial resistance to a motion in the PLP, moved by David Grenfell and seconded by Tom Williams, that Attlee, Lansbury's deputy, should carry on as leader.[58] The result of the election was: Conservatives, 432; Labour, 154; Liberals, 20; ILP, 4; Others, 4; Communists, 1.

Clynes, Dalton and Morrison returned to the House. Clynes was by now 66 and said he did not want to stand for the leadership. The candidates were Attlee, Greenwood and Morrison. Morrison was the favourite, even though his principal supporter was the not very popular Dalton. Dalton had originally thought of being a candidate himself and consequently aroused Morrison's suspicions – never a difficult feat. But by November 1935 Morrison had become reconciled to him.[59] Dalton said that, Morrison apart, the choice was between 'a nonentity and a drunk'.[60] On 14 November Morrison went to Dalton's flat and pored over the list of new Labour Members. Dalton recorded in his diary that the position seemed 'hopeful'. If Clynes did not run (as he did not), Attlee was the 'most dangerous'.[61] Morrison was viewed with some suspicion because fellow-Members thought he was more interested in the London County Council than in them. He was also a believer in the public corporation. Greenwood, by contrast, believed in workers' control. He was supported by Bevin and by many trade union Members, but was thought to be too much of a drunk. Attlee was supported by numerous MPs who had retained their seats and was described by the *New Statesman* as 'a natural adjutant, but not a general'.

On 26 November the Parliamentary Labour Party and the National Executive Committee met together at 11.30 in Committee Room 14 of the House of Commons. C.R. Attlee was in the chair. Emanuel Shinwell first moved that nominations and voting should be put off till later, but won only three supporters. J.R. Clynes was then asked whether he would accept nomination. He declined. Then Arthur Greenwood was nominated, followed by Attlee (who was supported by David Grenfell and the miners) and, finally, by Herbert Morrison. By prearrangement with Hugh Dalton, an MP called Arthur Hollins then asked whether the candidates would, if elected, 'give their full time to the job?' This was intended to reassure MPs who thought Morrison was preoccupied by his extra-parliamentary interests, notably the LCC.

As with most of Dalton's pieces of intrigue, it went awry. Morrison was prolix, saying he was in the hands of the party. There were shouts: 'It's not fair,' 'Very slick,' and 'Fancy putting up a new Member,' which was scarcely just, for Morrison had been MP for Hackney South in 1923-4 and 1929-31 before being returned for the same constituency in 1935. Indeed, it is probable that if he had kept his seat in 1931, he rather than Attlee would in due course have become leader. On the first ballot Attlee won 58 votes, Morrison 44 and Greenwood 33; on the second ballot Attlee defeated Morrison by 88 votes to 48. Dalton thought the Greenwood vote that went largely to Attlee on the second ballot had been organised by Freemasons.[62]

Dalton called it 'a wretched disheartening result! And a little mouse shall lead them.'[63] Mrs Webb noted that 'the irreproachable and colourless Attlee' had been 'elected Chairman of the Parliamentary Labour Party and Leader of His Majesty's Opposition'. This 'neutral and least disliked member of the front bench' might, she conceded, be 'better than Morrison, the dictator of policy'. All the same, he was 'a somewhat diminutive and meaningless figure to represent the British labour movement in the House of Commons!'[64]

4

Labour's Golden Age

This great Movement of ours.
Phrase used at Labour Party conferences *c.*
1945-75, attributed to Arthur Henderson

Henry Pelling writes that with the election of Attlee, for the first time the party's leader was not from the working class.[1] It was something for which Morrison, for one, would never forgive him. After the 1945 election, as we have seen, Morrison and Laski tried to supplant Attlee in Morrison's favour by seeking to have the leader re-elected by the new parliamentary party.* This was one reason for Attlee's suspicion of Morrison. In addition, as he observed – rather pettily, one may think – to the journalist Leslie Hunter: 'He stood against me in 1935, didn't he?'[2] In 1952 Attlee agreed with Hunter and his wife Margaret Stewart (who was also a journalist) that the party would elect Morrison if he retired:

> That's the one thing that worries me. I'd go at once if I thought Morrison could hold the party together, but I don't think he can. He's too heavy-handed, you know, and he might wreck the whole show. I may have to hang on a bit and see.[3]

Five years earlier there had been a revolt against Attlee which Morrison was asked to join, but he refused.[4] This did nothing to increase Attlee's charity. 'He never knew the difference between a big thing and a little thing,' he told Hugh Dalton later.[5] It is probable but by no means certain that Morrison would have won the leadership if Attlee had retired during the Churchill government of 1951-5. It is more difficult to make out the same case if we are thinking of the period between May 1955, when the recently appointed Anthony Eden won again for the Conservatives, and December 1955, when Attlee at last retired. Dalton believed that those who thought Morrison would have succeeded shortly after the 1955 election underestimated the damage which had been done to his reputation by his tenure of the Foreign Office in 1951.[6] This most unsuccessful period of Morrison's political career would have been even fresher in the memories of those exercising the parliamentary party's franchise after 1951 – even though they would have been more of Morrison's generation.

* See above, pp. 51-2.

HUGH GAITSKELL IN 1955

The idea that Attlee hung on after the 1955 election, just as he had in 1951-5, partly to keep out Morrison is deeply entrenched in the mythology of the Labour Party. Hunter certainly thought so: indeed, it is the principal theme of his book *The Road to Brighton Pier*, which R.H.S. Crossman reviewed, leading to the following exchange with Attlee:

> Crossman: I've just been reviewing a book about you.
> Attlee: Ah yes, I know. He says I hated Herbert. It's quite untrue. I pitied him and pity is a kind of affection. His trouble was vaulting ambition, which o'erleapt itself. Of course [referring to Hunter's book], it's all a pack of lies.[7]

This view of Hunter's work is incorrect. Most of his facts are right: it is his interpretation that is wrong. Attlee certainly disliked Morrison, wanted to keep him out of the leadership of the Labour Party and almost certainly put off his resignation in Labour's first post-war period of opposition to serve this end. But by May 1955 Morrison's decline in the party's esteem was already well advanced. Earlier, Attlee had wanted Aneurin Bevan to succeed him. In 1952 he had shown a clear preference for Bevan 'if only he wouldn't play the fool so much'.[8] In March 1955 he said to Crossman:

> Nye had the leadership on a plate. I always wanted him to have it. But you know, he wants to be two things simultaneously, a rebel and an official leader, and you can't be both.[9]

As late as November 1955 he said to Hunter:

> I'd like to see him get it. Trouble is he's so unstable, all over the place and you never know when you are with him. Anyway he's cooked his goose for the time being and the party would never stand for him.[10]

If Attlee had indeed possessed such a high regard for Bevan, he could have appointed him Chancellor of the Exchequer in 1950, before his resignation from the government. Many of the Labour Party's troubles in the 1950s flowed from this decision. In 1954-5 Bevan was perhaps in his most awkward and prickly phase. He resigned from the Shadow Cabinet over the South East Asia Treaty Organisation, and was replaced by Harold Wilson, greatly to his annoyance – though Crossman approved. In the autumn he was comprehensively defeated by Gaitskell for the Labour Party Treasureship. This was largely an honorific, even symbolic position, though Gaitskell did not treat it wholly as a sinecure.[11] Its principal advantage was that it carried automatically with it a seat on the National Executive.

Gaitskell would not have won the Treasureship so easily if he had not possessed the support of the big unions or, rather, of their leaders: Arthur Deakin of the transport and general workers, Tom Williamson of the municipal workers and Will Lawther of the miners. Bevan, as a former miner from Tredegar in Monmouthshire, was particularly hurt by the hostile position of the miners' union. In a sense, he had only himself to blame – though he did become Treasurer in 1956, when a peace of sorts had been imposed on the party. Ever since his arrival in the House in 1929, he had tended to shun and avoid the miners generally and the Welsh miners particularly. Naturally, this created some resentment. His close relationships with Lord Beaverbrook and others, combined with his taste for the better things of life, gave the impression that he had now detached himself from the working class. But the miners or, at any rate, the Welsh miners (in the 1940s and 1950s still a powerful group) would not have cared about his expensive restaurants, tailored suits and strong spirits if only he had paid them some attention. This he refused or neglected to do. If he had, they would have seen to it that he became leader.[12]

The union leaders' hatred (it is not too strong a word) of Bevan did not mean that they were passionately attached to Gaitskell. That is the other myth about the succession to Attlee: that the unions 'made' Gaitskell leader. How could they, when they did not have any votes? They had to wait till 1981 and the succeeding decade before that power was bestowed upon them. The union leaders had never loved Morrison, but he was still their candidate to succeed Attlee.[13] When, as late as October 1955, Crossman asked George Brown, a former transport workers' official, why a 'gaga Morrison' was preferable to a 'gaga Attlee', Brown replied that under Morrison's leadership the unions 'would be able to reassert their authority and smash the intellectuals'.[14] This, of course, may have reflected no more than Brown's dislike of (and desire to annoy) Crossman, who was certainly of that group which awaited Brown's hostile actions. Nevertheless, it does show that Morrison was still regarded by some trade unionists, who included Brown, as the natural successor to Attlee.

This is what Gaitskell thought too. In autumn 1954 he topped the poll for the Shadow Cabinet jointly with Jim Griffiths. Bevan, having resigned in April 1954, did not stand in the autumn. Gaitskell certainly saw himself in 1954-5 as a major figure in the party and a future leader. But he thought of himself in the first stage as deputy leader under Morrison. He genuinely had to be drafted.[15] In March 1955 Anthony Crosland, Roy Jenkins and Woodrow Wyatt wrote to him arguing that the leader should have the support of the centre 'which Herbert has not got'.[16] But Gaitskell refused to canvass in the tearoom. He left that to Dalton, who was described by Mrs Dalton as being 'like an elephant going through the jungle – clumsy, trumpeting but sly'.[17]

By March 1955 numerous figures in the party – certainly Gaitskell and

Deakin, probably Morrison and Williamson as well – had convinced themselves that Bevan would have to go. Attlee thought that Gaitskell and Morrison, either of whom might succeed him, wanted to inherit a disciplined party and that consequently both wanted Bevan eliminated (in the Labour Party's gentler usage of that word) well in advance. Attlee was half-hearted about the operation from the very beginning. Gaitskell was not, and composed an indictment for Attlee in which he set out the counts against Bevan. There were three of them. They were all based on his conduct in the House in 1954-5.

In April 1954 Attlee had indicated his approval of the government's support for a new anti-Communist alliance in South East Asia, SEATO. Bevan then rose and questioned his leader in a way which implied a lack of confidence in him. At a meeting of the Shadow Cabinet on the next day, Bevan was rebuked, though not formally censured, for his behaviour. He responded by announcing his resignation from the Shadow Cabinet.

Then in January 1955 Bevan had proposed that Labour should table a motion calling for talks with the USSR before ratification of the treaty on German rearmament. The parliamentary party rejected Bevan's proposal but nonetheless his allies had it placed on the Order Paper, as they were perfectly entitled to do. Gaitskell, however, wrote that though 'technically' there had been no breach of the Standing Orders, this was 'certainly contrary to their spirit'. A special meeting of the parliamentary party was called, when Bevan and his supporters were condemned for refusing to support majority decisions.

And, lastly, the parliamentary party had decided shortly afterwards to support the government over the construction of the hydrogen bomb. In the subsequent debate Bevan questioned the decision. He said that he and his friends would have to do the work of opposition in default of anyone else. Within hours he was interrogating Attlee vigorously in the House about whether the opposition agreed with the policy of making a nuclear response to a conventional attack. In the division, he and 61 others abstained on Labour's official motion.

A special meeting of the Shadow Cabinet was summoned. Gaitskell, Morrison and a youthful James Callaghan pressed for the withdrawal of the Whip. Attlee demurred but was over-ruled. The majority decided to make the question one of confidence. The whole Shadow Cabinet would resign if its recommendations were rejected by the parliamentary party, which met on 16 March 1955. Bevan was unrepentant. Opinon was evenly balanced. A compromise motion proposed by Fred Lee, calling for censure instead of withdrawal of the Whip, was defeated 138-124. The Shadow Cabinet's motion was carried 141-112.

The question was what to do next. Standing Orders said that the matter should be referred to the NEC. The majority of the Shadow Cabinet wanted to do this so that Bevan should be expelled by the committee (with, however, a right of appeal to the conference, which Bevan might well have exercised successfully). The majority argued that withdrawal of the Whip merely divested him of his duty to comply with it and imposed no real penalty upon him. He was bound to be readmitted to the parliamentary party – to have the Whip restored to him – before the election. So to the NEC the matter duly went.

The trade unions, through their representatives on that body (almost always the second-in-command figures), were now directly involved. Gaitskell, the Treasurer, himself believed, as he was to write in his diary, that the unions would be less munificent in disbursing the workers' pennies at the forthcoming election if Bevan remained unpunished. In explaining Gaitskell's conduct, there is no need to go quite as far as Brian Brivati who, in his life of Gaitskell, accuses him of carrying out Deakin's instructions.

The resolution to expel Bevan considered by the NEC was framed in terms of his refusal to comply with majority decisions rather than of his affronts to Attlee. When it began to look probable that Bevan would be expelled, Attlee stopped doodling and proposed that a special sub-committee should be set up to interview him. This was carried 14-13. The vote might have gone the other way. One of Bevan's supporters, Ian Mikardo, had gone to Israel for his daughter's wedding and was expected to be absent for the crucial meeting. In a tie that year's chairman, Dr Edith Summerskill, had intended to use her casting vote against Bevan. In the event Mikardo (whose name she could not bear to utter and whom she always called 'the man in the brown suit') came home early; while Mrs Jean Mann abstained.[18]

Bevan's pursuers had lost him to a temporary sanctuary which had been erected by Attlee and was to turn out to be permanent. At the sub-committee Bevan was accused of persistent attacks on party and union leaders, repeated refusals to accept majority decisions and the formation of an organised group with its own press (that is, *Tribune*). However, at the reconvened meeting of the NEC, Jim Griffiths moved and Attlee seconded a motion approving the withdrawal of the Whip from Bevan but accepting an apology from him (which had already been cleared with Attlee) together with an undertaking of future good conduct.[19]

Attlee and Griffiths were the peacemakers; both Gaitskell and Morrison wanted Bevan's extirpation. The union leaders blamed Attlee, for Griffiths then occupied the same position in the Labour Party as the Queen Mother was later to fill in the country. They thought Attlee had mishandled the situation. This was one reason why they wanted him to depart after the 1955 election. In late April the Whip was quietly restored to Bevan in preparation for this contest.

In the election of 26 May 1955 the Conservatives won 344 seats, Labour 277, the Liberals 6 and others 3. To Gaitskell's surprise, it was an election defeat that did not swing the party to the left.[20] Even Bevan commended Labour's 'good domestic programme' which, though not 'exciting or ambitious', was 'definite and practical'.[21] After the election Dalton began what he called his 'Operation Avalanche' to clear out the 'old gang', in which he included himself – he resigned from the Shadow Cabinet – but not Attlee.[22] Dalton wrote to Attlee that his own position was 'a very special one'. It was his 'strong hope that in the interests of party unity' he would continue as leader when the new Parliament met. The hope was shared, he knew, by many of their colleagues. No one else 'of whatever age' could 'do this difficult job' as well as he could.[23]

Bevan was, if anything, even keener for Attlee to stay. On 8 June 1955 the Shadow Cabinet, without a dissentient voice (for Morrison kept quiet), urged him to continue. Attlee said he would go on until October 1955, the time of the party conference, but no longer: the party, he said, must have a younger leader soon.[24] At this stage the Labour politicians thought the session would end in October 1955 and that they could then contemplate matters afresh in time for the parliamentary party's sessional elections in November. Instead the Eden government decided to prolong the session until autumn 1956. On the next day, 9 June 1955, Attlee announced to the parliamentary party meeting that he had told the Shadow Cabinet he wanted to go at once but had been asked to stay. Bevan urged him not to fix a date for his departure. That would only lead to 'speculation and intrigue'. An affecting exchange followed:

> Bevan: Clem, I implore you, put no limit. Just go on. (*Cheers*)
> Attlee: Is that the general wish? (*Cheers*) Anyone against? No? Very well.[25]

Dalton noted that this was 'almost entirely the end of Morrison' as a future leader. He was too old to succeed Attlee now.[26] The thought in many minds that day was that Bevan had ditched Morrison by prolonging Attlee's reign beyond the next 12 months and that, when Attlee finally went, Bevan would succeed him. However, things worked out quite differently.[27] Though Gaitskell was to prove the eventual beneficiary, it is clear that Attlee was not staying on specifically to keep out Morrison. In June 1955 – and up to the date of his departure in December – it was Bevan and his acolytes who wanted Attlee to stay on precisely for this purpose. On 21 June Attlee wrote to his brother Tom:

> It's high time the party found a new leader. I am too old to give a new impetus. I hoped to force their hand by fixing a date for retirement, but they would not have it. Twenty years is quite long enough, I think.[28]

Bevan's biographer and friend, Michael Foot, writes of a plan by the anti-Bevanites to push Attlee out and Morrison in and of Attlee's moving with 'astonishing agility' to safeguard his position.[29] This is not borne out by the evidence. Certainly Morrison's friends wanted Attlee to leave in June or July 1955, so allowing Morrison to take over in the autumn. This was before it was realised that the session would continue into 1956. But Morrison's friends were no match for Gaitskell's friends, notably for Dalton. By encouraging Attlee to stay, he intended to provide time to build Gaitskell's strength. This conflicted with Attlee's own wishes about his retirement.[30] In the session of summer 1955 Morrison, Attlee thought, tried 'too hard' in the House.[31]

Dalton refused to come to a firm conclusion about whether Attlee delayed to keep out Morrison. What he did know (he wrote) was that Attlee did not regard Morrison as likely to make a good Prime Minister or Labour 'a happy ship'. He was also dismissive of the view, advanced then and since, that Attlee's resignation was hastened by pressure from trade unions or from newspapers – some wanting Gaitskell, others wanting Morrison, none (apart from *Tribune*) wanting Bevan. Dalton doubted whether 'there was much in this'. He thought Attlee's health, and 'his wife's influence in the interests of his health', provided 'a much more likely explanation'.[32]

Indeed, on 8 August 1955 Attlee suffered a slight stroke, and his eczema recurred. Unlike Winston Churchill's more serious incapacitation of two years before, this was not kept secret. Speculation about his leadership increased. It grew still more in September when Percy Cudlipp – then writing a column in the *News Chronicle*, and brother of Hugh – visited Cherry Cottage in Buckinghamshire and was granted an interview.

Labour, Attlee informed the readers of the paper (officially an independent Liberal organ, in practice advocating a kind of enlightened Lib-Labbery), 'must have at the top men brought up in the present age', not, as he had been, in the 'Victorian age'. The party had 'nothing to gain by dwelling in the past'. Nor did he think it could 'impress the nation by adopting a puerile left-wingism'. He regarded himself as 'to the left of centre', which was 'where a party leader ought to be'. The world was 'constantly presenting new problems'. It was 'no use asking what Keir Hardie would have done'. He had had a long innings and would be glad when he could hand over to a younger man.[33] This appeared not in the Percy Cudlipp column's usual place but as the paper's main story ('lead' or 'splash' in Fleet Street argot) headlined Attlee Is Ready To Go.

Later that month, however, Barbara Castle told R.H.S. Crossman that she had seen Attlee, who had said he was willing to carry on for 12 months:

> With Barbara one is never sure whether Attlee hadn't merely grunted at intervals while she told him what to think. I tested her view by myself talking to Attlee ... He certainly has not committed himself to staying for the whole 12 months but merely to staying on if the party insists, which is slightly different.[34]

The party conference opened at Margate on the surprisingly late day of 10 October 1955. At this point Gaitskell hoped only to replace Morrison as deputy leader when Morrison replaced Attlee. He agreed with Patrick Gordon Walker that this outcome would be best both for the party and for himself.[35] The big trade unions wanted Attlee to go because he had, they considered, been weak in not expelling Bevan from the party in April 1955. They were moving towards Gaitskell as a successor – though they had no *locus* in choosing him – on account of Morrison's age and his ever-increasing apparent feebleness.

The *Daily Mirror* wanted Attlee to go and Gaitskell to succeed him. The paper's editorial director, Hugh Cudlipp, later wrote that Attlee, 'the chief architect of defeat, had to go, but Aneurin Bevan was not fit to take over the leadership'. Gaitskell, according to Cudlipp, supplied 'the brains and the zest' – the last not perhaps the quality which first came to the minds of those attempting to describe this intelligent, serious but prickly product of Winchester and New College. Unhappily, Gaitskell 'did not understand the *Mirror*. He assumed, rather imprudently, its automatic support as if it were a popular version of the unpopular *Daily Herald* [then Labour's official newspaper].'[36] The *Mirror* gave Attlee the name 'Lord Limpet'. Michael Foot wrote that the paper made his position 'intolerable'.[37] Attlee, who wanted to go anyway, was perfectly capable of standing up to the *Mirror*.

Foot is, however, frank that the Bevanites, of whom he was a leading figure, wanted Attlee to stay to give their candidate a better chance of succeeding him. By 1957, they thought – at any rate, hoped – Gaitskell's bubble, which weekly in 1955 they could see assuming alarmingly balloon-like proportions, would have burst. At the pre-conference demonstration Barbara Castle, another leading Bevanite, issued a fulsome invitation to Attlee to stay as long as he wished or could.[38] She 'drew a touching picture of evil forces being prepared to hustle poor deserving Clem Attlee off the stage before he was ready to go'.[39] Gaitskell again defeated Bevan for the Treasureship. For this reason and others, Bevan exploded. He chose the private session on the Tuesday afternoon (the traditional time in the conference calendar for such debates) which was ostensibly devoted to Harold Wilson's report on party organisation. Hugh Massingham recorded in his column in the *Observer*, which in those more self-effacing days he wrote as 'Our Political Correspondent', that:

> A time-bomb went off with a shattering explosion. It was the fearful noise of Mr Bevan blowing his top at what was comically called a private session. As every window was open and the loudspeakers on, even the quiet fishermen at the end of the pier could catch every word.[40]

According to Michael Foot:

> Delegates thumped out their enthusiasm so violently that the reporters who thought they might have had an afternoon off came rushing back to discover what explosion had shaken the Margate pavilion.[41]

While R.H.S. Crossman's version was:

> In the course of 12 minutes I do not recall Nye mentioning the [Wilson]
> report. He merely replied to Webber [William Webber, a trade union member
> of the National Executive Committee] on the subject of his expulsion, on the
> hypocrisy of the debates, on the trade union oligarchy and on anything else
> which came into his head. It was a brilliant and spontaneous tour de force
> and as Nye returned to his seat he was nearly mobbed by the delegates.[42]

Though Bevan won the cheers from the constituency delegates, his
support in the parliamentary party was not increasing, while former
supporters of Morrison were moving to Gaitskell. Dalton asserts that,
when the conference dispersed, Gaitskell had decided to stand.[43] This is
doubtful. Gaitskell's aim was to stop Bevan. He consented to stand himself
only when Morrison's political reputation and parliamentary performance
had declined so far that this course became the best means of accomplish-
ing his end. Alfred Robens said in a speech at Manchester that Attlee
would retire 10 days after Parliament reassembled. Eight MPs wrote from
the Council of Europe in Strasbourg urging Gaitskell to stand. The *Daily
Herald* was so excited that it dispatched the political reporter Hugh
Pilcher to interview Attlee in Malta, where he was on a brief visit. Attlee's
denial of any intention to resign was curiously equivocal.[44] He said:

> I have no intention whatever of resigning at the present time. There is
> nothing on the agenda of the parliamentary party meeting about it. I have
> heard of no one who intends to raise the subject.[45]

Morrison was urged by his friends, who were worried by Gaitskell's
growing support, to tell Attlee that, unless he resigned, most of the
Shadow Cabinet would resign instead. But though he was anxious for
Attlee to depart, Morrison himself – partly, no doubt, out of loyalty, partly
out of feebleness – was reluctant to cause a split.[46]

Gaitskell's speech in the autumn budget debate marked the end of
'Butskellism' – the word coined by the *Economist* to denote the alleged
unity of economic views between Gaitskell and the Chancellor, R.A. Butler. It was also the moment when Gaitskell himself became the clear
favourite to succeed Attlee. Crossman noted that Gaitskell's unwonted
aggression towards Butler 'made the headlines and in fact made his
speech'. He had taken the opportunity to destroy 'once and for all' the
figure of 'Mr Butskell'. This demolition was essential if he was to become
Leader of the Labour Party.[47] This was a significant entry in Crossman's
diary. It demonstrated that, by late October 1955, he (a Bevanite, or a
Bevanite of sorts) was prepared not only to contemplate the likelihood of
Gaitskell's becoming leader but also, by implication, to welcome that
outcome.

Attlee was equally pleased. He told Leslie Hunter that Gaitskell had 'done very well' and 'come on a lot'. Though he had 'the best chance', the party would have to decide.[48] Herbert Bowden, the Chief Whip, approached Harold Wilson and told him that Attlee was 'delighted'. Now that Wilson and Gaitskell were 'working so well together', he said he was 'ready to go'.[49] Attlee's biographer, Kenneth Harris, writes that it was at this point, in late October, that Gaitskell made up his mind to stand for the leadership.[50] This may be so: nevertheless, as late as 2 November Gaitskell would write to Douglas Jay that, though there was 'a continual fuss going on', as far as he could see Attlee had 'no intention whatever of moving on' and consequently the discussion was 'all rather academic as well as being regrettable'.[51] After Gaitskell's triumph in the budget debate came Morrison's failure in the censure debate. Crossman agreed with Bevan

> in feeling sympathy with the old boy for the treatment he got. The Tea Room [shorthand for the solid centre of the party: the Bevanites, like the Conservatives, favoured the Smoking Room] was utterly heartless. They were really like the spectators in a bullring, booing a matador who is past his years.[52]

It was after this failure that Gaitskell finally decided to stand.[53]

Both Morrison and Bevan took alarm. On 3 November they met together in the Smoking Room.[54] Morrison authorised first Eddie Shackleton and then Richard Stokes to negotiate with Bevan's representative, Leslie Hale.[55] Bevan sought the advice of the Conservative Minister James Stuart. It was to 'disentrench' his troops opposing Morrison and realign them in support of the older man in order to defeat Gaitskell.[56]

This was the first of two plots involving Morrison and Bevan which are often confused, partly, no doubt, because they contemplated the same outcome: that Morrison should be the Prime Minister in some future Labour government, unhappily as yet unelected, with Bevan as his Foreign Secretary, and that, after two or three years, Bevan should succeed him as Prime Minister. In this first plot, the assumption was that Gaitskell, Morrison and Bevan would all stand. The further assumption was that Bevan would come bottom of the poll – a creditable third, but bottom nonetheless. Neither Gaitskell nor Morrison would have won an absolute majority. If Morrison were first, Bevan's votes, redistributed virtually en bloc to him, would guarantee him the succession. If, however, he was second, and Gaitskell first, Bevan's votes would still give him a sporting chance. It was this double miscalculation – that no one would win an absolute majority, and that Bevan would be bottom of the poll – which kept Morrison in the contest, despite the advice of many of his friends that he should withdraw before he subjected himself to further and needless humiliation.

On 16 November Bevan 'berated' Crossman for the line he had been taking that it would be a 'disaster' if Morrison succeeded Attlee. According to Crossman, this led 'logically' to accepting Gaitskell as the next leader, 'though I never say so'.

> Bevan: You can't force the party to accept Gaitskell, and I must warn you that, if he is leader, I might not be able to collaborate.
> Crossman: But what's the alternative?
> Bevan: Well, there are times when no decision is best. The right thing to do now is to wait. After all, something may turn up. (*As an afterthought.*) Gaitskell might be more acceptable in nine months' time than now ....
> Crossman: But you've got to understand that many of us know all the drawbacks of Gaitskell but accept him as inevitable because you've ruled yourself out.

The 'whole conversation', Crossman records, 'was conducted in a perfectly rational way between friends'.[57] Towards its end Crossman blurted out to Bevan what he claimed never to say: that Gaitskell was the logical or inevitable successor. Both Bevan and Morrison were still resolved to prevent this from happening.

Later in the month Attlee called in Herbert Bowden, the Chief Whip, said he was going and asked him to fix a date. Bowden said they should 'get it over' before Christmas and suggested 7 December. Attlee agreed. Bowden asked whether he, as Chief Whip, should tell the contenders privately. Attlee told him to tell Gaitskell.[58] Morrison was understandably piqued and said, with a humour which was admirable in the circumstances, that he 'felt like Princess Margaret' (who had just renounced Group Captain Peter Townsend as a suitor). It was 'a bit hard' that he should be the only person that Attlee had not consulted in any way. He thought Attlee would go next day, 7 December, 'but he hasn't mentioned it to me'. He was 'a rum fellow'. He could, he said, tell his interlocutor, Crossman, 'a lot more about that if I wanted to'.[59] On 6 December Attlee wrote to his brother Tom:

> I am tomorrow giving up the leadership of the party. As you know, I wanted to go after the last election, but stayed on to oblige. There is, however, so much speculation as to the next leader going on that I think it best to retire now. The party is in good heart.[60]

Irrespective of whether the version given by Michael Foot and the Bevanites is accepted – roughly, that Attlee was forced out by a combination of popular newspapers and brutish trade unionists – it is evident that, having reluctantly agreed to continue as leader in June 1955, Attlee expected to carry on till the end of the session. This, through the decision of the Eden government, would occur in 1956, not, as had first been thought by Labour politicians, in 1955. When Attlee announced his resignation to the parliamentary party on 7 December, he said it was 'regrettable' that since June there had 'scarcely been a week pass' when 'one prominent member of the party or another' did not talk about his resignation. That certainly did not 'help the party'. He said 'Thank you' and left the meeting. Morrison took the chair. It was decided that nominations for the election would close on Friday 9 December at 11. Later that day, 7 December, it was announced that Attlee would be going to the Lords.[61]

On the evening of Attlee's resignation, Morrison and Bevan dined together. Next day's events, Dalton wrote, seemed to stem from 'this surprising love feast'. Bevan told the press on the Thursday that he would 'willingly accede' to a proposal of 10 MPs that he and Gaitskell should withdraw and allow Morrison to become leader unopposed.[62] The scheme originated with Emanuel Shinwell, a Morrison man; its supporters included David Grenfell, Richard Stokes and Tom Williams.[63] This was the second Morrison-Bevan plot. The first one, as we have seen, was that on any second ballot Bevan's votes would be switched to Morrison.* Now Bevan's votes could not be switched because Bevan, together with Gaitskell, would not – so it was vainly hoped – be contesting the election at all.

To Morrison's biographers, this was a 'curious and desperate manoeuvre'.[64] To Bevan's biographer, however, it was a 'feasible plan'.[65] The plan or manoeuvre certainly did not arouse much enthusiasm at the time. Twenty MPs who had formerly been Morrison supporters approached Gaitskell on the opposition front bench and urged him not to withdraw. More supporters of Gaitskell appealed to him in the Division Lobby.[66] Lena Jeger, then a young, leftist MP, had been present at the Morrison-Bevan dinner. She promptly told Harold Wilson (as a young, leftist MP likewise), who went immediately to see Gaitskell, said he was 'nauseated' and promised that, if Gaitskell withdrew, he would stand himself.[67] Morrison himself remained hopeful and went off to see his tailor at the Woolwich Co-op.[68] Barbara Castle continued to be his loyal supporter, explaining 'passionately' to the journalist Leslie Hunter that, though she had disagreed with many of his ideas on policy in the past – which was something of an understatement – his record had earned him a short period as leader. Attlee was 'crazy' if he imagined the party would accept Gaitskell.[69]

Mrs Castle rebuked her friend Crossman for his unsteadiness. On Thursday 8 December he had no doubt that Bevan and Gaitskell would both stand too. She reproached him with the rumour that he was going to vote for Gaitskell, which Crossman attributed to George Wigg. At this stage Crossman thought there was 'no problem'. On the first ballot, with three candidates standing, it was 'essential' that the Left should poll its full strength. If Gaitskell did not obtain the absolute majority on the first ballot, and he and Morrison remained in the contest, he would either vote for Gaitskell or tear up his ballot paper. Accordingly Wigg (if it was he who had started the rumour) was already half right. In any case, Crossman's

* See above, p. 107.

proposed actions were clearly contrary to the Bevanite line: that, if Gait-skell and Bevan both remained in the contest, the correct course to follow was to vote first for Bevan and then for Morrison but on no account for Gaitskell.

As he left the Smoking Room, where he had been having tea with Mrs Castle, Crossman ran into Bevan and said 'impetuously' that he heard there was a ridiculous rumour that he was going to vote for Gaitskell against him. This was completely untrue and he would like Bevan to know it was so. In his diary Crossman confessed himself 'a little bit baffled' that, though Bevan smiled, 'he looked a bit embarrassed but said nothing whatsoever and walked down the Lobby'.[70] Bevan was presumably being bashful about the Morrison-Bevan pact which, had it been successful, would have imposed the hated (by Crossman, at any rate) Morrison upon the party. The pact, though it did not come to anything, provided Cross-man with the pretext for voting for Gaitskell rather than for Bevan, a course he had really wanted to follow all along. He as good as announced his intentions in a special column in the *Daily Mirror* (for which he was then writing a regular column) on Saturday 10 December, four days before the MPs voted.[71]

The proposed pact, Crossman wrote, obviously put Gaitskell in an extremely embarrassing position. He was 'far too deeply committed' to consider Bevan's offer. The contest went on. Like 'many other left-wingers' Crossman himself would have preferred Bevan to have the leadership until he 'threw it away'. He could not support Morrison because he did not believe that the Labour Party 'in its present state of health' was 'strong enough to stand two or three more years of disintegration at the bottom and infighting at the top'.[72] The next day Hugh Massingham, the *Ob-server*'s political columnist, who was close to Bevan, Shinwell and Wigg, wrote more sympathetically of Morrison's decline:

> Those who owe everything to Mr Morrison, who would not even be in the House without his patronage, have deserted to Mr Gaitskell. No doubt they have their reasons, but it is not a pleasant spectacle and it is not a pleasant fact to record.[73]

The parliamentary party met at seven on the following Wednesday in Committee Room 14. Attlee was not in the chair on account of his swift and precipitate ascent to the peerage. Morrison was there in his place. The result was: Gaitskell 157, Bevan 70, Morrison 40. Gaitskell had won an absolute majority, Bevan had polled better than expected and Morrison had been humiliated. Attlee wrote to Gaitskell:

> I was delighted with your vote which was just about what I had anticipated. It was a pity that Herbert insisted on running. He had, I think, been warned of the probable result.

He concluded with the 'hope that Nye & Co will now go all out to support you'.[74] Nye & Co showed no such disposition, at any rate to begin with. Indeed, Bevan conducted himself with a conspicuous lack of grace or good humour. Gaitskell's succession, he wrote immediately afterwards in *Tribune*, was the result of an 'unworthy conspiracy'. Labour would 'rue the day' when it permitted 'the least reputable among newspapers' – the *Daily Mirror* – to 'fill the role of kingmaker'.[75] He did, however, announce that he would not stand against Morrison for the deputy leadership.

This small gesure of magnanimity proved barren. For Morrison slunk away like an old wounded animal. Bevan later stood against Jim Griffiths in January 1956 and lost 141-111. If Attlee had made Bevan rather than Gaitskell Chancellor of the Exchequer in 1950, or Bevan rather than Morrison Foreign Secretary in 1951 – Morrison was appointed in March of that year, whereas Bevan resigned from the Government in April – matters might have turned out differently. As things were, Gaitskell was never forgiven for defeating Bevan so comprehensively in 1955. Though there was a period of factitious concord in 1957-9 in readiness for the election, peace was restored only with the death of Gaitskell in 1963 and his succession by Harold Wilson.

In May 1959 R.H.S. Crossman recorded that Barbara Castle, the party chairman, was 'like the rest of them ... already reinsuring against defeat' in the forthcoming general election by 'preparing a case for blaming Hugh Gaitskell and the Right'. So also was George Brown, who, in contrast, was by implication criticising Gaitskell for what he considered to be his less than wholehearted support for the nuclear deterrent.[76] By July Crossman could see that Mrs Castle, Ian Mikardo, Anthony Greenwood, Tom Driberg and Wilson were 'all carefully preparing their positions to blame others for the defeat and to prove that they themselves were pure and undefiled'.[77] At this point the Conservatives were leading Labour by 45 per cent to 41 in the Gallup Poll. By September the margin had widened, with figures of 50 and 43 respectively. Nevertheless, Gaitskell honestly thought he could, should and would win. Bevan was not so sure. He certainly did not look forward to working with Gaitskell if a Labour government were elected on 8 October. Four days before polling day he confided to the journalist Geoffrey Goodman his opinion that Gaitskell was 'a stubborn man, always interfering', who would never leave him alone. He did not know how long he would 'be able to stand it'.[78]

To Gaitskell the result came as a terrible shock. The Conservatives had 365 seats, Labour 258 and the Liberals 6. On the verge of tears, he followed the American fashion and conceded defeat during the night of 8-9 October. Bevan was outraged by this further example of subservience to United States ways. On being told the news in his Ebbw Vale committee room, he said that he 'would never concede' but instead 'wait until the last vote was properly counted'.[79]

Immediately afterwards, on Friday 9 October, Douglas Jay had an idea

in *his* committee room. He would write an article and send it to *Forward*
for anonymous publication. *Forward* was the Gaitskellite popular weekly.
Oddly enough, it had started life as an organ of the Independent Labour
Party. It was intended to be a counterweight to *Tribune*, a publication
about which Gaitskell and his friends had always been abnormally sensitive – much more sensitive than they were about the *New Statesman*,
which was almost equally unfriendly towards the Labour leader and his
entourage, but was less populist in tone and had probably a smaller
influence in the constituencies. In 1959 it was edited by Francis Williams
(later Lord Francis-Williams), a former editor of the *Daily Herald* and a
widely admired press officer in C.R. Attlee's Downing Street.

On Saturday 10 October 1959 Jay began to write his article.[80] On the
Saturday, he and others were asked to come round next day to Gaitskell's
house in Frognal Gardens, London NW3, for pre-lunch drinks and 'to
discuss the lessons of the election'.[81] It is easy to forget that at this stage
Gaitskell's reputation in the party stood higher than it had at any previous
time. Crossman and Benn agreed that he 'had come out of the campaign
with tremendous prestige and could do more or less what he liked for a
bit'.[82] Just over a month later, Hugh Massingham wrote in the *Observer*
that, immediately after the election, 'it looked as if he could do anything
he liked ... his prestige was so great that it seemed he could arbitrarily lay
down the future party line'.[83]

Those who were present at the meeting were, in addition to Gaitskell,
Herbert Bowden, Anthony Crosland, Hugh Dalton, Patrick Gordon
Walker, John Harris, Frank Hayman, Douglas Jay and Roy Jenkins.
Bowden was the Chief Whip. Harris was then a rising young Gaitskellite
apparatchik who, Jenkins tells us in his memoirs, was nevertheless not a
particular friend of his, any more than Bowden and Gordon Walker were.[84]
Hayman, who has gone unspecified by name in all the accounts that have
so far been published, was described by Jay as 'a trade unionist'. In fact he
was a schoolmaster who had gone into educational administration and
been active in NALGO, the local government officers' union. He had
recently been appointed Gaitskell's parliamentary private secretary.
Though not a Wykehamist, he was as much a member of the middle
classes as Jay. But the meeting was clearly something more than the
haphazard gathering which Jenkins and Jay contrive to suggest. It was
also something less than Foot's view of it: that it was 'indisputable that a
bold initiative was set in motion by the right wing of the party' and that
'the lever which helped to let it loose was pulled at that Sunday night' – in
fact it had taken place on the Sunday morning – 'meeting in Frognal
Gardens, quite unpublicised, of course, at the time'.[85]

As it happened, the *Guardian* had wind of the meeting. The story was
given out that it was a party in honour of Dalton's retirement from
Parliament.[86] This is repeated by Philip Williams in his biography of
Gaitskell.[87] Susan Crosland, in her biography of her husband, asserts that

there was a dinner-party for Dalton at the Gaitskells' on the Saturday and that on the Sunday they all, or most of them, returned to Frognal Gardens to continue their discussion.[88] No such dinner party took place. It is unmentioned in Dalton's diaries. Indeed, on the Saturday evening in question Dalton dined with Jenkins and his wife.[89] Lord Jenkins denies that the Sunday morning gathering had anything to do with Dalton's retirement. They had all known that he was leaving the House of Commons for months, if not years, and he soon became a peer.[90]

Though the meeting was not held for his benefit, Dalton's account remains the fullest. He wrote that Jay 'started off with a great oration'. He wanted to 'drop' nationalisation, the trade unions, the name 'the Labour Party' (in fact Jay wanted to add to the name) and the independence of the party, and to make agreements, even including merger, with the Liberals. Dalton said he thought this was 'rather wild, pouring out the baby with the bath water and throwing the bath after them'. Others too were more cautious than Jay. Gordon Walker wanted a 'scientific inquiry'. He also thought the trade union connection might be loosened. Bowden was 'very practical', while Gaitskell 'said little in front of so many'. He was 'resolutely but cautiously revisionist'. The party constitution, Gaitskell thought, might be revised. Some new formula on public ownership could be substituted for the 1918 text. The party constitution might further be changed by having the National Executive Committee elected both by the unions, with the constituency parties represented regionally, and by the parliamentary party, with a shift of authority towards the parliamentary leadership. But any such changes would 'take time' and 'need most careful handling'. Dalton considered that Gaitskell 'very wisely' listened more than he talked – a view which was not universally accepted, then or subsequently.[91]

Jenkins's recollection, however, was that the talk was 'less taut than this' and that the question of a merger or an alliance with the Liberal Party was not raised.[92] Summarising the Frognal discussions afterwards, Gordon Walker had no doubt that the matters which had damaged Labour were nationalisation, the trade unions and local Labour councils. They were too closely tied to a working class which no longer existed.[93]

As a result of an interview with Tony Benn, Philip Williams asserts that after the Frognal meeting Gaitskell was determined to listen to (rather than to open) the debate in the party; was opposed to changing the name or weakening the trade union link; was convinced that Labour must 'adapt to the new affluent society'; and 'probably' intended to question Clause IV.[94] This was an accurate account of Gaitskell's general position from October 1959 to March 1960 – and, in particular, of his differences with Jay. But it is not quite what Benn recorded at the time, in the volume of his diaries which was published 15 years after the appearance of Williams's biography. Benn had arrived at Gaitskell's house on his own, after the departure of the leader's closer friends. Gaitskell 'thought we must review our relations with the trade unions'. He was 'not prepared to lose another election for the sake of nationalisation'. And 'he laid great stress on the disadvantages of the name "Labour", particularly on new housing estates'.[95]

Jenkins had been due to visit the United States for a month on 13 October as the guest of Kenneth Galbraith, the great economist. On the day before the Frognal meeting, he telephoned Galbraith to say he would not be coming owing to the political situation. This was a clear indication that Gaitskell was preparing for battle and wanted his friends around him. On Monday Jenkins appeared on the television programme *Panorama* and 'trailed the anti-nationalisation and trade union link-loosening line which four days later Jay was to set out more fully in an article in *Forward*'.[96] On his way home after the broadcast Jenkins called at Benn's house. According to Benn, they 'had a flaming row'. Jenkins said they 'must use this shock to drop nationalisation entirely' at the special conference which was due to be held during the last weekend of November.[97]

Whatever Jenkins's views on nationalisation, where he broadly agreed with Gaitskell, either he had misunderstood Gaitskell's true view of the trade union connection, or Gaitskell was later to change it. And, though Jenkins was fully involved in the launch of what became the Clause IV battle in the Labour Party, he did not actively approve of the choice of this particular piece of ground on which to fight. To amend a ritualistic statement of aim did not seem to him to be worth the trouble of a great argument. It would have been better, he thought, to concentrate on dropping specific proposals for nationalisation and on amending not the party's dogma, but the party's working constitution: so that, for example, the National Executive Committee became less the creature of the trade unions and more that of the parliamentary party.[98] Dalton agreed with him about Clause IV, while Crosland agreed with him about both Clause IV and the party constitution.[99]

Clause IV was composed by Sidney Webb (assisted by Arthur Henderson) for the party conference of 1918. In her diaries Beatrice Webb makes no reference to it, though she deals with the occasion. The words written by Webb intended to appeal, not to the trade unions, but to the City clerks and the like – represented in fiction by Mr Waller in P.G. Wodehouse's *Psmith in the City* and in reality by Malcolm Muggeridge's father – who were then joining the party in growing numbers and whose patron saint was H.G. Wells. The clause, strictly, sub-clause (4), laid down the principal object of the party:

> To secure for the workers by hand or by brain the full fruits of their industry, and the most equitable distribution thereof that may be possible, upon the basis of the common ownership of the means of production, distribution and exchange, and the best obtainable system of popular administration and control of each industry and service.

In 1929 'workers' had replaced 'producers' and 'distribution and exchange' were added.

Jay's article in *Forward* appeared on 16 October 1959. Though he had intended to publish it anonymously, Francis Williams persuaded him into having a byline.[100] He wrote that, if they were going to win, they must remove 'two fatal handicaps': 'the class image' and 'the myth of nationalisation'. They must modernise themselves quickly into a 'vigorous, radical, expansionist, open-minded party' representing – and being seen to represent – everybody who wanted 'reform and expansion'. The article did not propose a severance from the unions, which 'must remain an essential foundation of the Labour Party'. Nor did it propose relinquishing public ownership as such but only 'state monopoly' and the word 'nationalisation'. Nor, again, did it propose giving up the name 'Labour', which held 'the loyalty of millions'. But might there not be a case, Jay asked, for changing it to 'Labour and Radical' or 'Labour and Reform'? Clause IV was not mentioned. The article, Jay wrote 21 years later, was not inspired by Gaitskell 'or anyone else in Frognal Gardens' but by his 'party workers at 177 Lavender Hill' in his Battersea constituency.[101]

Naturally people thought the article had been inspired by the former group, and there was a tremendous fuss. But something else that happened at this time had a greater effect on the events of 1959-60. This was a complete breakdown in relations between Gaitskell and Wilson. Gaitskell made no secret of his wish to remove Wilson from the Shadow Chancellorship. This was a piece of intelligence which Crossman lost no time in passing on to Wilson, who was 'furious and insecure and even more furious at the suggestion he should be promoted to Leader of the House'. Wilson 'regarded this as a conspiracy to chase him out of the Shadow Chancellorship'.[102] Hugh Massingham wrote in the *Observer* that the atmosphere was no longer quite the same as it had been immediately after the election. Gaitskell now had his critics. He could hint, beckon and point: but the day seemed to have passed when he could insist and command.[103]

Certainly Dalton was concerned. He wrote to Gaitskell saying that Jay's article had given 'it all a bad start' and had 'struck the tuning-fork for all the Gregorian Chants of the Old Believers'.[104] By the end of November, on the eve of the party's special conference at Blackpool, Crossman was recording that the whole leadership of the party was 'stinking with intrigue and suspicion'. Everybody knew that Bevan was manoeuvring against Gaitskell and that Wilson, who did not 'forgive easily', was going to take his vengeance for Gaitskell's 'vague plot' – which, as we have noted, Crossman had revealed to Wilson – to remove him from the Shadow Chancellorship.[105]

Gaitskell, however, accepted Crossman's view that Bevan must have a veto on any proposed changes. On the Thursday before the conference he also agreed with the suggestion of his friend and admirer Charles Pannell that he show Bevan the speech. Gaitskell told Pannell later that he had done so and that Bevan had said he could not fault it in any way. Gaitskell's young aide John Harris recalled that Gaitskell had shown the speech to Bevan on the night before he made it and that Bevan had come into Gaitskell's hotel bedroom and said 'that's all right' or words to the same effect.[106] Nor was this approval wholly surprising or completely hypocritical. Bevan had long opposed both vague threats to nationalise and nationalisation on the pattern of the public corporation, as developed by his old political enemy Morrison.

> The trouble with the boards of the nationalised industries is that they are a constitutional outrage. It is not proper that a Member of Parliament should be expected to defer to a non-elected person. The Minister, by divesting himself of parliamentary responsibility, disfranchises the House of Commons; and this means he disfranchises the electorate as well. Part of the case for public ownership is public accountability. This can be effectively provided only if the Minister concerned can be questioned in the House. The present state of affairs reduces the Minister to the status of either a messenger or an apologist for the boards ... I have no patience with those socialists, so-called, who in practice would socialise nothing, whilst in theory they threaten the whole of private property. They are purists and therefore barren. It is neither prudent, nor does it accord with our conception of the future, that all forms of private property should live under perpetual threat.[107]

On Saturday 28 November Barbara Castle gave the chairman's address. She attacked the 'commercialised society' and the 'windfall state'; proclaimed the continuing indispensability of all the Labour Party's traditional attitudes, especially on public ownership; and concluded that the party was too good for the electorate.[108] Gaitskell opened the debate after lunch. He had imposed on himself an undertaking to reserve comment until the conference. Some friends of his thought this a mistake, as he had received a standing ovation at the first meeting of the parliamentary party. They, or some of them, thought also that he was mistaken in opening rather than summing up the debate. He said there was no Executive view: he spoke for himself alone.

Clause IV laid them 'open to continual misrepresentation'. It implied that common ownership was an end, whereas in fact it was a means; that the only precise object they had was nationalisation, whereas they had many other 'socialist objectives'; and that they proposed to 'nationalise everything'. But did they? The whole of light industry, the whole of agriculture, all the shops, every little pub and garage? Of course not. They had long ago come to accept for the foreseeable future some form of mixed economy. Had they better not say so, instead of going out of their way to 'court misrepresentation'?[109]

After Gaitskell had finished, Mrs Castle, blinded by the television lights, peered theatrically into the murk and cried 'Michael!'; whereupon – this is Bernard Levin's account – Foot emerged coincidentally from the blackest and most invisible quarter of the hall.[110] What was all this talk, he demanded to know, about ends and means? He could not understand it. It was beyond him. He was a simple socialist soul, to whom the Labour Party meant public ownership – a topic which, in its practical manifestation, had never exercised his mind to the slightest degree. This did not prevent his contribution from being greeted with loud and prolonged applause.

In private, Bevan was equally congratulatory.[111] In public, however, he was conciliatory. His speech was widely described as 'statesmanlike'. It won golden opinions for its refusal to attack Gaitskell. It was mostly great nonsense. He used to be taught as a boy, Bevan said, one of Euclid's deductions: if two things were equal to a third thing, they were equal to each other. On the previous day Mrs Castle had quoted from a speech he had made some years ago. She had said that he believed that Socialism meant the 'conquest of the commanding heights of the economy'. Gaitskell had quoted the same passage.

> So Barbara and Hugh quoted me. If Euclid's deduction is correct they are both equal to me and therefore must be equal to each other. So we have a kind of Trinity. I am not going to lay myself open to a charge of blasphemy by trying to describe our different roles. I am not certain in what capacity I am speaking, whether as the Father, the Son or the Holy Ghost.

Bevan had a particular liking for enlivening his orations with references to and from the Christian religion, especially Roman Catholicism, even though he was himself an unbeliever. His most famous was to deny any Immaculate Conception of Socialism. This caused some offence at the time among the conventionally pious. On this occasion, however, his observations aroused no adverse comment. He continued:

> Therefore I agree with Barbara, I agree with Hugh and I agree with myself that the chief argument for us is not how we can change our policy so as to make it attractive to the electorate. That is not the purpose of this conference. The purpose is to try, having decided what our policy should be, to put it as attractively as possible to the people: not to adjust our policy opportunistically to the contemporary mood, but to cling to our policy and alter its presentation in order to win the suffrage of the population.

The last sentence was reminiscent of what was often heard from the 'representatives' at Conservative conferences: that what was wrong was not the policy but the presentation, which was a recognised way of saying without giving too much offence that the policy was wrong too and that the politicians charged with putting it into effect were, if anything, slightly worse. This was more or less Bevan's view of Gaitskell. Benn thought the speech witty, scintillating, positive, conciliatory – 'the model of what a leader should do'. Bevan did not knock Gaitskell out but 'gently elbowed him aside'.[112] In the train to London afterwards, Bevan said he would overthrow Gaitskell and take over the leadership. He was convinced that the controversy over Clause IV marked a deliberate design to alter the nature of the Labour Party. Moreover, the scheme had been put in hand without any consultation with the recently elected deputy leader of the party, himself. 'We are living in the presence of a conspiracy,' he announced at a *Tribune* board meeting at the Café Royal shortly afterwards, and warned of 'great upheavals' ahead.[113]

Bevan himself, however, did little, not through indolence but through illness. Wilson told Crossman that it was impossible to conceive that Gaitskell would last another two years as leader. He had 'committed himself too far' and was 'too mulish and obstinate to give way'. It was 'essential' that he should not stay too long, preferably for under 12 months.[114] The editor of the *Guardian*, Alastair Hetherington, thought Gaitskell was finding it 'very difficult' to get on with Wilson, who was afraid his succession to the deputy leadership and hence to the leadership – this was Hetherington's view, though in fact only two deputy leaders, Attlee and Foot, have ever become leader – was in jeopardy, 'even if he was not himself altogether conscious of his motives'. Hetherington suggested that Gaitskell could safely go abroad at Christmas because Harold Macmillan would also be out of the country. Gaitskell replied: 'Yes, and Harold Wilson will be out of it too.'[115]

From Christmas 1959 the Clause IV battle became one that was increasingly fought within the National Executive Committee.[116] Crossman and Benn discussed the danger of a split in the party owing to Bevan's illness: he had cancer, though he did not know it.[117] On 20 January 1960 Benn heard that Bevan was 'critically ill' and that it looked as if he might not live.[118]

In February 1960 Crossman reported Wilson as 'pouring out his venom' against Gaitskell, not concealing his desire to get rid of him.[119] In public, however, Wilson appeared as 'the great mediator' and as 'the possible rival' if things went wrong for Gaitskell, who asked Benn, among others, what he thought about Clause IV. Benn replied he was '100 per cent in favour of modernisation and additions' but that he had 'a strong feeling' they should not 'delete the famous phrase'. Gaitskell was 'a bit surprised'.[120] The crucial meeting of the NEC was to be held on 16 March.

On 26 February Crossman wrote to the members of the committee saying that there was no decision by them to consider a revision of Clause IV. All they had was 'a powerful expression of opinion' by the leader of the party which he had been 'fair enough to emphasis was a personal view, presented to conference without authority and without even consultation with the Executive'. In those circumstances he could not understand how it was possible to question the right of any of them to express a different view.[121] Support of a kind, however, came from an unexpected quarter. Tom Driberg, High Churchman, promiscuous homosexual, *bon vivant* and man of the Left, wrote to Gaitskell saying the party constitution 'reads, and looks, like the rules of a provincial loan club in the 1880s'.[122]

On 16 March the National Executive assembled in a tiny room on the fourth floor of Transport House. As Benn arrived, Mrs Elizabeth Braddock looked out of the window and claimed she had spotted a journalist on the roof. So they pulled the curtains.[123] The events that were to follow hardly justified such concealment. Jenkins described them long afterwards as amounting to a 'a dreary draw'.[124] They were, rather, a clear defeat for Gaitskell. He failed to accomplish what he set out to do. Benn recorded that 'it soon became clear that people were looking for some way of bridging the gap'. Jennie Lee, Bevan's wife – soon to become his widow – suggested that 'the commanding heights of the economy' might provide such a bridge.[125] The suggestion was gratefully accepted. Clause IV remained, in embellished form. The added phrase was not Bevan's own. Though it had come to be associated with him, it had been employed in Labour debate for many years and in fact originated with Lenin.[126]

No period of calm followed the compromise. Nevertheless, Driberg, Greenwood and Crossman agreed with one another that they would rather keep Gaitskell than work for Wilson. It was clear to Crossman, however, that Mrs Castle would prefer to work for Wilson. When Crossman suggested that they might all start lunching together, they thought this 'terribly dangerous'.[127]

Opportunities to display a lack of comradely feelings were increased substantially with the government's cancellation of the Blue Streak missile, which was announced to the House of Commons in April 1960. The cartoonist 'Vicky' showed the Prime Minister Harold Macmillan as 'Supermac' saying: 'Ha, ha, this puts old Gaitskell in an awful dilemma.' This was meant to be funny: but, as so often with Vicky's cartoons, it turned out to be uncomfortably true.

In 1957 the government had embarked on the development of a liquid-fuelled rocket, the Blue Streak (a copy of the United States Argos missile). Its manufacture was suggested by the United States when Duncan Sandys, the Minister of Defence, was sent out to Washington by Macmillan after he had become Prime Minister. Derick Heathcoat Amory, the Chancellor of the Exchequer, was opposed to Blue Streak because of the cost. The Admiralty disliked it because the Navy wanted a submarine-carried nuclear deterrent of the kind the United States was developing. In October 1959 Harold Watkinson replaced Duncan Sandys at the Ministry of Defence, who went to Aviation. Watkinson reported that 'a large and ever-increasing number' of Russian missiles were targeted on Britain which 'could wipe out Blue Streak without any possibility of reply'.[128] In January 1960 Sir Richard Powell, the permanent secretary of the Ministry of Defence, stated that Blue Streak was 'vulnerable to pre-emptive attack' and was effective only if fired first in reply to a Soviet attack with conventional weapons.[129]

In February 1960 the Cabinet Defence Committee, which included both Watkinson and Sandys, discussed whether to cancel Blue Streak. After this meeting Macmillan, in a memorandum, recommended 'doing away' with the missile.[130] The Cabinet decided provisionally to abandon it and to try to acquire instead from the United States the slightly longer ranging Skybolt missile, which was discharged from an aircraft. An attraction of this course was that it would give our V-bomber force an extension of life. Macmillan recorded that the decision to abandon Blue Streak 'was not easy to make'. Nor, in retrospect – he was writing in 1972 – was he 'convinced that it was wise'.[131]

At the end of March 1960 Macmillan met President Eisenhower at Camp David, Maryland. Macmillan asked for and received assurances that the United States would try to develop an air-to-surface missile. He was also assured that, if the US found it technically feasible, the missile would then be produced for the US and Macmillan could place orders for the RAF. At the same time Macmillan pledged a base for US nuclear submarines. He offered Holy Loch on the Clyde in Scotland. 'In offering us Holy Loch,' the American political scientist Richard Neustadt writes, 'Macmillan had to suffer some abuse at home, but he apparently regarded it as cheap at twice the price.'[132] He conceived it, Neustadt continues, as the *quid pro quo* for Skybolt. The two transactions were not linked explicitly. The official documents on each said nothing of the other. But in Macmillan's mind the link was real. Eisenhower evidently thought likewise. At least he never disputed that the two of them had done a deal.[133]

At the time, Macmillan was more circumspect. Neither in his diary nor in his report to the Queen five days later did he refer to Holy Loch, though it troubled him, and was to be the subject of some acrimony between the United Kingdom and the United States in succeeding months. His diary referred to 'a very valuable exchange of notes about Skybolt and Polaris'. The United States undertook 'to let us have the *vehicles* (by sale or gift), we making our own nuclear heads. This allows us to abandon Blue Streak (rocket) without damage to our prospects of maintaining – in the late 60s and early 70s – our *independent* nuclear deterrent.'[134] (Italics supplied.)

As the following letter to the Queen demonstrates, by 'Polaris' Macmillan meant, not the US Polaris nuclear submarine base at Holy Loch on the Clyde, but the possibility of Britain's acquiring the Polaris missile from the US at some future time. He wrote to the Queen that he had been able to secure an assurance from the President that the government would be able to obtain either Skybolt or Polaris when it needed them. (This was not the United States' understanding of what had been agreed.) This would 'enable us without further hesitation to put an end to Blue Streak', a weapon which the Chiefs of Staff now felt to be 'obsolescent and unsuitable'. To complete the project would cost another £600 million 'and by the time it was ready it would really be out of date'. Moreover, 'for political and moral reasons' he was 'very anxious to get rid of these fixed rockets'. This was 'a very small country' and 'to put these installations near to large centres of population – where they have to be – would cause increasing anxiety to Your Majesty's subjects'. This was an objection which applied with equal force to the Polaris base at Holy Loch, as Macmillan was later to acknowledge. The French housed their nuclear deterrent both in the Massif Central and in the mountains of Provence. There seems to have been no good military reason why British land-based missiles should not have been located in the mountains of mid-Wales, in the Highlands of Scotland or in both, though there would have been justified objections from the Welsh and the Scots. Indeed, Macmillan tried unsuccessfully to persuade the US administration to have its Polaris base not at Holy Loch but at another loch in the Highlands. A bomber was 'somehow accepted on its bombing field', a curious point of view. A mobile weapon, either on a truck or 'better still' in a submarine, was out of sight. It had been made clear to him that no strings, 'to use the technical expression', would be attached. In other words, we should be able to buy the vehicle and make our own warhead. We could thus maintain our independent deterrent, first (if Skybolt proved satisfactory) by prolonging the life of the bomber force and later 'by acquiring a mobile weapon in some form'.[135]

After the announcement of the cancellation of Blue Streak had been made, Benn reported a 'big row in the House'. It would 'precipitate the growing crisis in the Labour Party on nuclear weapons'. Many trade unions (with the Transport and General Workers, led by the redoubtable Frank Cousins, well to the fore) were now 'supporting unilateralism'. The party would be 'under heavy pressure on this subject'. There was general talk of Gaitskell being forced out of the leadership.[136] The Labour Party was not primarily interested in the defence of the United Kingdom, which was not, after all, its responsibility. At the same time it was not interested in embarrassing the government, which *was* its concern.

Early in 1960, 48 Labour MPs had signed a unilateralist motion. On 1 March, 43, led by Crossman, Wigg and Shinwell, had abstained on a Labour defence motion, though Mrs Castle, Greenwood and Wilson supported the official line. When the cancellation of Blue Streak came to be fully debated on 27 April, Macmillan recorded that 'fortunately for us' the opposition was more divided than the government. Instead of uniting in a 'concentrated attack' on the Conservatives for 'accepting the objective of an independent deterrent but failing to achieve it and wasting large sums of money through their incompetence', Labour 'devoted a great part of the debate' to discussing 'whether we ought to have a nuclear force at all'.[137]

On 4 May Crosland wrote to Gaitskell with his customary brutal candour. In the seven months since the election they had suffered a 'major defeat' over Clause IV. They had achieved not a single one of the reforms which the moderates had wanted. Crosland cited a change in the composition of the National Executive Committee, accompanied by a change in the balance of power between that committee and the parliamentary party; a newly organised Transport House; and a 'systematic study of survey material'. Gaitskell's own position was weaker and he himself was more criticised than at any time since he had assumed the leadership. The morale of the right of the party was 'appallingly low'.[138]

The Amalgamated Engineering Union (as it then was) now came out for unilateralism. Benn recorded that people were 'seriously talking about the party breaking up in October'.[139] Crossman was certain that Gaitskell was 'heading for disaster'. He was 'now seriously beginning to think' that there might be 'a move to get rid of Gaitskell before the conference' (which was to be held at Scarborough on 3-7 October).

Crossman and Wigg, an old Army man, had put together a policy which, while not unilateralist – it accepted British membership of NATO – nevertheless rejected the British independent nuclear deterrent. But then, Jenkins and Crosland rejected it as well, while the United States administration would have preferred us not to have it either. Where Crossman-Wigg (later to be transmogrified into Crossman-Padley) really differed from Crosland-Jenkins remained unclear, except that both Crosland and Jenkins were content to allow the US unlimited base facilities in Britain. Crossman and Wigg glossed over this question. In addition, they appeared not only to contemplate but positively to relish the return of conscription: Wigg, because of his happy experiences in the Army, and Crossman, because of his general liking for bossing people about. None of these four – five including Gaitskell – knew anything very much about defence matters. The only senior Labour politician who did was Denis Healey. This was perhaps the first time, though it was certainly not the last, when he failed to provide any clear guidance at the requisite moment.

Crossman even went so far as to believe that Gaitskell might adopt his and Wigg's policy. Alas, 'it would be voted down by conference if Gaitskell were to move it', so real was 'the hatred and distrust of him'.[140] Gaitskell, however, wrote to his friend (and later his biographer) Philip Williams assessing that the likelihood of his having to resign was 'receding very fast as 'Mr K [Krushchev, the Soviet leader, who was behaving in a refractory manner] is generally thought to have rescued the Leader of the Labour Party'.[141] Gaitskell also tried to get Dalton to persuade Brown 'not to concoct some humbugging resolution with Cousins' as he 'wanted the issue clear cut'.[142] Unhappily Brown went into hospital after a fall and then dodged Dalton for a whole month.[143]

On 25 May Crossman lunched with Benn at one of the former's clubs, the Athenaeum. (His others were the Farmers' and, later, the Garrick.) Crossman said that Gaitskell was 'accident-prone'. He did not like or understand the party. Everything he did and said upset its members: Clause IV and, most recently, defence were two current examples. Benn asked Crossman whether there was a move against Gaitskell. Crossman replied there was not. But he thought Gaitskell would get into one mess after another and then would come a time when his colleagues would not want to save him. There was no intrigue but Brown had decided that he did not really have confidence in Gaitskell.[144] Crossman described Benn as 'full of gaiety and excitement and pretty clear that Gaitskell couldn't last very long'.[145]

On the same day Macmillan wrote in his diary that Watkinson was shortly off to Washington, with a directive which would enable him to make a 'definite agreement' for Skybolt, if the United States authorities would sign it. He could 'open up the more difficult problem' of allowing the United States a nuclear base on the Clyde.[146] Accordingly Macmillan told the Defence Committee of the Cabinet that it would be preferable 'to refrain from taking any initiative' in reply to the US proposal for a submarine base in Scotland until Watkinson had made satisfactory arrangements for the provision of Skybolt.

Quite apart from anti-Polaris demonstrations in Scotland and elsewhere, the Cabinet was alarmed by the misunderstanding with the US over the precise nature of the agreement which Macmillan and Eisenhower had reached at Camp David. The US wanted to install a dry dock on the Clyde in summer 1960. On 1 June Watkinson met the Defence Secretary, Thomas Gates, in Washington. Watkinson emphasised the political difficulties for the government. He said they could be overcome only if the scheme could be presented as a joint US-UK enterprise. Watkinson reported to Macmillan from the aeroplane taking him back to London. He pointed out the differences between the United Kingdom and the United States. He emphasised that the US considered Skybolt to be closely linked to Holy Loch and that, additionally, the Americans were likely to press the British to accept a NATO joint project for a European nuclear deterrent.

Watkinson found it impossible to get the Americans to accept an exchange of Holy Loch facilities for a Polaris submarine: for Macmillan thought that, in return for giving away Holy Loch, he should receive not only Skybolt but Polaris as well. The Americans were reluctant at this stage to give Britain Polaris on account of congressional opposition. In addition they claimed that we had committed ourselves to supporting a European submarine force. They were prepared to exchange Holy Loch for the right to buy Polaris missiles without warheads provided these were assigned to NATO. Philip de Zulueta, Macmillan's private secretary, noted that this arrangement did not seem 'a very good bargain' from Britain's point of view. It also had the 'presentational disadvantage' that the Americans would like to put their equipment on the Clyde in 1960, whereas Britain's submarines would not be available until 1966. Consequently the Holy Loch base 'could not at all easily be presented' to the public as a joint effort 'unless we bought a nuclear submarine from the US'.[147]

Meanwhile, in a speech at Hinckley, Woodrow Wyatt felicitously described Frank Cousins as 'the bully with the block vote'. Tony Benn wrote that the party was in 'a deplorable state' and that Wyatt's speech had 'disheartened members'.[148] Macmillan wrote in *his* diary that he had agreed 'in principle' at Camp David to 'do what we could, more or less in return for Skybolt'. But Watkinson had 'managed to disassociate' the two deals.[149] When he brought this to the attention of the Cabinet, there was a good deal of anxiety, and he did not press for an immediate decision. His colleagues naturally wished to include as a *quid pro quo* Britain's right to buy or build the Polaris submarine 'should we later decide to do so'.[150]

With the Secretary of State for Defence out of favour with the Prime Minister, and both the Prime Minister and the Cabinet in a state of confusion about what had, or had not, been agreed with the United States President at Camp David in March, the Labour Party was concerning itself with less practical matters. The crucial dispute was about stating explicitly that NATO must retain nuclear weapons so long as the USSR had them. Brown and Crossman agreed with that policy and claimed that Cousins also was prepared to tolerate it. But Cousins's condition was that any Labour Party-Trades Union Congress document should not say so.

Gaitskell wrote to Crossman saying that the argument or interpretation which would follow would 'tear the party in shreds' long before the conference had met. At one point Crossman had written of the desirability of not 'disturbing the convictions of a large number of active workers in the party'. If, Gaitskell replied, he was thinking of 'unilateralists, pacifists and fellow-travellers', he did not see how they could avoid coming out in clear opposition to them. (Gaitskell was to re-use the phrase in his speech to the Scarborough conference in October 1960, just as he was to re-use Crossman's phrase about fighting and fighting again, drafted for him in the immediate aftermath of the 1959 election, in the same speech.) As for the others, Gaitskell saw no reason why they should not be able 'without too much difficulty' to have a draft accepted, first, by the National Executive Committee and, later, by the conference, which was 'both clear cut on principles and also sensible from a technical, economic and military point of view'.[151]

But there was little prospect of peace at this stage. The organisation Victory for Socialism – which bore much the same relationship to the old Bevanite movement as did the Wee Frees to the Presbyterian Church of Scotland – demanded Gaitskell's resignation. Of the 15 Labour MPs who were members of VFS, three (Judith Hart, Walter Monslow and Bert Oram) resigned in protest. VFS also attacked Jay, Crosland and Jenkins, none of whom had wanted Gaitskell to raise the Clause IV question and of whom the last two were urging him to repudiate the British bomb. At the end of June the parliamentary party passed a vote of confidence in Gaitskell by 179 votes to 7, which was not as impressive as it looked because there were 258 Labour MPs. Gaitskell's defence statement was approved 97-15.

On 15 June Macmillan wrote to Eisenhower saying that, over Polaris, he would do his best 'about a suitable arrangement for the use of Scottish ports'. The President would realise that this was 'a pretty big decision for us to take'. It would 'raise political difficulties for us in view of all the pressures and cross-currents of public opinion here'. He had to put it to his Cabinet colleagues and hoped it would 'be possible for us to make a mutually satisfactory arrangement'. Eisenhower replied on 20 June, hoping Macmillan would 'find it possible to proceed this year with the arrangement' on which they had 'reached agreement in principle at Camp David'. Macmillan noted: 'I did not, repeat not, agree to this at Camp David.'[152]

On 22 June the National Executive Committee agreed to 'express our full confidence in the elected leader of the parliamentary party'. Gaitskell wrote to the Labour MP E.L. Mallalieu (a friend of his who did not take much active part in internal Labour Party quarrels, and was not to be confused with his affable, left-wing relation, the journalist J.P.W. Mallalieu) that it was 'wiser at the moment to keep rather quiet on the (Labour) constitution' – a subject which, to the distress of Crosland and Jenkins, had never engaged his attention – 'and leave Morgan Phillips (the party's general secretary) to explain the position'.[153] On 28 June the *New Statesman*, which was opposed both to unilateral nuclear disarmament and to Gaitskell's leadership of the party, said that the new defence policy was in itself acceptable but would not do because Gaitskell would continue to support the British bomb.

Macmillan wrote to Eisenhower that there was 'serious public controversy' in Britain. The people were 'inevitably conscious that this duty of providing the advance base' exposed them to 'special risks'. It meant that the government must be able to present the project in a way which would command public support. To use the Clyde would be 'a serious mistake from your point of view as well as ours'. It would surely be a mistake to put down what would become 'a major nuclear target so near to the third largest and most overcrowded city in this country'. Macmillan suggested that Loch Linnh would be better. It was near Fort William and 'a robust people of three or four thousand highlanders' – who would presumably view the prospect of nuclear incineration with greater fortitude and equanimity than the inhabitants of Glasgow. Fort William would be 'much more to my taste'.

Holy Loch 'should be run as a partnership'. It should be made clear from the outset that the British should have an option to come in themselves on the 'operation of Polaris submarines'. Britain had a firm understanding that US bombers would not undertake operational missions from British bases without our prior agreement. With the submarines, all that had been suggested so far was that they should not without consent fire their missiles from within United Kingdom territorial waters. Macmillan wondered 'whether this could for presentational purposes be extended to something like a hundred miles'. On 30 June 1960 Eisenhower replied rebuffing Macmillan on all the matters he had raised.[154]

In July Bevan died. There was a meeting of the National Executive at Transport House about the state of the party. The whole of the morning was taken up with a discussion of what to do about Clause IV. It was agreed that the party should jettison any idea of constitutional change and should instead recommend the new 'statement of aims', incorporating control of the commanding heights of the economy, to the Scarborough conference.[155]

In August Wilson and Crossman had dinner at the Athenaeum. Crossman had by now come to the conclusion that, in the interests of the party, it would be a good thing if the official defence policy were to be defeated at Scarborough 'so heavily and ignominiously that Gaitskell had to resign'.[156] He was sure that Gaitskell would not get away with using the parliamentary party against the conference.[157] Two days later he, Wilson and Mrs Castle agreed to revive the Bevanite group. After dinner, 'miracle of miracles', Wilson seized the bill and 'himself paid £6'. This made Crossman think that Wilson was 'really seriously out for the leadership'.[158]

On the same day Crosland wrote to Gaitskell saying they had been wrong to 'go for doctrine' when they should have 'gone for power'. In the then 'bloody-minded state of the party', Gaitskell, the 'Hampstead group' and 'occasional trade union leaders' were not strong enough to force 'major changes'. The conclusion had to be that, first, in 1961 they must 'go for power' and, second, Gaitskell needed 'systematic alliances'. Crosland suggested that after the conference Gaitskell should invite Brown, Wilson and Callaghan for a talk. Clause IV was 'all water under the bridge'. But they were all intelligent enough to realise that major changes were needed if the party was ever to win another election.[159]

Gaitskell was dismissive. The three people whom Crosland had named could not 'really be regarded as just rational human beings' simply because they were 'principally interested in winning the next election. They are all able and talented, but they are *not* like that!' A discussion with them on the lines Crosland had suggested 'would be inhibited by an unwillingness to speak frankly in front of each other or even to him'. There was no need for Gaitskell to explain why. Crosland must surely understand this because he knew both them and the circumstances of the moment. It would not even be safe for him to speak frankly to them. He could not 'rule out the risk that one or other might use this against us in the present struggle'. The attitude of 'at least one of them' – obviously, Wilson – was 'by no means clear' and might 'well be hostile'.[160]

On 15 September the Cabinet formally approved the base at Holy Loch, having to be content with the broad assurance which Eisenhower was prepared to give. There now began to circulate the first hints that Skybolt might not prove to be satisfactory. On hearing these rumours Macmillan sent an urgent message to Eisenhower asking for more details.[161]

Crossman telephoned Benn saying that Gaitskell was 'ready to fight it out on defence' and that the conference would be 'a big showdown'.[162] Two days later Crossman and Peter Shore came to dinner and discussed the conference. They concluded that the Left was determined to crush Gaitskell and that the Right was determined to crush the Left on defence. Benn, Crossman and Shore represented the 'centralists' who hoped that the crisis could be averted if the National Executive accepted Cousins's resolution instead of making a fight of it. The resolution in question rejected any defence policy based on the threat of the use of strategic or tactical nuclear weapons and called for the cessation of manufacture and banning of aircraft carrying nuclear weapons and of nuclear bases.[163]

On 23 September the Skybolt agreement was signed. Watkinson minuted to Macmillan that an Anglo-American planning conference on the project had just ended when the Americans had given an assurance that it was being given 'top development priority'. Delivery of the first four missiles to the RAF was planned for March 1964. Britain had accepted the American proposals to establish a base at Holy Loch. It would be 'most helpful if in welcoming these mutually advantageous arrangements' Macmillan could emphasise to Eisenhower that Britain had accepted the American proposals for Holy Loch, which would 'certainly cause us some difficulties', in view of the arrangement they had agreed to for the supply of Skybolt, and that Britain regarded the whole transaction as a reciprocal arrangement in accordance with what had been agreed at Camp David. It was important that the Americans should recognise that, if Skybolt should meet with serious troubles and have to be abandoned, they would have a moral obligation to overcome in one way or another, 'the difficulties which this would cause for us'. After all, they had Holy Loch, while Britain certainly did not have Skybolt 'for some years yet'. This would give Britain the necessary standing to re-open the Polaris submarine question or to 'take any other action that seemed necessary' if Skybolt failed.[164]

On the Monday before the conference Benn decided that it might be necessary to resign from the NEC at Scarborough – as he duly did – 'in an attempt to make peace'. At Scarborough, before the weekend, he dined with Wilson, Crossman and Mrs Castle. Wilson was 'busy composing his speech' for the eve-of-conference rally on the Sunday evening. All he was interested in was 'turning the situation to his own advantage'. He thought Gaitskell could be dislodged. The more he saw of him, the more Benn's opinion of him dropped. Next day Benn noted that the 'real issue' was that Gaitskell and Cousins would not have a compromise, each being anxious to destroy the other. Benn and his allies had to 'try to strengthen the middle and make its pull irresistible'.

It is often forgotten that at that eve-of-conference weekend, 1-2 October, when the whole National Executive Committee, together with other leading figures in Labour politics and in journalism, were gathered at the Royal Hotel, all the talk was of compromise, of some genie from the bottle who would suddenly appear and bring peace and concord to the party. Benn, Brown, Gunter, Wilson, Crossman and Mrs Castle all wanted some formula to be produced: the last three, admittedly, for reasons of their own, not least because it would be the first step on the road that would end with the disappearance of Gaitskell. James Margach of the *Sunday Times*, the most experienced political correspondent present (Hugh Massingham of the *Observer* was absent owing to illness), thought a compromise of some kind would be stitched together at the last minute as it had so often been in the past. Virtually the only correct forecast of Gaitskell's uncompromising approach came from the *Sunday Dispatch*, whose reporter was not a proper political correspondent at all but had been sent to Scarborough to see what was going on.

On the Saturday Gaitskell told Benn that defence was 'a much better issue on which to fight than Clause IV'. On the latter the parliamentary party did not care one way or the other. The trade union leaders were tied by their own constitutional provisions, which pledged them to support a specifically Socialist party. But now on defence he had the support of the trade union leaders and the majority of the parliamentary party. It was a much better issue on which to have it out. He admitted to Benn that his attempt to jettison Clause IV had been 'a tactical error'.

On the same day Cousins told Benn that he had always wanted to form a trade union political party. He had 'half a mind to put up against that man' – as Cousins customarily referred to Gaitskell – in his own constituency. 'And as for you,' Cousins went on, 'you've burned your boats now and you've no future with that man.' This analysis, if correct, certainly did not cause Benn to view Wilson in any more favourable light. He 'thought of nothing but how he could turn the developing crisis to his own advantage'. For Benn, Wilson's speech on Sunday evening at the rally was to be his great bid for the leadership. He had 'concocted a lot of phrases which were full of significance but took no stand'. Benn's 'contempt for him grew' each time he met him. He did not think he had 'one-tenth of the character of Gaitskell'.[165]

On the night before the speech, Gaitskell told his wife that probably he would lose, in which event he would retire to the back benches and carry on the struggle from there.[166] In his speech Gaitskell said that you could not escape the issue of defence. If you were a unilateralist in principle, you were driven to becoming a neutralist. Either the sponsors of the resolution meant that they would follow the 'cowardly, hypocritical course' of saying 'we do not want nuclear bombs, but for God's sake, Americans, protect us' – which, as we have seen, was precisely what the Americans wished to do, provided they could have bases on British territory – or they meant we should get out of NATO.

It was 'not in dispute that the vast majority of Labour Members of

Parliament' were 'utterly opposed to unilateralism and neutralism'. Were they expected to change their minds overnight? If 'all of us, like well-behaved sheep, were to follow the policies of unilateralism and neutralism', what kind of impression would that make on the British people? He did not believe that Labour MPs were 'prepared to act as time servers'. They were men of conscience and honour, 'honest men, loyal men, steadfast men, experienced men, with a lifetime of service to the Labour movement'. There were others too, not in Parliament but in the party, who shared these convictions.

What sort of people do you think they are? What sort of people do you think we are? Do you think we can simply accept a decision of this kind? Do you think that we can become overnight the pacifists, neutralists and fellow-travellers (*boos and jeers*) that other people are? How wrong can you be? As wrong as you can about the attitude of the British people.

The result of the debate might deal the party a grave blow, but there were

some of us, Mr Chairman, who will fight and fight and fight again to save the party we love. We will fight and fight and fight again to bring back sanity and honesty and dignity, so that our party with its great past may retain its glory and its greatness.

The speech was crude, vulgar, abusive and intellectually negligible. Inevitably it was a great success. Though he lost the vote, Gaitskell had expunged the popular picture of him which derived from Suez and showed him as somehow lacking in patriotic zeal. He had controverted this view, and in the best possible way: by attacking his own party. For, as Neil Kinnock was to demonstrate in 1985, and Tony Blair to confirm ten years later, a Labour leader is taken seriously in England (Scotland and Wales adopt different criteria) only if he has had a good set-to inside his own party.

Benn was particularly impressed with the first part of the speech, 'a magnificent defence of multilateralism' which 'captured the conference'. But he 'threw the whole lot away' at the end with his attack on pacifists, neutralists and fellow-travellers and with his intention to fight and fight again. Benn and Shore agreed that Gaitskell could not 'really ever lead a united Socialist Labour Party'. Kenneth Robinson, on the other hand, thought that Gaitskell was the only person who emerged from Scarborough with honour.[167]

Meanwhile Wilson was contemplating what his next move should be. Crossman thought that, 'poor little man', he had 'really cornered himself this time'. He had known he would be pressed to stand against Gaitskell, 'in which case he would be committing political suicide'. He wanted to stand as deputy leader instead. But he also knew that, if he did not stand against Gaitskell, he would be accused of cowardice. And he might well be defeated for the deputy leadership, as Brown had Gaitskell's support. Here was the object lesson for the 'master-tactician' and the 'super-opportunist' who was so clever that his tactics were disastrous and he destroyed his opportunities.

What (Crossman asked rhetorically) could he say about somebody who 'throughout all these talks' had been 'utterly trivial, complacent and vain'? They had started with Greenwood's saying that he had decided to resign from the Shadow Cabinet and reading out a letter of resignation protesting against Gaitskell's leadership in 1959-60. Crossman said this made sense only if Greenwood was resigning to stand against Gaitskell, at which Mrs Castle said: 'But Harold must do that.'[168]

Greenwood's intention was indeed, in Crossman's words, to 'smoke out' Wilson.[169] On Sunday 16 October Crossman, at his (or, rather, his wife's) substantial property, Prescote Manor in Oxfordshire, was telephoned by Greenwood, who said that Wilson had been suggesting that he should in due course stand down and that Wilson should challenge Gaitskell.[170]

On 17 October Gaitskell wrote to Commander Stephen King-Hall, then a well-known publicist who had made his name on the *Brains Trust* radio programme. He was a supporter of the Campaign for Nuclear Disarmament. Gaitskell wrote that the issue was 'clear cut and straightforward'. On the one side, there was unilateralism, which equalled neutralism. On the other, there was collective security, with Britain 'ceasing to be an independent nuclear power by remaining an important and loyal member of the alliance'.[171] Gaitskell, however, would still not commit himself on this.

It would form virtually the whole of Wilson's platform. First of all Bevan's widow, Jennie Lee, had led a deputation urging him to stand against Gaitskell. But he resisted until Greenwood had decided to leave the Shadow Cabinet to stand instead. He went badly off his sleep and showed an unprecedented short temper.[172] Foot, unlike Mrs Castle, was certainly prepared to see Greenwood stand rather than Wilson. Greenwood now became reluctant to withdraw. But he became so not out of pique, as both Philip Williams and Ben Pimlott imply – for he had, after all, resigned from the Shadow Cabinet precisely to force Wilson's hand – but because he was beginning to have doubts about Wilson's credentials as a true unilateralist, which, indeed, should have been obvious to him long before if he had had his wits about him.[173]

But withdraw Greenwood duly did, and on 20 October Wilson announced he was standing as an opponent of unilateralism who could nevertheless unite the party. He told his allies that what really mattered was getting votes, the votes of the Centre, and he could get more than Greenwood because he was a multilateralist, whereas Greenwood would get only the votes of the unilateralists. In his opening statement, Wilson said it was a tragedy that the party, united as it was on all other issues, should be torn apart by differences on defence policy, which 'by the very nature of things' changed from year to year and even from month to month. But the issue facing them was not defence but the unity, indeed the survival, of the party. Twice within the past 12 months – at Blackpool over Clause IV and at Scarborough over the call for defiance and the reversal of conference decisions – they had been 'plunged into deep and bitter controversy, and some of us, despite our disagreement with these actions [Wilson did not mention Gaitskell by name], have done everything possible to secure compromise and maintain unity'.[174]

Crosland wrote to Gaitskell saying that in the next 10 days they had 'one single over-riding object': to ensure that Wilson's vote was as low and Gaitskell's as high as possible. The next 12 months would depend entirely on this. To achieve it they 'must resort to any degree of chicanery, lying, etc, etc'.[175] In practice Crosland neither cared for nor was adept at the blacker political skills. But from time to time he enjoyed pretending to be a brutal political realist.

Crossman, by contrast, both liked and fancied himself at these dark practices. But he was not really much good at them either, partly because he became tied up by his own ingenuity and partly because he was disliked and distrusted by the majority of those he was attempting to convert to his point of view. He wrote to Wilson saying the most important lesson he drew was that they had now thrown Gaitskell on the defensive on the issue of unity. 'Thank God for the Tory Press' which on this occasion had dubbed Wilson the unity candidate. Crossman now felt that, 'with really hard work and consistent plugging of the unity line', they could achieve a better result than even Wilson in one of his more optimistic moods had calculated.[176]

On 25 October Wilson said that he believed the crisis of confidence arose from the feeling that 'some of our leaders' did not unequivocally reject the idea of the independent British bomb and that they were waiting for Skybolt or Polaris to come along, with the idea of returning to a separate British deterrent with an American rocket to deliver it. He believed it was 'essential' that the leader of the party should state 'beyond all doubt' that, as the policy statement had intended, he accepted that there would be no British hydrogen bomb. This argument addressed itself to the weakest part of Gaitskell's position, as both Jenkins and Crosland recognised. But it had little effect on Labour MPs, and on 3 November Gaitskell defeated Wilson for the leadership by 166 votes to 81. In the election for deputy leader Brown defeated Fred Lee by 146 votes to 83, James Callaghan (with 55 votes) having been eliminated in the first round.

Crosland remained worried about defence policy. He wrote to Gaitskell complaining that 'the Tories never went into this degree of written detail' which might at any time be rendered obsolete by new weapons or new strategic thinking. But the Labour Party seemed to feel the need 'to bring out frequent new policies, each causing endless argument and wasting an immense amount of valuable time'. Moreover, the greater the detail, the stronger the pressure for 'compromise formulae and papering over the cracks'. All these disadvantages were unnecessary, as they did not need a detailed defence policy while they were in opposition.

Nor was defence the only subject about which Crosland was concerned. There was, he wrote, a limit to the amount of disaffection which any party could stand and still be successful in the country. Relying always on 'the trade union hatchets' was fatal electorally in the long run. The task for the next year was to isolate the extreme Left and to win back or consolidate the Left-Centre. Benn (who, Crosland informed Gaitskell, had voted for him against Bevan in 1955) was 'a more controversial case'. But Crosland could see nothing against consulting him on the whole question of public relations, propaganda and reform of the machine, on which he had 'quite enlightened views'. Of course he was 'a hopeless neurotic'. But he could be won back to help in a crucial field of reform.

They must face the fact, Crosland went on, that the impression had got around – and, alas, he himself largely shared it – that the middle-class leadership of the party (such as Gaitskell, Gordon Walker and Soskice) were 'leading from an extreme and rather rigid right-wing position' and had 'no emotional desire to change any major aspect' of the society in which they were living. The 'element of radicalism and discontent', which even the most moderate left-wing party had to possess, seemed to be lacking. Even J.F. Kennedy (who was to be inaugurated as US President in January 1961) sounded more radical than Labour did.[177]

These spirited observations elicited no very clear response from Gaitskell. Still less did Macmillan's statement in the House of Commons on 8 November about Polaris. Wherever these submarines might be, Macmillan said, he was 'perfectly satisfied' that no decision to fire the missiles would be taken without 'the fullest possible previous consultations'. The version which had been agreed with Eisenhower had gone:

> As regards control we shall continue to rely on the close co-operation and the understanding which exists [*sic*] between us and the United States on all these defence matters and which the President has recently reaffirmed.[178]

Macmillan had not stuck to the form of words agreed with Eisenhower. There was a certain amount of diplomatic toing and froing in which the Labour Party did not participate and from which Macmillan emerged with his confidence unimpaired. On 13 December 1960 he recorded in his diary that in a defence debate over 50 of the anti-Gaitskellites sat 'defiantly' in their seats and refused to vote for the opposition motion. It was thought that over 70 had abstained. This was 'a very large number' and he remembered 'nothing like it since the vote which led to Neville Chamberlain's fall from power in 1940'. In the text of his memoirs, he added that he was certain we would obtain Polaris 'one way or another if we needed it, but it would cost a great deal of money'.[179]

The principal event of early 1961 was the formation of the Campaign for Democratic Socialism to reverse the Scarborough decision. The moving and organising spirit was William Rodgers, then best known as the General Secretary of the Fabian Society.* It consisted of young candidates, especially young MPs and trade unionists of a modernising cast of mind. The growing pressure to dislodge Gaitskell made CDS more of a defence of his leadership than its sponsors had at first intended: but, if Gaitskell fell, the party was bound to swing to the left. The organisation played the principal part in bringing the Centre of Labour back to the leadership. The whole process took 18 months.[180]

The Crossman-Wigg compromise was now revived as Crossman-Padley. Walter Padley was an affable, muddled, popular MP who prided himself on his international socialism and whose chief subjects of conversation were cricket (he claimed to have kept wicket for Gloucestershire on one occasion) and Rosa Luxemburg. He wished to reverse the out-and-out unilateralism of the union of which he was president, USDAW, the shopworkers'. Crossman-Padley included a commitment both for NATO and against the first use of nuclear weapons of any kind. Its opponents maintained that this commitment – or these two commitments – necessarily implied a return to conscription. On bases there was a somewhat muddled formula.

Nevertheless, in January 1961 Crossman-Padley (or Crossman-Wigg) nearly became party policy in the NEC by two votes; in February it was rejected 133-69 by the parliamentary party. Crosland told Gaitskell he thought Crossman's compromise preferable to another defeat. Gaitskell disagreed. He found the style 'demagogic' and the phrases 'ambiguous and bombastic'.[181] He also told Rodgers that he was against its views on bases and its pledge not to use nuclear weapons against a conventional attack.[182] He confided to his friend and biographer Philip Williams that everybody was 'behaving pretty much as expected – Mr Cousins impossible – Mr Crossman petulant and treacherous – Mr Driberg like a tired snake'. On their side there had been 'more loyalty and firmness and successful planning than for a long time'. By the end of March they should have 'scored a useful advance' but this did not mean they had 'won the civil war'.[183] Crossman, however, thought they had. He told David Wood, the political correspondent of *The Times*, that there was no prospect of any change in the leadership in the autumn. Wilson had more enemies than Gaitskell. The only chance lay in a coup by Brown 'and that would cost us a million votes'.[184]

At this time there was also a US National Security Council Paper saying the United States 'must try to eliminate the privileged British status'. Their minimum objective should be to persuade Macmillan to commit his atomic warheads to the NATO atomic stockpile and his delivery weapons to NATO commanders. They should also try to persuade him

---

* The fullest and best-informed account of CDS is in Brivati, *Gaitskell*, 380-400.

'to cease the production of fissile materials for weapons purposes'. President Kennedy minuted: 'It would be desirable for the British in the long run to phase out of the nuclear deterrent business since their activity in this field is a standing goad to the French.'[185]

Gaitskell did not concern himself with such matters. Perhaps he felt he had no need to. 'Things are going fantastically well,' he wrote to the Durham miners' leader Sam Watson. 'If you can swing the NUM (the National Union of Mineworkers), I think we can even win on Polaris.'[186] Whether Gaitskell should have accepted Crossman-Padley, or something very like it, rather than gone on to secure a virtually outright victory – as he did – is a debatable question. Certainly Gaitskell himself regarded this as a battle for power, as he had regarded the struggle between him and Bevan over teeth and spectacles in 1951. Cousins told his executive committee on 10 March 1961 that Crossman-Padley would be 'a step forward' but no substitute for the union's policy. And Foot told the readers of *Tribune* on 9 June that it would be only 'a bad second best'. They would still have 'the right and the duty' to argue for their own policy.[187]

And yet Wilson fought the 1964 election on a policy of rejecting the 'so-called British nuclear so-called' deterrent and of 'renegotiating' the Nassau agreement under which Macmillan had obtained Polaris in place of the Skybolt missile. This had been jettisoned by the US. Defence convulsed the Labour Party in 1960-1. Everything was more or less calm in 1962, at any rate as far as defence was concerned. Wilson fought the 1964 election on a policy that was closer to Crossman's than it was to Gaitskell's, but tried to keep as quiet as he could about it, for he was discomfited by the attacks made upon it by Sir Alec Douglas-Home. Then, in office in 1964-70 and 1974-6, he not only omitted to renegotiate the Nassau agreement but actually embarked on a programme of improving Polaris, a policy which was continued by Callaghan in 1976-9.

As the 1961 conference approached, Dalton wrote, it became clear that Gaitskell, largely by a 'single-handed effort marked by great courage, personal integrity and inexhaustible patience, had given an example of distinguished and clear-cut democratic leadership, very rare in modern politics'.[188] It was not quite true to say that Gaitskell won a complete victory at the 1961 conference. He was defeated over the Polaris base at Holy Loch about which he was, if anything, slightly less cautious than Macmillan. It was not all quite over yet. On 2 November 1961 Gaitskell defeated Greenwood for the leadership 171-59, and 10 days later Brown defeated Mrs Castle for the deputy leadership 169-56.

The 1959-61 period has been gone into at length because a Labour leader in opposition could have been deposed. In some ways Gaitskell brought the risk on himself, both by raising the Clause IV controversy himself and by refusing to accept various elaborate compromises on defence put together by Brown, Benn, Wigg, Padley and, above all, Crossman. In the Clause IV controversy he had the parliamentary party and the unions against him: in the defence controversy they were on his side. The crucial event was Gaitskell's clear victory over Wilson in the PLP election in November 1960. But it was a necessary and not a sufficient condition for his survival. The sufficient condition was that he should reverse the Scarborough vote of 1960 at the Blackpool conference of 1961, which he duly did, except in one respect. Gaitskell was quite clear in his mind that, if he lost at Blackpool, he would have to resign the leadership.

In the next year, 1962, there was another row, about the Common Market (as the European Community or Union was then called). Gaitskell came out against joining the market and if anything united the party thereby. He also cut himself off from some of his closest supporters, though Jenkins and Rodgers more than Crosland who, as usual, found arguments on both sides. Indeed, the breach between Gaitskell and Jenkins over Europe in 1962 was comparable to the breach between Bevan and Foot over the British hydrogen bomb in 1957. And it was not only politicians such as Jenkins who were saddened. 'He'll live to regret it,' Ray Gunter, the Welsh trade union MP and later Minister, said in the bar of the Grand Hotel, Brighton, immediately after Gaitskell had delivered the second greatest – some would maintain it was the greatest – conference speech of his life, against British membership of the Common Market.[189]

In fact he lived for just over three months. At a dinner party at his home on 7 December he said he had to be careful with his diet that evening as he had picked up something in Paris.[190] No one imagined this was anything serious, but his wife kept pressing him to see a doctor, which he had not done for years: indeed, he had no regular general practitioner. He refused until the House rose on 14 December. On 15 December he went into the trade union hospital, the Manor House, partly out of union loyalty, partly because he knew its head. The doctors were not happy about his blood tests but had no grounds for keeping him in hospital. On 23 December 1962 he was discharged but fell ill again at home. On 3 January 1963 he entered the Middlesex Hospital, where he died on 18 January from pulmonary congestion brought about by lupus erythematosus, a rare immunological disease in which tissues may be damaged by antibodies circulating in the blood.[191]

HAROLD WILSON IN 1963

Gaitskell's death was as shocking as it was because few had realised how seriously ill he was, until the hopeless hospital bulletins of the last days. But politics went on. Even before his death, Crossman had been proposing the formation of a 'regency council' of five to act in the leader's absence.[192] Benn recorded in his diary that Gaitskell's death 'seems a disaster' because it looked as if Brown would succeed him and 'for a number of reasons' he was 'totally unsuitable' to be leader.[193] Crosland was equally unenthusiastic. 'Are we going to be led by a neurotic drunk?' he asked.[194] Wilson began as the outsider: not only had he been defeated by Gaitskell for the leadership in 1960 but he had also been defeated 133-103 by Brown for the deputy leadership in November 1962, only two months before. On 21 January Brown as acting leader (under present-day rules he would have been leader until a successor had been elected) chaired a meeting of the Shadow Cabinet. Afterwards Brown and Wilson talked. The conversation left each with a different impression. According to Brown, they simply agreed to fight cleanly. According to Wilson, they agreed that each would serve the other loyally. It may be that, according to the Wilson version, each agreed also to serve the other as deputy leader. But Wilson knew as well as anyone that the deputy leadership was not in the leader's gift. At any rate, Wilson leaked the story that each had agreed to work with the other to the papers: 'Labour Rivals In Unity Pact.' Brown denied that he had entered into a pact with anyone. This was regarded as a tactical coup for Wilson. If it was, it was the only one of the campaign.[195]

The strategist of Wilson's campaign was Crossman. His advice to Wilson was that there should be no overt campaigning. In his memoirs of 1972, Wigg stated that he had attached only one condition of his offer to help Wilson. He mentioned it only because of the suggestion that Crossman had 'played the role of kingmaker'. Crossman, he had insisted, 'must be excluded from any knowledge of our plans because he could not be relied upon to keep his mouth shut'.[196]

All the allegations of undue pressure and bullying tactics were made against the Brown campaign. This was not altogether surprising. Though Charles Pannell, a respectable but irritating trade unionist, was its leader, its – largely self-appointed – deputy leader was Desmond Donnelly, an intelligent but unreliable character who finally committed suicide in a bleak hotel just outside Heathrow Airport after finding himself in a financial queer street from which even he could not manage to effect an escape. His slogan was: 'To keep the spirit of Gaitskell alive, vote Brown.' This did not greatly help matters. Nor did the rumour (whether it was initiated by Donnelly is unclear) that Wilson did not believe in God, which Wilson promptly denied with some credibility, for, in a party that was even in 1963 largely godless, Wilson was distinguished by his Christian faith.[197]

But the old Gaitskellites, the remnant of CDS, could not agree on whether to unite behind Brown. Crosland's attitude to Brown as leader has already been noted. He and his friends met both at his flat and at Jack Diamond's. Wigg claimed to have had a spy at these gatherings. After a meeting in Diamond's flat, his representative reported that they were no nearer agreement than they had been at the beginning in their search for a third candidate.[198] Surely, however, the only realistic possibility was Callaghan? So it was. Crosland called on Callaghan but told him, somewhat discouragingly, that he would be knocked out of the contest in the first ballot. George Thomson urged him to stand, which seemed 'to clinch Jim's decision'. From then on the Callaghan campaign was led by Crosland.[199] Callaghan wrote that the quality of his principal nominations,

Crosland and Thomson, was not enough. Wilson 'automatically got the vote of the left' and Brown 'scored heavily with the right' while Callaghan 'secured only the votes of those who preferred neither candidate'.[200]

At first Wigg (according to Crossman) was afraid of Callaghan's candidature and thought Wilson would do better in a straight vote. The Callaghan candidature had been brought about, Crossman thought, by the 'strong-arm methods of the Brownites' and by the 'agonised awareness of some of Gaitskell's closest friends that, if Harold Wilson was an odious and impossible man, George Brown was plain impossible'.[201] Brown responded with 'especial vigour' to Callaghan's decision to run. Like Crossman, he saw that what Wilson had to fear more was a contest against himself alone, who could get some of the respectable vote on account of his position as deputy leader.[202]

How far is it true to say that Callaghan – or, if you prefer it, Crosland – made Wilson leader? Consider PLP multi-candidate elections for leader or deputy leader from 1945 to 1980 (after which the PLP alone ceased to be the electorate). In 1960 Brown led on the first ballot for the deputy leadership and duly won the second ballot. In 1971 Jenkins was ahead in the first ballot for the deputy leadership and won it in the second. In 1972 Short was ahead in the first ballot for the same post and again won in the second. In 1976 Foot was ahead in the first ballot for the leadership, was second to Callaghan in the second ballot (when three candidates remained) and was again defeated by Callaghan in the third ballot. In 1980 Healey was ahead in the first ballot for the leadership but lost in the second ballot to Foot. Both in this election and in that of 1976 there were more than three candidates – four in 1980, six in 1976. The rule seems to be that, in a three-candidate contest, he who tops the poll in the first ballot also tops it in the second, assuming he has not already won an absolute majority; while, in a contest with more than three candidates, the leader in the first ballot does not win the final one.

So, at any rate, it was on this occasion. In the first ballot Wilson had 115 votes, Brown 88 and Callaghan 41. As Wilson had not gained an absolute majority, Callaghan dropped out, and in the second ballot Wilson defeated Brown by 144 votes to 103. At Crossman's house after the first ballot, Wilson said: 'There is one toast we must drink, to the man who is not here, the man who should have done it, Nye Bevan.' Wilson said later that Gaitskell had wasted too much time on the press – a most bizarre charge for Wilson to make in view of his later close connection with many editors and political correspondents. He added that Gaitskell had also wasted too much time on social life. 'A leader cannot afford it. Mary and I will have none of it whatsoever. We have a serious job to do.'[203]

When the result of the second ballot was announced, Wilson tried to speak but Brown waved him down and read out a written announcement saying he wanted time to think things over. He then disappeared for a short period and was incommunicado until he returned to serve as Wilson's deputy leader.[204] When Wilson formed his first Cabinet in 1964, Wigg counted eight who had voted for Callaghan, seven for Brown and six for Wilson.[205]

JAMES CALLAGHAN IN 1976

The circumstances surrounding Harold Wilson's resignation in 1976, the resignation itself and its constitutional consequences are dealt with elsewhere in this book.[*] As Michael Foot's biographer, Mervyn Jones, put it: 'For the first time in British history the Monarch had to wait for a party election before appointing a Prime Minister.'[206] Meanwhile Wilson simply carried on until the election had been completed. What had once been thought to be the impediment to an elective process – the gap between the resignation of one Prime Minister and the appointment of another – turned out to be no impediment at all. There was no hiatus. Her Majesty sent for Callaghan as she was to send for John Major 14 years later.

On Tuesday 16 March, the day of Wilson's resignation, Tony Benn told his private secretary at the Department of Energy that he must not say to anybody that he was standing for the party leadership because he had not made up his mind. But he wanted 'the decks completely cleared of all engagements. Just tell Bernard Ingham' – then Benn's Director of Information – 'that you don't know what I'm doing.'[207] Stanley Orme, an affable left-winger who was devoted to Michael Foot, advised him not to stand. Orme said that Eric Heffer and Dennis Skinner, who were both of them further to the left but less affable, agreed with him. Skinner, however, supported Benn later on.

Barbara Castle, who had not got on with Callaghan since the battle over *In Place of Strife* in 1968-9 and, indeed, long before that, wanted to inaugurate a 'Stop Jim' movement by limiting the contest to Denis Healey and Foot. Benn thought this 'a typically defeatist view'.[208] Indeed, Mrs Castle urged Foot to stand as soon as the Cabinet at which Wilson's resignation was announced broke up. Peter Shore endorsed her view. Foot said, according to Mrs Castle: 'Perhaps. We must discuss it.' From this Mrs Castle happily and correctly concluded that 'he had made up his mind to stand'. She told Benn that the future was with him, 'but not this moment', from which she incorrectly concluded that he 'seemed to agree'.[209]

Next day Foot said he would like to see Benn, who told him he was 'fighting purely on the issues'. Foot replied that he thought Benn was 'wrong to campaign in the open for a new policy', which, according to Benn, consisted of policies on industry, on open government and party democracy, and on industrial democracy. That evening, the television interviewer Robert McKenzie put it to him that what he believed was contrary to Cabinet policy. Benn replied that he was 'collectively responsible for everything', but the public was 'entitled to know' his view. He

---

* See below, pp. 203-11.

'jumped through the burning hoop' and 'came out the other side. It was amazing.' He was 'a free man'. He did not know what the Cabinet would say tomorrow – Benn's broadcast did not turn out to cause much disturbance – but this was 'a completely new development. Besides, Harold can't do anything to me now.'[210]

By Wednesday afternoon the candidates were Benn, Callaghan, Crosland, Foot and Jenkins. Healey had not yet decided whether to stand. Roy Hattersley was supporting Callaghan for fear of splitting the Right's vote and letting in Foot. Jenkins said he quite understood and hoped this would not affect their friendship, though they 'have had the most perfunctory of relations since'.[211] Hattersley then called on Crosland at his Ministry and asked whether he would like to know why he was not voting for him. Crosland said: 'No. Fuck off.' On the ground floor Hattersley had a message awaiting him, asking him to return to Crosland's room, where he was asked to 'keep in touch' and a drink was arranged.[212]

On Thursday Mrs Castle was concerned because Healey had not yet put his name forward. There was talk – such was his recent unpopularity in the party – that he might stay out of the contest altogether. 'This thought worried me no end. To be left with Jim would be too terrible!' She asked her office to ask Healey's office to arrange for him to telephone her, which he did as soon as he had emerged from Thursday's Cabinet. She told him she was 'rooting for Mike [Foot]' but that she thought he ought to stand, as he would certainly be her second choice. The advice of Healey's friends at this stage was that he should desist.[213]

On 20 March Benn received a note from Wilson saying that political advisers were not to be active in the leadership campaign. This was not a precedent that was followed when John Major sought re-election as leader of the Conservative Party in 1995. Healey allowed his name to go forward. Jenkins appeared on *Panorama*: 'By that time even an unproductive boost to morale was welcome, for we were running up against a disappointing wall, not of hostility, but of cautious regret.'[214]

Callaghan told Benn that he 'had given up ambition years ago' but, when the opportunity to become leader came, the heart was 'bound to quicken' and he was 'really fighting to win'.[215] According to Susan Crosland, shortly before the list for the first ballot was to close, Hattersley came to Crosland's room in the House. Callaghan, Hattersley reported, was in 'a particularly aggressive mood'. It was no good, he had said, for Crosland to come along after the first ballot offering his support: he must offer it before the first ballot, by refraining from standing.[216] Callaghan denied this. He had been, he wrote in 1987, 'somewhat surprised' to read in Mrs Crosland's 'splendid biography' that Hattersley had told Crosland that he was angry that Crosland was standing and that Crosland must give him his support before the first ballot or else he would have 'no interest' in Crosland. 'If this happened, it was a piece of private enterprise' done without the agreement either of his election team or of himself.[217]

On polling day, 25 March, Benn told Ian Mikardo, a scrutineer, that he had decided to announce withdrawal from the ballot at the party meeting even if he had qualified for the second ballot. Mikardo approved. The result of the first ballot was: Foot 90, Callaghan 84, Jenkins 56, Benn 37, Healey 30 and Crosland 17. Under the rules of the exhaustive ballot, only Crosland would have been compelled to withdraw. To compel both Healey and Crosland to withdraw, Benn would have needed to obtain 48 votes (one more than the sum of Healey and Crosland's votes). And, to compel Benn, Healey and Crosland to withdraw, Jenkins would have needed to obtain 85 votes (one more than the sum of Benn, Healey and Crosland's votes).

It was the relative placing of Callaghan and Jenkins which secured the headlines. In Jenkins's opinion, Callaghan's lead, while not overwhelming, was nonetheless enough to settle the issue. The country, he thought, needed a new Prime Minister quickly, and not the long-drawn-out agony of a third, or even a fourth, show round. From 56 votes that Prime Minister was not going to be Jenkins. He therefore immediately decided to withdraw. Healey, 'with characteristic pugnacity, decided to fight on, but that in no way unsettled' Jenkins's mind.[218] Crosland said to his friend Bruce Douglas-Mann that he was not sure he even wanted to be Prime Minister but was perfectly clear he did not want to come bottom of the poll.[219]

Benn thought that Foot 'did extremely well', that Callaghan did 'less well' than he had expected, that Jenkins obtained 20 votes fewer than he had expected, that Benn had 20 votes more than many people had thought, that Healey did very badly and that 'Crosland did marginally better than the disastrous result that had been forecast'. The Jenkins camp, Benn recorded, was in disarray. It was 'a terribly disappointing result' for him. When he thought of 'the fantastic press' Jenkins had had over the years, and 'all the banging' Benn had had, it was 'gratifying' that he should have won only 19 (Benn writes '18') more votes than he and that Healey should have had seven fewer. That was 'amazing'. Benn thought Callaghan would 'romp home' in the second ballot.[220]

Mrs Castle was not disposed to give Jenkins any credit for his public spirit. She described it as 'this further display of political daintiness' which proved 'conclusively' what she had always known: that Jenkins would never lead the Labour Party. 'I bet Denis stays in the ring, despite his derisory 30 votes. But then, he's a pugilist, not a patrician' – an odd way, perhaps, to describe the son of a miner who had gone to Abersychan County School, but one sees what Mrs Castle meant. Benn's withdrawal in Foot's favour (she went on) was a 'foregone conclusion'. His votes would now almost certainly switch to Foot. She had not been surprised by Crosland's vote. 'Despite the endless build-up he gets in the press' he was not 'a serious contender at all'.[221]

In the second ballot the figures were: Callaghan 141, Foot 133, Healey

38. Healey's vote – only one more than Benn had obtained in the first ballot – gave Benn 'great pleasure'. It appeared to him that Callaghan was 'going to make it' but that there were 'still uncertainties one way or the other'.[222] Callaghan remained untroubled, or so he maintained afterwards. At no time, he wrote in 1987, did he have real doubts that he would be elected. This determined his 'public attitude during the three successive ballots that were necessary'.[223] In the third and final ballot Callaghan had 176 votes and Foot 137.

Callaghan was not the last Leader of the Labour Party to be elected by the parliamentary party alone: that was Foot. Nevertheless, it is probably right to regard either his election in 1976 or his fall from office in 1979 as the end of Labour's golden age. Foot's election was preceded by loud calls for and complicated manoeuvres towards an extended franchise. These proved successful in January 1981, two months after Foot's election as leader by his fellow MPs. To these matters we now turn.

5

Fancy Franchises

In February 1859 Disraeli introduced a Franchise Bill ... to
create a number of franchises – 'fancy franchises' was the name
which Bright fastened on the proposal – for doctors, clergy,
graduates, East India Stock holders, State pensioners of £20 a
year and upwards, and other nondescript superior persons.
G.M. Trevelyan, *The Life of John Bright*, 1913

Electoral college? Sounds more like a comprehensive to me.
Jeffrey Thomas, QC, to the author, 1981

The character of the Labour Party changed between, roughly, the late
1960s and the mid-1980s. The best viewing platform from which to discern
this change was the party conference. The conference of the mid-1960s had
hardly altered in 20 years. It was predominantly male; working or lower-
middle class; suited or sports-coated; cigarette- or pipe-smoking; and
middle-aged or elderly. Towards the end of the decade it began to change.
It became younger. Clothes were more casual. There were more women.
Even smoking was finally prohibited in the hall, though the Labour Party
held out against the ban for longer than any other political party. These
tendencies became more pronounced during the 1970s. There were other
developments too. The floor became less deferential towards the platform.
And it expressed itself – whether against the platform or against fellow-
inhabitants of the floor – in increasingly strident and intolerant tones.

For much of this, Tony Benn was blamed. But though his tastes were
philistine, his political discourse was civilised. His disputes were always
conducted rationally or, at any rate, politely. True, Benn came to represent
something, and to represent it consciously: the Labour belief in betrayal
by its leaders. It went back to 1931 (when, oddly perhaps, Benn's father,
Wedgwood Benn, had as a member of Ramsay MacDonald's Cabinet been
part of the majority supporting cuts in benefit). It went back to Harold
Wilson, to the 'July measures' of 1966 and his ambivalence towards the
Vietnam war.

This was not fantasy or conspiracy theory by the Left. These things had
happened: they, or something like them, might happen again. Outside was
the Movement: the brothers and sisters in their branches, the comrades,
male and female alike, in their ward and general management committee
(later changed to general committee) meetings. Inside were Ministers, or

Shadow Ministers, and Labour Members of Parliament, and the leader himself, who might even be Prime Minister, though he was more likely to be Leader of the Opposition merely. The solution was obvious. It was to make those on the inside subject to the control of those on the outside.

Oddly enough, it was assumed either that Labour Ministers and Labour MPs were as one or – what was, if anything, even more questionable in practice – that a Labour majority could control the operations of a Labour government. The Labour Movement would accordingly try to control Labour MPs by means of mandatory reselection; a Labour government through acquiring the editorship of the election manifesto; and a Labour Prime Minister by choosing the leader. Though these great constitutional changes came about through the efforts of individuals, notably Vladimir Derer, they would not have been accomplished without the support of the trade union movement, wielding its block vote at the conference. Nor was this surprising: for in the end it was the trade union leader rather than the party activist who possessed the greater power over the choice of leader.

The Campaign for Labour Party Democracy was founded in 1973, when Labour was in opposition. The occasion was the publication of *Labour's Programme 1973,* when Harold Wilson made clear that a Labour government had no intention of carrying out one of its main proposals, the nationalisation of Britain's 25 largest companies. The campaign's initial statement of aims included neither mandatory reselection of MPs nor the election of leader by a wider franchise. It was concerned solely with conference decisions and their implementation by the parliamentary party. Quite soon, however, the former topics asserted themselves. In December 1973, for instance, there were disagreements because at that time the campaign insisted on concentrating on mandatory reselection rather than on the election of the party leader.

At the 1976 conference the Rushcliffe Constituency Labour Party, encouraged by the campaign, moved a resolution inviting the National Executive Committee to set up a 'working party' on new methods of electing a leader. The conference agreed to this proposal. Next year there was no report from the NEC. Ian Mikardo, on its behalf, apologised for the delay and promised to come back next year, 1978.[1] On 3 October 1978, Mikardo proposed three choices: the *status quo*, the election of the leader by the whole conference and election by means of an electoral college. All the resolutions favoured the third choice, the electoral college – not surprisingly, because they would have been co-ordinated by the campaign – but the conference voted overwhelmingly in favour of the existing system. Benn recorded that 'it was a good debate but there was no doubt that the trade unions had been kept in step by Jim [Callaghan]'.[2]

Under the party's rules, this should have been the end of the matter until 1981. For this was a constitutional change. And such changes, if they were defeated at the conference – as this one was – had to wait three years before they could be raised again. What seems to have happened here was that simultaneously the conference accepted an NEC proposal to transform the leader of the parliamentary party into the leader of the whole party. The Left thought this change would make a Labour Prime Minister or Leader of the Opposition more 'accountable' (a word that gained in popularity in left-wing circles as the 1970s progressed) to the conference and the NEC. As one of its leading representatives, Jo Richardson, put it: he or she would 'feel a commitment to the Movement which some of our party leaders have lacked'. The NEC was duly instructed to produce proposals in 1979 which would make the leader of the Parliamentary Labour Party the leader of the whole Labour Party. By this means was the whole question kept alive.[3]

MICHAEL FOOT IN 1980

In May 1979 Callaghan was inclined to retire after the election. 'I was sick of it,' he said to Foot's biographer, Mervyn Jones. But Foot begged him to stay on.[4] Callaghan wrote that had he followed his 'personal inclination' in May 1979 he would have resigned. A new leader would be elected 'who would face the Conservative government without the taint of defeat'. He was told that the parliamentary party was ready to re-elect him unanimously. He felt that if he resigned it might appear that he was 'leaving at the moment of defeat', unwilling to account for himself or 'the inevitable inquest which always follows'. He therefore decided to remain as leader for one session of Parliament in the 'vain hope' that by then some of the 'bitterness of defeat would have drained away. It was not a happy period.'[5]

David Owen took the same view as Callaghan. He talked to his friend Peter Jay on the telephone. As Jay was about to speak to his father-in-law, the defeated Prime Minister, Owen said he hoped Callaghan would resign immediately: 'If he went now, he could go with dignity and hand over to Denis Healey.' Jay promised to pass on Owen's views.[6] On 9 May the former Labour Cabinet met in the Commons. Foot suggested that Callaghan should be re-elected unanimously. All agreed. Later that morning the parliamentary party met. Foot moved Callaghan as leader, which was carried unanimously. Callaghan said he was going to carry on: 'There is no vacancy for my job.'[7]

In the Shadow Cabinet elections in June, Denis Healey was top, John Silkin second and Peter Shore third. James Callaghan told David Owen that he wanted to appoint Shore Shadow Foreign Secretary because he wished the parliamentary party to have a choice in the leadership election. Owen thought this showed that Callaghan had doubts about Healey as leader. Callaghan said he thought Foot would not want to be leader. He seemed to Owen to be exalting Shore in order to take Foot's place 'as leader of the centre left'. Callaghan's doubts about Healey were not new to Owen: he 'had picked them up on a number of occasions in the past'. He also knew that Callaghan liked Shore and 'recognised in him his own robust patriotism'. It had been noticeable in the late Cabinet that Callaghan had taken trouble to ensure he carried Shore's support. Now he was giving Shore the opportunity to promote his chances.[8]

Whether the question of the election of leader should go to the conference was debated by the NEC in July. It was decided by 14 votes to 11 that it should. 'A triumph,' Benn recorded. Later in the month there was a joint meeting between the NEC and the Shadow Cabinet. Owen, according to Benn, was doubtful about any change in the method of election, though one might have expected him to oppose it unless it was to a system of one member, one vote – for which Owen can fairly claim to have been the first enthusiast. Foot was doubtful about any constitutional change whatever on account of the party's experiences over Clause IV in 1959-60.

Four days later Larry Whitty (then of the municipal workers' union, later to be general secretary of the party) outlined the attitude of the trade union leaders. It was broadly that all constitutional questions should be postponed at the 1979 conference and referred to an inquiry. Benn was prepared to accept postponement but thought the conference should vote on the principle of a manifesto written by the NEC, of an electoral college for the leadership and of mandatory reselection for MPs. Next month, in August, Clive Jenkins of the white-collar ASTMS union gave Benn to understand that David Basnett of the municipal worker was offering Benn support over the electoral college provided he dropped his other demands. But what Benn really cared about at this stage was 'the manifesto and accountability: the party leader issue won't make any difference'.[9]

Basnett and Jenkins were the trade union leaders who were to play the principal parts in the events of 1979-81. Basnett was tall, thin and lugubrious; Jenkins short, stout and voluble. Both were vain. But their vanity took different forms. Basnett regarded himself as an intellectual and a trade union statesman: his intentions were both lofty and good. Jenkins likewise had no doubts about his mental powers, but was happy to be looked upon as a plotter and a maker of mischief. By no stretch of language could Basnett be regarded as being on the left, whereas Jenkins took some pride in being so placed. Both had a disastrous influence on the course of events, but Jenkins's influence was more so. It lasted longer and crucially affected three changes: the election of Michael Foot as leader in 1980, the creation of the electoral college in 1981 and the election of Neil Kinnock as leader in 1983. For the party's lamentable electoral performance in 1979-92, the primary responsibility must rest not with Benn but with two Welshmen, both called Jenkins: Clive, who forced these changes, and Roy, who by setting up the Social Democratic Party split the anti-Conservative vote and so guaranteed certainly two and possibly three elections for the Conservatives.

In 1978 the Labour Co-ordinating Committee had been founded. It was more concerned with Labour's industrial policy and withdrawal from

Europe than with constitutional matters. Nevertheless it drew closer to the Campaign for Labour Party Democracy. In 1980 the Militant Tendency and a similar Trotskyist organisation, the Socialist Campaign for a Labour Victory, were brought together in the Rank and File Mobilising Committee, an umbrella organisation dedicated to changing the party constitution. This took its leadership mainly from the Campaign for Labour Party Democracy.[10]

The campaign's newsletter for September 1979 said that 'the need for greater democracy within the Labour Party was brutally emphasised by the shattering general election result which heralded Britain's most reactionary post-war government'. For the first time in its history, the newsletter went on, the campaign was confident that all the constitutional issues – the election of the party leader, control over the manifesto and reselection of MPs – could be 'fought out' at the conference. The campaign had by now, however, changed its earlier opinion. It now believed that there should be an electoral college. It had earlier believed in the sovereignty of the party conference (or 'conference', without the definite article, as it is *de rigueur* to call it in Labour circles, left and right alike). Jon Lansman, an official of the campaign who was not as important as Derer but received much more publicity (indeed, Derer received hardly any) said they had changed their position because election by the conference was 'unwinnable'. The decision to support the electoral college was 'entirely tactical'. They had been compelled to take into account the opinion of the trade unions.[11]

There is no doubt that this was the view both of the campaign and of the unions. But it was distinctly odd all the same. For at this time the unions controlled 90 per cent of the conference vote. Accordingly one would have expected them to support the system which would give them the greatest power, that is, election of the leader by the conference; whereas, by the same process of reasoning, one would have expected the campaign to support the system which would give individual members in the constituencies the most power they could reasonably expect, that is, election of the leader by some form of electoral college.

At this point we must, unhappily, have a look at the block vote. It is not the most alluring of subjects. The Labour Party divided its members into individual members and affiliated members. The latter was by far the larger group. It consisted mainly of trade union affiliated members – both the Fabian Society and the Co-operative Society affiliated smaller numbers as well. But the number of members which an organisation chose to affiliate was a matter for that organisation to determine. It was a question of paying the affiliation fees: truly, of buying votes at the party conference.

With a trade union, there were three figures to be taken into account: first, the number of members who were in the union; second, the number of members who paid the political levy; and, third, the number of members who were affiliated to the Labour Party. That a member paid the political levy – or, rather, refrained from going through the complicated and frequently oppressive procedures involved in 'contracting out' of paying the levy – did not strictly or necessarily mean that he or she wanted to be affiliated personally to the Labour Party. It meant that the member wanted to contribute to the Political Fund and accordingly approved of the union's involving itself in political activities, which could in theory include support for the Conservative Party. Nevertheless in practice the number paying the political levy provided a rough guide to the number which it was proper to affiliate to the party.

Most unions chose to under-affiliate, in that the number affiliated was smaller than the number paying the political levy. They did this partly to save money and partly – as with the transport and general workers – to avoid giving themselves too dominant a position in the conference. Other unions affiliated precisely the number paying the levy, as the National Union of Mineworkers did in those faraway days when, though led by Communists such as Arthur Horner and Will Paynter, it was the most punctilious of unions. Others, anxious to preserve their political influence, such as the old National Union of Railwaymen, over-affiliated. Others again, wanting to increase their influence, such as ASTMS, affiliated more members than in fact existed.

The block vote was not split to reflect the divisions within a union: that was why it was called the block vote. The procedures for determining how it should be cast varied from union to union. Certain unions had a tradition of 'strong', that is, dictatorial leadership. The transport workers had it, with leaders ranging from Ernest Bevin through Arthur Deakin and Frank Cousins to Jack Jones. The engineers under William Carron were famous either for casting their vote for two contradictory resolutions or for switching their vote at the last minute. The woodworkers likewise were well-known for changing their minds at the last, or for casting their vote in unexpected directions.

On 10 September 1979 the NEC's organisation sub-committee met the trade union general secretaries. Basnett said he hoped the NEC would not press for change at the conference. Reselection, he thought, might possibly be handled in 1979. But he hoped the NEC would agree not to put the electoral college or the drafting of the manifesto to the vote. He thought a special conference should take place before the 1980 conference. The NEC finally voted 18-0 to have both an inquiry and votes at conference. Earlier Foot had been in a minority on having the conference votes. Barbara Castle supported both the electoral college and reselection but abstained in the NEC vote, which was carried 9-2. The minority consisted of Michael Foot and John Golding. Two days later James Callaghan agreed that reselection should be discussed by the conference but had an 'open mind' on the electoral college. 'Of course Healey wouldn't become leader if there was a college,' Benn wrote in his diary.[12]

The transport workers, controverting Lansman's opinion of what the unions wanted, were worried that the electoral college would not give the unions sufficient weight in choosing the leader. Benn thought that all he and those who agreed with him had to do was 'get an electoral college accepted in principle at conference and go on from there'. At the pre-conference NEC meeting the trade unionist and chairman of the party Alex Kitson brought the transport workers' general secretary Harry Urwin over to talk to Benn. Urwin said he would support Benn on mandatory reselection and the electoral college but not on control over the manifesto.[13]

It has been suggested that one reason why the party changed as much as it did during the 1970s lay in the abolition of the 'proscribed list' in 1973. This was a list of organisations which bore such innocuous, even laudable titles as Housewives (or Scientists) for Peace but were in reality Communist 'front' bodies. Ever since the 1920s the party had understandably been obsessed about the danger of being taken over surreptitiously by the Communists. But it had never been concerned to the same degree or sometimes, it seemed, at all with the danger of infiltration by groups which were not officially Communist but nevertheless of the extreme left. By 1973 the danger from the Communists was virtually non-existent; whereas the danger from the extreme left was increasing.

There were several reasons for this increase. The class of 1968, who had been unformed revolutionaries in their early twenties, were now in their early thirties. They were part of what Keith Waterhouse christened the Polyocracy. They tended to be in public – particularly local authority – employment of one sort or another, where they felt themselves to be underpaid and regarded with less esteem than they thought was their due. And, since 1973, there had been a change in the nature of politics in the United Kingdom: they were harder and more polarised and were to be exploited by Margaret Thatcher after 1979.

All these new characteristics were on display at the 1979 conference. It was a most unpleasant gathering. Its one light moment occurred when the ancient Philip Noel-Baker was called to speak in a debate on the economy, and proceeded to give a detailed account of the Battle of the Somme before embarking on a lengthy peroration about the urgent need for world-wide disarmament. Noel-Baker went uninterrupted by the chairman, which was a rare example of toleration in that week. The Labour MPs were corralled in a kind of pen to the left of the platform as one looked out from it. They were at right-angles both to the platform and to the audience in the hall. In this position they resembled the enemies of the people in the dock during a Moscow show-trial of the 1930s and were, indeed, treated in the same fashion, with much jeering and finger-pointing from the speaker on the rostrum and from his (or, more often, her) auditors in the hall.

Nevertheless, on 2 October 1979 the electoral college was defeated – the engineers union once again filling its traditional role of proving unreliable from the Left's point of view – whereas mandatory reselection was carried.

The Right, Benn recorded, were 'furious' about the latter defeat. Even if the election of leader were confined to the PLP, mandatory reselection changed 'the whole balance of power in the party'. In one sense, Benn proved to be wrong about this. Relatively few MPs were deselected, and those who did meet this fate did so more on account of indolence or other deficiencies than of doctrinal impurity. In another sense, however, Benn proved to be right: for it is probable that the MPs would not have proved so abject in 1979-81 in surrendering their power to elect the leader if the constituencies had not already possessed the power to remove them from their seats. On the electoral college, Benn wrote that the 'fixers' would not win. 'We'll come back next year and put it right.'[14] Owen, however, 'hoped this would be the last we heard of it'.[15]

But the 1979 conference also resolved to set up the Commission of Inquiry. The commission's remit was 'to bring forward proposals to ensure that the party is open, democratic and accountable at all levels, and to ensure that all levels of the party leadership and all aspects of the work of the party are fully accountable and responsive to the wishes of the membership'. A small group of trade union leaders and representatives of the NEC, at this point unchosen, were empowered to mount a detailed investigation into the constitutional changes already being advocated by the Left. Basnett and Jenkins had played into their hands: the former thinking that what he was doing was retaining the responsible power of the unions, the latter acting in an altogether more mischievous spirit. The Left could hardly believe their luck and duly set up the Rank and File Mobilising Committee, which brought together the Campaign for Labour Party Democracy, the Socialist Campaign for Labour Victory, the Labour Co-ordinating Committee, the Militant Tendency and similar Trotskyist organisations.[16]

On 24 October the commission was set up. At the NEC Eric Heffer moved that it should consist of five trade unionists, five NEC representatives and the leader, James Callaghan. Tony Benn moved the addition of the deputy leader, Michael Foot, of the chairman, Alex Kitson, and of the Treasurer, Norman Atkinson. This was carried 13-8. Benn calculated that 'the left-right balance is potentially ten to four in our favour – a great victory'.[17]

Of the five NEC members, four were of the hard Left: the distinction between 'hard' and 'soft' Left, as represented respectively by, say, Eric Heffer and Joan Lestor, was established in the late 1970s. Of the five trade union members, three were associated with the Left. Only Terry Duffy of the engineers was firmly on the right. Callaghan could rely on the automatic vote of Duffy only and on the general support of Foot and Basnett. Following representations Michael Cocks, the Chief Whip, was put on as an 'observer' as a sop to the parliamentary party. David Owen believed that a new leader would have been forced to fight but that Callaghan saw his task as one of 'damage limitation'. If he had resigned earlier, Denis

Healey would have had self-preservation as an incentive to mobilising the parliamentary party and refusing 'to have anything to do with such a grotesquely unrepresentative commission'.[18] Healey himself subsequently described the commission as 'rigged'. He also claimed to have 'led the attack' on the way this had been contrived. But the truth is that in the whole 1979-81 period Healey's trumpet was muted, as also were those of several other leading members of the parliamentary party.[19]

On 31 October 1979 Fred Willey moved that the parliamentary party should be represented independently of and additionally to those MPs who were already members of the commission. This was carried 133-61 but had no effect apart from the addition of the Chief Whip. Dennis Skinner of the hard Left later correctly pointed out that the commission was not the creation of the NEC but of 'right wing trade union leaders like Basnett'. Benn thought he did not have a chance of being elected leader by the parliamentary party if the election took place before the establishment of an electoral college, which the commission was likely to recommend. Callaghan would be pressed to retire by those whose hopes rested on the support of the parliamentary party but who would not be elected by a college.[20]

By May 1980 it was generally recognised that the electoral college would be accepted by the October conference. Arguments ensued about its composition. Paradoxically, the followers of Benn, whose base was in the constituencies, wanted the unions to have most of the votes; whereas the union leaders, notably Basnett and Duffy, wanted to hand as much power as possible to Members of Parliament.[21] Clive Jenkins's idea was that the college should be 150 strong and comprise 50 representatives of the parliamentary party, 50 of the unions and 50 of the constituencies. Benn wrote that he would make clear that he was interested only in a Labour Party which was 'collectively led'. It would not matter who was leader but he would be one of the candidates.[22]

By the summer it became clear that trade union leaders such as Moss Evans of the transport workers and Clive Jenkins of ASTMS did not want Healey to be leader. They also wanted Callaghan to stay until the question of the electoral college could be resolved. On the weekend of 13-15 June 1980 the commission met at Whitehall College, Bishop's Stortford, described by Benn as the 'ASTMS country club'. Those present were James Callaghan (the leader), Michael Foot (the deputy leader), Frank Allaun, Terry Duffy, Moss Evans, Eric Heffer, William Keys, Joan Lestor and Jo Richardson. Basnett, not Callaghan, was in the chair.

On the Sunday Foot moved the *status quo*. They had had, he said, two conference decisions (in 1978 and 1979) in favour of it; the parliamentary party wanted the system to stay as it was; he therefore moved election by the PLP. Duffy seconded. Richardson seconded the proposal that they adopt the principle of the electoral college. Basnett said he favoured a 'National Council of Labour' which would deal with the manifesto and 'approve' the leader. Evans said that what they were meant to be discussing was the electoral college. His union favoured such a body and the other unions and the constituency parties agreed. Callaghan raised the position of the Queen. For whom did she send? She might send for someone else if the parliamentary party refused to accept the nominee of the electoral college. Callaghan was here calling in aid the principle that the Prime Minister must command the confidence of the majority of the House of Commons.

The commission was in no mood for such constitutional niceties. Foot's proposal was lost 9-3, the minority consisting of himself, Callaghan and Duffy. Evans then proposed an electoral college of 50 per cent to the parliamentary party, 25 per cent to the unions, 20 per cent to the constituencies and 5 per cent to the affiliated societies. This was carried 7-6. David Owen (who was not present) thought that, if Callaghan had put up a fight, as he had not, it would have meant defying the unions and the conference, which he was not prepared to do at that late stage of his leadership. He would, Owen considered, have been wise to resign 'there and then' and to place his weight behind Healey as his successor: 'no one could blame him for wanting to retire to his farm in Sussex, but many would blame him for putting his authority behind the electoral college'.[23]

At the next meeting of the Shadow Cabinet, Owen and William Rodgers attacked Callaghan for betraying the parliamentary party. Callaghan responded by accusing them of complicity in a speech which Roy Jenkins had just made recommending the creation of a new centre party.[24] This was Healey's account. Owen recorded that Callaghan 'clearly had a guilty conscience over what he had done and was behaving in an unusually furtive way'. He called Owen 'a political infant'. Owen was so angry with Callaghan that he felt that, if he did not stand down, Healey should challenge him for the leadership. Owen thought that Healey was also angry but 'did not know exactly how to get out of the mess we were in without offending Jim'. He was 'loath to do that for he knew Jim could still influence his chance in any leadership selection'.[25]

It is possible, as Owen himself hinted, that Callaghan did not want Healey to succeed him. Healey himself curiously advanced 'Labour's strength in the country' as one of several reasons why he resisted pressure from the Manifesto Group of right-inclined Labour MPs to break with Callaghan and lead a campaign against the decision reached at Bishop's Stortford. Over half intending Labour voters, Healey wrote, wanted Callaghan to lead Labour into the next election – though it must have been clear to Healey, as it may not have been to the prospective voters, that Callaghan had no intention of doing any such thing. The fight Healey was being asked to lead, he thought, 'would have had no prospect of victory'. It would have meant 'splitting the party' and 'throwing away the clear majority Labour had' in the country, so 'guaranteeing' Margaret Thatcher's victory at the election.[26]

At the beginning of July, Callaghan made a speech at Brecon in which he urged the party to persist with the old electoral college of MPs only but urged them to consult their constituencies. Benn interpreted this to mean that Callaghan wanted all constitutional changes to be defeated at the conference.[27] The Liberal David Steel and Owen agreed that Healey was so compromised in his attempt to win votes in anticipation of Callaghan's departure that the chances of persuading him to fight the electoral college were 'very slim'.[28]

The Campaign for Labour Party Democracy wanted to give, not 50 per cent to the parliamentary party (which was what had been decided at Bishop's Stortford), but 50 per cent to the trade unions, with 25 per cent each to the parliamentary party and the constituencies. The Tribune Group wanted to give a third each to the three sections, the affiliated socialist societies having fallen by the wayside in the general excitement. On 7 July Joan Maynard moved the first of these choices at the organisation committee of the NEC. She was more or less a Communist and had been described by Ferdinand Mount in the *Spectator* as Stalin's nanny. This was subsequently vulgarised by the Conservative politician and journalist Jock Bruce-Gardyne into Stalin's granny. Joan Lestor moved the second choice. She oscillated between the hard Left and the soft according to the mood of the moment. Neither she nor Benn felt bound by the Bishop's Stortford formula, even though both of them had been members of the commission. By now Benn favoured Miss Maynard's position. The *status quo* was rejected, as was Miss Lestor's motion 7-2, while Miss Maynard's motion was carried.

The 50-25-25 formula, with the trade unions taking the half-share, was considered by the full NEC on 23 July. Shirley Williams wanted to refer it back to the organisation committee. Michael Foot said that the parliamentary party still had the right to elect the leader. But Mrs Williams's proposal – the 'reference back' was an old Labour device for stalling proceedings – was defeated. The NEC accepted the formula of the Campaign for Labour Party Democracy.

The date of Callaghan's resignation now became crucial. The Bennites in 1980 were in much the same position as the Bevanites in 1955. In 1980, however, the Left were looking forward to a change in machinery rather than to a change in opinion. Benn was told that at a *Guardian* lunch Foot, the paper's guest, had made it clear that Callaghan would resign after the conference.[29] Callaghan had told Foot that the 1980 conference would be his last and that he had made up his mind to retire immediately afterwards. Callaghan's recollection was that Foot had said he would not be a candidate.[30]

On the eve of the conference Foot dined with three experienced journalists of leftish inclinations: Ian Aitken of the *Guardian*, Richard Clements of *Tribune* and Geoffrey Goodman of the *Daily Mirror*. They all urged him to stand for the leadership. Foot said he would be supporting Shore, but agreed to give more thought to the matter when his companions told him that Shore could not defeat Healey.[31] The conference before which they were meeting turned out to be the most unpleasant in the history of the Labour Party. Screaming women in boiler suits and shouting men in woolly hats were much in evidence. The conventions of civilised debate – notably that of allowing your opponent to speak – were suspended. The atmosphere was horrible: intolerant and vengeful. Let us now turn to what happened.

On 1 October the conference voted by a narrower majority than had been expected to support the principle of an electoral college. It also voted down both the 50:25:25 ratio and the 33:33:33 ratio for the college. Further consideration was adjourned until the following afternoon. On Wednesday evening the NEC met and instructed the party's officials to return with a new set of proposals to be put to the conference. At 11 that night a meeting of the hard Left (which included a representative of the Militant Tendency and also Margaret Beckett, later to be deputy leader and temporary leader of the party) decided to switch its support to a 40:30:30 ratio, with the unions taking the larger share. It decided this because it thought the new ratio had the best chance of being accepted on the following afternoon. It would look, misleadingly, like a compromise. That night and early next morning those who had attended the meeting and others of the same persuasion lobbied the members of the NEC at the Imperial Hotel.

The lobbying was successful, and the NEC decided to support the new ratio. Callaghan then said that if this was implemented he would withdraw what he had said about party unity and campaign for the Labour MPs to elect their own leader. This was a course which he and Foot could have followed from the very beginning, but chose not to. Neil Kinnock said that Callaghan's approach was 'rather regrettable'.

On the Thursday afternoon all the proposals for the electoral college were defeated, leaving only the principle intact. David Basnett of the municipal workers (the joint architect of this sate of confusion) and Tom Jackson of the postal workers objected that they had not had time to consult their members. Basnett successfully moved an emergency resolution that there should be a special conference in January 1981 to resolve the method of electing the leader. Tony Benn wrote: 'So we are back where we started.'[32]

But it was only to be a matter of time before Benn was successful, a success from which, owing to the operations of the national electoral system, he was to derive no personal benefit. The 1980 conference also witnessed the beginning of – and, to a large extent, was the cause of – the Social Democratic Party. On the day the conference voted to widen the franchise for electing the leader, there was a lunchtime meeting of the group Campaign for a Labour Victory, in some ways the forerunner of the SDP. David Owen said they were 'fed up with this fudging and mudging, with mush and slush'. They needed 'courage, conviction and hard work'.

They could not 'turn this party round' unless there was much clearer and more decisive leadership. They must ask their leaders to 'stand up for their beliefs with the same conviction and passion and the same skill used by others' who had won on countless issues at the conference.[33]

Owen and his allies considered that they could not defeat the case for a wider franchise by advocating a return to the old system of election by Labour MPs only. The best course, they thought, was to exploit the opportunity which the conference had left them. The party had not been able to agree a mechanism for the election of the leader. It had only committed itself to a wider franchise. They had to ensure that one member, one vote became the way of choosing the leader.

In a speech in North Wales, Owen said that they could not have a Prime Minister chosen by trade union block votes which did not accurately reflect the number of members paying the political levy or by block votes cast in line with a union's overall policy, which might be determined by Communists, Conservatives and people who did not pay the levy. They could not have a Prime Minister chosen by the switching of a block vote merely because the general secretary of a union happened to be absent, or allow the choice of Prime Minister to pass 'from Parliament to the caucus, to unrepresentative block votes and to unrepresentative delegates'.

But in Owen's opinion there was very little chance that Healey would 'come out of his shell' and champion one member, one vote. 'His strategy, such as it was, was to lie low and hope people could be frightened by the sheer implausibility of Michael Foot as Prime Minister.' Shirley Williams agreed enthusiastically with Owen about one member, one vote. William Rodgers could see tactical advantages in supporting it but genuinely believed it was better for MPs to choose the leader. He agreed, however, not to attack one member, one vote.[34]

The Right of the party was fragmented. The union leaders were not steadfast in opposition to an electoral college. Tom Jackson of the postal workers said he was prepared to accept it. Roy Hattersley commented that for some reason which he could not explain his half of the party was always in a mood to accept defeats and to 'lie down under them'.[35] The Campaign for a Labour Victory imitated the Campaign for Labour Party Democracy and produced a 'model constitutional amendment' providing for the leader to be chosen by secret ballot of all party members. Those trade union leaders who accepted the principle of an electoral college differed about the precise proportions which should be adopted. Thus Terry Duffy and John Boyd of the engineers wanted the parliamentary party to have an absolute majority of 51 per cent or more; while David Basnett of the municipal workers proposed that the parliamentary party should have 50 per cent, which Michael Foot was eventually to support. On 6 October a note in Benn's diary recorded that Callaghan had indicated he would resign and prefer Foot as his successor.[36]

Benn's position was difficult. The electoral college was not yet set up.

The election for Callaghan's successor would be fought in the parliamentary party under the old rules. Benn's supporters considered this an illegitimate election lacking in authority and smacking of sharp practice. Should Benn stand? Or should he stay away? There is little doubt that his inclination was to stand but that he was dissuaded by his supporters. On Sunday 12 October he held a party for them at his house. Jo Richardson proposed that if Foot stood no one else from their group should. Stuart Holland agreed. The unanimous view was that Benn should not, as he recorded, 'stand yet'.[37]

On 16 October Benn made a speech saying that whoever the parliamentary party elected would be an interim leader whose term of office would automatically expire when the election 'under agreed procedure' for 'choosing the leader of the whole party' took place. Foot's biographer, Mervyn Jones, suggests that Benn was anticipating two leaders: one of the parliamentary party, the other of the whole party. But Benn's words surely made clear that he was expecting any leader chosen by the old procedure to step down once a new procedure had been first set up and then used to produce a new leader. The phrase 'stand yet' lends persuasiveness to this interpretation; Benn was perhaps naïvely expecting to be given his chance in 1981, when the electoral college was set up, rather than in 1983, when Foot retired after the general election and Benn could not stand in the subsequent contest because he had lost his Bristol seat.

After Callaghan's resignation on 15 October the Shadow Cabinet met and authorised an election under the old rules. Healey announced his candidacy. Callaghan gave no endorsement but, according to Mervyn Jones, decided to vote for Healey and said that he expected him to win.[38] This contradicts other accounts that Callaghan preferred Foot. But it was by no means clear at this stage that Foot wanted to be a candidate.

On 16 October Ian Mikardo telephoned him and told him it was his duty to stand because Peter Shore could not win. Foot promised to think it over. Mikardo then spoke to Clive Jenkins, who said he was busy already on Foot's behalf. Every half hour or so the doorbell of Foot's house in Hampstead rang for the delivery of more telegrams urging him to stand. Foot and his wife Jill (who had long been more ambitious for him than he was for himself) read them together. He finally wondered aloud to her whether he might not be letting a lot of people down if he failed to stand. Mrs Foot agreed. Jenkins had prompted some of these messages, but many came spontaneously from members in the constituencies.

Stanley Orme, a friend of Foot, arranged a meeting of Peter Shore, John Silkin and Albert Booth, and proposed that they should all urge Foot to stand. Silkin refused, saying he himself was bound to win.[39] Shore did not go as far as this. Nevertheless, he still thought at this point that he and not Foot would be the candidate to oppose Healey.

On the same Thursday Jenkins was at a union meeting with Moss Evans and David Basnett. They went on afterwards to discuss the leader-

ship at Basnett's office in Duke Street, St James's, and agreed that they
did not want Healey because they thought he was too aggressive and
would split the party. Jenkins suggested Foot; both Evans and Basnett
thought this a good idea too. Jenkins then organised the flood of telephone
messages, letters and telegrams to Foot's house. What moved Foot most
strongly was the argument that he more than any other candidate was the
best qualified and equipped to unite the party.[40]

On 18 October Foot received yet another telegram. It was from the
present writer and asked him whether it would be possible to talk on the
telephone. Foot obliged within half an hour and indicated clearly – though
without committing himself precisely – that he intended to stand for the
leadership owing to the pressure under which he had been placed by his
friends and admirers. He then flew to Dublin to deliver a lecture com-
memorating the death of one of his many unlikely heroes, Jonathan Swift.
On the following day the *Observer* reported exclusively that Foot intended
to contest the leadership. This came as a surprise to many people, not least
to Peter Shore.

On the same day, Sunday 19 October, the Labour MP Stuart Holland
pushed a note through the Foots' letter box listing 20 MPs who would vote
for him but not for Shore. Already Foot had told Orme from Dublin that
he would be standing. Jenkins was unaware of this. He had organised a
supper party at the Foots' house that evening for Ian Mikardo, Jo Richardson, Moss Evans, Alan Fisher of the public employees, William Keys of the
printers and Arthur Scargill of the miners. Foot contrived to give the
impression that he was still listening to advice and allowed the union
leaders to think they had persuaded him. At the end of the evening they
were sure he would run.[41] Shore, however, was still unaware of Foot's
intentions. Foot did not tell him, and Shore did not ask.

On Monday Shore went to Foot's room in the Commons to confirm he
had Foot's support and was much put out when Foot told him he was
standing. He said later that he had no feelings of resentment and did not
consider he had been let down or betrayed, which may indicate that this
is what Shore did indeed feel. On the same day, 20 October, Foot announced his candidature, saying he had yielded to pressure and that his
wife 'might divorce me' if he did not stand. Neil Kinnock became the
organiser of Foot's campaign.[42] The preposterous John Silkin told *The
Times* that, if Foot did not stand – Silkin would have talked to the paper
on the previous day, before Foot announced his candidature – he would
beat Healey in the first ballot. If Foot did stand, it would only delay the
outcome. Silkin said that he would beat Foot and that he had already told
him so.[43]

On 22 October a motion was put at the National Executive Committee
asking the parliamentary party to suspend the leadership election. Foot
said that the Shadow Cabinet had considered the matter. Suspension was
'feasible' but 'we didn't want to have a conflict'. Neil Kinnock spoke in

favour of the motion for suspension, which was carried by 16 votes to 7.[44] It had little effect on the parliamentary party, who met six days later. They rejected by 119 votes to 66 a motion to postpone the election until after the conference of January 1981.

John Morris, the Member for Aberavon and Shadow Attorney-General, said that nobody had any authority to take away the power of the parliamentary party to elect their leader without their consent. If legitimacy was to be conferred on the new system, it was obligatory on those who wanted it to come about to carry the support of the parliamentary party. The only person with the right to become Prime Minister was he or she who had the confidence of the House of Commons (a point Callaghan had raised on previous occasions). No outside body, Morris said, whether conference or electoral college, had any power over Labour Members of Parliament.[45] Writing in *Tribune*, Foot was less firm than Morris. A new system, he considered, would 'involve a serious erosion of parliamentary authority'. However, to say that it was impossible to contrive a fair system struck him as 'absurd'.[46]

The last election held under the old system took place on 4 November 1980. In the first ballot Healey had 112 votes, Foot 83, Silkin 38 and Shore (who persisted in standing, as he was entitled to do, though it seemed a little pointless in the circumstances) 32. As Silkin and Shore between them had fewer votes than Foot, under the rules of the exhaustive ballot they both dropped out. Benn's opinion was that Foot would be the leader, 'and that will be a tremendous event'.[47] On the afternoon of 10 November, when the second ballot was held, Healey was warned five minutes before the announcement of the result that he had lost by 129 votes to 139. He composed his features into a cheerful grin as he walked past the political correspondents assembled in the corridor on his way to Committee Room 14, where the figures were being announced. Foot was looking nervous and unhappy, so it was assumed that Healey had won. Benn made this assumption because Healey was 'red in the face' – though he was normally so anyway – 'and smiling', while Foot was 'white as a sheet'.[48] Wilson told Healey that he had voted for him on the first ballot but for Foot on the second: 'I suppose this was an existentialist *acte gratuite* – he did not explain.'[49]

Healey believed that, though more MPs who were later to join the Social Democrats had voted for him, several had voted for Foot so as to be able to justify their subsequent defection. He also believed that 'their few votes alone' were enough to explain his defeat.[50] William Rodgers and David Owen, who voted for Healey despite their doubts about him, took the precaution of having their voting slips witnessed. Owen thought that two or three right-inclined MPs might have voted for Foot.[51] One of them was Neville Sandelson, the Member for Hayes, who later joined the Social Democrats.[52] But Owen did not think they changed the result. He thought Healey was deluding himself in his apparent belief that these few votes were enough to explain his defeat. When Owen, Rodgers and Shirley Williams had talked to him in September 1980, before the conference, they had warned him that, by failing to fight, he was heading for defeat.[53] But Mrs Williams told Foot's biographer that she could name several MPs, on Healey's side politically, who nevertheless voted against him on personal grounds. Callaghan, however, voted for Healey.[54] Healey congratulated Foot and said he was willing to serve as deputy leader. He was elected without any further nominations.

The new leader then set about helping to construct the new system of which, in his heart, he disapproved but which – together with his new deputy leader and his former leader – he declined to fight. On 18 November he told Benn that he wanted the parliamentary party to have the largest percentage possible in the electoral college. Benn suggested a third each for parliamentary party, trade unions and constituencies. Foot said: 'I'll live with that.'[55]

At the Wembley conference of January 1981 the Left had won, and showed it. There was, however, nothing of the clenched-fist-saluting triumphalism which had been on display at Blackpool three months previously. The mood was conspiratorial and grave. There were five choices before the conference: an electoral college to be held at the conference; an electoral college to be conducted by post; an electoral college that was separate from the conference; a ballot of individual members; and miscellaneous provisions. David Owen and Frank Chapple of the electricians favoured the individual ballot. Moss Evans of the transport workers wanted the electoral college to assemble at the conference. The individual ballot was defeated by a ratio of 15:1. The proposal for an electoral college at the conference was carried overwhelmingly.

Eric Heffer for the National Executive Committee then proposed a ratio of 33:33:33 in the electoral college, with equal shares for unions, constituencies and MPs and with the extra one going to affiliated socialist societies. David Basnett of the municipal workers and Tom Jackson of the postal workers then proposed a ratio of 50:25:25, with the MPs taking the half share. Just before lunch the ubiquitous Clive Jenkins of the technical and managerial staffs brought his union's vote behind the shopworkers' proposal of a 40:30:30 ratio, with the largest proportion going to the unions. Lunch saw numerous cabals. The Campaign for Labour Party Democracy's representative said it was essential that everyone should support the shopworkers and abandon the National Executive Committee's proposal. After lunch the 40:30:30 ratio was fixed.[56]

Michael Foot said he could not pretend that 'absolutely all the results this afternoon' – one of Foot's jokes, more effective in speech than in print – were the ones he had wanted. He had agreed with the case put by Basnett. He did not disguise from the conference and had not disguised from anybody that he wished the conference had reached the same conclusion. He believed that 'very often the rights and duties and the performance of the

Parliamentary Labour Party' were 'quite improperly derided in our movement'. If Basnett's option had been adopted, it could have made 'some of
our other problems' more easy to deal with 'readily and speedily'.[57]

To Roy Hattersley, the fight for one member, one vote was 'temporarily
over'. Shirley Williams, Tom Bradley and he (the first two were shortly to
leave the Labour Party and join the Social Democrats) had put the idea to
a joint meeting of the Shadow Cabinet and the National Executive Committee. It had been, in Hattersley's words, 'slaughtered' by a 'co-ordinated
assault on both the principle and the practice led by Neil Kinnock'.[58]

Tony Benn thought that no praise was high enough for the 'enormous
skill' of the Campaign for Labour Party Democracy, which had worked
'tirelessly' to persuade constituency parties and smaller unions to vote for
the shopworkers' resolution. He thought the organisation had been 'really
triggered off' by the votes of certain Labour MPs in 1971 against a
three-line whip, to give Heath the majority needed to take us into the
Common Market'. He had been chairman of the party in that year and had,
he claimed, identified party democracy as the crucial question. In the same
year, in a Fabian lecture, he had raised the matter of the leader's being
elected in a different way. It had been, Benn concluded, 'an important day'.
What had been decided would 'never be reversed', and nothing would be
the same again.[59] This illustrates the danger of politicians' saying 'never'.

Next month, at a meeting of the Shadow Cabinet, Peter Shore proposed
a motion calling for a 50:25:25 ratio, the half-share going to the parliamentary party. Benn proposed one supporting the decision arrived at by the
Wembley conference. He said he had already given his reasons, one of
which was that he thought the Shadow Cabinet should support the
conference. His motion found no seconder. Roy Hattersley, Denis Healey
and Merlyn Rees all argued against the Wembley decision. Healey now
wanted to go back to election by the parliamentary party. Stanley Orme,
seconded by Neil Kinnock, and supported by John Silkin and Albert Booth,
proposed a transposition of the Wembley formula of 40:30:30 whereby the
largest share went to the parliamentary party rather than to the unions.
This was rejected. Foot said they could not have different members moving
different things at the parliamentary party's meeting. They could not all
vote the way they liked. Accordingly he himself would propose Shore's
motion to the parliamentary party on behalf of the Shadow Cabinet. They
would 'minimise the quarrel' and the parliamentary party could 'put the
matter to conference'.[60]

At the parliamentary party's meeting John Morris said they had 'gone
down the wrong road' in lending any support at all to the electoral college.
The role of the parliamentary party in the choice of leader was a very
important one. The smaller it was, the greater the possibility of conflict. If
the leader was not accepted by the parliamentary party after being elected
by the college, the result would be 'a disaster'. Constitutionally the Prime
Minister, when appointed by the Sovereign, had to carry the support of the

House of Commons. By the end of March 1981, however, Foot was prepared to retreat slightly from his previous position. He told Benn that they
might persuade the conference to support a 33:33:33 ratio. Benn replied
that they might or might not. For his part, he was not particularly
concerned about percentages. That was not the point, which was that the
election for deputy leader would take place under the existing system,
decided at Wembley.

Benn was correct. In Labour politics, the period from February to
September 1981 was dominated by the question of whether he would – or
should – challenge Healey for the deputy leadership. He had wanted to
stand for the leadership when Callaghan resigned but had been dissuaded
by his followers from contesting an 'illegitimate' election held under the
old rules. Now, from the constitutional point of view adopted by his
followers, he was free to stand. He was determined to do so. Others wanted
to stop him.

Thus in mid-April Benn was invited to lunch, a 'fancy meal' as he
disapprovingly called it, by the ever-active Clive Jenkins, who tried to
persuade him not to stand against Healey. Jenkins admitted that there
had been an agreement between the union general secretaries and the
organisation Trade Unionists for a Labour Victory that there would be no
contest for the deputy leadership. Benn records Jenkins as saying that
they had agreed there would be no contest for the *leadership*. This is
perfectly possible, in which case the leadership would *a fortiori* have
included the deputy leadership. The unions had told the Shadow Cabinet
in late 1980 (when Benn was not a member). Benn had suspected a
'general understanding' but not realised there was a more specific agreement.

He concluded it was 'scandalous' that, while the union leaders had been
arguing at Wembley for a new franchise, they had agreed secretly that the
franchise should not be used. Now they were 'acutely embarrassed' by
what had happened. In June Foot sought to avert the embarrassing
election by proposing another one instead. He said that Benn, whom he
was finding increasingly troublesome, should stand against him instead.[61]
But Benn persisted in his course and, far from showing the hostility to
Foot which by now Foot undoubtedly felt for him, claimed repeatedly that,
of the three candidates for the deputy leadership – himself, Healey and
Silkin – he was the only one who had voted for Foot in 1980.

In the election for the deputy leadership, the transport workers consulted their regional organisers, who had themselves adopted a variety of
methods. Whereas the majority of regions had voted for Healey, the
union's executive committee decided to recommend a vote for Benn on the
basis that most of the largest regions, and presumably – though one
cannot be sure about this – an absolute majority of members had preferred
him. Despite this recommendation, however, the union's delegation at

Brighton decided to vote for Silkin on the first ballot and, after consultation among themselves, for Benn on the second.

The public employees, by contrast, had consulted their members individually, probably against the wishes of their general secretary, Alan Fisher. They voted for Healey. Reg Race, a member of the union and the MP for Wood Green, said that the only fault in the procedure was that the union's executive council had not made a recommendation. He was sure that, had they done so, it would have been for Benn. The result of the union's internal ballot would then have been different. The trade union movement, Race considered, had 'a responsibility to state its views to its members'.[62]

The result was extraordinarily close. In the first ballot Healey had 45 per cent of the college, Benn 37 per cent and Silkin 18 per cent (figures rounded). In the second ballot Healey had 50.426 per cent and Benn 49.574. There was a clear majority for Healey among the unions and MPs, and an overwhelming majority for Benn in the constituencies. Thus 83 per cent of the constituency party votes went to Benn and only 28 per cent of the parliamentary vote. If Benn had won, as he might well have done, he would have been imposed on the parliamentary party.

The working of the electoral college created doubts about its future. The methods employed by the unions to consult their members and cast their votes had been shown to be questionable. Some had consulted individual members. Others had gone through regional offices but no consistent method was applied to each region. Others again had consultations which were countermanded by delegations at the conference. And many delegations were swayed conclusively by the personal opinions of their presidents or general secretaries.[63]

NEIL KINNOCK IN 1983

This travesty of democracy was attacked but it remained obstinately in place throughout Foot's period of leadership. It was there when he resigned – or was pushed into resigning – as leader after the general election of 1983. After 9 June the Conservatives had 397 seats, Labour 209, the Liberals 17, the Social Democrats 6, the Scottish Nationalists 2, the Welsh Nationalists 2 and Northern Ireland 17.

Before the overnight votes had been counted Clive Jenkins was on the telephone to Moss Evans. Both agreed that they would support Foot if he wished to stay as leader. But if he did not they would – in the phrase of that moment, used by Jenkins and David Basnett – 'have to jump a generation'. Evans asked Jenkins somewhat coyly whether they were 'both thinking of the same person'. They were: Neil Kinnock. Jenkins then telephoned Foot, who invited him and his wife to supper on the next day, the Saturday. Foot had already decided he would not seek re-election at the October conference but had not planned an immediate announcement.

Jenkins's concern was to prevent the Right from mobilising and to give Kinnock a favourable start. Foot had already asked him whether he was prepared to stand for the leadership and he had said Yes. At supper that evening Foot asked what would happen if he resigned. His wife Jill replied that they would 'nominate Neil'. Jenkins said that the interest of both Kinnock and the party would be best served by an immediate announcement giving time for Kinnock to establish himself. By the end of the meal Foot had decided not to accept the nomination and to inform Kinnock accordingly. He telephoned Kinnock's home at once, to find that he and his wife Glenys were out for the evening. Foot gave the message to the baby-sitter, who forgot to pass it on.

On the Sunday morning the executive of Jenkins's union were to meet. As Foot's biographer put it: 'Having (so he believed) stage-managed Michael's decision to stand in 1980, he was happy to stage-manage Michael's departure.'[64] Jenkins explained later that the executive 'happened' to be due for a meeting and that it 'happened' to be the right time for them to consider nominations for the leadership. No one believed that what occurred was pure chance. Jenkins told the executive that Foot would not be standing. They then nominated Kinnock. Jenkins telephoned him at Broadcasting House, where he was about to be interviewed for *The World This Weekend*.

The news of Foot's resignation took the other potential candidates by surprise. Peter Shore was giving a television interview on *Weekend World* when he was told by the presenter, Brian Walden. Roy Hattersley was watching the programme at home and proceeded to announce his own candidacy on the television programme *Face the Press* early that evening. Denis Healey attributed these manoeuvres to a desire for revenge on Jenkins's part against him, and cited Stendhal's *Le Rouge et le Noir* where, on the last page, Julien Sorel is sentenced to death in revenge for a slight suffered many years earlier.[65] Healey was referring to the attack he had made on Jenkins at the 1974 conference. This may – who knows? – have rankled still. Certainly Jenkins wanted to keep him out of the leadership in 1980. But by 1983 his chance had gone, as he himself recognised. What happened in that year was, he wrote, 'no disappointment' to him: 'the bulk of the movement wanted a younger man'. And he shared the blame for the defeat in the election.[66] What really finished Healey's chances was the setting up of the electoral college in 1981. It is still possible, however, that he would have lost in the college as a whole but, even at this stage, won in the parliamentary party. This would have caused certainly embarrassment, maybe a crisis.

Altogether the right of the party were in confusion. Terry Duffy, the president of the engineers, came out for Peter Shore; Gavin Laird, his general secretary, for Roy Hattersley. Duffy was forced to change his mind when Basnett endorsed Hattersley. Duffy said afterwards that he had telephoned 'the big unions' – in practice their presidents or general secretaries – but had been unable to gain their support. In such circumstances supporting Shore was 'no use'. Basnett said they had to 'skip a generation' and 'put young men in charge'.[67] Duffy said that, if Hattersley wanted a membership ballot, they would have to give 'the most serious consideration' to one. He would ask the general secretary to examine the proposal at once. The union would still vote for Hattersley. That was what the executive committee had decided and there was 'no more to be said'.[68]

Following the same principle but producing a different result, the executive committee of the transport workers met four days after Foot's resignation, and decided they would be supporting Kinnock. When the union met later for their once-every-two-years conference in the Isle of Man, 'they decided that their members were obviously Kinnockites and that it was a waste of time and money to ask them to confirm what everybody already knew'.[69] Since there was no request and, in most cases, no particular wish to seek the views of trade unionists or party members, the election was decided by the preferences of general secretaries and their executive committees, and by the 50 or so members of the general management committees of constituency parties.[70]

The Left certainly believed Kinnock would win. They were also in some confusion. On the Sunday evening they met in Chris Mullin's Brixton flat. One of their non-parliamentary number, Jon Lansman, had budgeted for a candidates' list of Benn, Healey and Kinnock and had concluded, not unrealistically, that Benn would beat Healey in the second ballot. But Benn had lost his seat at Bristol South East and was accordingly ineligible to be a candidate. Tony Banks, who had just been elected for Newham North West, offered to resign so that Benn could fight the by-election. Benn would not hear of it, for the proposed course 'would be manipulative' and he would not 'contemplate such a thing'. But he had '*never* [italics in diary] known anyone make such a generous offer before'.[71]

They then discussed candidates for the leadership. Lansman believed that Kinnock would win on the first ballot; they would accept this and concentrate again on the deputy leadership, as they had in 1981, and not contest the leadership. Accordingly Michael Meacher, the industrious but uninspiring Member for Oldham West, who had served as a junior Minister in the last Labour government, was drafted to fight the deputy leadership.[72] Eric Heffer drafted himself to fight the leadership, to no very great enthusiasm from his comrades. Kinnock and Hattersley agreed that each would stand for the deputy leadership as well, should the other win the principal bout. Kinnock thought it would be an advantage to have Hattersley cemented to his leadership. Hattersley felt he had no alternative but to make a reciprocal gesture, though he did so reluctantly.[73]

Foot, though perhaps surprised at the rapid turn of events, accepted them with equanimity. Whatever helped Kinnock had his approval: that seemed to be his approach. His friends were not always so benign. They thought the old bibliophile had been shamefully – and shamelessly –

manipulated by Clive Jenkins. The head of his office, Tom McCaffrey, who had previously worked for James Callaghan, was particularly annoyed because Foot had been due formally to announce his resignation to the National Executive Committee on the Wednesday. Jenkins's manoeuvre had, he thought, robbed the occasion of its dignity.[74]

Evidently Foot thought, with Jenkins, that the less consultation there was, the better it would be for Kinnock. The Shadow Cabinet – 'operating', as Hattersley candidly put it later, 'at the very margin of its responsibilities' – carried by a large majority a motion calling on local parties to ascertain the opinions of their individual members. Despite Foot's protests, the motion was dispatched to the parliamentary party for further discussion. Max Madden, MP for Bradford West and a member of Kinnock's campaign team, proposed a procedural motion which meant that the matter would not be further considered. Foot fell upon it, saying: 'This is none of our business.' The meeting finished. On the way out, Hattersley told Foot that he had 'betrayed us'. Foot lost his temper and said to Hattersley: 'I'll have the skin off your back.' Hattersley responded with: 'You couldn't knock the skin off a rice pudding.' There the matter ended.[75]

Hattersley left the meeting with his team leader, John Smith; Kinnock's team was led by Robin Cook. Kinnnock gained the support of traditionally moderate unions such as the steelworkers and the shopworkers. On 1 August 1983 the less moderate electricians, who had moved to the right first under Frank Chapple and then under Eric Hammond, decided through their executive committee to boycott the election because it was 'already a foregone conclusion for Mr Kinnock'. Kinnock arrived at Brighton with his wife on the Saturday before the election.

The conference began at five on Sunday 2 October. Kinnock won 71 per cent of the electoral college, Hattersley 19 per cent, Heffer 6 per cent and Shore 3 per cent. Of the 30 per cent of the college allocated to MPs, Kinnock had 15 per cent and Hattersley 8 per cent: there was accordingly no question of Kinnock's being imposed on the parliamentary party. Hattersley did conspicuously badly in the constituencies, though he did better than Shore. In the election for deputy leader Hattersley had 67 per cent, Meacher 28 per cent, Denzil Davies 4 per cent and Gwyneth Dunwoody 1 per cent. Hattersley had a clear majority in the parliamentary party. (All figures are rounded up or down.)

The combination of Kinnock and Hattersley was known as the 'dream ticket', mainly because one represented the Left, the other the Right, but also because they were thought to embody complementary virtues: the poetry of Wales and the common sense of Yorkshire; mastery of the public meeting and command of the House of Commons; and so forth. The combination did not work as effectively as had been expected. Why that was so is outside the scope of the present study.

On the last day of the conference, 7 October, it defeated a proposal to introduce 'one member, one vote' into the electoral college. Kinnock's period of leadership saw various perfunctory and piecemeal attempts to change Labour's internal constitutional arrangements. In the general election of 11 June 1987 the Conservatives had 376 seats, Labour 229, the Liberals 17, the Social Democrats 5 (making 22 for the Alliance), the Scottish and Welsh Nationalists 3 apiece, and Northern Ireland 17. There was another leadership election on 2 October 1988, when Benn challenged Kinnock for the leadership and both Heffer and John Prescott challenged Hattersley for the deputy leadership. Kinnock won 89 per cent of the vote in the electoral college and Benn 11 per cent. Hattersley was 67 per cent, Prescott 24 per cent and Heffer 9 per cent. With both posts, the winner had an absolute majority among Labour MPs.

To prevent a repetition of these contests, a change in the rules was introduced whereby any candidate had to be nominated by at least 20 per cent of the parliamentary party. This requirement was not only stringent but ambiguous: it was not clear whether a Member could nominate more than one candidate. In 1992 more than five Labour MPs were initially to put their names forward, so making it arithmetically impossible for them all to be properly nominated if a Member was to be restricted to one candidate only. Appeals to the party's general secretary and its director of organisation failed to resolve the matter satisfactorily. Eventually some of the candidates withdrew, rendering further arbitration unnecessary. The other change was the introduction of new voting rules into constituency parties giving all individual members the right to vote for the leader and his deputy. This had previously been left to the members of general management (later called general) committees.

JOHN SMITH IN 1992

In the election of 9 April 1992 the Conservatives had 336 seats, Labour 271, the Liberal Democrats 20, the Welsh Nationalists 4, the Scottish Nationalists 3 and Northern Ireland 17. Kinnock had been leader for nine years and lost two elections, though he – with most others – had expected to win this one. He was distressed and disappointed; his wife was devastated. In his post-poll speech at the party's headquarters in Walworth Road he said it was his last as party leader. Many did not immediately take his meaning. Among them was Bryan Gould.

Gould had been Kinnock's principal assistant in the election of 1987. He was a native of New Zealand who had gone to Oxford and become successively a diplomat, an academic lawyer, a Labour MP, a television presenter after losing his seat at Southampton Test, and an MP again after winning Dagenham. He was physically unarresting – he looked more impressive on television than in the flesh. But intellectually he was formidable. Quite why Gould's stock fell as it did between 1987 and 1992 is still a slight mystery. Partly it was jealousy; partly his hostility to the European Community after Labour's position had shifted; partly his failure to make much impact either on events or on opinions when he was in charge of opposition to the poll tax before 1990. But mainly, perhaps, it was the difficulty he presented to those who wished to categorise him as on the right or on the left. Peter Shore had suffered from a similar disability. British political parties are, like British newspapers, uneasy with people who cannot be put into boxes, tied up neatly and labelled.

John Smith, by contrast, was easier to categorise. He was the son of a Scottish schoolmaster and was a practising Scots lawyer, one of the group of Scottish Labour MPs who had, in the 1980s, overtaken the Welsh as the dominant group in the parliamentary party. His formidable debating skills had been displayed to the best advantage when he was Shadow Minister for Trade and Industry. During the Westland affair in 1986 he had embarrassed the government more acutely than had Neil Kinnock. As Shadow Chancellor, however, he had proved less sure-footed. His plodding manner and owlish appearance belied his quick wit and liking for convivial company. Unfortunately he had suffered a heart attack. Though he had recovered from it and pursued his recovery by climbing Scottish mountains, he had already begun to put on weight again.

Kinnock telephoned Gould on the Sunday after the election. Gould had not realised what he meant when he said at Walworth Road that he had made his last speech as leader. It came as a surprise to him when Kinnock said he would resign next day. Gould said he would probably contest the leadership. Kinnock advised against, saying that 'Smithy' had 'got it all sewn up'. Gould, in Kinnock's opinion, would win only a fraction of the vote. It would be 'better to let him have it'. Smith, Kinnock said, would not last the course, which turned out to be correct, though the beneficiary in the end was Blair, not Gould. At that stage, however, Kinnock thought it important that Gould should be 'there to pick up the pieces'.[76] This suggests that Kinnock was predicting that Smith would not last because of his politics rather than because of his health.

Smith's election was inevitable, Kinnock thought. That did not mean he was specially well-disposed towards the new leader. He had been compared and contrasted with Smith too often, to his own disadvantage. But the speed with which Kinnock moved worked in Smith's favour. Perhaps he thought that, as Smith was bound to win anyway, it did not matter. He announced he would be proposing to the NEC that the election should be held as quickly as 'proper organisation' allowed. It would accordingly take place in the second half of June. There were some cries of 'rush'. The committee put off the contest for a further three weeks.[77]

On the previous day, Sunday 13 April 1992, Gould had appeared on the television programme *On the Record*. Though he did not formally declare his candidature – Kinnock had not yet resigned officially – it was obvious he intended to run. It was equally clear that Smith would not willingly have him as his deputy; not least because of their differences over Europe. Kinnock did not want Blair to stand for the deputy leadership because he favoured Gould. Hattersley concurred, because he thought Blair should eventually be leader. Brown was excluded because it was agreed that the leader and his deputy should not both be Scots.[78] This was one reason why Margaret Beckett became the favourite for the deputy leadership: that she was not a Scot. Another was that she was a woman. And another was that she had leftist credentials: accordingly the combination of Smith and Beckett could be presented, not perhaps as a 'dream ticket', but certainly as a balanced one.

John Edmonds of the municipal workers appeared on television to say that there was 'one name on everybody's lips' when it came to choosing a successor to Kinnock. He was joined by other union leaders, notably Bill Morris of the transport workers, in his enthusiasm for Smith. About 10 per cent of the electoral college had been pledged to Smith even before the party knew officially that there was to be a contest. He claimed, however, that he would have preferred Kinnock to stay on.[79] Gould announced his candidature on the day after Kinnock's resignation. Smith had already declared. Gould was reasonably confident, though no more, of winning the support of the 55 MPs required to enable him to stand. He thought the requirement had been set at too high a level for the good of party democracy – that it acted as a 'real bar' to candidates who might not have a chance of winning but were nevertheless legitimately entitled to stand.[80]

The preliminaries were enlivened by a letter to the *Guardian* by Colin Byrne.[81] He had resigned as Labour's press officer in autumn 1991. What, he asked, had the Labour Right done about Militant in the 'bitter years' before Kinnock? What had they done about reforming the party's relationship with the trade unions? These were perfectly fair questions to ask – though the persons most at fault had been James Callaghan, Denis Healey and, up to a point, Roy Hattersley rather than John Smith. And what had they done about Europe? The answer, as he had seen for himself during those years of 'crucial policy review and National Executive Committee meetings, was usually to sit on their hands and let the Kinnocks and the Blairs take the flak'.[82] The point was generally sound, though Blair was not a member of the NEC during the period in question.

The Member for Pontypridd, Kim Howells, introduced a note of funerary elegiacism. The defeat in the election, he wrote, had 'felt like the death of a loved one'. They had 'wandered like sleepwalkers through last weekend only to be woken on Monday by the realisation that apparently there was to be no funeral'. They were being informed that Kinnock's successor was 'bound to be John Smith'. Members both of the party and of Parliament had been telephoning him to 'express anger' and to ask: 'Why the rush?'[83]

The tone of bereavement was maintained by the member for Birmingham Ladywood, Clare Short. Before they had 'had time to mourn', she wrote, they had been 'told the result of the next leadership election'. They felt 'stunned and angry'. The 'instigator of the plan' to elect a new leader 'with indecent haste' had been Kinnock, who 'appeared to be acting alone'. Many 'suspected that he just could not bear it any more and wanted to go quickly'. He did not 'trust the party to have a civilised election'.[84]

As matters turned out, the election – precipitate as it was, though not quite so much so as Kinnock had first wanted – was conducted with the greatest civility by Labour or, indeed, by any other standards. Gould, it is true, said in an interview that he would not be persuaded to stand for the deputy leadership alone. He said he intended to fight on economic policy. The election provided a chance he had been awaiting to attack United Kingdom membership of the exchange-rate mechanism of the European Monetary System, which we had joined in the last phase of Margaret Thatcher's premiership. He had, he said, 'loyally not opened up on any of these issues over the past three years'. The party had 'placed a premium on self-discipline and party unity' to win the election. What he was not prepared to do was to say that, as they had just lost that election, they 'ought to go back into purdah on this kind of issue'.[85]

Smith's campaign did not enjoy the happiest of starts. The *Sunday Times* reported that 'the normally unflappable Scots lawyer had an uncomfortable time'. He 'appeared badly briefed and was reluctant to give a clear statement of his views on issues such as the unions' block vote and proportional representation. His lacklustre performance was even more apparent when Gould launched his campaign in the same room five hours later.'[86] This did nothing to affect Smith's position as the clear favourite. Long before nominations closed on 26 April 1992 he had received the blessing of the leaders of the engineers, the transport workers and the municipal workers. Though Ken Livingstone, who had been MP for Brent East since 1987, wished to contest the election, as others did also, only Gould managed to collect the 20 per cent or 55 MPs necessary to qualify as a candidate.

There was little public interest. The Fabian Society gallantly tried to drum up some. It organised a debate on 20 May where Gould said that 'the leadership of our party must have some experience' of what it meant 'to fight and win in those areas outside our heartlands'. (Smith was Member for Monklands East and had been Member for Lanarkshire North; Gould was Member for Dagenham and had been Member for Southampton Test.) There was a certain amount of speculation about Tony Blair's becoming John Smith's deputy and eventual successor. On television on 31 May Jack Cunningham was asked by Sir David Frost whether he believed the next Labour Prime Minister would be Smith or Blair. Soon the talk was that Labour had got it wrong once again: they were choosing the leader they should have had at the last election rather than the leader who would win the next.[87]

Policy played little part in this sleepy contest, though at the beginning of June Smith – worried by the charge that he was over-indulgent towards the European Community – issued a statement saying that the exchange-rate mechanism was 'a fixed but adjustable system', membership of which did not 'preclude the possibility of a general realignment'. He believed this was 'indeed likely'. Smith repeated his view in the House of Commons at the beginning of July.[88] Neil Kinnock pursued the matter in a letter to the *Financial Times*, saying that he could write without having his 'words treated as Labour Party policy'. He gravely urged the government to take a 'real lead' in 'pressing for an immediate revaluation of the deutschmark'.[89]

Nothing seemed to make any difference. On 18 July the results were announced to a special conference meeting in the Royal Horticultural Hall, Westminster. The construction workers, with 160,000 votes, were the only sizeable union to vote for Gould. Smith won the municipal workers by 110,200 to 30,300 but the union's entire block vote went to Smith. The shopworkers split 76,000-10,000 with the same consequence. Gould's vote in the parliamentary party was 68. The surprise was that Smith had won an overwhelming majority in the constituencies. For deputy leader, Margaret Beckett had 57 per cent of the electoral college, John Prescott 28 per cent and Bryan Gould 15 per cent. Mrs Beckett's share split in a 25:19:13 ratio for, respectively, unions, constituencies and MPs; Prescott's in a 12:7:9 ratio; and Gould's in a 3:4:8 ratio. For leader, John Smith had 91 per cent of the electoral college and Bryan Gould 9 per cent. Smith's share split in a 39:29:23 ratio and Gould's in a 1:1:7 ratio.

It had been predicted that Kinnock would vote not for Mrs Beckett but for Gould as deputy leader.[90] As things turned out, he abstained in both elections. Once again, Labour had been lucky, in that the fancy franchise had produced the leader the party wanted, even more overwhelmingly than in 1983. In particular, the parliamentary party had not been at odds with the two other components of the electoral college – as it would have been if Benn rather than Healey had won the deputy leadership in 1981. In 1992 Gould, though he polled better among his parliamentary colleagues than with the unions and the constituencies, was still behind both Mrs Beckett and Prescott in the poll of Labour MPs. And yet, the feeling remains that a injustice was done to him, that his talents were insufficiently recognised. He evidently shared this sentiment, for shortly afterwards he returned to his native New Zealand to re-embark on an academic career.

Despite his hesitant campaign, in which he was reluctant to discuss sensitive matters, particularly if they involved the trade unions, Smith turned out to be the most innovative leader constitutionally in the party's history, and the most original politician since Tony Benn in 1979-81. The story is often difficult and sometimes tedious to disentangle. Fundamentally, however, it was to do with the power of the trade unions – in particular, with the power of their leaders to cast a large block of votes behind a person or policy. This power was exercised in three areas: first, the choice of party leader; second, the formation of policy through resolu-

tions passed at the party conferences; and, third, the selection of parliamentary candidates. This book is primarily concerned with the first of
these, but the others will put in an appearance from time to time.

In May 1992, before John Smith had been elected, John Prescott was
moved to say at the annual conference of the white-collar union MSF that
it was 'a sad reflection of the political climate in Britain today' that it was
necessary for him to say that he was 'proud to be a trade unionist'. At the
beginning of June, the public employees held their conference. Their
deputy general secretary, Tom Sawyer – later to be general secretary of
the Labour Party – said that as long as the unions continued to fund the
party, so long would they have a say. It was 'as crude as that'. He
summarised the position: 'No say, no pay.'

Smith was emollient. In the *Tribune* debate of 26 June 1992, which was
an attempt to enliven the torpid leadership election, he had promised that
no changes would be made until the 1993 conference. In any case, he said,
it had already been agreed that, in 1993, the union block vote would have
been cut from 90 per cent to 70 per cent of the conference's vote. It is
interesting to speculate that these various changes involving block votes
and electoral colleges which were made during the 1981-93 period would
not have been implemented so readily had it not been for the invention of
the pocket calculator. In July Sawyer returned to his theme. It was, he
wrote, 'puzzling at first' but, reading the articles that had been written and
the speeches that had been made at the time of the general election, and
talking also to journalists about briefings that had taken place, he now
understood 'that there were influential people in the party who were
preparing, in the event of a defeat, for a concerted attack on the union
link'.[91]

Smith was polite but none the less determined to change the constitution. A fortnight before being elected leader under the 1981 system, he told
the BBC's *On the Record* television programme that the party would
introduce one member, one vote for all its 'key decisions'. But a way had
to be found whereby the new system would be consistent with organisations' being 'in' – that is, affiliated to – the party. If 'radical changes'
involved the party in 'subverting its principles and aborting its mission',
then he was 'conservative in that very narrow sense'. He did not 'want to
abort our mission'. When he was elected leader he said in his acceptance
speech that they must base their 'internal democracy on the principle of
one member, one vote and not on the basis of block votes'. By January 1993
he felt confident enough to tell Sir David Frost that 'one trade union
general secretary casting millions of votes' would not 'happen in the
future'.

A committee called the Union Links Review Group was duly set up. It
consisted of Margaret Beckett, John Prescott, Robin Cook, Clare Short,
representatives of the four largest unions, and Lewis Minkin, author of
The Contentious Alliance and a conservative in matters constitutional.

With the exception of Nigel Harris of the engineers, indeed, they were all to a greater or lesser degree opponents of one member, one vote, with Prescott and Mrs Beckett well to the fore in opposition. Tom Burlison of the municipal workers produced a compromise. Levy-paying trade union-ists would be able to vote as individuals in choosing parliamentary candidates. This scheme would produce two classes of members: full party members and what Burlison called 'registered supporters'.

The group's report proposed no change to the block vote system at the party conference, except to allow each union delegate to cast a portion of his or her union's vote instead of having one official casting the whole lot. This would be called 'one delegate, one vote'. Larry Whitty, the then general secretary (who was to be succeeded by Tom Sawyer), admitted that the change was 'largely presentational'. It would avoid television pictures of votes being thrust into a box. The party could then say: 'We don't have the block vote.' The trick was exposed at Tony Blair's first conference in 1994, when the unions insisted that on matters of 'union policy' delegates would all be instructed which way to vote, as a block. An additional presentational change would be to express conference votes in percentages rather than as millions of non-existent individuals.[92]

Blair was unsure of John Smith's position. Smith was said to be 'persuadable' on the registered supporters scheme, which Blair opposed. He said in *On the Record* that he believed the system should be one member, one vote: 'there should not be two classes of membership'. In February 1993 the review group reported to the National Executive Committee. It was agreed to hold a 'consultation exercise' in the party and among the unions on the options available. According to the NEC minutes, Smith 'expressed his preference for selection by the party membership on the basis of one member, one vote; but this option need not preclude aspects of the registered supporters system from being considered for beyond the next election'.[93] Whitty said it would be impossible to introduce the registered supporters scheme until after the general election (which was four years away).

Prescott and Sawyer, Whitty's successor, then developed a plan called 'levy plus'. Gordon Brown had proposed a similar idea in a Tribune Group pamphlet in 1987. The name was suggested by Phil Wilson, Blair's assis-tant in his Sedgefield constituency, in a report to Blair in 1992. In return for a small payment above the political levy paid to the union, the member of the union would become a full member of the party. It is difficult to see why this system was considered so very different from the registered supporters scheme. In the latter, the union member was required to pay nothing extra but merely to indicate his support for the party. Between the two there was in truth no difference of substance.

In the document *New Paths to Victory* of 1992 Smith had proposed replacing the electoral college with a new one with 50 per cent repre-sentation for constituency parties and 50 per cent for Labour MPs. The constituency parties would use one member, one vote instead of delegating the decision to general committees. The schemes both for registered supporters and for 'levy plus' were essentially devices to keep trade union influence more or less intact. But the unions' chief interest lay in the selection of parliamentary candidates rather than in the choice of leader. The third area where there was a flagrant lack of democracy – the voting on policy resolutions at the party conference – was relatively calm. It was generally agreed that the unions' proportion of the total vote should slowly decline from 90 per cent through 70 per cent to 50 per cent.

On 24 February Smith issued a statement saying he did not believe that work on the registered supporters scheme could be completed in time for the rule change which would have to be made at next year's conference. 'For this practical reason,' he concluded, he would 'recommend a one member, one vote system to conference.'[94] The registered supporters scheme having been ruled out, the unions divided about what to do. The six largest unions, which were all opposed to one member, one vote, met at the Trades Union Congress's headquarters in Bloomsbury to agree a common policy. The transport workers wanted no change, the municipal workers refused to accept that the registered supporters scheme would not work and the rest wondered whether to support 'levy plus' (which had been provisionally fixed at £3 a year instead of the £15 which full party membership cost). At the end of May, Smith appeared at the conference of the Manufacturing, Science and Finance Union. The delegates nevertheless insisted on retaining the union vote both in the selection of candidates and in the choice of leader.

In the early summer all the big unions at their conference came out against change. Tom Burlison of the municipal workers and Treasurer of the party said Smith had 'lost the fight for reform'.[95] A spokesman for his office let it be known that 'the view of all of us' was that they did not want him to remain as leader 'in a position where he had been so completely defeated, to a point where people could say' that he 'was leader only so far as he was allowed to be by John Edmonds'.[96]

It was not only the trade union movement which was discontented. Tony Blair was none too happy either. He wrote that 'simply allowing any trade union levy payer to have voting rights in the Labour Party' led to the 'quite eccentric situation' that those who did not even vote Labour but might vote Tory 'should have the right to decide' who the Labour candidate should be'.[97] Blair was here referring to 'levy plus' in connection with the selection of parliamentary candidates rather than with the choice of leader. But *a fortiori* his criticism would apply to the latter as well. On 11 July Smith told *On the Record* that there would be a case 'for individual trade unionists' taking part in the election of leader and deputy leader of the party provided they could 'get certain principles established'. These were that they 'get an end to block voting' and that 'the people taking part' were Labour supporters – which went some way, though Smith did not say so, towards meeting Blair's objections.[98]

In July the review group met for the last time. Smith surprised everybody by turning up. He had now – to the indignation of Brown and Blair – abandoned both the 50:50 electoral college and the pure milk of one member, one vote. He calculated that he would have a better chance of securing one member, one vote in the selection of parliamentary candidates if he conceded the unions some continuing say in the choice of party leader. Accordingly he proposed an electoral college with a third of its strength allocated to the trade unions, a third to the constituency parties and a third to the Labour MPs. This looked, and was intended to look, like a retreat. In reality it was a change of revolutionary proportions. For the unions were to cast their vote not in blocks – as they had when Kinnock, when Healey and when Smith himself had been elected to their positions – but as collections of individuals, on the basis of 'levy plus': it was not one member, one vote but certainly one person, one vote.

As one of Blair's biographers, John Rentoul, put it: 'In choosing the party leader, the power of the unions' activist and official structures was broken.'[99] The meeting lasted six hours. Some of the time was taken up with debating Smith's demand that only he would speak for the group. On 19 July 1993 the National Executive Committee approved the changes. The trade unions or, at any rate, some of them held a demonstration. Smith said that these were 'new proposals' which had 'not yet been considered by the Labour movement'. Nevertheless, 'I recommend them'.[100] They were as follows:

The leader and deputy leader would be elected separately. If there was a vacancy for either post, the nomination had to be supported by 12.5 per cent of the parliamentary party. If there was no vacancy – if there was a challenge, which could take place annually – the nomination had to be supported by 20 per cent. Trade unions and other affiliated organisations, constituency parties, and Labour members of the European Parliament could also nominate candidates. But they had to be Labour members of the Commons. Presumably (the new rules did not say so explicitly) the same requirements about levels of support from Labour MPs would also apply. Voting would take place so that the result could be declared at the annual conference.

However, when the party was in government and the leader was Prime Minister, and he or she 'for whatever reason' became 'permanently unavailable', the Cabinet in consultation with the National Executive Committee would appoint one of its members to serve as party leader (and presumably as Prime Minister as well, though the new rules did not say so) until a ballot could be carried out. When the party was in government, and the deputy leader became unavailable, the Cabinet in consultation with the NEC would appoint one of its members to serve as deputy leader, who would hold office until the next party conference. Alternatively the

Cabinet or, in opposition, the Parliamentary Committee – the Shadow Cabinet – could leave the post vacant until the party conference.

When the party was in opposition and the leader for whatever reason became unavailable, the deputy leader would automatically become leader temporarily. The NEC would decide whether to hold an immediate ballot or to elect a new leader at the next conference. When the party was in opposition and the leader and deputy leader both became unavailable, the NEC would order a postal ballot. After consulting the Parliamentary Committee, the NEC might choose to appoint a member of that committee to serve as leader until a new one was elected.

Voting would take place consecutively in three sections. The first would consist of Labour MPs and Labour MEPs; each would have one vote. The second would consist of all individual members of the party; each would have one vote. The ballot would take place nationally and be counted as an aggregate vote broken down by constituency parties. The third would consist of those members of affiliated organisations, chiefly trade unions, who had indicated that they supported the Labour Party and were not members or supporters of any other party or ineligible to join Labour; voting would be by means of one person, one vote, recorded by each organisation and added up nationally. If no previous declaration of eligibility and support had been made, the ballot paper would provide for one.

Each section would have a third of the total vote. The votes of every candidate would be calculated as a percentage in each section. The votes so proportioned would be added up, and the candidate receiving more than half of these would be declared elected. If no candidate reached this total on the first ballot, further ballots would be 'held on an elimination basis': that is, the party would employ its traditional exhaustive ballot. When the party was in opposition, the election of leader and deputy leader would – subject to the exceptions already noted – take place at the conference. When the party was in government and the leader was Prime Minister, the election would take place only if requested by the majority of the conference on a card vote. Presumably this would apply to the deputy leader as well. The trade unions, owing to the size (even if reduced) of their block vote at the party conference, accordingly retained some element at least of their old power, to be exercised only over the dismissal of a Labour Prime Minister.

At the Trades Union Congress in September 1993 the delegates were impressed by Smith's 'obvious sincerity and came away believing that, at heart, the Labour leader was a friend of the union movement'.[101] On the Sunday evening before the start of the Labour conference, Blair, Brown, Prescott and Kinnock all spoke at a fringe meeting (in a hall which was too small, and from which many had to be turned away) in favour of one member, one vote.[102] It should be remembered that at this stage and, indeed, throughout the one member, one vote controversy, union indignation was directed less at the proposals about the election of party leader than at those about the selection of party candidates.

It was by no means certain that Smith would win over either or both. It was rumoured that he would resign if defeated. There was much skulduggery, long familiar to students of the Movement. For instance, the white-collar union, MSF, was neutralised by a procedural device. The rule changes introducing one member, one vote were lumped together with another change which laid down that there must be one woman on every parliamentary shortlist. Roger Lyons, the general secretary, persuaded the union to abstain.

Margaret Beckett, the deputy leader, gave no support to Smith. She wanted him to lose, both because she was honestly opposed to most of and maybe all the changes he was introducing and also because she was ambitious to succeed him if he resigned. John Prescott behaved differently, though his instincts were probably closer to Mrs Beckett's than to Smith's. His speech was generally believed to have swung the vote in Smith's favour. It concluded:

> There's no doubt this man, our leader, put his head on the block when he said he believes of [in] a relationship and a strong one with [between] the trade unions and the Labour Party. He's put his head there, now's the time to vote, give us a bit of trust and let's have this vote supported.[103]

The changes were passed by a majority of 0.2 per cent. If he had been defeated Smith would have arrived at the NEC meeting that evening with a proposal that there should be a second vote the next day, the Thursday. If he had lost that one too, he probably would have resigned. But, as things turned out, there was no need to put his resolution to the test. As Smith's biographer wrote:

> his victory was possibly the most important and most lasting legacy of Smith's short period as party leader. It meant that the leadership election which followed his death would be played out under a set of rules which made it impossible for anyone to win by fixing votes in smoke-filled back rooms. The votes would be cast by individual supporters of the Labour Party, rather than [be] nominated totals on ballot papers submitted by union leaders and constituency party delegates. It could be said therefore that Smith scored his biggest success 10 weeks after his death.[104]

TONY BLAIR IN 1994

Smith died of a heart attack on 12 May 1994. Ten days later Mrs Beckett appeared on *Breakfast With Frost* and saw herself described as 'acting leader' on Sir David Frost's teleprompter. She asked for it to be changed to 'leader', as it duly was. As she correctly pointed out, there was no such title as 'acting leader' in the Labour constitution.[105] On the Wednesday afternoon following Smith's death, the Shadow Cabinet agreed that no contenders for the leadership should declare until after the European elections on 9 June. This injunction had little effect. By the weekend after Smith's death each of the candidates had a campaign team. Nigel Griffiths and Nick Brown were working for Gordon Brown; Richard Caborn and Derek Fatchett for John Prescott; Alun Michael, Peter Kilfoyle, Jack Straw, Andrew Smith and Marjorie ('Mo') Mowlam, who appointed herself campaign manager, for Blair, with Anji Hunter and Barry Cox, the fundraiser, from outside Parliament. Peter Mandelson became Blair's press adviser straightaway, and was known as 'Bobby', after Bobby Kennedy, not as a sign of affection, though it may have been that as well, but to preserve his anonymity. He told some journalists not to write Brown off; he told others that the new leader would be Blair. Blair and Brown met on the Sunday after Smith's death for their first discussion. Both were embarrassed. Blair was prepared to concede that Brown could defeat him for the leadership but maintained that he was better placed to win a general election.[106]

This was a new form of election. It was not clear how much – or how little – influence union leaders would have over their members. Jack Dromey of the transport workers and John Monks of the TUC tried to prevent union executives from making recommendations. In this they were largely successful. However, Blair's sponsoring union, the transport workers, decided to recommend Mrs Beckett. The municipal workers, Unison and MSF made no recommendations to their members.

Ms Mowlam enlivened the campaign by telling John Patten, the then Conservative Education Secretary, that Blair was worried about the restricted or otherwise inconvenient space for his family at No. 10.* She told him this as they were travelling together on a train. Patten immediately made her remarks public, to general amusement.

On 24 May Blair gave a speech to a conference on the family and crime, in which he said that the break-up of 'family and community bonds' was 'intimately linked' to a breakdown of law and order. Family and community alike relied on notions of mutual respect and duty. It was in the family that people first learnt to 'negotiate the boundaries of acceptable conduct' and to recognise that they owed responsibilities to others as well as to themselves. They then extended themselves from the family to the community and to society as a whole. The values of a decent society were in many ways the values of the family unit, which was why helping to re-establish 'good family and community life' should be a 'central objective of government policy'. That could not be done without policies, especially on employment and education, which improved 'society as a whole'. We did not 'show our children respect' or 'act responsibly to them' if we failed to provide them with the opportunities they needed 'with a stake in the

---

* She turned out to be right. After the 1997 election Mr and Mrs Blair found No. 10 inconvenient as far as accommodation went, and exchanged places with the Chancellor, Gordon Brown, at No. 11.

society' in which they lived. This was perhaps Blair's first reference to that stakeholding society which was to play such a large part in his subsequent pronouncements. As early as 24 May, there could be no doubt about his candidature.

There was more doubt about the ambitions of Mrs Beckett, formerly Smith's deputy, now, as she had firmly pointed out to Sir David Frost, leader; though she had omitted to tell him that, under the new rules of the previous year, she was leader *pro tem*. At the National Executive Committee she said that she wanted an election for the deputy leadership to take place at the same time as the election for the leadership. Normally it was uncontested at the party conference. Mrs Beckett would almost certainly have occupied the deputy leadership unopposed (the more so in view of her impressive parliamentary and other public performances in the weeks after Smith's death), even though Blair would have preferred somebody else. Her only reason for wanting to hold both elections simultaneously was that she wanted to contest both the leadership and the deputy leadership. It was a gamble on her part: she might lose both, as she proceeded to do. It also allowed John Prescott to enter the contest as the representative – embodiment, even – of the old Labour Party.[107]

Gerald Kaufman, one of the most experienced Labour MPs, asked Peter Mandelson to see him in his room at the House of Commons. He told Mandelson that the Labour Party was lucky to have two first-rate candidates in Gordon Brown and Tony Blair. However, there was only one vacancy. So would Mandelson please tell Brown that he would be 'crushed' if he stood against Blair and that accordingly he should announce his withdrawal from the contest?[108]

On Bank Holiday Monday, at dinner at Joe Allen's restaurant, Covent Garden, Brown told his supporters Nick Brown and Charlie Whelan (who was not an MP but his press officer) that he had decided to withdraw. Next evening, on 31 May, Brown had his more famous dinner, with Blair at the Granita restaurant, Islington, within walking distance of the Blairs' house in the same borough. It was the kind of modern restaurant which charged hefty prices for fresh pasta with shaved parmesan and wilted spinach. In effect Brown surrendered to the inevitability of Blair's victory. He did not eat much at the Granita, and was later spotted having a second dinner at Rodin's restaurant, Westminster.[109]

Brown formally announced his withdrawal on the next day, 1 June. He said he was doing so because the news had already become public. He added that he would be supporting Blair. On *Channel 4 News* Neil Kinnock expressed 'relief' at not having to choose between the two of them. Brown did not blame Blair but resented Mandelson's activities: he had, so Brown thought, changed sides abruptly. Brown also thought, correctly but perhaps inconsistently, that Mandelson had been backing Blair all along. Anyway, Brown's relationship with Blair survived, whereas his relationship with Mandelson did not.[110]

On Saturday 11 June Blair formally announced his candidature at the Trimdon Labour Club in his Sedgefield constituency. On 13 June the candidates debated on the BBC television programme *Panorama*. Mrs Beckett argued in favour of the trade unions' having a continuing 'collective voice' in the affairs of the Labour Party. Blair differed markedly in tone, saying that he did not agree that the party should support the repeal of 'all trade union law' since 1979. Most of the audience were members of the transport workers' executive. Only two of them hissed under their breath. Altogether the campaign avoided the examination of points either of emphasis or of difference. Blair and Mrs Beckett clearly disagreed on trade unions; Prescott advocated a target for reducing unemployment; there was not much else.[111]

The National Executive Committee's instructions for the election stated that everyone entitled to vote would be balloted individually using a ballot paper specified by the Labour Party. Unity Security Balloting Services would conduct the ballot on behalf of the NEC in the MPs-MEPs' and individual members' sections of the electoral college. Voting would be by postal ballot using preference voting on a single ballot paper: instead of using a cross, individuals would have to list their preferences, 1, 2, 3, ...

This was to embrace the alternative vote. The system that had been endorsed by the 1993 party conference specified the exhaustive ballot. This was the method used by the parliamentary party for electing a leader before 1981. The bottom candidate (or candidates, if their combined votes were fewer than those of the candidate immediately above them) dropped out and had second and, if necessary, third preferences redistributed until one of them obtained an absolute majority. Under the alternative vote the voter's preferences were fixed for the duration of the election; under the exhaustive ballot he or she could change them as the election proceeded. The failure to follow the rules aroused no adverse criticism or, indeed, comment of any kind, except in the political column of the *Independent on Sunday*. Leading members of the party explained casually that to follow the rules exactly would take up too much time and prove too expensive.[112]

Ballot papers would be dispatched on 30 June 1994. Individual party members would be eligible to vote if they had been members on 25 May 1994. The NEC asked all affiliated organisations such as trade unions to conduct postal ballots. Why their ballots also could not be conducted by Unity Security Balloting Services was never adequately explained. But each individual from the affiliated organisations' section would be asked to sign this declaration: 'I support the principles and policies of the Labour Party, am not a supporter of any organisation opposed to it and pay a political subscription to the body that issued the ballot paper.'

If any affiliated body were unable to conduct a full postal ballot, they would have to consult the NEC Procedure Committee to ensure that the proposed ballot met with the committee's requirements. The results would be totalled and then calculated as a percentage of that third of the electoral college. 'There will be no block votes.' If no candidate received more than

50 per cent of the electoral college in the first round, the candidate who came bottom would be eliminated and his or her votes redistributed according to the second preference on the ballot paper. This process would continue until a candidate received more than 50 per cent. If finally two candidates tied, the person with most first preferences won. The result would be announced at a special meeting called by the NEC of representatives from each section of the electoral college. There would be no special conference.

The results were declared on 21 July 1994. Tony Blair had won an absolute majority in every section of the new third-third-third electoral college: among the affiliated organisations, 52 per cent to John Prescott's 28 per cent and Margaret Beckett's 19 per cent; among the constituency parties, 58 per cent to Prescott's 24 per cent and Mrs Beckett's 17 per cent; and, among the MPs and MEPs, 60 per cent to Prescott's 20 per cent and Mrs Beckett's 20 per cent. Aggregated, these proportions worked out as 57 per cent for Blair, 24 per cent for Prescott and 20 per cent for Mrs Beckett, who also lost the deputy leadership to Prescott by an aggregated total of 43.5 per cent to 56.5 per cent. In the parliamentary party, Blair's support was not as overwhelming as Smith's had been but it was greater than Kinnock's had been.

Once again, the choice of the Labour MPs had corresponded to the choice of the Labour Movement. The Movement had not imposed an unsympathetic figure on its representatives in Parliament – one of the principal arguments used before the adoption of a new method of choosing the leader in 1981. Once again, Labour had been lucky with its newest fancy franchise.

Part III

The New System

6

Tory Democracy

More appropriate for the enstoolment of an African tribal chief.
Humphry Berkeley, on the old method of choosing
a Conservative leader, 3 July 1963.

On 1 January 1964 a young Conservative MP, Humphry Berkeley, wrote to the Prime Minister, Sir Alec Douglas-Home, saying that in March 1963, 'before the leadership of the party was in dispute' – and, incidentally, before the epigraph to this chapter – he had declared in public that he felt that the party should 'adopt a more formal method of choosing a leader'. The events of Blackpool 1963 and after had 'emphasised this need and would have done so, whoever had emerged as leader of the party'. Since then, he had had 'many talks with our colleagues in the House', including 'senior members of the government'. He had discovered a 'widespread view' that they should not continue with the present system which 'in any event, as practised a few months ago, bore little resemblance to what has been known as the customary process'.[1]

He asked Sir Alec, as leader of the party, to consider setting up a small committee to consider the matter, hear opinions and make recommendations. He added that nothing he had said implied 'any criticism of your leadership of the party' and perhaps presumptuously but nevertheless typically took 'this opportunity of sending you every good wish for an outstandingly successful year'.[2]

At this time Berkeley (who died in 1994) was 37 and the Member for Lancaster. He had represented it since 1959. He was the son of Reginald Berkeley, the playwright (author of *French Leave*), and had been educated at Malvern and Pembroke College, Cambridge, where he had been President of the Union. In his last year at the university he had assumed the character of H. Rochester Sneath, a fictitious headmaster. As such he had written to numerous dignitaries, asking for their views on various matters of concern. The letters and the replies are much funnier than Henry Root's productions – not least because the joke is maintained with consistency – and almost as funny as *The Diary of a Nobody*.[3]

He possessed a scornful expression and a superior manner, products of his masterful nose and curling lip, and was not universally popular among his fellow-Members. Once, leaving a Chinese restaurant where he had lunched with Anthony Howard, the journalist, and noticing that his shoelace was undone, he summoned a waiter to retie it. Howard was so embarrassed by his companion's demand that he knelt down and retied it himself. This behaviour owed more to Berkeley's imperious and demanding nature than to any prejudice against those with differently coloured skins. On the contrary: he was renowned not only for his political and business connections with Africans but also for the affection in which he held them. An elderly fellow-Member once asked him why he was so fond of them. 'I simply love their little woolly heads,' he replied. Afterwards the Member could be heard musing to his friends about whether Berkeley was wholly sane. There could, however, be no doubt about his courage, which had been demonstrated both over Commonwealth affairs and with his campaign to implement the Wolfenden proposals for reform of the law on homosexuality.

Redoubtable though he was, it was perhaps surprising, nevertheless, that Sir Alec replied to him in so friendly and accommodating a manner. He wrote on 14 January 1964 that he was 'not averse' to the idea of a 'private study' which might be used on some future occasion. But he did not think it would be wise to initiate this study before the election. It would inevitably become known, and would then be taken 'as evidence of dissatisfaction with the present leadership', though Sir Alec appreciated his 'assurance that it does not'.[4] Sir Alec ended by inviting Berkeley to get in touch with him later in the year. On 21 January 1964 Berkeley indicated that he and his friends, who included Peter (later Sir Peter) Tapsell, were 'happy to leave the matter in abeyance until after the election'. He added masterfully that the prospective study 'should not be so private as to prevent all interested parties from giving their views quite freely'.[5]

Sir Alec's view was that, for the sake of any future holder of his position as leader, the processes of choice must be reviewed, even though the 'magic circle' of selectors had 'almost everything to be said for it'.[6] The Whips 'knew the form of every runner in the field'. Some people felt, however, that 'candidates favourable to the establishment' had the advantage over 'anyone who might at any time have been rebellious'. There were always those who, 'stirred up by the media', were ready to charge the magic circle with 'rigging the result'. He had not been worried until this accusation 'began to reverberate through the constituencies and to affect party morale outside Parliament'. He then concluded that, 'with all its disadvantages', it was necessary to adopt a system of election, 'where from start to finish everything was seen to be open and above board'. He was 'in the best position to see that business through'.[7]

After the surprisingly narrow Conservative defeat in the general election of 1964, Sir Alec kept his word. On 5 November 1964 he told the 1922 Committee that he proposed to review the mechanism for choosing a leader. Berkeley at once resumed his correspondence.[8] In December he submitted a memorandum. Sir Alec consulted principally Lord Blakenham, formerly John Hare, and the new Chief Whip, William Whitelaw.[9]

On 26 February 1965 he came down to the 1922 Committee and announced his decision on the procedure to be followed in future for the selection of the new leader of the party.

The leader would be elected by Conservative (and National Liberal) Members of Parliament, and the machinery supervised by the Chairman of the 1922 Committee. Candidates would be proposed and seconded in writing. If, on the first ballot, a candidate received both an overall majority and 15 per cent more of the total number of votes cast than any other candidate (what soon became known as 'the surcharge'), he would be elected. If no one satisfied those conditions, a second ballot would be held. Nominations made for the first ballot would be void and new nominations, under the same procedure as for the first ballot, would be submitted, if required, for the original candidates and any others who might be nominated. When Margaret Thatcher was challenged by Michael Heseltine in 1990 it was incorrectly stated in several newspapers that the 1965 procedure had restricted the entire election to those candidates who had originally been nominated, and that late entrants – in effect a new election – had been allowed only with the 1975 changes.* This was not so. If, as a result of any second ballot, one candidate received an overall majority, he would be elected. If no candidate received an overall majority, the three candidates with the highest number of votes would go forward to a third ballot. Each voter had to indicate two preferences, marking his paper '1' and '2'. 'Plumping' – voting for one candidate only – was not allowed; nor is it today. The second preference of the bottom candidate would then be redistributed between the top two. The candidate so elected would be 'presented for election as party leader to the party meeting constituted as at present'.[10] There was no provision for annual re-election. George Hutchinson, the journalist, asked Sir Alec about this. He replied that he 'hadn't discussed it much' or 'thought a great deal about it at the time'. The idea was that 'once a party had elected a leader that was that' and 'it had better stay with him'.[11]

EDWARD HEATH IN 1965

Sir Alec did well in the 1964 election: but opposition suited him less comfortably than government had done. Harold Wilson, the new Prime Minister, did not treat him with much respect. Though relations between Prime Minister and Leader of the Opposition were nothing like as brutish as they were to become (particularly between Margaret Thatcher and Neil Kinnock in 1983-90), it is fair to say that the collapse of civility occurred in this period. It had begun with the elevation of Sir Alec to the premiership in 1963. It was Wilson who was responsible for the collapse. He had previously been in some awe of Harold Macmillan. By 1965 there were

* See below, pp. 189-90.

murmurs of dissent about Sir Alec, whose 'reaction was boredom with the whole business'. Had he been ten years younger – he was then 62 – he might have put up a fight, but he had 'no stomach for it'.[12]

There was no coup. The Executive of the 1922 Committee had considered Sir Alec's position several times and concluded, even though by a majority, that he should stay. On 5 July 1965 a motion signed by 25 backbenchers was put to the 1922 Committee asking for a debate on the leadership. Sir William Anstruther-Grey, the chairman, said he would tell Home. There was no vote.[13] On both 9 July and 13 July 1965 Sir Alec said he was not standing down.[14] But there were grumbles about him on the back benches and in the newspapers. William Rees-Mogg wrote in the *Sunday Times* of 18 July 1965, in one of the few political articles of recent years which have had a discernible effect on the course of events – another was Iain Macleod's article in the *Spectator* – that Sir Alec had played a 'captain's innings', of a kind sometimes to be seen at Weston-super-Mare before the war, when the amateur, usually a 'Blue', would come in to bat at No. 7 or 8 and knock up a small but useful score. It was time, Rees-Mogg wrote, for Sir Alec to surrender the crease.

Though Sir Alec had already decided to go when this piece appeared, it nevertheless concentrated the minds of backbenchers. William Whitelaw, the Chief Whip, and Edward du Cann, the chairman of the party, were constrained to agree – the latter did not require much persuasion – that numerous Conservatives were at one with Rees-Mogg.*[15] On 22 July 1965, at a crowded meeting of the 1922 Committee with Sir William Anstruther-Grey in the chair, he announced his intention of resigning. 'We've been bulldozed into this by the press,' exclaimed Greville Howard, the Member for St Ives.[16] What finally made up Sir Alec's mind, however, was not a newspaper article but an opinion poll which disclosed that a majority of the British people considered Harold Wilson to be more honest and sincere than he was.[17] Sir Alec said that 'I myself set up the machinery for this change, and I myself have chosen the time to use it'.[18]

These words anticipated the fate of Edward Heath in 1975 and of Margaret Thatcher in 1990. Conservative leaders since 1963, excepting John Major, have played a part in – have, in a sense, almost invited – their own downfall. Major invited it in 1995 but successfully resisted it. Unlike his two successors, however, Home himself was not an unsuccessful candidate. The candidates were Edward Heath, Reginald Maudling and Enoch Powell. Iain Macleod was nowhere, as he had been in 1963: Humphry Berkeley estimated he might have obtained 40 votes.[19] Heath had impressed with his handling of the Finance Bill: the adjectives commonly

---

* John Campbell, Heath's most recent biographer, states that it was this article which decided Sir Alec on his course of action. Other evidence is that he had already made up his mind. It is, of course, consistent with both views to conclude that, while Sir Alec had already decided to go, it was the article which finally settled him in his course of action.

applied to him at that time were 'rough', 'abrasive' and 'gritty', all qualities which Harold Wilson was then thought to possess.

But Maudling remained the favourite, even though he had fallen back in esteem since 1963. There was an inchoate belief among Conservatives of a certain sort (more common in 1965 than in later years) that violence had been done to the natural order of succession, which should have been first Butler and then Maudling, with no place for either Macmillan or Home. And yet, even though he was only 48, Maudling's time might have come and gone.

The result was: Heath, 150; Maudling, 133; Powell, 15. To satisfy the 15 per cent rule Heath should have obtained a majority of 45 or more; in fact it was 17. 'That was a turn-up for the book,' Maudling remarked in his usual affable way, and promptly withdrew from the contest.[20] Powell did likewise. At mid-morning on the next day the second ballot closed and there was only one nomination, for Heath. Sir William Anstruther-Grey formally declared him the winner. His election was duly confirmed at the ceremonial party meeting six days later.[21] One of Sir William's successors, Cranley Onslow, neglected to follow this punctilious procedure 25 years later, when John Major failed to satisfy the rules by two votes, and both Michael Heseltine and Douglas Hurd withdrew.[*]

These rules were not properly understood by many Conservative MPs, either in 1965 or on the five subsequent occasions on which a modified procedure was used. It was not merely that they tended to become glassy-eyed whenever percentages were mentioned: they were also what Anthony Crosland would have called 'frivolous' in their attitude to elections. They failed to understand that elections were a serious business which produced important results. They regarded them much as dissatisfied Conservative voters looked upon by-elections, as an opportunity to register a protest. Thus several Conservatives voted for Heath, not because they wanted – still less expected – him to win, but because they wished to administer a shock to 'the old gang' as represented by Maudling. There were signs of greater electoral awareness 30 years later, when a third of the parliamentary party refused to support John Major, who nevertheless declared (or had it declared on his behalf) that he had won a famous victory.[†]

MARGARET THATCHER IN 1975

Ten years later the instincts which had operated for Heath worked against him and for Margaret Thatcher. Inevitably there were differences. In 1965 the Executive of the 1922 Committee had maintained a position of benevolent neutrality, a majority favouring Sir Alec's continuation in office,

* See below, p. 233.
† See below, pp. 239-40.

though without any great enthusiasm on their part. In autumn 1974 the Executive wanted Heath to go. Indeed, from the moment the October 1974 election was lost, it was clear to most observers that Heath could not expect to retain the Conservative leadership for much longer.[22]

On the weekend after the defeat, every member of the 1922 Executive received messages, telephone calls and letters from MPs demanding early consideration of Heath's position. When they met they were unanimous that there should be a contest, not necessarily at once, but certainly in the foreseeable future.[23] John Campbell conjectures that, if he had offered himself for re-election at the very beginning of the new parliamentary session in November, he would have been confirmed in office.[24] It is possible that, if a challenger had presented himself – or herself – at this stage, the sitting leader would still have been victorious.

Instead Heath was distant with du Cann. The Executive responded by inviting him to address the first meeting of the whole committee on 30 October 1974. Heath declined, offering to meet the Executive instead, but only after their re-election, so implying that they had no authority until then. The Secretary, Philip Goodhart, wrote an authoritative letter to *The Times* stating that this was an erroneous view of the Executive's position.[25]

Personal factors were also involved. In 1967, when Heath had been leader for two years, du Cann had been displaced as party chairman and replaced by Anthony, later Lord, Barber. Du Cann and Heath did not like each other. Nigel Fisher insisted that du Cann, placed as he was in a delicate position because of his known antipathy to Heath, conducted the entire procedure over the next few months with 'complete rectitude'. However, William Whitelaw thought with Heath that du Cann was motivated by personal grievance.[26]

At a packed meeting of the 1922 Committee on the day after the Queen's Speech in November 1974, Kenneth Lewis, the Member for Rutland and Stamford, said that the Conservative leadership was 'a leasehold not a freehold'. According to John Campbell, Heath now realised he would have to submit himself to re-election. As he had no intention of resigning, the old 1965 rules would have to be revised. That procedure was applicable only when there was a vacancy. In Nigel Fisher's words: 'It had not occurred to anyone when the rules were first devised in 1965 that a leader who had lost the confidence of a substantial section of his party would wish to continue in office.'[27] According to this interpretation, it was Heath's refusal to resign – when he could have availed himself of the 1965 procedure, if any candidates had presented themselves against him – which led to the changed rules that were to dispose not only of him but of Margaret Thatcher as well.

The suggestion for a review had come originally from du Cann, and Heath accepted it.[28] On 14 November he told the 1922 Committee that it was 'perfectly natural' that, after the election, they should want to discuss the leadership. What the party asked was that this should be done 'reasonably' and with 'restraint and dignity'. The Chairman of the 1922 Committee had reported the committee's view to him. As he understood it, they wished to have a review of procedure. This seemed to be perfectly reasonable. There was no reason why there should be any delay. He 'would wish to get on with it at once'.[29] To carry out the inquiry he appointed Lord Home, as he was once again (he had been granted a life peerage in 1974 as Lord Home of the Hirsel).

The objections to Heath were not primarily doctrinal, even though the first candidate who was thought of as a possible rival and who rapidly disqualified himself was Sir Keith Joseph. They were, rather, that he had mistimed the first election of 1974, had lost both elections of that year and, above all, was rude all the time. 'So *you're* here, are you?' he said to Peter Jenkins, then of the *Guardian*, on noticing him about his reporting tasks in a Hampstead committee room during the first 1974 campaign. He noticed a table of refreshments at the far end of the room. 'So this is where we get the sandwiches, is it?' he said, before moving purposefully in their direction. Stories of his brusqueness, his gaucheness, his lack of small or indeed any talk, his sheer bad manners – omitting to stand up, neglecting to offer a drink, failing to ask about his interlocutor's more pressing concerns – were famous at Westminster. It was one of them which led indirectly to the success of Margaret Thatcher. Airey Neave had suffered a heart attack as a junior Minister in a previous Conservative government. Heath had said to him: 'So that's the end of your political career, then.' Neave now undertook the leadership of Mrs Thatcher's campaign.

In December 1974 Lord Home's committee reported to Heath. It recommended three substantial changes in the voting arrangements: first, that the annual election should, if requested, take place – a challenger required only a proposer and a seconder – so removing the leader's entitlement to stay on at will; second, that the 15 per cent 'surcharge' should be of the whole electoral college, all Conservative MPs, rather than of those actually voting; and, third, that while the electoral college remained unchanged, the arrangements for consulting extra-parliamentary sections of the party should be formalised. The first two changes were of some importance.

Campbell states that the first was for the party in opposition only.[30] This was not so. It was subsequently asserted – at the Conservative leadership elections of 1989, 1990 and 1995 – that this had been the intention, assumption or understanding. But if this had been so, the rules could have said it clearly, whether in 1975 (when the Home proposals were accepted by the party) or on the three subsequent occasions on which they were brought into play. They could have been modified to provide for the possibility of challenge to the leader only when the party was in opposition. They were not so modified, which suggests that the party in Parliament (its protestations to the contrary) cherished the power which it possessed to dislodge a Prime Minister. The party in the country, by contrast, disapproved of this power, and on every occasion since and including 1975 has supported the incumbent against his or her rivals.[*]

The second change made it more difficult for the incumbent to win on the first ballot, as Mrs Thatcher was to discover in 1990. It also made it harder for Heath (who was by now certain to be challenged) to win on the first ballot. Accordingly it immediately became known as 'Alec's revenge'.

In 1974-5 Sir Keith Joseph insisted that he was making way for Mrs Thatcher ('Margaret will stand') rather than for du Cann, whose claims were being advanced by a group led by Peter Tapsell. Du Cann declined, partly because he was not certain to win on the first ballot, but mainly because his then wife Sallie did not want him to allow his name to go forward.

The prevailing theory at the time was that Mrs Thatcher would play the part of that favourite Conservative creature, the stalking horse. She would not beat Heath outright but would do well enough either to deprive him of victory under the rules or, failing that, to shame him into resignation. The way would then be open for William Whitelaw to enter the contest. He could not stand on the first ballot because he was a loyal old soul. But with Heath out of the way he would defeat Mrs Thatcher easily on the second ballot. That was what many people thought. Hugh Fraser also announced his intention of entering the contest as the representative of traditional Conservatism, but he did not campaign.

On 25 January 1975 Heath announced that he accepted Lord Home's proposals, that nominations would close on 30 January and that the election would be held on 4 February. The result of the first ballot was: Thatcher, 130; Heath, 119; Fraser, 16. This was a much bigger upset than that of 1965. Sir Geoffrey Howe, John Peyton and Jim Prior now entered the second ballot, in addition to Whitelaw. The result was: Thatcher, 146; Whitelaw, 79; Howe, 19; Prior, 19; Peyton, 11. She had won an absolute majority of 18. It was an even bigger upset than that of the first ballot.

Margaret Thatcher was to remain leader for 15 years, 11 of them as Prime Minister. The last years were not very successful for her and were difficult all round. The year 1989 was especially troublesome. She dismissed a Foreign Secretary and lost a Chancellor of the Exchequer. During the summer the talk grew about challenging her in the autumn. Michael Heseltine was adamant that he would not do it. Sir Ian Gilmour was hesitant. In the end Sir Anthony Meyer decided to have – or, rather, was persuaded into having – a go himself.

Sir Anthony was a rich, vague, handsome baronet whose manner was at once diffident and self-assured. He sat for Clwyd in North Wales, which used to be Flintshire West until the Welsh-language-crazed boundary commissioners managed to lay their hands on it. He had previously sat for Eton and Slough. When he was offered Clwyd he thought it was in

---

[*] In 1997 John Major resigned immediately after losing the general election. Whether he would have continued to enjoy the constituencies' support if he had stayed is a matter for speculation.

Scotland. His wife Barbadee accompanied him on all his public engagements.[31] He had been a professional diplomat, serving in Moscow, Paris
and London. His instincts were decent and his one political cause was
Europe. When he challenged Mrs Thatcher, he was 69. He was persuaded
into – some might say, put up to – this course by Chris Moncrieff, then the
indefatigable political correspondent of the Press Association.

He was treated with much scorn and some abuse by the cheap press,
but displayed himself to advantage on television. Not for the first or last
time, BBC and ITV acted as a counterweight to the *Daily Express*, the
Daily Mail and the *Sun*, which supported the Prime Minister with a
vehemence that was to be exceeded only in the next year.

If Sir Anthony was dignified, Mrs Thatcher was regal. There was no
campaign to speak of. Its ostensible leader, George Younger, merely let it
be known that the Prime Minister expected all good Conservatives to do
their duty. This method of approach turned out to be an unfortunate
precedent – though Tristan Garel-Jones worked for Mrs Thatcher in 1989
as he declined to do in 1990.* The result of 5 December was: Thatcher, 314;
Meyer, 33; spoilt, 24; abstentions, 3. Sixty (or 16 per cent) of her parliamentary party had refused to support their Prime Minister. This was certainly
damaging enough. What was even more damaging was that Sir Anthony
had demonstrated that a Conservative Prime Minister could be challenged
constitutionally.

The fall of Margaret Thatcher is discussed in detail later on in this
book.† Her supporters, together with a few others who adopted a more
theoretical approach, objected to the removal of a Prime Minister by his or
her backbenchers. But when a sub-committee of the 1922 Committee came
to examine the question in 1991, it made no proposals for any change in
this respect. In particular, Mrs Thatcher's supporters objected to the 15
per cent 'surcharge' which had by four votes deprived her of victory in the
first ballot. But here again no change was proposed. The only substantial
change which *was* proposed – and put into effect in July 1991 – was that,
in default of a vacancy, a contested election could take place only if the
chairman of the 1922 Committee was 'advised in writing by not less than
10 per cent of the members of the parliamentary party' that they believed
such an election to be necessary. In addition, the procedure for consultation was made ostensibly more thorough and more democratic; though,
as before, the final decision about how to cast his or her vote was for the
individual Member. For example, in the period between the close of
nominations and the first ballot it would be the responsibility of the
constituency association 'in conjunction with the Member' to discover 'the
views of their membership regarding the candidates by the most effective
means available'. And the procedure on the third ballot, if any – in the five

---

* It is fair to say that Garel-Jones would have worked for Mrs Thatcher in 1990 if he had
been approached on her behalf before rather than after the first ballot.
† See below, p. 211ff.

elections up till then, none had been held – was tidied up. If no candidate received an overall majority on the second ballot, any candidate might withdraw by informing the chairman of the 1922 Committee. Of those remaining, the two candidates who had received the highest number of votes at the second ballot would go forward to a third ballot. The candidate receiving a majority of the votes cast in this ballot would be elected. If this third ballot resulted in a tie, a fourth ballot would be held 'unless the two candidates are able to inform the chairman of the 1922 Committee that they have resolved the matter between themselves'.

On 9 July 1995, after John Major's challenge to himself, Douglas Hurd supported proposals to end challenges to a Conservative Prime Minister. He told the BBC's *Breakfast With Frost* programme that he had wanted a change ever since the fall of Margaret Thatcher in 1990: 'I think a Prime Minister should be removed either in an election [a general election] or by the House of Commons openly.'[32] In January 1996 a sub-committee of the 1922 Committee began to re-examine the rules. In practice nothing happened. In May 1997, when the Conservatives suffered their worst defeat of the 20th century and were left with 165 MPs (164 after the death of the Member for Uxbridge), they had more or less the same system which Lord Home had bequeathed to them in 1975 and which had replaced Edward Heath with Margaret Thatcher and Margaret Thatcher with John Major. The only substantial change was that an election had to be requisitioned by 10 per cent of Conservative MPs, who had to write to the Chairman of the 1922 Committee.

WILLIAM HAGUE IN 1997

Neither Heath nor Mrs Thatcher had departed voluntarily. Major, like Home in 1965, went of his own choice. Home went nine months after losing an election, Major at once. There were some who criticised him for following this course. John Biffen, for instance, the retiring Member for Oswestry, thought during the general election campaign that Major ought to carry on for a few months at least to allow passions to subside – Biffen was clearly expecting defeat.[33] Major, for his part, felt he had done enough and certainly had suffered enough. On the Friday after the election he announced his resignation and departed for his favourite cricket ground, the Kennington Oval.

Amid the carnage, Major had retained his seat in Huntingdon. So had Michael Heseltine kept his in Henley. But Michael Portillo, to ill-natured but understandable satisfaction all round, lost his in Enfield Southgate. He was an ex-MP. Few conditions are more deserving of the prefix. He could neither vote in the election nor be a candidate for the leadership of his party. The latter disqualification was galling not only to Portillo but also to his supporters, who had recovered their spirits since his less than heroic performance in the election of summer 1995 in which John Redwood had stood against Major. The new contest they had in their sights was Portillo against Heseltine, a straight competition between right and left;

two views on Europe; economic libertarianism and old-fashioned Tory corporatism. It was a competition between youth and age as well, for Heseltine had been 64 in March. Owing to the youth of the new Labour Prime Minister, the younger candidate might well have won it.

Portillo having been eliminated from the competition, there was a case for Heseltine to be elected without opposition. Some Conservatives, including his former supporters, welcomed this prospect unreservedly; though Heseltine in government from 1990 to 1997 had done little enough to deserve such continuing support, having behaved in a scrupulous fashion in omitting to secure any preferment for them. Others thought of him as a caretaker leader: to which those who were less friendly responded that caretakers in politics had a habit of turning themselves into permanent residents. Others again, who were less friendly still, said they would not have Heseltine at any price. He resolved any difficulties when, soon after the election, he went into hospital with a recurrence of heart trouble. He announced he would not be contesting the leadership. It was widely believed that his wife Anne had been crucial in making up his mind for him.

Then occurred a small revolt against the method of electing a leader which had in modified form existed since 1965. It was led by Robin Hodgson, the Chairman of the National Union of Conservative and Unionist Associations, the umbrella organisation of the party's voluntary wing.[34] He wanted every member of the party to have a vote. One difficulty was that it had never been entirely clear who was a member of the party. Quite apart from everything else, its legal existence was full of doubt. But in May 1997 the Conservative Party was in no mood for juridical arguments of this nature. In practice a ballot would, it was reliably stated by Sir George Young, take two years to organise. Even those who had wanted Major to carry on, such as Alan Clark, thought this too long. Clark considered that there should not be a party election till November 1997. Other ingenious proposals were advanced for electoral colleges of various kinds. The party chairman, Brian Mawhinney, suggested that the party's 700-odd constituency chairmen should take part in electing a new leader. Their votes would comprise 15 per cent of the new electoral college, while the rest of it would be composed of MPs.[35]

There were several reasons for this call at this time. One was the Somme-like scale of the Conservative defeat. The mood was that anything should now be tried to prevent any repetition of the catastrophe. Another, perhaps more rational reason was that it was thought that 164 MPs was too small a constituency. Yet another reason was that Labour had an electoral college which had produced Tony Blair, the most successful leader of any radical party in the 20th century, more successful even than Harold Wilson in 1966, C.R. Attlee in 1945 or even (though few went as far back as this) Sir Henry Campbell-Bannerman in 1906. Politicians are like publishers, generals or film producers. They want to imitate the last big success in their field. Labour had enjoyed a great triumph with Blair, who had been produced by an electoral college. The Conservatives could perhaps enjoy a lesser triumph with a leader produced by similar means. That was the way the argument went.

At this stage the candidates were Kenneth Clarke, Stephen Dorrell, William Hague, Michael Howard, Peter Lilley and John Redwood. Dorrell soon withdrew owing to lack of support and the risk of humiliation. He gave his backing to Clarke, who was clear that he wanted the election to take place under the existing rules, though he promised a review once he had been safely elected. The other candidates adopted much the same approach. Some became stronger enthusiasts for party democracy as the contest progressed and the depth of frustration in the local associations became evident. On 7 May, for instance, Hague said he would not change the rules, which had 'stood the test of time' and ensured that the leader was 'chosen by the people who knew the leadership candidates the best'. But on 16 May he promised that if the Conservative MPs elected him he would call a special conference of party representatives to endorse him.

With Major having resigned so precipitately, and Heseltine – virtually the only possible stopgap candidate – having ruled himself out, it is doubtful whether the necessary mechanisms of mass democracy could have been put together in reasonable time. As things turned out, further dispute proved otiose on account of the election of Sir Archie Hamilton as the new Chairman of the 1922 Committee in succession to Sir Marcus Fox, who had lost his seat at Shipley (though it is possible that, even it he had retained it, he would have had to make way for someone else).

Sir Archie had retained his seat at Epsom. He was a very tall Etonian former Guards officer but could be distinctly on the short side in his manner. It was said that if he was unlocatable during a division the Whips would advise one another: 'Look everywhere except the Library.' He resembled a Conservative member of the 1950s, notably in his aversion to and abruptness with journalists. Sir Archie was opposed to any change in the rules. After his election he said that his opposition was 'well known' but whether his views prevailed or not remained to be seen. It was a matter for the whole executive.[36] Unsurprisingly this body supported the new chairman. There was, however, a promise of 'fundamental' reform after the election which was to be held in June. The National Union nevertheless persisted in its plans to give its association chairmen a vote and to publish the results on the day before the first ballot. Hodgson said tactfully that there had been a 'breakthrough' and that an agreement would be reached by Christmas. A new system would be in place for the next contest. But he remained 'very sad and disappointed that not enough MPs could be persuaded to make a change'.[37]

The first ballot was enlivened by an attack on Michael Howard by his former junior minister at the Home Office, Ann Widdecombe. She had been in charge of prisons and was well known – indeed something of a joke – in political circles for steadfastly taking the blame for or even trying to justify assorted grotesqueries which had been perpetrated under Howard's regime, notably the placing of women prisoners in fetters while they were giving birth. Another enormity over which Howard had presided during his period of office was the dismissal of Derek Lewis, the Director of the Prison Service. Miss Widdecombe certainly thought so.

Lewis's expertise lay not in incarceration but in television. In the Granada company he had been highly regarded, loftily placed and munificently rewarded. As a businessman he was, in the fashion of the time, thought by politicians to be efficient. He was in charge of one of those government agencies which had sprouted like broccoli since 1979.[38] Whether efficient or not – and there were those who had their doubts – they certainly caused problems of ministerial responsibility which were similar to those brought about by the newly nationalised industries after 1945.

These unresolved problems were at the core of Miss Widdecombe's complaints against Howard: that he gave specific directions to Lewis which he was not entitled to give but – unlike Miss Widdecombe with her manacled female prisoners – refused to accept the blame when things went wrong, as they frequently seemed to do. For with the privatisations of various aspects of custodial punishment, in particular the coming and the going in a selection of vehicles, prisoners appeared to effect their escape virtually at will. It was such a dash for freedom, in this case from Parkhurst Prison on the Isle of Wight, which was the cause of Howard's dismissal of Lewis. The merits of the case need not concern us here. They were debated in the Commons when Howard, as Home Secretary, scored a notable triumph over the Labour spokesman, Jack Straw. It was almost though not quite as comprehensive a victory as that of Roy Jenkins over Quintin Hogg after George Blake had escaped from Brixton.

Now Miss Widdecombe claimed that Howard had misled the House. Nor was that all. He was, according to her, a thoroughly bad lot. His character had about it, so she told her friends – in a phrase that was to become widely quoted – 'something of the night'. Howard's friends retaliated by claiming she had been infatuated with Lewis; maybe still was. Her opportunity to attack Howard came in the lengthy debate on the Queen's Speech. The consensus was that she had won on points but had failed to deliver the knockout punch. Nevertheless it was agreed that Miss Widdecombe's assault had done Howard's prospects no good.

Certainly Howard did worse than expected in the first ballot on 10 June. Clarke had 49 votes, Hague 41, Redwood 27, Lilley 24 and Howard 23. The National Union had also carried out its promised poll. Among constituency (including Scottish) chairmen Clarke had 322 votes, Hague 188, Redwood 25, Lilley 24 and Howard 23. Among Conservative peers Clarke had 177 votes, Hague 45, Lilley 37, Redwood 13 and Howard 10. Aggregated, with MEPs and 'Eurochairmen' added, Clarke had 608 votes, Hague 278, Lilley 84, Redwood 49 and Howard 26.[39]

Clarke's predominace both with the peers and with the European Conservatives was not perhaps surprising. What was surprising was his popularity with the constituency chairmen. Clarke was a Europhile. They were or were assumed to be Europhobes virtually to a man or woman. Moreover, Clarke was accused in some quarters of having 'lost us the election' by refusing to allow Major to rule out a single currency for the duration of the next Parliament. The lack of evidence that this was a factor in the Conservatives' catastrophic performance did nothing to cause the accusation to be withdrawn. But the constituency chairmen did not believe it; or, if they did, they did not allow it to influence their votes.

The principal reason why Clarke was the overwhelming choice of the party outside the House of Commons was probably that he was better known than any of the other candidates. The party activists invariably support the continuation in power of the existing incumbent. Thus in 1975 they supported Heath, in 1990 Mrs Thatcher and in 1995 Major. In 1965 they would have preferred Home to stay. Whether in 1997 they would have wanted Major to stay is more doubtful. He had, after all, led them to a terrible defeat; whereas in 1964 Home had nearly beaten Wilson. Clarke was not the leader but he was the next best thing currently available.

Under the Conservatives' curious rules the 'second ballot' was not really a second ballot at all but a new election. All the candidates who had stood in the first ballot could in theory stand again, however badly they had done in that first round. Moreover, additional candidates could put themselves forward. In 1975 Edward Heath and Hugh Fraser had withdrawn, while Geoffrey Howe, John Peyton, Jim Prior and William Whitelaw had unsuccessfully joined the contest with Margaret Thatcher. In 1990 she had departed straightaway, and Douglas Hurd and John Major had come forward for Major to win on the withdrawal of Heseltine and Hurd – even though he failed by two to obtain the requisite absolute majority of all those entitled to vote.

In 1997, by contrast, the candidates behaved much as their Labour equivalents would have done in a parliamentary party election before 1981. Michael Howard and Peter Lilley withdrew, as Peter Shore and John Silkin did in 1980, or Tony Benn, Anthony Crosland and Roy Jenkins in 1976. Howard and Lilley then behaved as their Labour equivalents would not have done – not, at any rate, so openly. They jointly urged their supporters to vote for Hague. This was regarded not only as a rebuff for Redwood, who was the sole unequivocal representative of the Tory Right remaining in the contest, but also as a guarantee of victory for Hague in the second ballot.

It became evident that Howard and Lilley could not command their supporters in this peremptory fashion. People believed too that Hague had lost support after saying to a meeting of backbenchers on 16 June that Clarke would have to agree to rule out joining a single currency for ten years if he wanted to be a member of his Shadow Cabinet. This was held to be cheek rather in someone of Hague's youth. At all events, in the election on 17 June Clarke had 64 votes, Hague 62 and Redwood 38. Once again Clarke had surprised his detractors. But he remained well short of the 83 needed to give him his absolute majority.[40]

Within minutes of the result Redwood announced that both Clarke and Hague had already telephoned him. He said Clarke had 'got in first'. Accordingly one 'could say that Kenneth Clarke was a little better organised than William Hague, which might be a reason to vote for him'.[41] A further reason in Redwood's eyes, it soon appeared, was that Clarke had agreed to make him Shadow Chancellor in return for his support.

Norman Lamont, who had failed to be returned at Harrogate, but supported Hague, accused Redwood of 'breathtaking cynicism' and said the arrangement was an 'alliance built on sand'. Sir Peter Tapsell, who *had* been returned for Louth and Horncastle and was a Hague supporter likewise, described Redwood's move as 'one of the most contemptible and discreditable actions by a senior British politician I can recall during my 38 years in the Commons'.[42] But Lord Tebbit – who like Lamont did not have a vote – supported the pact, which was widely compared to the one between Molotov and Ribbentrop. He would, he said, have like Redwood to win 'cleanly'. That had not been possible. The party was not prepared to do it. He believed that 'at the end of the day' it was 'better to have a union between these two men'.[43]

Lady Thatcher, who did not have a vote either, disagreed with her old ally. She had previously refused to declare her hand. There was now, however, a clear possibility that Major's successor would be Clarke. She remained a woman of strong emotions. If there was one Conservative politician she hated above all others – more than Howe, more even than Heseltine – it was Clarke. Previously Hague had solicited her support. She had told her friends that he had failed to impress her. But these were desperate times. She stood outside the House of Commons with Hague and said that she 'most earnestly' hoped he would win and that the Clarke-Redwood pact was 'an incredible alliance of opposites' which would 'only lead to further grief'. To curious reporters she said: 'The name is Hague. Have you got that? Hague.'[44]

Whether because of this endorsement, because MPs were repulsed by the pact or because of both considerations, Hague did better than expected in the third ballot on 19 June 1997 – the first occasion when a Conservative election had reached this stage. He won by 92 votes to 70. Clarke immediately announced that he was returning to the back benches and politely refused Hague's offer of a frontbench job. He said he had decided before the contest (it was well known at Westminster) that, having served on the front bench in opposition and government for 26 years, he would retire to the back benches if he did not win.

Hague went off to be crowned at Conservative Central Office in Smith Square, London SW1, with John Major, the retiring leader, and Brian

Mawhinney, the retiring chairman, filling the archiepiscopal roles. He talked of a 'clean slate' and of an end to factions. He even quoted General Montgomery's appeal to his troops before the battle of El Alamein. But, as Peter Riddell wrote in *The Times*, the Conservatives were not yet at their Alamein. They were still retreating across the desert.[45]

A document entitled a 'green paper' was presented to the Conservative party conference at Blackpool in October 1997. It was a basis for discussion, the name picked up from Whitehall usage. It had been compiled under the auspices of Archie Norman, a prominent businessman who had become an MP at the election. Hague invited the representatives to be as radical and outspoken as they liked about it. They duly were. On 8 October the conference erupted, the match having been applied to the fuse by Lord Archer. He, together with numerous other representatives, blamed Conservative MPs for the party's recent defeat. He demanded a 50 per cent share for the constituencies in any electoral college to choose a new leader. Sir Archie Hamilton said it was essential that any such leader should have the confidence of Conservative Members. They should accordingly have the preponderant voice in any new body. For this view he was jeered. He was jeered even more noisily when he correctly stated that Margaret Thatcher would not have become leader if the decision had been left to the constituencies in 1975 (they had wanted Edward Heath to stay in place). There the matter uneasily rested for another six months.

7

A Fettered Prerogative

Constitutional theory always has and always will emerge from
the hard facts of politics rather than from the textbooks of
professors.

The Times, 24 December 1985

After 1964 there was, as we have seen, a complete change in the Conservative method of choosing a leader. Labour's system was fundamentally
altered in 1981, and then again in 1993.* In 1990, following the deposition
of Margaret Thatcher, the new Conservative system, as modified in 1974-
5, was used effectively to appoint John Major. In 1976, following the
retirement of Harold Wilson, the old Labour system of election by the
parliamentary party alone was used to appoint James Callaghan. In the
first of the 1974 elections Labour did not have an absolute majority over
the Conservatives. Edward Heath could possibly have continued in office.
This episode is discussed later on.† It was an example of a situation when
the old politics were relevant – as, indeed, they might still be. But the first
of the post-1965 examples was straightforward enough.

HAROLD WILSON IN 1966

In the general election Labour won 363 seats, the Conservatives 253, the
Liberals 12 and others 2. Harold Wilson continued in office without the
need for formal reappointment.

EDWARD HEATH IN 1970

When the Sunday papers appeared on 14 June 1970, four days before the
election, there was almost total unanimity about the likely result. The
Sunday Times's weekly summary of five opinion polls recorded variations
in the Labour lead from Gallup's 2.5 per cent to NOP's 12.4, with an
average of 6.4. Wilson tells us that our leading national bookmaker ceased
taking bets on Labour, having imposed odds which, allowing for tax,
represented 34 to 1 on. He, however, 'was one of the few who had doubts',
though he 'would have found it difficult to rationalise them'.[1]

---

* See ch. 5 above.
† See below, pp. 200-3.

At 1 a.m. on Friday 19 June the Wilsons left the Adelphi Hotel, Liverpool, for the count in his nearby constituency, Huyton. His result was declared just before two, but results in the rest of the county were far less satisfactory. Indeed, it was by now evident that, contrary to most expectations, Labour had lost the election. At three the Prime Minister set out by car for Downing Street. He arrived just after seven. His political secretary, Marcia Williams, had already telephoned the staff there to tell them to start packing.[2]

At 11.30 a.m. Roy Jenkins, the Chancellor, called and stayed for 20 minutes. Jenkins found him 'looking appallingly battered', but he was 'wholly calm and unrecriminating'. Recriminations would have been understandable because, within the Labour Party, Jenkins was accused of sacrificing the party's prospects of re-election to his own wish to be considered a man of honour, as demonstrated by his refusal to introduce a tax-cutting pre-election Budget. Whether such recriminations would have been justifiable is outside the scope of this book. At all events, Wilson said 'Well, there it is' and proceeded to rehearse to Jenkins the speech which he proposed to make in the debate on the Address.[3]

Soon after lunch on the Friday, Wilson publicly conceded that Labour had lost. But he could not resign formally until the early evening because the Queen was at Ascot. The crowd in Downing Street laughed, clapped and shouted 'Out, out, out' as Ministers arrived to say goodbye.[4] Meanwhile Heath was waiting in the Albany, watching television. The final result was Conservatives 330, Labour 287, Liberals 6, SNP 1, Others 6. At 6.50 p.m. he was driven to the Palace to kiss hands and then, shortly before seven, to No. 10.[5]

HAROLD WILSON IN MARCH 1974

The result of the election was Labour 301, Conservatives 297, Liberals 14, SNP 7, Plaid Cymru 2, Northern Ireland 12, Others 2. On Friday 1 March 1974 it was clear that no party would have an adequate majority in the House of Commons. In the afternoon the Labour Shadow Cabinet met at Transport House and decided to make a statement. This emphasised the need for the government 'to deal decisively with the economic and industrial crisis facing the nation'. In these circumstances, it continued, 'the Labour Party is prepared to form a government and to submit its programme for the endorsement of Parliament'.[6] According to Jenkins, there was 'no mood of euphoria'. The only excitement was provided by the news that Heath was not resigning but trying to cobble an arrangement with the Liberals.

Wilson became agitated at this and talked about issuing a denunciation of constitutional impropriety. Callaghan and Jenkins were both strongly against this course.[7] In his memoirs, however, Wilson made no such charge against Heath. Indeed, he went out of his way to emphasise the correctitude of the course adopted by him. He was still the Prime Minister 'and there was no vacancy'. The position traditionally taken by Buckingham Palace in this kind of situation, following an 'unclear' election result or (Wilson added) a vacancy occurring during the lifetime of an elected Parliament, was 'not always understood'. There were suggestions in March 1974 that, as Labour had more seats than any other party, the Sovereign should have sent at once for the Leader of the Labour Party. This was not so. A government was in existence, and until it resigned, following an election or a defeat on the Queen's Speech, the Palace could only observe the classical doctrine: 'We have a Government.'[8]

To Marcia Williams, however, Wilson said that Heath's conduct was 'rather as if the referee had blown the whistle and one side had refused to leave the field'.[9] Wilson's reflections on constitutional propriety were *ex post facto*. At the time, it appears, he had to be restrained by his colleagues. It was resolved that no one would 'make any news comment, claim or forecast' over the weekend – a self-denying prescription which, exceptionally for the Labour Party, was followed – and that the Shadow Cabinet would meet in the Leader of the Opposition's room on Monday morning.[10]

On the Friday morning Heath held a quick Cabinet meeting which authorised him to see what he could do about staying in office. He then went to Buckingham Palace to report to the Queen, who had returned hurriedly from Australia. Heath persuaded himself that an agreement with the Liberals was possible and would make sense. It would not, however, have provided an absolute majority. For this, he needed 318 votes. An alliance with the Liberals, however firm, would have given him only 311. Cecil King – a witness to be treated with caution – recorded that Heath was trying to make up the deficit by offering the Conservative whip to seven of the 11 Ulster Unionists (that is, those who had not become Democratic Unionists).[11]

But first Heath telephoned the Liberal leader, Jeremy Thorpe, who returned from Devon for a meeting in Downing Street that lasted two hours. Robert Armstrong, then the Prime Minister's private secretary, was also present. Heath offered what he inaccurately called a 'coalition' with the Liberals. They would be allocated only one place in the Cabinet, which would be occupied by Thorpe. Both he and Heath seem to have assumed that this would be the Home Office, though no specific post was mentioned. Heath also offered a Speaker's Conference to examine the case for electoral reform. Thorpe replied that he must have time to consult his party. He would have liked to be able to accept. The Liberals in the country were, however, angry at the idea that their party might sustain a discredited Conservative government. Many of Thorpe's parliamentary colleagues were annoyed. The only terms which might have been acceptable would have included a specific promise to introduce proportional representation. Late on the Saturday, David Steel drove Thorpe to the side door of No. 10. Heath confirmed that only a Speaker's Conference was on offer: there was no promise to accept its recommendations.[12]

What the Liberals' response would have been if such a promise had been made is a matter for speculation. It would have amounted to something less than a commitment to proportional representation. The conference – the traditional British way of settling these matters and no more than a committee of MPs under the chairmanship of the Speaker – might have recommended no change, or some new system which was unsatisfactory to the Liberals, such as the alternative vote.[13] The Liberal mood against 'keeping the Tories in office' was strong. On Monday morning the 14 Liberal MPs met and agreed a final rejection of Heath's offer. They called instead for an all-party government of national unity – an idea which was to be taken up by Heath himself seven months later at the second general election of 1974. Thorpe wrote to Heath: 'I do not believe that a Liberal presence in the Cabinet, designed to sustain your government, would be acceptable.'[14]

Jenkins believes that 'in a hung Parliament there is a lot to be said for getting your opponent to lose his room for manoeuvre first'.[15] The view of Heath's biographer is that he was 'tactically inept'. Had he resigned immediately and allowed Wilson to form a government, he would have retained the right to try again if Wilson failed. The Queen, Campbell asserts, would not automatically have had to grant Wilson a dissolution, but could have turned back to Heath.[16] While this expresses the constitutional position accurately enough, it is doubtful whether the Queen would have followed the course indicated. There is no question that Wilson could have 'formed a government' in the sense of assembling a Cabinet and filling other ministerial posts. He was vulnerable to defeat in the House. If this had occurred, he could have asked for a dissolution. In modern conditions, there is little doubt that the Queen would have granted one, however inconvenient this might have been to her loyal subjects and to herself.

On Monday the Shadow Cabinet met again. The tone, Wilson wrote subsequently, was 'more than a little impatient'. Shirley Williams and Tony Benn were dispatched to prepare a press release. While they were still at work, messages arrived saying that the Cabinet meeting had broken up and that Ministers were 'clearing their cupboards'. The Shadow Cabinet adjourned. The private secretary at No. 10 telephoned Wilson's office, as he had on Friday, to ask where he might be found.[17] He also said that Heath was going to the Palace at 6.30. Sir Martin (now Lord) Charteris, the Queen's private secretary, telephoned: 'Would it be convenient, Marcia, for Harold Wilson to be at the Palace at 7.00 p.m.?'[18] The Queen asked Wilson whether he could form a government. He replied that he could. He was confident that, on its first test – the adoption of the Queen's Speech – it would be supported by the House of Commons.[19]

HAROLD WILSON IN OCTOBER 1974

In the second general election of 1974 Labour obtained 319 seats, the Conservatives 277, the Liberals 13, the SNP 11, Plaid Cymru 3 and others 12, of whom 10 were Ulster Unionists. This gave Labour one more seat than the 318 which was required to provide an absolute majority in a House containing 635 Members. Wilson continued as Prime Minister but was disappointed at the result; while his entourage of Joe Haines, Marcia Williams and others were distinctly unhappy with it.[20]

JAMES CALLAGHAN IN 1976

No domestic political event of modern times aroused as much suspicious interest as Harold Wilson's resignation. All kinds of fanciful tales were made up about it: he was shortly to be arrested as a Russian spy, the government was on the point of collapse, he was suffering from a mortal disease. The last two of the then current stories were not, perhaps, completely exaggerated. For Wilson's health was already a cause for concern, certainly to himself; and he was later to undergo and survive an operation for cancer. Moreover, during the IMF crisis later that year James Callaghan's administration very nearly did come to pieces.[21] It is entirely possible that Wilson foresaw the sorry happenings that were to follow, and wanted no part of them. The general course of events leading to his resignation was, however, clear enough, and possessed no sinister quality.

The reason why people thought the event required further explication lay partly in the modern notion – which was to reach its apogee in the succeeding decades – that no one ever voluntarily resigned from anything, certainly not from what was in theory the most powerful position in the land. But it lay more in the climate of the time.[22] People were prepared to believe the most strange stories about politicians. These tales concerned not so much the routine corruption which was to become the small change of political discourse 20 years later as, rather, events partaking of a quality of fantasy. And, at a time when the Leader of the Liberal Party was to be arraigned on a charge of conspiracy to murder (of which he was acquitted), who was to say that the stories were as strange as all that?

In fact Wilson was fed up with politics, particularly Labour politics. And who could blame him? He had wanted to resign for a long time. On 13 May 1970 he told Roy Jenkins, the then Chancellor, that though he would be well short of 60 he was determined to hand over the premiership in the next Parliament. He said there were two possible dates: the Labour Party conference in October 1972, or just before midsummer 1973. On 14 June 1973 he would have been in office for a day longer than H.H. Asquith and accordingly (in that pre-Thatcher era) the longest serving Prime Minister of the century.[23] In August 1970 the political columnist of the *New States-man* reported that, if he had won the June election, as he had expected to do, it was his intention to resign in two years or so.[24] In these circum-stances his successor would probably have been Roy Jenkins. The information in this article was neither denied nor the occasion for much surprise. It came not, as some quite reasonably supposed, from the newly appointed editor of the paper, R.H.S. Crossman, but from the then more junior Labour figure, Roy Hattersley.

In 1972 Wilson told Denis Healey that he did not intend to serve another full term as Prime Minister.[25] In February 1974 Labour won the election called by Edward Heath and in March Wilson formed his third administration, for the first time as a minority government. He decided that he would not continue in office for more than two years, even if he won the second election which was inevitable.[26] That was Wilson's own account. When Bernard (now Lord) Donoughue joined his Downing Street staff in March 1974, Wilson told him to arrange two years' leave from his academic post at the London School of Economics. He intended to retire in Spring 1976 on reaching his 60th birthday.[27] He said to Donoughue: 'I have been round this racetrack so often that I cannot generate any more enthusiasm for jumping any more hurdles.'[28]

Soon after the general election of October 1974, Wilson approached Dr Thomas Stuttaford in the Athenaeum. Stuttaford, Conservative Member for Norwich South from 1970 to February 1974, had just fought the Isle of Ely unsuccessfully as a Conservative and been readopted as candidate. Wilson wished him good luck in his future contest, adding that he would not be in the House to welcome him, as he planned to retire in two years. Dr Stuttaford asked him why. Wilson replied that there were several reasons, but the best was that his late mother had started to suffer from senility at about the age he would attain in 1976.[29]

Joe Haines, one of Wilson's entourage, tells us that one of the reasons was that he wanted people to ask 'Why did he go?' rather than 'Why did he stay?'[30] Early in 1975 it became increasingly clear to Haines that Wilson was determined to proceed with what Haines described as 'his oft-expressed ambition' to resign. In March 1975 Wilson's political secre-tary, Marcia Williams (already Lady Falkender), asked Haines and other familiars whether they realised that Wilson intended to resign within a few months. This was earlier than they had expected. She asked them what they 'were going to do about it', presumably with a view to persuad-ing Wilson to stay in office longer rather than to finding a congenial successor. But answer, it appears, came there none. Haines, for his part, thought it right for Wilson to resign for his health's sake. In his account he made no reference to senility as such but wrote that Wilson's strength was no longer inexhaustible.[31]

At this stage Heath had just been dislodged from the Conservative leadership. As Leader of the Opposition he had enjoyed the use of an official car. He had inaugurated this practice when, as the new Prime Minister, he had given Wilson a car in 1970. Wilson had repaid the courtesy in 1974, when he had become Prime Minister for the second time round. Now Wilson made a ruling that all former Prime Ministers should have a car. He foisted one on Lord Home, who did not want one, and on Lord Avon, who had no need of one. The drivers of the Government Car Service concluded that the reason he had done this was that he himself was shortly to retire. Tony Benn put this story to Wilson during one of his numerous farewell dinners in March 1976. Wilson maintained that the change had been made 'for security reasons'. Marcia Williams, however, confirmed Benn's version, describing him as 'a naughty man' for having brought it out.[32]

For some time Wilson had had the party conference of October 1975 in mind as his retirement date. Mrs Williams was opposed to this: both because she wanted him to stay and because the resignation of Harold Macmillan during the Conservative conference of 1963 was not a happy precedent. This is what Mrs Williams subsequently wrote.[33] But Macmillan had resigned at the very start of the conference, so throwing the event into the utmost confusion. If Wilson had resigned on the last day, before the rendition of 'The Red Flag' or thereabouts, that consideration would not have applied.

Wilson's first self-constructed hurdle was the European Community negotiation, followed by the referendum. This was successfully surmounted in June 1975. But his plans were put out by the balance of payments crisis in the following month.[34] It nevertheless became apparent to Mrs Williams that he really was going to resign on or near his 60th birthday in 1976, 'as he had said all those years ago'.[35] In the summer of 1975 he discussed the details with Kenneth Stowe, his secretary at No. 10, and with Joe Haines. Haines compiled a detailed 'resignation timetable' – which was, however, to be disrupted by Princess Margaret's divorce.[36]

In September 1975, on the Prime Minister's annual visit to Balmoral, he informed the Queen's private secretary that he intended to submit his resignation six months later. George Thomas, the Speaker of the House of Commons, spent the first weekend of October at Chequers; Wilson told him likewise of his intention. On 9 December 1975 he formally told the Queen at his weekly audience that 11 March 1976 'or thereabouts' would be the date.[37]

This was also the evening of the annual dinner of the Newspaper Publishers' Association. Lord Goodman was in the chair. At the end of the festivities he turned to the host and said: 'Oh, Arnold, I mentioned that matter to the Queen.' This suggests, though Wilson does not say so explicitly, that Goodman had already been told.[38] The Queen, as has been noted, was first told through her private secretary in September 1975. Later, Barbara Castle asked Goodman when Wilson had told him that he was going. Goodman said it was 'well before' Christmas 1975, though he had not given a precise date, except to say that he did not want to stay after Easter.[39] Wilson had said this at a dinner party of Goodman's, though he may also have told Goodman separately.[40] Goodman thought that Wilson had been a little blatant and that his meaning would immediately be understood by the newspaper proprietors who were within earshot. This was what Wilson wanted:

> The 9 December exercise was designed to make [medical] stories less likely, and also to discourage others attributing my 'sudden' resignation to an impending national crisis, or ... some great revelation.[41]

Alas, those present failed to comprehend what Wilson was getting at. Far from being crude, he had – not for the first time – been too clever for his own good. The 'Wilson Resignation Mystery' stories, which he had correctly anticipated, were unabated. In the same month Harold Lever told Denis Healey that he thought Wilson would announce his resignation soon.[42] On Boxing Day 1975 Roy Jenkins and his wife lunched with Ann Fleming at her country house, Sevenhampton. Lord Goodman was also present. He took Jenkins aside and told him that Wilson was determined to resign in March, probably on his 60th birthday. Though this was 'a great secret', Goodman had decided to tell him because he preferred Jenkins rather than anyone else as Wilson's successor.[43] Wilson, however, did not take Jenkins into his confidence, any more than he did Healey.[44]

He did not tell Callaghan either. Callaghan found out as Healey had, from Lever, who telephoned on Boxing Day 1975. He said that what he had to tell Callaghan must be treated in the 'strictest confidence'. The Prime Minister had made a 'firm decision' to resign in March 1976, and Callaghan must prepare himself to take over. This last part of the message presumably had Wilson's authority, for Lever had held out no hopes of the succession when talking to Healey. Callaghan decided to tell only his 'closest friend', Merlyn Rees, who advised him to stand. Nevertheless Callaghan, as Foreign Secretary, decided to carry on with his overseas trips for the first part of 1976.[45]

Marcia Williams refused to accept Wilson's decision, even in the early months of 1976.[46] Wilson replied that he had always taken the view that Ministers should retire at 60, when they were still young enough for another political post (though Wilson himself neither accepted nor, as far as is known, was offered a major position of this nature). Besides, when a Minister had been in office for a long time, he inevitably became stale. With the same problems coming up again and again – in 1974-6 this was the most frequently given of Wilson's reasons for resignation, in conversations both with Mrs Williams and with others – government and

Prime Minister lost their original vigour. A certain enthusiasm disappeared.[47]

Yet Wilson's 60th birthday, 11 March 1976, was marked not by his resignation but merely by a dinner party given for him by his publisher George Weidenfeld. Wilson and Callaghan, who was also at the dinner, had to leave before ten to vote in a Commons division on public expenditure. Wilson asked Callaghan to travel with him to the House. Wilson now told Callaghan what Lever had already told him on Boxing Day 1975, though in greater detail. He intended to call a special Cabinet meeting on the morning of 16 March to tell Ministers of his intention to resign. Meanwhile Callaghan should begin to make preparations for the forthcoming contest.[48] Mrs Williams was told three days later, on Sunday 14 March at Chequers. This was the first time she had been informed of the precise date.[49]

In the debate on public expenditure 37 Labour Members abstained and the government was defeated by 28. Healey had a row with the Left which almost certainly affected his vote adversely in the election that was to follow.[*] In the car, returning from the House to Weidenfeld's dinner party in Chelsea, by now in its closing stages, Callaghan urged Wilson not to resign at such a moment. But he could see that his mind was made up.[50]

At 9.30 on 16 March Wilson had an audience with the Queen and tendered his resignation 'to take effect as soon as a successor was appointed'.[51] At 10.30 the Cabinet met. Wilson told Healey beforehand in the lavatory outside the Cabinet room.[52] He told Edward Short, the deputy leader, in his study.[53] Tony Benn recorded that those Ministers who had not been taken into Wilson's confidence, as the majority had not, were 'stunned'. But they were so 'in a curious way, without emotion'.[54] According to Roy Jenkins, 'there were one or two cloying statements round the table, which Wilson rather elegantly brought to an end by withdrawing to prepare some necessary statements'.[55]

Barbara Castle was 'all unsuspecting that Harold's time-bomb was about to go off'. But when Eric Varley, the Secretary for Industry, passed her a note asking whether she had been aware that Wilson was going to do this, she replied: 'I can't answer that question.'[56] This was odd, because it implied, if anything, that Mrs Castle had indeed been told, and did not want to hurt Varley's feelings or to cause any division in the Cabinet over who had and had not been told. Yet it appears that she was in the majority who had not been told by Goodman, by Lever or by Wilson himself. It was five days later when she discussed the resignation with Goodman.[57]

Contrary to Jenkins's account, Mrs Castle tells us that Wilson, far from bringing the proceedings elegantly to a close, embarked on a detailed story of the background to his resignation. He had, he said, made up his mind to resign when he won the election two years previously, in February

---

* See above, pp. 140-1.

rather than in October 1974. Healey later maintained that Wilson lost heart after having failed to do in October 1974 what he had managed in 1966 – that is, significantly to increase his majority. This contention is at odds with Healey's own claim that as early as 1972 Wilson told him that he would not serve another term as Prime Minister.[58]

There was, Wilson continued, never a 'right time' to implement such a scheme. But he thought he had chosen the 'best possible' moment. He had considered resigning before the 1975 conference or at Christmas 1975 but decided that the government's pay policy was in 'too delicate a balance'. It was, however, right to go before he became enmeshed in the next pay policy round. He had thought of his 60th birthday on 11 March 1976 as an 'excellent moment'. But unfortunately there turned out to be two by-elections on that day. He had also thought of waiting till summer 1976, but decided that this would be 'awkward' for his successor, who ought to have a chance to 'play himself in' before the House rose for the recess and the next party conference.

These explanations may have been prolix but they were both reasonable and consistent one with another. Mrs Castle, however, found them 'casual' and 'almost incredible'. We must remember that Mrs Castle's political life, at any rate in the higher reaches of the Labour Party, was – no doubt unjustly – drawing none too peacefully to its close. So was that of Mrs Marcia Williams. The difference was that Mrs Castle had been taken by surprise by the sudden departure of her patron and protector; whereas Mrs Williams had not, even though she had not been told the exact date until the last minute.*

Wilson having left the Cabinet to prepare some statements of his own, it was another Mrs Williams, Mrs Shirley Williams, who proposed that the remaining Ministers should minute a tribute to Wilson immediately. Mrs Castle added that they 'ought to issue something to the press'. She and Shirley Williams were sent away to draft a suitable document, 'which we did', Mrs Castle tells us, 'short and sweet but making it quite clear that the Cabinet had been taken by surprise'. After some amendment by Callaghan and Jenkins it was agreed and issued. Sir John Hunt, secretary to the Cabinet, added a short preface to the effect that the statement had been agreed by the Cabinet in the Prime Minister's temporary absence.[59]

The subsequent election, which Callaghan won, has already been discussed in chapter 4.† Other Prime Ministers had resigned in office: Anthony Eden in 1957, Winston Churchill in 1955, Neville Chamberlain in 1940, Stanley Baldwin in 1937, Ramsay MacDonald in 1935. Baldwin was at the end of his political career and departed voluntarily. His was perhaps the nearest precedent to that of Wilson in 1976. Eden and Churchill were both forced out, on the ostensible grounds of, respectively,

---

* See above, p. 207.
† See above, p. 138ff.

ill-health and old age; though Churchill put up a longer, harder and more successful fight than Eden.[*] Chamberlain likewise was forced out, and put up a fight of sorts for a few days.[†] What distinguished Wilson's case was not so much that he resigned voluntarily in office as that his successor was chosen by election and presented to the Queen.

In 1945, as we have seen, Harold Laski led a plot to have the leader re-elected by the new parliamentary party whose members had been the beneficiaries of Labour's landslide. The party was quite different in numbers and composition from the one that had elected C.R. Attlee in 1935. But Laski, though a great theoretician, was less concerned with implementing any theory of democracy within the parliamentary party than with having Attlee replaced by Herbert Morrison. As we have also seen, Laski's scheme was frustrated by Ernest Bevin.[‡] If it had succeeded, with Morrison leader in Attlee's place, it is by no means certain that George VI would have accepted the change and summoned Morrison instead. For one thing, Attlee had been Churchill's deputy – and, in effect, Prime Minister of the home front – during the war and was known to the King. And, for another, it was he and not Morrison who had been leader when Labour won the election.

Neither of these arguments was brought up at the time. The Laski conspiracy was short-lived and, from Attlee's point of view, not specially serious. The latter argument – that it was the sovereign people who chose a Prime Minister, at a general election – was heard more strongly in the 1990s: in 1990, when Margaret Thatcher was dislodged in favour of John Major, and in 1995, when Major successfully sought to have himself confirmed in office both as Leader of the Conservative Party and as Prime Minister. But of this argument surprisingly little was heard in 1976. It may have been because Callaghan was seen as the inevitable and somehow correct leader of the Labour Party, and also because (perilous though the Labour government's position undoubtedly was) the new Prime Minister was seen by the Conservative Party as a dangerous opponent in any election for the inexperienced new Leader of the Opposition, Margaret Thatcher.

Accordingly the cries for a general election to confirm Callaghan in office were muted. Instead the criticism was of the usurpation of the Queen's prerogative to choose her Prime Minister. Norman St John-Stevas (later Lord St John of Fawsley) – biographer of Walter Bagehot, editor of his collected works, confidant of several members of the royal family and admirer of all things regal – was, perhaps inevitably, the most prominent and hostile critic.

But the cry was not taken up. The cock refused to fight. Who, after all,

---

[*] See above, p. 53ff.
[†] See above, pp. 47-8.
[‡] See above, pp. 51-2.

could object to Mr Callaghan? The Labour Party's position was certainly clear enough. It had been laid down with magisterial dignity in January 1957 after Harold Macmillan had succeeded Anthony Eden in what were, by and large, unedifying circumstances.* James Callaghan was chosen by the parliamentary party, as Harold Wilson and others had been before him and Michael Foot was to be after him.

Neil Kinnock and John Smith were chosen by the electoral college set up after the Wembley conference of 1981 in which trade unions and constituency parties could in theory comprehensively outvote Labour MPs. In fact the majority of Labour Members clearly supported the person voted in by the electoral college. So likewise did they support Tony Blair, who was elected by something approaching a universal party franchise. Even so, it was fortunate, in a way, that Kinnock did not succeed Foot as Prime Minister, or Smith succeed Kinnock in the same circumstances. For the prerogative argument would then have carried more weight. It could plausibly have been claimed that our Prime Minister was being chosen not by Her Majesty but by assorted Bills and Berts, operating the corrupt system of the block vote, whereby voting strengths were calculated on the number of affiliated members, which often bore the most arbitrary relationship to the number of members who paid the political levy or, sometimes, were members of the union in total.

Happily, or alas, it did not happen. Neither Smith nor Kinnock was called upon to submit himself for election as leader while a Labour government was in office or after a Labour Prime Minister had died or resigned. Callaghan was so required and, under a different electoral system, the occasion went off splendidly, from a constitutional point of view.

Cledwyn Hughes (later Lord Cledwyn), the chairman of the parliamentary party, came to Wilson's room in the House bearing the result of the final ballot. Wilson telephoned the figures to the Queen's private secretary. At the party meeting Callaghan made a speech of acceptance and thanks.[60] He also went to Transport House to meet the party officers because he 'wished to make the symbolic gesture of linking the party in the country with the Labour Members of Parliament who had elected me'.[61] Wilson went immediately from the party meeting to Buckingham Palace to tender his resignation. He did not recommend Callaghan as his successor. He said that the Queen was already aware of the voting figures he had sent her, which meant that Mr Callaghan was the elected leader of the Parliamentary Labour Party.[62]

While he was still at Transport House, Callaghan was telephoned by the Queen's private secretary, Sir Martin Charteris, who asked: 'When would it be convenient for you to come to the Palace?' He left immediately with Mrs Callaghan, who waited in an ante-room as the Queen received

* See Appendix A.

him and invited him to form a government. The kissing-of-hands ceremony took place a week later.[63]

MARGARET THATCHER IN 1979, 1983 AND 1987

In March 1979 James Callaghan's government was the first since 1924 to be defeated on a vote of confidence. At the subsequent general election the Conservatives won 339 seats, Labour 269, Northern Ireland Members 12, Liberals 11, Scottish National Party 2 and Plaid Cymru 2. Margaret Thatcher became Prime Minister. The audience at which a politician receives the sovereign's authority to form a government comes to most Prime Ministers only once in a lifetime. Authority is unbroken when a sitting Prime Minister wins an election. So it was with Mrs Thatcher.[64] In 1983 the Conservatives won 397 seats, Labour 209, Alliance 23 (Liberals 17, Social Democrats 6), Northern Ireland Members 17, Scottish National Party 2 and Plaid Cymru 2. In 1987 the Conservatives won 376 seats, Labour 229, Alliance 22 (Liberals 17, Social Democrats 5), Northern Ireland Members 17, Scottish National Party 3 and Plaid Cymru 3.

JOHN MAJOR IN 1990

The displacement of Margaret Thatcher in November 1990 was the most shocking political event of modern times. For it overturned the beliefs of a whole generation (perhaps of several generations) of political scientists and constitutional analysts in the impregnability of a United Kingdom Prime Minister with an adequate parliamentary majority and in good physical and mental health. In 1990 Mrs Thatcher satisfied all these criteria except perhaps the last, though the doubts concerned not so much her sanity as her mental balance.[65] Almost a year afterwards Professor Anthony King of the University of Essex said that he still had difficulty in coming to terms with the event. Professor Philip Norton of the University of Hull persisted in maintaining, in the face of evidence, that the Cabinet had played a subsidiary part – if, indeed, any part at all – in events, and that Mrs Thatcher's downfall had been brought about by the Conservative MPs.[66]

As Francis Bacon wrote, it were infinite to judge causes, or the causes of causes. If Mrs Thatcher had not taken the line she did on Europe, and said 'No. No. No' in the House on 30 October 1990, Sir Geoffrey Howe would not have made the speech he did, and Michael Heseltine would not have stood in the first ballot, where Mrs Thatcher obtained an absolute majority of those entitled to vote, so clearing the first hurdle set up by the rules, but failed to obtain the 15 per cent 'surcharge', so falling at the second hurdle. It is a matter of opinion whether she would have won conclusively in the second ballot. It can also be argued that the very need for a second ballot demonstrated such a lack of confidence in her that she should not have allowed her name to go forward.

This was not the argument which most of that fatal procession of Ministers who saw her on 21 November put directly to her. What they said was that, if she decided to stand – which they devoutly hoped she would not – they would of course support her. But they did not think she would win. Mrs Thatcher was not deceived, even if Professor Norton was. On television, in one of a series of programmes designed to publicise the first (chronologically the second) volume of her memoirs in 1993, she memorably described the Cabinet's behaviour as treachery with a smile. And when, shortly after the event, a colleague said that they were 'going to pin regicide on Heseltine', she replied: 'Oh no, it wasn't Heseltine. It was the Cabinet.'[67]

The fall of Margaret Thatcher had numerous causes extending over many years. She should probably have left office in 1989, having served for a decade. In April 1990 Lord Carrington, her former Foreign Secretary, annoyed her over dinner at his house when he said that the party wanted her to leave office both with dignity and at a time of her own choosing. She took this to be, as she was later to put it, 'a coded message'. 'Dignity' might suggest 'a rather earlier departure than I would otherwise choose'. Carrington was, she suspected, 'speaking on behalf of at least a section of the Tory establishment'.[68]

She fell out with her most senior Ministers, Geoffrey Howe and Nigel Lawson. She and Lawson agreed about the role of the state in general – both were on the minimalist side – but they came to differ about monetary and exchange rate policy. Her view was that a government could concentrate either on the money supply or on the exchange rate but not on both. It was 'an entirely practical issue'. In her opinion, the only effective way to control inflation was by using interest rates to control the money supply. If a government set interest rates to fix a particular exchange rate, it was 'steering by a different and potentially more wayward star'.[69]

In the early months of 1988 her relations with Lawson worsened. She sought to discourage excessive exchange rate intervention on his part 'but without much success'. It seemed to her 'contradictory' to raise interest rates while simultaneously intervening to hold down the value of sterling.[70] On 10 March 1988 she told the House of Commons that the Chancellor and she were absolutely agreed that the paramount objective was to keep inflation down. The Chancellor never said that aiming for greater exchange rate stability meant total immobility. Adjustments were needed, as we had learnt when we had a Bretton Woods system, and as those in the EMS had learnt.

Mrs Thatcher has asked herself whether she should not have dismissed her Chancellor at this stage. She writes that he was pursuing a policy without her 'knowledge or consent' and that he 'continued to adopt a different approach from that which he knew I wanted'.[71] The second count of the indictment against Lawson may be true. The first – that Mrs Thatcher did not know of her Chancellor's policy of 'shadowing' the German mark – is more difficult to justify. Indeed, in a newspaper interview she admitted that she knew about Lawson's policy, and went on to say that to allow it was her 'great mistake'.[72]

Mrs Thatcher left Lawson where he was. He resigned in October 1989. Quite apart from the position of Sir Alan Walters as the Prime Minister's economic adviser – something to which the Chancellor not unnaturally took exception – there was a clear difference of policy. Lawson believed that the exchange rate should be 'an essential element of financial discipline, with the rider, incidentally, that exchange rate stability is itself an economic benefit'.[73] Mrs Thatcher later told Kenneth Baker that she feared Lawson would not have gone quietly.[74] Instead she decided to move the apparently less dangerous Geoffrey Howe from the Foreign Secretaryship to the Leadership of the House.

This change deprived him of the government-owned country house, Chevening in Kent, to which he and Elspeth, Lady Howe, had become much attached and which, indeed, they tended to treat as the ancestral home of the Howes of Aberavon. Howe was punished because, with Lawson, he threatened to resign at the Madrid European summit meeting if Mrs Thatcher did not give a firmer commitment to join the exchange-rate mechanism of the European Monetary System. Howe resigned not from the Foreign Secretaryship (as some erroneously believe) but from his new post after the Rome summit meeting, after which Mrs Thatcher found herself in a vociferous minority over a single currency. Europe was accordingly part – a most important part – of the course of events which were to lead to her resignation. Bernard Connolly, a European civil servant, has written:

> Mrs Thatcher said 'no' ... to a single European currency. For the rest of the Community, and for the Euro-enthusiasts in her own country, she had committed a political capital offence. She had to be got rid of quickly.[75]

There is not the slightest evidence that European political leaders or civil servants played any part whatever in Mrs Thatcher's downfall. Indeed, the former group were surprised by the event, some even saddened. True, all the United Kingdom politicians who played the principal roles in her fall – Geoffrey Howe, Michael Heseltine and Tristan Garel-Jones – were enthusiastic Europeans. It is also the case that they were all Welsh: Howe from Aberavon, Heseltine from Swansea and Garel-Jones from Llangennech near Llanelli. As well describe the Fall of Thatcher as a Welsh conspiracy as a European one! As the constitutional historian F.W. Maitland wrote, what is now in the past was once in the future. Or, as the former Minister John Biffen put it shortly afterwards:

You know those maps on the Paris metro that light up when you press a button to go from A to B. Well, it was like that. Someone pressed a button, and all the connections lit up.[76]

If we are looking for one cause which brought Mrs Thatcher down, it was the poll tax. Backbenchers refused to support her in the numbers they did because they feared they would lose their seats at the election, not because they possessed views on Europe which were different from hers or, indeed, views on Europe of any description. She herself wrote that the opposition to her approach towards the Community was 'very much a minority view'.[77] The unpopularity of the poll tax was compounded by the result of the Eastbourne by-election on 18 October 1990, which the Liberal Democrats won after Mrs Thatcher had compared them to a 'dead parrot' – it is doubtful whether she herself understood the reference – at the Bournemouth conference shortly beforehand. The effect of the defeat was to strengthen further the belief among MPs that Mrs Thatcher could not win an election.[78]

Meanwhile, at the Rome summit, Mrs Thatcher was fighting what she described as 'a lone battle'.[79] Geoffrey Howe went on television and told Brian Walden that Britain did not oppose the principle of a single currency. This implied that Mrs Thatcher 'would probably be won round', which was 'either disloyal or remarkably stupid'.[80] In the summer Lady Howe asked her husband whether he should press on with his challenge to the Prime Minister to dismiss him if she dared. Or should he resign? And, if so, when and in what circumstances? Howe himself was 'deeply reluctant' to play a part in allowing the government to 'slip still further in the direction of prime ministerial domination'. Nor did he relish the prospect of mounting hostility towards what he called a 'balanced view of Britain's role in Europe'. Nevertheless, in July 1990 he decided to stay in the government.[81]

In early October, paradoxically, Britain finally joined the ERM, following pressure on the Prime Minister by the Foreign Secretary, Douglas Hurd, and the Chancellor, John Major; Hurd having partially converted Major to his own high opinion of the scheme. Far from being properly grateful, Howe was piqued because he was the last to be told. It was a 'dramatic signal' to him personally of the 'impossibility of securing the sort of effective working arrangement' with the Prime Minister for which he had 'genuinely hoped' when he decided to continue in the government.[82] It was Mrs Thatcher, so Howe believed, who was being disloyal to the Cabinet by advancing the 'clear view' that the United Kingdom would never participate in any future arrangements for European monetary union.

Howe was unhappy about the situation that was emerging. He consulted his personal assistant, Anthony Teasdale, and his parliamentary private secretary, David Harris. They confirmed his instinct to wait till the afternoon of Tuesday 30 October 1990, when Mrs Thatcher would be making a Commons statement on the Rome summit.[83] Howe sat on her right. At first, reading from a prepared text, she was moderate enough:

> On economic and monetary union, I stressed that we would be ready to move beyond the present position to the creation of a European monetary fund and a common Community currency which we have called a hard ecu. But we would not be prepared to agree to set a date for starting the next stage of economic and monetary union before there is any agreement on what that stage should comprise (*Hear, hear*). And I again emphasised that we would not be prepared to have a single currency imposed upon us, nor to surrender the use of the pound sterling as our currency.[84]

The Leader of the Opposition, Neil Kinnock, was combative but not specially so. In the course of his observations he mentioned Sir Leon Brittan, a European Commissioner, and his divergence from the Prime Minister's views. This appeared to annoy her disproportionately:

> Leon Brittan is a loyal member of the Commission. Yes, the Commission wants to increase its powers. Yes, it is a non-elected body and I do not want the Commission to increase its powers at the expense of the House, so of course we differ. The President of the Commission, Mr Delors, said at a press conference the other day that he wanted the European Parliament to be the democratic body of the Community. He wanted the Commission to be the Executive and he wanted the Council of Ministers to be the Senate. No. No. No.[85]

Howe was particularly exercised by the attack on Jacques Delors. He could not, even if he had wanted to, 'feign enthusiasm for this stuff'. His discomfiture was obvious. No less obvious, he thought, was 'the increasingly nationalistic crudity of the Prime Minister's whole tone'. On the next day, 31 October, he decided to resign; attended his last Privy Council meeting as Lord President; and went out to lunch with John Cole of the BBC.[86] Mrs Thatcher heard nothing from him.

At Thursday morning's Cabinet meeting she berated him, in her opinion 'probably too sharply', about the preparations for the legislative programme in the new session.[87] One of the confusing elements of the 1990 Conservative crisis was that it was played out in the period when the old, 1989-90 session was ending and the new, 1990-1 session beginning. Howe's last Cabinet marked the administrative, as distinct from the formal, start of the new session. As it also marked a display of prime ministerial beastliness to the Lord President, who resigned later that day, it has acquired a certain mythological status. Howe wanted a Cabinet directive to departments to get their Bills ready. Mrs Thatcher had only to 'utter four or five words' to meet his point. Ministers would do the rest. But to his 'astonishment' Mrs Thatcher turned on him: 'Why aren't these Bills ready? Isn't it the Lord President's responsibility to see that this kind of thing has been done?' Colleagues, according to Howe, were as amazed as he was by this outburst. Having already decided to resign, he said to himself: 'What the hell. This is positively the last time.'[88]

According to Cecil Parkinson, Mrs Thatcher gave Howe 'a very rough ride'. He felt the performance was 'unjustified and unnecessary'. The atmosphere was 'distinctly cool' but 'not noticeably more so than usual'.[89] According to Kenneth Baker, Mrs Thatcher was 'unnecessarily rude', and for about ten minutes asked a series of 'niggling questions' about which Bills were and were not ready for introduction.[90]

By this time her differences with Howe, unlike the rows she had had with Lawson, were 'as much a matter of personal antipathy as of policy'. They found each other's company 'almost intolerable'. She was, however, surprised at the immediate grounds of his resignation. She did not know, and in 1993 claimed still not to know, whether he was in favour of a single currency.[91] Mrs Thatcher was relieved by Howe's resignation but at the same time had no doubts about the political damage it would do: 'All the talk of a leadership bid by Michael Heseltine would start again.'[92] She retired to her study to consult the colleagues: Kenneth Baker, the party chairman; John Wakeham, the Energy Secretary; Tim Renton, the Chief Whip; and Alastair Goodlad, his deputy.

Mrs Thatcher wanted Norman Tebbit in the Cabinet as Education Secretary. He refused. Renton wanted William Waldegrave instead. She demurred. The post went to Kenneth Clarke, with Waldegrave at Health and John MacGregor as the new Leader of the House in Howe's place.[93] Baker found Mrs Thatcher 'peering rather myopically' at Howe's letter of resignation. She 'suddenly looked a lot older'. What could the party chairman say? 'There wasn't very much.' But he emphasised a phrase in Howe's letter about 'mood'. He did not like the Prime Minister's 'style'.[94]

Baker repeated this analysis, if such it can be called, several times, on television and elsewhere. It was taken up by Sir Bernard Ingham, the Prime Minister's press secretary, and was approved by the Prime Minister. It is believed by her, or so she says, to this day. Not only was it manifestly untrue. It was also a political error. It greatly annoyed Howe. Admittedly he was annoyed anyway. Otherwise he would not have resigned. But his resignation speech – at this stage ten days away – would almost certainly have been different if Baker had not pursued the course he did.

On the next day, Friday 2 November, Heseltine telephoned Howe. He began by saying that he was sorry about but not surprised by Howe's resignation. He went on to say that he was on the point of leaving for a short but long-arranged visit to the Middle East. But on the next day he intended to issue an open letter to his constituency chairman. Howe confirmed to Heseltine that he had no intention of standing against Mrs Thatcher for the leadership. Heseltine said 'that that remained his position also' – presumably meaning that he did not intend to stand against

Mrs Thatcher *simpliciter* rather than that he did not intend to stand against her if Howe was a candidate also.[95]

On Saturday 3 November Mrs Thatcher was working at Chequers on her speech on the Loyal Address. That evening Ingham telephoned to read out Heseltine's open letter. It said, among other things, that if decisions continued to be taken and imposed which did not carry 'the collective endorsement', the strains would 'continue to show and be our undoing'. Ostensibly the letter was about the need for the government to chart a new European course. In fact – as Mrs Thatcher saw on that Saturday evening – it was Heseltine's 'first tentative public step' on his way to the leadership.[96]

On Sunday the papers were full of stories about the coming contest. There were the opinion polls taken after Howe's departure, which showed Labour with leads of 14 and 21 per cent. Alan Clark advised Mrs Thatcher on the telephone to sack Tim Renton and make Tristan Garel-Jones Chief Whip instead. She refused, saying: 'Oh, but he's enjoying his present job so much.' She was clearly referring to Garel-Jones, who had recently been transferred from the Whips Office to a junior post at the Foreign Office, rather than to Renton, who never gave the impression of enjoying his job at all, and was, indeed, an inexplicable appointment for Mrs Thatcher to have made, the more so in view of his long association with Howe. Clark recorded: 'I don't think she realises what a jam she's in.'[97]

On Monday 5 November Kenneth Baker and Kenneth Clarke dined together. Clarke, according to Baker, 'had no time' for Heseltine and thought he should 'stop messing about'.[98] On 7 November Howe issued a statement to counteract the assertions of Baker and Mrs Thatcher: 'When I come to speak I shall be dealing with matters of substance as well as style.'[99]

By 6 November Mrs Thatcher certainly realised that a challenge of some kind was being discussed. A contest had to take place within 28 days of the opening of the new parliamentary session. But the leader, in consultation with the Chairman of the 1922 Committee, could nominate an earlier date. This Mrs Thatcher and Cranley Onslow, the then chairman, proceeded to do. Mrs Thatcher claims that it seemed best to 'bring matters to a head' and to 'get the leadership campaign, if there was to be one, out of the way quickly'.[100] It might equally be said that, with the connivance of Onslow, she was trying to forestall a contest of any kind. They agreed to bring forward the date for the closing of nominations to Thursday 15 November with the first ballot on Tuesday 20 November. This meant that she would be in Paris for the European summit when the first ballot occurred, if there was to be one. It was to prove a costly error, and a course from which Onslow, who was surprised by her choice of 20 November on account of her absence abroad, tried to dissuade her.[101]

Meanwhile Heseltine's constituency officers had, with some misguided help from a Central Office agent, prepared a less than enthusiastic reply to him. Ingham imprudently added to the pressure on Heseltine with a typical sentence: 'He'd better put up or shut up.' By the second half of the week beginning Sunday 4 November, Heseltine was once again in touch with Howe. According to Howe, Heseltine's 'thinking had moved on from the previous Friday'. If he did decide to stand against Mrs Thatcher, he asked, would Howe be prepared to support him in the ballot? Heseltine emphasised that he had not yet taken any decision. Howe replied that he would have to think very carefully.

On Saturday 10 November Howe returned Heseltine's call. He told him that he did not feel able to give him the assurances he wanted. For he was determined to remain innocent of any charges of conspiracy. He could not be seen to be acting in a way which implied, even though falsely, that he might have resigned in order to hand the leadership over to Heseltine. As for his own chances, his advisers knew as well as he did that his position was by now weaker than it had been in July 1989. Fifteen months in the 'ambiguous role' which Mrs Thatcher had forced upon him had 'taken its toll'.[102]

On 12 November Mrs Thatcher spoke at the Lord Mayor's Banquet. She was wearing an Elizabethan cloak, a black velvet dress and pearls. She looked like Mary Queen of Scots on her way to the scaffold. In the course of her observations, which were chiefly about events in the Gulf, she said:

> I'm still at the crease, though the bowling's been pretty hostile of late (*Applause*). And, in case anyone doubted it, can I assure you that there will be no ducking the bouncers, no stonewalling, no playing for time? The bowling's going to get hit all round the ground. That's my style.[103]

Why, some observers wondered on hearing these preposterous remarks, did our politicians turn to cricket for their imagery when they had never shown the slightest interest in the game, still less any knowledge of it? What was more interesting, however, was that at this stage Mrs Thatcher clearly expected a challenge from Michael Heseltine. On the same day Alan Clark recorded:

> The Whips have totally clammed up. A bad sign. Already they have gone into 'neutral' mode. Secret policemen burning the old files, ready to serve.[104]

Parliament had assembled for the State Opening and the Queen's Speech on Wednesday 7 November, the first such occasion in 15 years when Geoffrey Howe had no frontbench position. He had no need to appear in the House till the time came for his own intervention. He decided to speak on 13 November after Prime Minister's Questions. The House would, he hoped, be reasonably full. By that stage of the all-purpose debate, the better-known politicians would already have spoken: there would be less competition for the attention of the press. He penned the first version of the speech on 10-11 November, and revised it over the next two days. The text from which he spoke for 15 minutes was the fifth or sixth version. His wife Elspeth – contrary to much jocular speculation at the time – played no part in the writing. She did, however, hear successive drafts. Of one of the later ones she said: 'Geoffrey, are you sure you need to go that far?'[105]

Just before mid-day on 13 November the Speaker's Office telephoned. The subject chosen for the fifth day of the Debate on the Queen's Speech was Education. It would 'set a bad precedent' for a former Leader of the House such as Howe to speak on more general matters, though he could so if he insisted. However, there was a way out of the difficulty. As he was making a resignation speech, there was no reason why he should not make it in the form of a personal statement, at the start of business. But it was not to last for more than 20 minutes.[106]

Just before 4.20 on 13 November Mr Speaker Weatherill introduced him with: 'I remind the House that a resignation statement is heard in silence and without interruption.'[107] Howe was wearing a grey suit, a white shirt and a grey-blue tie with white spots. Nigel Lawson sat on his right scowling, as was his habit when he considered that a serious expression was required. Mrs Thatcher wore dark blue and a fixed smile, which became more strained as proceedings developed. She had John Major on her right hand on the front bench, Kenneth Baker on her left. Howe was by now of course on a back bench, diagonally over Mrs Thatcher's right shoulder. He held his notes as if sheltering them from the rain. He began by rebutting the charge laid by Baker:

> It has been suggested, even, indeed, by some of my Right Honourable and Honourable Friends, that I decided to resign solely because of questions of style and not on matters of substance at all. Indeed, if some of my former colleagues are to be believed, I must be the first Minister in history who has resigned because he was in full agreement with government policy (*Loud and prolonged laughter*). The truth is that, in many aspects of politics, style and substance complement each other. Very often, they are two sides of the same coin.[108]

Then came the most important part of the speech. He had agreed with Lawson not only a year previously, at the time of the Chancellor's resignation, but five years previously, when entry into the ERM was first mooted. He had concluded that the policy against inflation 'could no longer rest solely on attempts to measure and control the domestic money supply'.[109] The former monetarist Chancellor, author of the 1981 Budget, was rejecting monetarism. It had worked once, maybe: but it was not working by 1985. Lawson had been right not only in 1989 but all along. The delay in entry into the ERM had actually brought about inflation.[110] Accordingly it was not Lawson who was to blame for its recrudescence, as Mrs Thatcher and her friends alleged. It was Mrs Thatcher herself.

This was powerful stuff. Inevitably it was largely ignored, both at the time and afterwards. So also, though to a lesser extent, was Howe's revelation that at the Madrid summit he and Lawson had made it clear that they 'could not continue in office unless a specific commitment to join the ERM was made'.[111] Howe quoted that Prime Minister to whom Mrs Thatcher referred familiarly as 'Winston' on the merging of sovereignty:

> I have to say that I find Winston Churchill's perception a good deal more convincing, and more encouraging for the interests of the nation, than the nightmare image (*Gasps*) sometimes conjured up by my Right Honourable Friend, who seems sometimes to look out upon a continent that is positively teeming with ill-intentioned people, scheming, in her words, to 'extinguish democracy', to 'disown our national identities' and to lead us 'through the back door into a federal Europe'. What kind of vision is that?[112]

Mrs Thatcher had been dismissive of the hard ecu – a common as distinct from a single currency. She had said that no one would want to use it.

> How on earth are the Chancellor and the Governor of the Bank of England, commending the hard ecu as they strive to, to be taken as serious participants in the debate against that kind of background noise (*Gasps*)? I believe that both the Chancellor and the Governor [John Major and Robin Leigh-Pemberton respectively] are cricketing enthusiasts so I hope there is no monopoly of cricketing metaphors [a reference to Mrs Thatcher's Mansion House speech the evening before]. It is rather like sending your opening batsmen to the crease only for them to find, the moment the first balls are bowled, that their bats have been broken before the game by the team captain (*Laughter*).[113]

He concluded with a call to insurrection:

> The time has come for others to consider their own response to the tragic conflict of loyalties with which I have myself wrestled for perhaps too long.[114]

Margaret Thatcher said to Kenneth Baker: 'I didn't think he would do something like that.'[115] Cecil Parkinson watched the speech on television with a dozen Conservative Members who had come to talk to him about transport. At the end they all knew that a contest was inevitable and that Heseltine would be a candidate.[116] Baker went to Major's room in the Commons and found him 'pacing nervously up and down' and 'quite devastated'. Major said she 'must go on' and repaired to Mrs Thatcher's room to offer comfort and support, where Baker joined them. She thought a contest 'inevitable'.[117]

Parkinson met Heseltine at seven that evening. He tried to persuade him not to stand against her. He said he would lose, split the party and destroy any chance he might have of ever becoming leader. He urged Heseltine to put out a statement explaining that, though he was under pressure to stand against Mrs Thatcher, he had decided not to. He suggested that he give as reasons the interests of party unity, the 'severe economic difficulty' and the position in the Gulf. Heseltine was unmoved by this appeal. 'Cecil,' he said, 'she is finished. After Geoffrey's speech, she's finished.' Next day, Heseltine declared his candidature.[118]

That evening Baker dined with Norman Tebbit, who thought Mrs Thatcher would win any contest but that above all Heseltine had to be stopped. He was not tempted to enter any election himself but never completely ruled out the possibility.[119] Alan Clark derived a more belligerent impression from Tebbit. They should not go for a compromise candidate but 'fight all the way, to the death. This appeals to me. Leonidas at Thermopylae' – a classical allusion to which Clark was to return several times during the contest, notably in his interview later on with Mrs Thatcher. From the beginning he thought Mrs Thatcher would not win. That was the point of the reference.[120]

Lord Whitelaw thought that if a third of the parliamentary party (124) voted against Mrs Thatcher she would have to go. But he was determined to stop Heseltine.[121] At a meeting in John Wakeham's room in the Commons on 15 November, Wakeham, John Gummer and Kenneth Clarke agreed that, if Mrs Thatcher did not win outright on the first ballot, she could not continue in the contest.[122] In view of the general agreement about the peril Mrs Thatcher was in and the necessity to 'stop Heseltine' – something about which Whitelaw and Tebbit concurred, though Tebbit was unprepared to support Hurd, who was Whitelaw's favourite candidate – it is surprising that so little was done.

Mrs Thatcher had already taken the view that she must be in Paris during the election: not only because she had promised to be there and, in addition, considered the event to be a commemoration of her part in winning the Cold War but also because, in an odd way, her absence from Westminster would enhance her position there. She would be seen to be above the battle and, accordingly, people would vote for her. It was an extraordinary miscalculation.

Apart from this, there was the question of her campaign or, rather, her lack of a campaign. There has been a disposition to blame her parliamentary private secretary, Peter Morrison, for the neglect. He was certainly an extraordinary choice as PPS, let alone as a campaign manager. But following the departure of her first PPS, Ian Gow, she had come to take the view that it was unfair to expect Members to accept the post unless they were persons of substantial private wealth. Morrison was certainly that. And – unlike his brother Charles, and other rich Tories – he was in more or less complete sympathy with what Mrs Thatcher was trying to do.

Norman Fowler had been approached by Morrison and agreed to be part of the campaign team, but dropped out immediately, Mrs Thatcher tells us, claiming past friendship with Howe. George Younger was supposed to

captain the team but was about to become chairman of the Royal Bank of
Scotland, and was consequently 'heavily involved in his business affairs'.
Michael Jopling also – in Mrs Thatcher's phrase – 'bowed out'. John Moore
'was not always in the country'. Subsequently several of her younger
supporters in the No Turning Back Group, alarmed at the way her
campaign was going, drafted themselves.[123]

Formally, both Central Office and the Whips Office behaved with
complete propriety, which was more than the former had done in 1975,
when it had unsuccessfully led Edward Heath's campaign to remain
leader. At that time the officers of the 1922 Committee had worked against
Heath: in 1990 they were more or less neutral, not so much because of any
carefully arrived at decision about what constituted proper conduct as
because they did not know what was going on. There remained a difference
between Central Office and the Whips Office – or, at any rate, between
their respective heads, Kenneth Baker and Tim Renton. Baker, though not
personally close to Mrs Thatcher, considered that as chairman of the party
he had to give her his complete support. Renton was, to put it at its lowest,
not a Thatcher supporter.

On 14 November Baker issued a statement saying that his own position
was 'clear'. He was '100 per cent' behind Mrs Thatcher. It was to her
'political skills' and 'unprecedented electoral successes' that Conservative
MPs owed their position. She was entitled to expect their loyalty in return.
Her qualities of leadership were the 'greatest political assets' which the
Conservative Party and the nation had.[124] Nevertheless, the chairman was
determined that Central Office should not be used to influence the way
MPs voted. He issued written instructions to this effect to the staff, which
became known as the Baker Rules; or so, at any rate, Kenneth Baker
claims.[125]

The Whips Office was, according to Baker, in a similar position. Renton
knew the parliamentary party was divided and that he 'could not use the
usual processes of persuasion'. In a situation like this the Chief Whip was
'in a very difficult position'. Renton summoned a meeting of the Whips and
told them that they had to remain neutral. One of them asked whether
that meant that they could do nothing to help the Prime Minister. Renton
replied: 'You do nothing.'[126]

On Saturday 17 November Mrs Thatcher and her husband gave a
dinner at Chequers for her most trusted advisers. The party consisted of
Peter Morrison, Alistair McAlpine, Gordon Reece, John Whittingdale,
Kenneth Baker, Tim Bell, John Wakeham, Michael Neubert and Gerry
Neale, the last six accompanied by their wives. Morrison said he had 220
for, 110 against and 4 abstentions. Mrs Thatcher said she remembered
Heath thinking the same thing when he stood against her. She advised
Morrison not to trust his figures, for some people were 'on the books of both
sides'. Everybody else seemed far more confident than she and spent the

time discussing what should be done to unite the party after her victory. She hoped they were right, but 'some instinct' told her otherwise.[127]

Baker shared Mrs Thatcher's doubts. He told her that when it was all over they would have to 'do something' about the poll tax or, as Mrs Thatcher insisted on calling it, the community charge. He had raised this matter previously and been repulsed. This time he was not. After dinner Reece stayed and made a last attempt to persuade Mrs Thatcher not to go to Paris. Baker had previously urged her to stay at home. She replied that, if she were to 'pull out now', MPs would think she was 'running scared' and was going to lose. 'No, the decision is made.'[128]

On Monday and early on Tuesday several meetings took place at Westminster in the Prime Minister's absence. They were concerned not with maximising Mrs Thatcher's vote on 20 November but with the form of words she would use in Paris. Thus on 19 November Baker spoke to Wakeham and told him that it was going to be 'very close' and that they should prepare for a second ballot. They agreed to meet later that morning in the Prime Minister's room in the House, together with Younger, Moore, Tebbit, Onslow, Renton, Morrison and Neale. Renton said that, if she won only 187 votes, she could not go on to a second ballot because only half the party would be supporting her. Morrison said she would want to fight on even with those figures. Baker said she ought not to sound so definite about her future intentions. He thought his colleagues considered his views 'too defeatist'. Morrison was 'clearly impatient at having to discuss all this, since he believed that such an outcome was beyond the bounds of possibility'.[129] The form of words agreed for use in Paris, if she won on the first ballot but failed to win outright, was:

> I am pleased that more than half the parliamentary party voted for me and I would like to thank all my supporters. Nevertheless I am disappointed that it is necessary to have a second ballot. According to the rules laid down by the 1922 Committee nominations are now open for the next round. I can confirm that it is my intention to let my name go forward to the second ballot.[130]

Next morning, the day of the vote, Mrs Thatcher's team reassembled at 11.15 and confirmed the statements which Mrs Thatcher had by now agreed. Baker again urged a more modest and accommodating approach on her part. His view was still that she should return from Paris as leader and consult the colleagues about remaining in the contest. A decision made – or apparently made – in Paris would be seen as high-handed; as, indeed, it turned out to be. Baker was proved right. Tebbit, however, was vigorously opposed to the course he was recommending, saying that, if she did not at once declare that she was going on, her support would (in a word much used throughout these events) 'haemorrhage'.[131]

Morrison spoke to Mrs Thatcher on that Monday evening on the telephone and was full of confidence. It had already been arranged that he would fly to Paris to be there to give her the good news. Just before six on the day of the first ballot she went upstairs to a room at the ambassador's residence to have her hair done. Just after six she went to a room set aside for her to hear the results. Those present were Bernard Ingham, the press secretary; Charles Powell, her private secretary; Sir Ewen Fergusson, the ambassador; Cynthia Crawford ('Crawfie'), her maid; and Peter Morrison. He had a telephone line to the Chief Whip and Powell another to John Whittingdale.[132]

At Westminster the company gathered in the Prime Minister's room was larger: Wakeham, Tebbit, Neale, Neubert, Bell, Reece, Whittingdale, Waddington, Moore, Lennox-Boyd, Newton, McAlpine, Brendan Bruce (the press officer at Central Office), Tony Kerpel and Baker. At 6.30 Ian Twinn, the MP for Edmonton, came in with the figures.[133] Renton telephoned Morrison, who passed the result to Mrs Thatcher, saying: 'I'm afraid, Prime Minister, that these figures are rather disappointing.'[134] In fact Powell had received the result first and given the thumbs-down sign out of Mrs Thatcher's sight.[135]

The result of the first ballot was Thatcher 204, Heseltine 152, abstentions 16. Mrs Thatcher had gained the absolute majority (187 or over) which was required by the rules but fallen 4 short of the 15 per cent 'surcharge' of those entitled to vote (56) which was also required. The Labour MPs Dennis Skinner and Tony Benn were standing on benches in the crowded corridor outside the committee room in which the results had been announced. Benn recorded:

I could see everyone – Tory, Labour and Liberal MPs, clerks, secretaries, journalists – a sea of faces. There was a bit of scuffling further up, and then all of a sudden, through the crowd, came a number of journalists, who ran by so quickly I could hardly recognise any of them. The crowd opened like the Red Sea. One of the journalists said to me: 'Second ballot. Can you comment?' So I said: 'It is appropriate that it should have happened to her when she was in Versailles' – a point Caroline [Mrs Benn] had made to me.[136]

Within minutes, and in full view of the British television audience Mrs Thatcher was bouncing down the steps of the Paris Embassy, Ingham in close attendance. John Sergeant of the BBC said: 'Prime Minister, Mrs Thatcher, it's here, this is the microphone.' Mrs Thatcher knew perfectly well where the microphone was and seemed to think that Mr Sergeant was preventing her from reaching it. Pushing him aside, she said:

I'm naturally very pleased that I got more than half the parliamentary party and disappointed that it's not quite enough to win on the first ballot so I confirm it is my intention to let my name go forward for the second ballot.

This version was slightly different from the one set out in Kenneth Baker's memoirs. Nevertheless, it was close enough for Wakeham to be able to observe laconically afterwards: 'She picked up the right piece of paper.'[137] Douglas Hurd, who as Foreign Secretary was in Paris too, said:

> I would just like to make a brief comment on the ballot result. The Prime Minister continues to have my full support, and I am sorry that this destructive, unnecessary contest should be prolonged in this way.

In fact Hurd was none too happy at the course which events were taking in Paris. He was particularly annoyed when Powell told him to sign Mrs Thatcher's nomination form for the second ballot – which, however, he proceeded to do – thinking it improper for a civil servant temporarily assigned to No. 10 so to instruct a Cabinet Minister.[138] He was angry because he thought he was being forced into giving support to Mrs Thatcher when all the circumstances had not been properly considered. He had told his parliamentary private secretary Tim Yeo not to go 'scurrying round the House' on his behalf. Though some Conservatives, notably Whitelaw, favoured him as the 'stop Heseltine' candidate, others, such as Tebbit, preferred Major.[139]

Baker had already spoken to Major on the previous day, Monday 19 November. Major was in his Huntingdon home recovering from an operation on his wisdom teeth. Baker had heard that Robert Atkins and Norman Lamont had been promoting him as the candidate if Mrs Thatcher were to be defeated. It is unclear whether Baker mentioned these two to Major. He certainly said that so many people were 'talking up' Major's chances that he assumed there was some 'campaign running' on his behalf. Major 'vehemently denied' this and said he had been discouraging friends from promoting him.[140]

After 6.30 on Tuesday the temperature at Westminster was even more febrile than it had been in the Imperial Hotel, Blackpool, in October 1963, when Harold Macmillan announced his resignation. The main event of the evening was the meeting at Tristan Garel-Jones's house at Catherine Place, SW1, not far from Buckingham Palace. Garel-Jones was a friend of Major's who was also close to Hurd, not least because he was now a junior Minister in the Foreign Office. Those present were Chris Patten, John Patten, William Waldegrave, Malcolm Rifkind, Norman Lamont, Tony Newton, Douglas Hogg, Richard Ryder, Tim Yeo and Alan Clark.

Garel-Jones invited Clark during the ten o'clock vote that night, saying that 'a few mates, Chris [Patten] and people' would be talking about the next steps and ways of supporting the Prime Minister.[141] However, he turned down the suggestions Clark made about prospective fellow-attenders: Jonathan Aitken, Francis Maude, David Davis, Andrew MacKay and Peter Lilley. In fact Lilley had long rejected Mrs Thatcher as a candidate for the second ballot, but Clark did not know that.

Waldegrave was the only person to express sympathy for Mrs Thatcher. Lamont, 'Mepistophelian in his black tie', shocked Clark by saying at the beginning that he could conceive of Heseltine as both an effective and a tolerable Prime Minister. Clark said that a Baldwinesque figure was needed and suggested his chief at Defence, Tom King. Chris Patten laughed. John Patten said: 'I presume you're joking.' Garel-Jones said: 'Come on, Al, you'll have to do better than that.' Clark had expected Garel-Jones 'to try and rig it' for Major. In practice a consensus built up 'quite rapidly' for Hurd. Clark was doubtful about this choice, because Hurd was too much an 'establishment candidate' – and also perhaps, though Clark does not say so, because Hurd's views were antipathetic to his own. The 'really sickening thing,' however, was 'the urgent and unanimous abandonment of the Lady'.[142]

In the opinion of Baker, who was not at the meeting, some genuinely believed that Mrs Thatcher could not win the second ballot. Others saw it as an opportunity to get rid of a leader whom they disliked and who was, they thought, an electoral liability. The only factor uniting the two groups was a determination to stop Heseltine. Baker confirms Clark's account that a majority of those present supported Hurd as a successor. This surprised Lamont, who was fully committed to Major and resented some disparaging remarks which had been made about him.

There was some surprise that Clark had been at Catherine Place, because he was an ardent admirer of the Prime Minister. Baker thought Garel-Jones had been 'astute' in inviting him, as this gave the impression that the Right was deserting Mrs Thatcher, 'which it was not'.[143] But Clark was a long-standing friend of Garel-Jones, and it was unsurprising that he should have been invited. Employing some of the legal terminology which he had no doubt picked up during his spell as Home Secretary, Baker concluded that where a 'collective course of action' had been agreed upon to 'achieve a common goal', there was 'that sense of purpose which every plot has to have'.[144] After the Catherine Place meeting (at which he had not been present), Baker was passing through the antechamber behind the Speaker's Chair when he met a group of Ministers: Chris Patten, Waldegrave, Rifkind and Newton, with Lamont at their head. They told him they had met earlier and gone on to see Renton. They were 'looking worried, and a bit flushed and flustered'. Lamont, as spokesman, said it was their unanimous view that Mrs Thatcher should now withdraw, as she would lose the second ballot, though they would all vote for her. The 'clear impression' which Baker received was that the group were searching for an 'executioner'. That he 'was not prepared to play this role dismayed them all and angered some'.[145]

On her return to London on the Wednesday morning, Mrs Thatcher met Tebbit and Wakeham. They were joined later by Baker, Renton, Onslow and MacGregor.[146] Earlier that morning Baker had met Tim Bell, Gordon

Reece and other familiars at Central Office. All of them wanted Mrs Thatcher to go on: the rallying cry for the second ballot was that only she could stop Heseltine.[147] Mrs Thatcher herself was receiving less encouraging news. Her private office told her that, following her request, they had telephoned Peter Lilley to ask him to help with the drafting of her speech for Thursday's No Confidence debate. Lilley had replied that he 'saw no point' because she was 'finished'. This upset Mrs Thatcher, who concluded that the second ballot was going to be 'even more difficult' than she had imagined in her 'worst nightmares'.[148]

Both she and Baker agree that it was Morrison, in Paris, who had suggested that she should see members of the Cabinet individually, to 'gee them up', as he was to put it.[149] Mrs Thatcher implies that she immediately accepted this advice: arrangements were made 'as soon as we got back to London'.[150] Baker, by contrast, writes that on her return to London she had still not accepted Morrison's advice and asked Wakeham for *his* advice. He reinforced Morrison, saying 'quite decisively' that she should see Ministers individually. Her firm response was that she would not be able to do so because she had to make a statement to the House that afternoon about events in Paris and then see the Queen – to say nothing of drafting a speech for Thursday's censure debate. She did not have the time. Wakeham replied that she would have to make the time.[151]

At mid-day on the Wednesday Mrs Thatcher's husband was definite in his advice: 'Don't go on, love.' [152] Her colleagues were less clear. They gathered in the Cabinet Room: Tebbit, Wakeham, Morrison, Baker (who later left to lunch elsewhere), MacGregor, Renton, Onslow and Moore. Baker said she alone could stop Heseltine. But her campaign needed a 'major overhaul' and she must give an undertaking to look 'radically' at the poll tax.

MacGregor then spoke. He had been given the task of trawling Cabinet Ministers because Wakeham was busy with electricity privatisation. Evidently Wakeham did not feel the obligation to 'make time' where his own activities were concerned. MacGregor had also asked Ministers about the views of their junior Ministers, to which several of the former group had replied: 'Why don't you ask them yourself?' He said there were very few Ministers who were proposing to shift their vote. The 'underlying problem' was that they had no faith in Mrs Thatcher's ultimate success. They were concerned that her support was eroding.

This was less than wholly candid, as Mrs Thatcher was later to discover.[153] MacGregor had already told Baker that no fewer than ten Ministers already thought Mrs Thatcher would be defeated if she went on. They felt it would be better if Hurd, Major or both were to stand instead. Immediately after the No. 10 lunch, MacGregor explained to Wakeham that he had 'not had a chance' to tell her that the Cabinet was not unanimous.[154] Mrs Thatcher thought he had not been able to tell her this in front of Renton and Onslow and had not managed to see her in advance.[155] This was certainly the explanation which MacGregor gave to others too.[156]

Onslow said that he brought no message from the 1922 Committee that Mrs Thatcher should stand down. But nor did they wish to convey any message to Heseltine. They were, as Mrs Thatcher was to write, declaring their neutrality. Renton, for his part, 'gave a characteristically dispiriting assessment'. He reported that the Whips Office had received 'many messages' from both backbenchers and Ministers saying Mrs Thatcher should withdraw. He also brought news of Lord Whitelaw's opinions. Whitelaw was worried that Mrs Thatcher might be humiliated in the second ballot: 'it was touching that so many people seemed to be worried by my humiliation'. If Mrs Thatcher had known the true picture immediately after lunch on the Wednesday she might have, as she was to put it later, 'thought twice' about asking her colleagues individually for their support.[157]

While the frugal and dispiriting luncheon at No. 10 was proceeding, Baker was lunching with two surviving supporters of Mrs Thatcher. Afterwards he telephoned Major, still at home in Huntingdon, and urged him to return to London 'immediately' and to appear on television expressing strong support for Mrs Thatcher. Major replied: 'I'll have to think about it.'[158] He was also telephoned by Mrs Thatcher herself. She asked him to second her nomination for the second ballot. There was 'a moment's silence' and 'the hesitation was palpable'. Then Major said that if that was what she wanted, yes, he would do it.

Later, when urging her supporters to vote for Major in the second ballot, she was to claim that he had not hesitated to second her nomination, 'but both of us knew otherwise'.[159] In her memoirs, Mrs Thatcher implies that Hurd also agreed to nominate her on the Wednesday.[160] This may be so. But Hurd's hand had already been forced by Charles Powell in Paris on the previous evening: an action which was to bring about a resentment in Hurd whose dimensions Powell clearly did not realise.

Mrs Thatcher asked Wakeham to take charge of her campaign. He agreed, but said he needed people to help him. George Younger, who had been a kind of phantom campaign manager for the first ballot, 'clearly' could not spare the time. Wakeham suggested Kenneth Clarke, which Baker thought 'utterly unrealistic' because he had been told that Clarke's views were the same as those of the people who had attended the Catherine Place meeting, where Clarke had not been present. He had not been there because he could not be found, occupied as he was in touring the television studios expressing the warmest support for Mrs Thatcher.

Wakeham was then 'amazed' to find that he could not persuade Alastair Goodlad, Tristan Garel-Jones, Richard Ryder or his own PPS, Andrew Mitchell, to join him in running Mrs Thatcher's campaign. They all thought she would lose. By mid-afternoon on Wednesday 21 November

1990 Wakeham's campaign was finished; if, indeed, it had ever started. But as she left No. 10 to make her European statement, Mrs Thatcher gave to assembled reporters the message (which was also put up outside the house, as if on a notice board): 'I fight on, I fight to win.' This was Ingham's idea. It expressed a confidence Mrs Thatcher did not feel.[161] Tebbit, however, put out a statement saying that Wakeham was to be Mrs Thatcher's campaign manager. This was 'an announcement which considerably surprised John'.[162]

Mrs Thatcher went to the Palace for an audience with the Queen at which she informed her that she would stand in the second ballot. She then returned to her room in the House to see the Cabinet one by one. This procedure began at six. Peter Morrison sat in throughout. Her first visitor was Cecil Parkinson. This was a personal call and separate from the list of scheduled appointments. He said it would be a 'hard struggle' but that she could win. He found her 'full of enthusiasm' and determined to do so.[163] The next caller was Francis Maude. As Financial Secretary to the Treasury, he was not a Cabinet Minister at all. He had come to see Morrison, but was ushered in. He told Mrs Thatcher that he 'passionately' supported the things she believed in. He would support her as long as she went on. But he did not believe she could win. He left in a 'state of some distress' and did not succeed in cheering up Mrs Thatcher.

Kenneth Clarke's manner was 'robust in the brutalist style he has cultivated'. He tried to be the candid friend. He said that the Conservative method of changing Prime Minister was 'farcical' and that he would be happy to support her for another five or ten years. 'Most of the Cabinet', however, thought she should stand down. If she lost, the party would be led by Heseltine and end up split. Hurd and Major should be released from their obligations. According to Mrs Thatcher, Clarke did not threaten to resign – which, at the time, he was widely credited with doing. It is certain that, with others, he was sweetening the medicine.[164] He did, however, threaten to resign on the following morning.

While the interviews were being conducted, Baker went to Chris Patten's office at the end of the Ministers' corridor. There he found Clarke, Garel-Jones, Ryder and Goodlad. Of these, only Patten and Clarke were members of the Cabinet. Patten said that her decision to go on was 'disastrous'. Baker replied that in a contest with Heseltine, with only two candidates standing, she was the only one who could beat him. If she stood, she would win. What would she have won, Patten asked Baker, if she had a majority of a few? What sort of victory was that? She should stand down and let other people come forward. In any case (Patten continued), the evidence he was getting was that she would not win. Baker concluded that 'this group of Ministers really did want a change of leader'.[165]

Peter Lilley was, Mrs Thatcher thought, 'obviously ill at ease'. From the message she had received in Paris about his unwillingness to help with her speech, she 'knew roughly what to expect from him'. He said he would support her but it was 'inconceivable' she would win. Heseltine must not be allowed to gain the leadership. The only course was to make way for John Major. Other visitors, notably Clarke, had said that both Major and Hurd should be – this was the favourite word – 'released'. Lilley plumped for Major. Malcolm Rifkind was in Mrs Thatcher's estimation her 'biggest critic' inside the Cabinet. He said that she could not win and that Major or Hurd would do better. She asked him whether she would have his support if she did decide to stand. Rifkind said he would 'have to think about it', but promised not to campaign against her.

Peter Brooke was wearing full evening dress because he was going on later to a formal dinner, though he was to joke subsequently that one should always be so attired when taking grave decisions. Mrs Thatcher, at any rate, found him 'charming, thoughtful and loyal'. He believed she could win if she went on 'with all guns blazing'. Michael Howard was 'altogether stronger and more encouraging' than other members of his ministerial group such as Lilley. He doubted her prospects but promised to support her and to campaign for her. William Waldegrave was 'very formal'. He said he would vote for her so long as she was a candidate but had a 'sense of foreboding' about the result.

At this point Mrs Thatcher received an urgent message from Wakeham. The position was much worse than he had thought. John Gummer then came in and 'reeled off the standard formula'. He also mentioned both Major and Hurd. Chris Patten told her he would support her but she could not win.[166]

Alan Clark arrived. Like Maude, he was not a member of the Cabinet but, unlike Maude, had no very plausible reason for being there.

'I am a fighter,' Mrs Thatcher said to him.

'Fight then,' Clark recounts. 'Fight right to the end, a third ballot if you need to. But you'll lose.'[167]

As Mrs Thatcher 'had no particular fondness for Wagnerian endings, this lifted my spirits only briefly'.[168] Wakeham and Baker then appeared together. Wakeham said that he doubted whether Mrs Thatcher could gain the support of the Cabinet. He told her about the refusal to serve of Garel-Jones and Ryder. She was disappointed in the latter but not surprised by the former. Baker said the position had 'deteriorated' since the morning. He had found ten or twelve members of the Cabinet who did not believe she could win. However, he still thought she should go on. He also tried a suggestion by Tom King that, if she won, Mrs Thatcher should stand down after Christmas 1990. She rejected this.

Norman Lamont repeated the formula: the position was beyond repair. John MacGregor said the same. So did King, 'though more warmly than most'. When Baker saw her at 7.30 she was already saying: 'It's a funny old world.'[169] David Waddington arrived 'in the deepest distress'. As a former Chief Whip, whose departure from the post was now regretted by the Prime Minister, he could see that support had collapsed in the Cabinet.

He promised his own backing for whatever she was going to do, said that in his view she would lose and left with tears in his eyes.[170] Tony Newton was, according to Mrs Thatcher, nervous and 'just about managed to get out the agreed line'.

Wakeham then re-entered and elaborated further on what he had already told her. She had lost the Cabinet's support. She could not even muster a credible campaign team. 'It was the end. I was sick at heart.' She dictated a brief statement of resignation to be read out at the Cabinet on the next morning, but said she would return to No. 10 to talk to Denis before finally taking the decision. While she was preparing to leave, Norman Tebbit arrived with Michael Portillo. They tried to convince her that the Cabinet was misreading the situation. Then a delegation from the 92 Group arrived: George Gardiner, John Townend, Edward Leigh and Christopher Chope. They said much the same as Tebbit. Mrs Thatcher then returned to No. 10.

At around midnight Michael Portillo turned up with Michael Forsyth and Michael Fallon. At first Peter Morrison tried to bar their entrance because she was writing her speech for next day's censure debate. When Mrs Thatcher was told they had been repulsed, she said she would see them, and they were summoned back. Neil Hamilton joined them. They tried to convince her that all was not lost. But it was no use. John Gummer, who was also present, contradicted them.[171] In the meantime, Jeffrey Archer's chauffeur had driven to Huntingdon to secure Major's signature on Mrs Thatcher's nomination paper. He returned with it to Archer's flat on the Albert Embankment. But Archer could not sleep with the precious document beside him. He took it round to No. 10 himself, arriving at about 1.30. He did not see Mrs Thatcher but Morrison, who took the unopened envelope and put it aside as if it would not be needed.[172]

At 7.30 next morning Mrs Thatcher telephoned Andrew Turnbull, the principal private secretary to the Prime Minister, and told him she was going to resign. The Private Office then put into effect a plan which had already been agreed for an audience with the Queen. Morrison telephoned Major and Hurd to tell them of the decision. Wakeham and Baker were also told. She then had a 'rather desultory' briefing from Ingham, Powell and Wakeham for that afternoon's Questions in the House.[173]

The Cabinet met shortly after nine to enable Ministers to attend Lady Home's memorial service at St Margaret's, Westminster, later that morning. Ministers looked grim, said little and avoided one another's eyes. An exception was Kenneth Clarke. He was telling anybody who would listen that, if Mrs Thatcher did not resign, he would resign himself before mid-day. At 9.10 the doors of the Cabinet room were opened. Mrs Thatcher was already there, sitting in her usual place. Sir Robin Butler, the Cabinet Secretary, was next to her. She had clearly been crying: her eyes were red and swollen. A carton of tissues was placed beside her on the table. She picked one out of the box and wiped away some tears.

Mrs Thatcher began by saying that before the formal business of the Cabinet she wanted to make her position known. She read: 'Having consulted widely among my colleagues ....' Then she broke down. She tried again and failed. 'I am so sorry,' she said. Cecil Parkinson said to the Lord Chancellor, James Mackay: 'For God's sake, James, you read it.' Various colleagues dissented, which broke the tension. Most of them, however, could not look at her, and sat drilling holes with their eyes into the Cabinet table. Mrs Thatcher regained her composure, and read out the statement, which continued ' ... I have concluded that the unity of the party and the prospects of victory in a general election would be better served if I stood down to enable Cabinet colleagues to enter the ballot for the leadership. I should like to thank all those in the Cabinet and outside who have given me such dedicated support.' Lord Mackay, having been forewarned, then read out a tribute thanking Mrs Thatcher on behalf of the Cabinet for her services to the nation.

Mrs Thatcher was by now in tears again, but composed herself sufficiently to lay down firmly that the Cabinet should unite to support that person who was most likely to defeat Michael Heseltine. Kenneth Baker, on behalf of the party, and Douglas Hurd, as the most senior Minister, added tributes of their own. Mrs Thatcher could stand no more. She moved next business – a strengthening of British forces in the Gulf.[174]

That afternoon in the House she made perhaps the best parliamentary speech of her career. She then set about securing the succession for Major. She wanted – perhaps needed – to believe that he was the man to safeguard her legacy and advance her policies.[175] Norman Lamont was Major's chief campaign manager, with John Gummer as his assistant. He had already been promoting Major's candidature: certainly since the Wednesday morning, when he had canvassed Parkinson on Major's behalf, and probably since the Tuesday evening.[176] Hurd's campaign was organised by Sir Giles Shaw; Heseltine's by Michael Mates, Keith Hampson and Sir Peter Tapsell.

Mates said afterwards that he would give 'anything' to know who had persuaded both Major and Hurd to put up against Heseltine.[177] And, indeed, it is probable that Heseltine would have beaten Hurd alone, possible that he would have beaten Major also. There is an analogy with the Parliamentary Labour Party's election in 1963 following the death of Hugh Gaitskell, when supporters of Harold Wilson against George Brown thought it was helpful to their cause that James Callaghan was standing as well; while, conversely, Brown's supporters considered Callaghan's candidature worse than unnecessary.*

In 1990 there was what amounted to a Cabinet agreement that Heseltine had to be 'stopped'. David Hunt breached it by voting for Heseltine. Mrs Thatcher would doubtless have preferred Major alone to do the

* See above, p. 137.

stopping. On the other hand, the consensus at the Catherine Place meeting had been that Hurd was the man – even though Garel-Jones, in whose house the meeting had been held, was an old friend of Major's, and Lamont, who had attended it, was already thinking of him as Mrs Thatcher's successor, as was Lilley also. Between the Wednesday evening and the Thursday morning the Cabinet came to an unexpressed agreement that both Major and Hurd should be put up as candidates in the second ballot. Some members simply wanted a choice. Others thought it was not possible either to know in advance or to find out in the time available which of them alone had the better chance of defeating Heseltine.[178]

It was not realised then that Hurd would poll as disappointingly as he did. Partly this may have been his own fault. He played the game of lowlier-than-thou with some vigour, describing his father (a Conservative MP, Sir Anthony, later Lord, Hurd) as a 'tenant farmer' of 500 'not particularly good acres' on the Marlborough Downs, and saying that he would not have been able to go to Eton if he had not won a scholarship. This claim to a boyhood of rural privation was oddly reminiscent of Michael Meacher contesting the deputy leadership of the Labour Party seven years previously.[179] However, though Hurd may not have been aristocratic or patrician, as many newspapers said he was, he was manifestly at the upper end of the English upper-middle class. It was to this that many Conservative MPs objected, casting their votes accordingly.

The result was: Major, 185; Heseltine, 131; Hurd, 56. Under the Conservative Party's elaborate rules, which were properly understood by few, the 'surcharge' requirement, which had fatally wounded Mrs Thatcher and made a second ballot necessary, was not a requirement likewise in that second ballot. The absolute majority, however, remained necessary. Whereas Mrs Thatcher had met this criterion in the first ballot, Major had – by two votes – failed to meet it in the second. Mrs Thatcher was later to make much of this in a jocular manner which nevertheless had an edge to it. Still, the rules were clear. In the event of no candidate's obtaining an absolute majority on the second ballot, the contest went on to a third ballot with the bottom candidate or candidates, in this case Hurd, dropping out.

Heseltine forestalled this event by withdrawing. Hurd 'conceded defeat', though there was no need for him to say anything. Cranley Onslow then decreed that there would be no third ballot. When challenged about whether he had the power to do this, he replied that, as Chairman of the 1922 Committee, he was empowered by the rules to be the sole arbiter of elections.[180] Whether this meant that he was entitled to jettison the requirement for a third ballot in the circumstances of November 1990 remains doubtful. It was equally uncertain (a separate but analogous argument) whether Heseltine was entitled to withdraw as he did. The short answer is that Conservative MPs, never very happy with elections, were by this stage thoroughly fed up with casting their votes and – guilty at having helped with the assassination of Mrs Thatcher – were now happy to settle for John Major.

He was confirmed as leader at the traditional mass meeting, held this time at the Queen Elizabeth Conference Centre, in the week after he had become Prime Minister. He became Prime Minister the day after the announcement of the result of the second ballot. Until then, Mrs Thatcher remained in office. The Wilson-Callaghan precedent of 1976 was followed. Mrs Thatcher did not resign but informed the Queen of her intention to resign after her party had elected a new leader.

JOHN MAJOR IN 1992

The general election of 1992 was held on 9 April, three months short of the last permissible day. Contrary to the expectations of all the polls, most of the pundits and the entire Kinnock family apart from Neil Kinnock himself – who later confessed to feeling doubt in the last few days of the campaign – the Conservatives won with 336 seats. Labour obtained 271, the Liberal Democrats 20, Northern Ireland parties 17, Plaid Cymru 4 and the Scottish National Party 3. John Major continued in office.

JOHN MAJOR IN 1995

In 1922 Bonar Law refused to become Prime Minister until he had been elected leader of the Conservative Party, and caused King George V some annoyance in the process.* In 1995 John Major resigned the leadership of his party, remained Prime Minister and, as far as we know, went unrebuked by Queen Elizabeth II. Indeed, the whole episode produced surprisingly little comment of a constitutional kind, apart from an article by Enoch Powell in the *Daily Mail*.[181]

The genesis of Major's bold decision lay in the United Kingdom's forced exit from the exchange-rate mechanism of the European Monetary System in September 1992. However unjustly, the Conservative claim to be the party of financial competence was destroyed. Major compounded the party's embarrassment by refusing to dismiss his Chancellor, former campaign manager and intriguer on his behalf in 1990, Norman Lamont. He eventually required Lamont's resignation in May 1993, when it was too late.

In that year the Maastricht Treaty was ratified, after greater parliamentary difficulty than had been foreseen by the government or by most of the press. As a Community treaty it required approval by the UK Parliament under the European Parliament Elections Act 1978. The royal prerogative was over-ridden. The effect of the Maastricht debates was to give confidence to those Conservatives who were hostile to UK member-

* See above, pp. 9-10.

ship of the European Community, or 'Union', as it had, in a blatantly propagandist use of language, officially become. It was claimed that Major's position was in peril: for the machinery which had toppled Margaret Thatcher remained in place in substantially the same form, modified significantly only to the extent that 10 per cent of the parliamentary electorate had to requisition a contest by writing to the chairman of the 1922. The government continued to lose by-elections – another cause of Major's precarious position.

November 1993 came and went, and there was no election for leader. The same happened in 1994. But the then Chief Whip, Richard Ryder, deprived eight Members of the whip following their abstention in a post-Maastricht European vote. Another Member, Sir Richard Body, resigned it voluntarily. Altogether 20 MPs caused trouble by abstaining or voting against the government in two divisions (on Value Added Tax and on fishing) succeeding the main European vote which had caused the withdrawal of the whip from the eight. After a few months the whip was restored, the dissentients making no substantial concessions. The truce between government and Europhobes remained fragile. It was taken for granted that someone, probably Lamont – who had become an increasingly hostile critic of the Prime Minister and the government – would stand against Major in November 1995.

Two events were crucial in Major's decision to seek re-election. One was his reception at an afternoon meeting of a Conservative backbench group which, though not 'right wing' in any doctrinaire sense (one of its leading members being Sir Peter Tapsell), was nevertheless suspicious of Europe. This reception was not only by and large hostile but, in the eyes of many of those present, impertinent, in that the Prime Minister was treated as a guest speaker of dubious credentials. The other event was his attendance at a heads-of-government conference in Halifax, Nova Scotia. While he was out of the country the level of enmity in the Conservative Party reached a new height. Alighting from the aeroplane in London, he appeared a man who had had enough.

Major had discussed the ploy with Douglas Hurd before the Cabinet meeting on Thursday 22 June. But he made no mention of it at the meeting itself. Hurd afterwards considered this to have been a mistake. Nicholas Soames, who was outside the Cabinet, knew on the Wednesday evening. Sir George Young, who was then outside the Cabinet likewise (he was promoted to it in the reshuffle that followed Major's re-election), knew about ten minutes before the announcement on the Thursday afternoon. Altogether about half the Cabinet were told confidentially about Major's intentions before the meeting. John Redwood, however, was told by Michael Howard at half past three on Thursday. Howard himself had learnt on the Wednesday. He agreed to be part of Major's campaign team before the Cabinet meeting. In addition to Howard, Major's team included Lord Cranborne (who led it), Sir Graham Bright, Alastair Goodlad, Sir Archie

Hamilton, Ian Lang, Brian Mawhinney and Tony Newton. Also involved on the Prime Minister's behalf were Michael Jack, David Maclean, Sir Michael Neubert and John Ward.

That afternoon Major had a press conference in the garden of No. 10. He said he had been 'deeply involved' in politics since the age of 16. He saw public service as a duty. If one could serve, he believed one was under an obligation to do so. He had been Prime Minister for five years. In that period the government had achieved a 'great deal'. But for the last three years he had been opposed by a 'small minority' in the party. During that period there had been 'repeated threats' that there would be a leadership election. In each year they had turned out to be 'phoney threats'. Now the same thing was happening again. He believed it was 'in no one's interest' that this should continue until November 1995. It undermined the government and damaged the Conservative Party. He was not prepared to see the party he cared for 'laid out on the rack like this for any longer'. To remove the uncertainty, he had that afternoon tendered his resignation as Leader of the Conservative Party to Sir Marcus Fox, the Chairman of the 1922 Committee, and requested him to set the machinery in motion for the election of a successor. Under the party's rules, it was by no means clear that he was entitled to ask the Chairman of the 1922 Committee to do this, or that the latter was justified in complying with his request.

He had confirmed to Sir Marcus that he would be a candidate in the election. If he won, he would continue as Prime Minister and lead the party into and through the next general election. If he were defeated, which he did not expect, he would resign as Prime Minister and offer his successor his 'full support'. The party 'must make its choice'. Every leader was leader only with the support of his party. That applied to himself. It was why he was 'no longer prepared to tolerate the present situation'. It was 'time to put up, or shut up'.

At that stage the balance of probability, in the opinion of most Ministers, was that no one would choose to put up and that Major would be elected unopposed. However, someone, 'some crank', might choose to stand. If that happened, abstentions might occur in such numbers as to weaken the Prime Minister and perhaps destroy him. Less likely still was that Norman Lamont would stand. Major was undoubtedly taking a risk. But no one thought he would be opposed by a member of his own Cabinet.

On 24 June he told the constituency chairmen that he had resigned 'to clear the air'. It was 'the right thing to do'. They should 'settle our differences and turn our fire on Labour'. If they did not, they might lose the election. If that happened, it would be a 'calamity' for the country. They would 'see all the gains of 16 years drift away'. The Conservative Party won elections 'from the centre right of politics' (a phrase that went on to put in periodical appearances in the Prime Minister's speeches). But he also wanted to talk about what angered him: 'that a tide of trivia, of rumour, of insubstantial stories and of froth has been drowning out the real political issues'.

While Major was saying this, John Redwood was in the process of making up his mind about whether to stand. Redwood belonged to that group in the Cabinet whom Major had previously stigmatised as 'bastards' on account of their hostility towards the European Community. He was a Fellow of All Souls and had been a historian specialising in 17th-century history. He was affable but distant and somehow not quite of this world. He played village cricket and, indeed, turned out over the weekend when he was making up his mind.

He was cross because Major's decision to stand had not been collective but taken by Major alone. He was further annoyed because he had learnt of it only at 3.30 on the Thursday afternoon. To make matters worse, he had been told of it not by Major but by Michael Howard. There was an element of justifiable pique in Redwood's decision. There was something else too, though perhaps it could be classified as pique in a different form. He had become increasingly irritated by the assumption that Major's legitimate heir – or, at any rate, the candidate of the Tory Right in any contest for the succession – was Michael Portillo.

Redwood appointed as his campaign manager his special adviser at the Welsh Office, Hywel Williams, a Welsh-speaking former Rugby school-master who was fascinated by the life of politics. He resigned his position at the Welsh Office to help Redwood. Other special advisers, such as Tim Collins, resigned similarly to perform the same service for Major, though they were taking less of a risk than Williams. Redwood announced his candidature at a press conference held in a small room in Westminster. The consequence was that his supporters – substantially those Conservative MPs who had earlier lost the whip – had to crowd behind him in undignified fashion. Teresa Gorman was wearing a particularly garish outfit, and Anthony Marlow an Old Wellingtonian blazer and a deranged grin. According to several experienced observers, it was Marlow's blazer that put people off.

Even so, Major's colleagues were not disposed to minimise the threat presented by Redwood's candidature. It had upset their plans. Lamont they could have dealt with; even a breakaway from the Cabinet by Portillo was within the scope of their imagination. For Redwood to stand was quite unexpected. As a Minister put it later on, Major's friends were 'running about like a lot of headless chickens'. This did not, however, prevent Major, Douglas Hurd and Kenneth Clarke from leaving for Cannes to attend a European Community meeting.

On 26 June Major was interviewed at the door of their hotel by the BBC. He said that, when he resigned, he did so to provide the opportunity to 'clear the air'. He welcomed and looked forward to the contest. The party would have the chance to 'discuss policies' and to 'make a clear-cut decision'. He would continue to advocate 'common sense Conservative policies from the centre right'. On that basis he expected to win the election. When it was over, he would ask the Conservative Party to unite, determine that its 'common opponent was the Labour Party' and carry on governing the country. He did not think (he said to his interviewer) that Redwood's entry had destroyed his objective of winning a decisive victory in the first ballot. There was now an 'election that people would take seriously'. It provided an 'admirable opportunity to clear the air'. He believed he would win 'comfortably'.

Redwood (the interviewer said) had suggested that there had been a 'failure of leadership' and asserted that no Conservative should consider abolishing the pound. Major replied that Redwood had sat in the Cabinet for the last two years. He knew what the government's policies were. He had 'just sat there' accepting them throughout that time. He and Major had discussed policy on many occasions. He had 'put policy suggestions', all of which were being considered, into their study groups. It was rather surprising that he should suddenly 'take a different position from the rest of the Cabinet'. But Major had no doubt that they would debate this over the next week. He did not feel angry about Redwood's decision to stand against him. But he was 'intrigued' by it, because Redwood had sat in the Cabinet for so long. He was every bit as confident as he had been on the previous Thursday. He expected to win; stay as Leader of the Conservative Party; and go on to the election, through it and after it as Prime Minister.

Others were not so sanguine. There were 329 Conservative Members who were entitled to vote. Accordingly Major had to obtain, first, an absolute majority, 165 or more and, second, a margin of 15 per cent or 50 over Redwood. It was wholly within reasonable contemplation that Major would fail to meet either or both criteria owing to the number of abstentions. In 1990 Margaret Thatcher had failed by four votes to meet the second, 'surcharge' criterion. On that occasion the beneficiary had been John Major; the challenger, Michael Heseltine. Nearly five years later the challenger was Redwood. But the beneficiary this time might turn out to be Heseltine.

There was another possibility. If Major failed to win on the first ballot, Michael Portillo, then Employment Secretary, might allow his name to go forward. Publicly, all members of the government were naturally constrained to adopt a demeanour of the utmost loyalty to Major. While Heseltine behaved impeccably, having concluded that this was not the most propitious time for him to become Prime Minister, Portillo did not demonstrate that degree of enthusiasm for Major's cause which might have been thought appropriate in the circumstances. Even more damagingly to him, it was discovered that telephone lines were being installed in a house in Westminster, to be used by him as a headquarters in a second ballot.

Enoch Powell was one of the few to break the silence on constitutional matters. He wondered why nobody had yet responded to these aspects of

Major's 'self-immolation'. He had said to the Sovereign that he was no longer leader of the majority party in the House of Commons but was nevertheless carrying on as her Prime Minister. Powell did not think anybody could say that; not, at any rate, 'without inflicting damage on the constitution'. The Queen governed only on the advice of a person who, in tendering it, was able to assure her that he believed it had the support of a majority in the Commons. That was not what had happened here. The position of Prime Minister and Leader of the Conservative Party did not represent separate or separable positions: one or other of them could not be renounced at pleasure without affecting the other.[182]

Certainly Redwood and his supporters did not pursue this line. On 29 June he issued a statement saying that the country was based on one currency, one Parliament, a common language and a common law. These were our 'birthrights'. Co-operating, trading or even 'sharing some policies' with 'our European neighbours' did not jeopardise them. Transferring more power to European institutions did. Europe had in embryo one court, one Parliament and one currency. If we went too far down the road of giving powers to the court and the Parliament, and if we adopted a single currency, our capacity for self-government would have gone. Labour would 'sleepwalk us' into a federal union. In the forthcoming inter-governmental conference the United Kingdom should 'lead with its positive vision of Europe'. This was

> a Europe of free peoples, when trade grows ever greater, regulations are reduced, diversity flourishes. We must press for more things to be done nationally and locally, and put some restrictions on the power of the (European) court to develop law.[183]

There was some disappointment with Redwood's ideas on the future direction of a Conservative government under his leadership. The best he could manage was a general proposal for economy all round. At Cannes, Douglas Hurd and Kenneth Clarke both thought that Redwood would be more of the doctrinaire Right than he turned out to be. That aspect of politics was better represented by the *Sunday Telegraph* and the *Daily Telegraph,* which both urged Conservative Members to vote for Redwood. Nor was the *Daily Mail* enthusiastic for the Prime Minister. There was no evidence of a campaign on Heseltine's behalf in anticipation of a second ballot. On the morning of the election, however, Heseltine was closeted with Major for about three hours; and it was noticeable that the bulk of Heseltine's supporters did not vote till the late afternoon. Afterwards Ministers were adamant that no deal had been struck between the two.

The result was: Major, 218; Redwood, 89; abstentions, 8; spoilt ballot papers, 12; MPs not voting, 2. Major had over half (165) of the parliamentary electorate on his side. His majority was 129 rather than the 50 required by the party's rules. Nevertheless, his was hardly a spectacular victory. He had won 66 per cent of the vote; 34 per cent – 111 Conservative Members – had declined to support him. This did not inhibit his colleagues, in an operation planned by Lord Cranborne, from proclaiming a famous victory. Who gets to the microphone first, wins.

On the doorstep of No. 10, Major claimed that when he had called the election, he had known that it would be contested. So it had been, by a 'heavyweight candidate'. They now had the verdict of the parliamentary party, a 'very clear-cut decision', a decision in which he had 'received the largest share of votes' that any candidate had in 'any seriously contested election'. He believed that this had put to rest any question or speculation about the leadership of the party up to and beyond the general election. He thanked all those under Robert Cranborne who had worked so hard. He also offered a 'special vote of thanks' to 'those tens of thousands of silent people in the constituencies up and down the country' who made clear their belief 'by a truly overwhelming majority' that the government's policies were correct and that they wished him to continue in Downing Street as Prime Minister. He concluded by saying that the election had been decided by Members of Parliament in Westminster, not commentators outside Westminster with their own particular views. He believed that this was the right democratic way to determine these elections. The matter was concluded and he would 'begin this evening' – it was 4 July 1995 – to reconstruct the government.

There were resignations from David Hunt, Jonathan Aitken, Richard Ryder and Douglas Hurd, respectively Minister for Government Information, Chief Secretary to the Treasury, Chief Whip and Foreign Secretary. The Departments of Education and Employment were merged under Gillian Shephard. Brian Mawhinney was made Minister without Portfolio. Michael Heseltine became First Secretary of State and Deputy Prime Minister, with Roger Freeman, Chancellor of the Duchy of Lancaster, as his assistant in the Cabinet.

It was said that the Prime Minister's action in summer 1995 in throwing himself on the mercy of his own party was unprecedented. So it was. But there had been a near-precedent. In 1954-5, when he was being urged to hand over to Anthony Eden, an irascible Winston Churchill had several times threatened to take his case to the 1922 Committee, consisting of all Conservative Members of Parliament.[*]

TONY BLAIR IN 1997

The general election campaign of 1997 was characterised by its length and by its decisiveness. The longest Parliament since 1945 had ended with the longest campaign of modern times, which in turn produced the largest majority of the 20th century for any radical party.

[*] See above, p. 53ff.

After the 1992 election John Major had a majority of 21. By February 1997 it had disappeared through deaths or defections. Nevertheless he managed to go to the country at a date of his own choosing. At the beginning of the year there were three possible days: 20 March, 10 April and 1 May. Major considered the first, but the obstinate Conservative deficit in the opinion polls always made the last the most likely choice. So it was. On 17 March Major went to the Palace to ask for a dissolution, having first presided over a meeting of the Cabinet. He then announced that Parliament would be prorogued on 21 March but not dissolved until 8 April and that the election would take place on 1 May.

Parliament is adjourned on most weekdays and for the recess. It still exists and can be recalled for the outbreak of war or some similar emergency. It is prorogued at the end of a session, which begins with the Queen's Speech and the State Opening of Parliament, a traditional ceremony created for the benefit of the ancient Dimbleby family. After prorogation Parliament ceases to exist – it comes to an end – until the new session begins. Thus in 1996, as in most parliamentary years, the 1995-6 session continued after Parliament reassembled in late October; whereas the new 1996-7 session began with the Gracious Speech in early November 1996.

However, Parliament is dissolved at the end of a Parliament. The Parliament of 1992-7 was dissolved on 8 April but prorogued on 21 March, an interval of 18 days. The 1945-50 Parliament was prorogued on 20 January and dissolved on 3 February, 14 days later. That was the only recent comparable period. In 1970 and 1972 Parliament was prorogued and dissolved on the same day. In October 1974 and in 1979, 1983 and 1987 it was not prorogued at all: dissolution followed a period of adjournment. The same course could have been pursued in 1997. That it was not led to the accusation that Major was trying to prevent the publication of the almost completed report by the parliamentary Commissioner for Standards, Sir Gordon Downey, into allegations (in the event largely justified) that certain Conservative MPs had accepted money in return for asking questions in the House.

The final, bad-tempered session of Prime Minister's Questions took place on 20 March. Earlier Major had challenged Tony Blair to a televised debate, but negotiations broke down. The Conservatives hired an actor to dress up as a chicken and follow Blair about, suggesting (or so they supposed) that he had 'chickened out' of the debate. Labour retaliated by hiring another chicken, this time headless, to embody the Conservatives. The Liberal Democrats proceeded to present the leaders of the two main parties as Punch and Judy.

The second weekend after the calling of the election was Easter. Full campaigning started on 1 April. The campaign was marked by the use of modern technology, particularly by Labour in their new headquarters at Millbank on the Thames; by the refusal of the polls to shift much or, indeed, at all; and by a certain lowness of tone even by the standards of previous elections. Thus before the election the Conservatives had disclosed plans for a drastic revision of State pensions which by the year 2040 would virtually privatise the system. This was unwise of them. During the campaign Labour accused them of wanting to abolish the State pension. In the rough old trade of politics, this was understandable. Up to a point it was even true. What Labour omitted to mention was that they had very similar changes up their own sleeve – as the appointment of Frank Field was shortly to demonstrate after they had won.

Of the few episodes that rose above name calling, on 3 April Blair gave an interview to the *Scotsman* in which he compared the proposed Scottish Parliament to an English parish council to the extent that both had the right to levy taxes. He went on to say that having a power was not the same as using it, and that even after a Scottish Parliament had been created it would not raise tax rates because 'sovereignty rests with me as an English MP, and that's the way it will stay'. These observations caused some offence in Scotland, though they were not to win the Conservatives one seat in that country.

On 16 April Major used his morning press conference to make a for him impassioned plea to be allowed the freedom to decide on the single European currency at the appropriate time and (in Aneurin Bevan's slightly adapted phrase) not to be left naked going into the conference chamber. He predicted that Blair would 'sell out' at the forthcoming summit conference at Amsterdam. This belated resolve by Major to make Europe the 'central issue' – even though there was no objective or important difference between Labour and Conservatives on the single currency – did not, however, embolden him to discipline or even substantially to rebuke several Conservative MPs, one of them a member of the government, who diverged from his own policy of, as he claimed to see it, rational procrastination.

Election day was fine and sunny. On the previous day Blair had told his closest colleagues not to be complacent. He expected a majority of between 60 and 70 and would have been happy with 50. In the event Labour won 418 seats, Conservatives 165, Liberal Democrats 46, Northern Ireland parties 18 (including Sinn Fein 2), Scottish National Party 6, Plaid Cymru 4, Independent 1, and the Speaker, giving Labour an overall majority of 177. Major saw the Queen shortly after mid-day on 2 May and later announced he would be resigning as Conservative leader.

At one o'clock Blair and his wife Cherie walked instead of being driven to No. 10 Downing Street and were cheered on their way by crowds who had been carefully assembled by the Labour Party but whose applause was none the less heartfelt for that. One of those shifts in British politics had occurred again, as it had in 1906, 1945 and 1979.

8

The Dissolution of Parliament

Another matter which is now never discussed in Cabinet is the exercise of the prerogative of dissolving Parliament ... No dissolution since 1918 has been brought before the Cabinet.

Sir Ivor Jennings, *Cabinet Government*, 1959

Harold said 'We needn't, of course, decide anything yet' and then he made a 20-minute speech. The most interesting point was that he had got Roy's certificate that it would be just as safe to have the election in October as in June. Nevertheless Roy had decided that in the circumstances June was right.

R.H.S. Crossman Diary, 14 May 1970

The dissolution of Parliament is one of those areas of government in which high and low politics lead happily separate existences. It involves, on the one hand, the exercise of the royal prerogative and, on the other, the maximisation of party advantage, brought about, if necessary, by cuts in rates of interest and of income tax and by such other means as are thought effective in securing the object in view.

In practice, dissolution causes surprisingly little difficulty, though Prime Ministers judge wrongly on numerous occasions, as C.R. Attlee did in 1951, Harold Wilson in 1970 and Edward Heath in 1974. In 1964 Sir Alec Douglas-Home was probably right to hang on for as long as he did; whereas in 1978 James Callaghan was probably wrong to delay the election until the next year when, as things turned out, he was forced into one at a time not of his own choosing. In the 1960s, the high-water mark of the theory of prime ministerial power, flexibility over dissolution was widely held to add to that power and on that account to be undesirable. But, as the examples cited show, Prime Ministers can get it wrong. Equally, they can get it right by mistake. Though Neil Kinnock was a late convert to fixed-term Parliaments, it is unlikely that the elections of 1987 and 1992 would have turned out differently if they had taken place in a more rigid system.

THE THEORY OF DISSOLUTION

But if the low politics are fairly simple, subject only to human error and the vagaries of political fortune, the high politics (in the sense in which that phrase is used here) are quite difficult. For they involve two matters which are often – indeed, usually – confused: the powers of the Prime Minister in relation to his colleagues, and the powers of the Prime Minister in relation to the Crown. Only the Prime Minister, it is said, can ask for a dissolution; from which it is deduced that only the Prime Minister can decide on a dissolution. But a channel of communication is not the same as the request which is being communicated. A message does not necessarily tell us anything about the means whereby it has been composed.

Victorian Cabinets arrived at a collective decision to dissolve: it was not a matter for the Prime Minister to decide alone. But the decision would still have been communicated to the Sovereign by the Prime Minister. And the reason for collective decision – for an unambiguously, even ostentatiously collective decision – was surely easy to understand. It was that the alternative to dissolution was resignation.[1] Resignation as a course of action has fallen into disuse, though it may revive if we have a House of Commons in which no party has an absolute majority, or if we return to a three-or-four-party system such as existed for most of the 19th century.

As recently as 1950, however, Attlee considered resignation as a possibility. Patrick Gordon Walker tells us that he attended his first Cabinet meeting in the Prime Minister's room in the House of Commons. They were meeting there because an opposition amendment to the Queen's Speech was being moved that night and Ministers had to be on hand to vote. The newly re-elected Labour government had a majority of six – then regarded as dangerously small, and likely to lead to all manner of constitutional troubles. Attlee said they might be defeated that night and, if so, should resign. After a period of silence, Gordon Walker (the least experienced member) said that he was 'inclined to think that all serious votes in the House should carry their consequences' and that, if defeated, the government 'should think in terms of another immediate general election'. Herbert Morrison then said that they should wait until the arrival of the Foreign Secretary, Ernest Bevin, who had been delayed. Bevin 'strongly and robustly' supported Gordon Walker's view, which was then adopted as the Cabinet's.[2]

Even today, no Prime Minister would arrogate to himself the decision about whether each member of his Cabinet was going to resign, to make way for another Cabinet, composed of politicians of another party. The matter would be decided collectively. The decision to dissolve Parliament and to hold a general election is different because to politicians it feels different. They are in practice prepared to cede greater authority to the Prime Minister. But this is very different from asserting that he or she solely has the constitutional power to decide the date of the election.

An episode in 1992 will perhaps make this clearer. In November of that year the Whips thought they might lose the (constitutionally unnecessary) 'paving' debate to the Maastricht Bill. It was given out that John Major would go to the Queen and demand a general election if he was defeated in the vote. During Margaret Thatcher's years such a threat proved unnecessary, largely because she had such big majorities. Even big majorities, however, do not always obviate the use of the threat. In 1966-70, for instance, Harold Wilson was comfortably off in the voting lobbies: but that did not mean that in 1969, when his and Barbara Castle's proposals for trade union reform incorporated in the White Paper *In Place of Strife* appeared imperilled by the Parliamentary Labour Party, he did not think it helpful to deploy the threat of dissolution. In fact it availed him nothing – the Cabinet retreated first. The same threat had been taken perhaps slightly more seriously earlier in the 1960s, when he and the Labour government had been in difficulties of one kind or another. By 1969 the novelty, such as it was, had worn off.

In 1992 Major and his associates revived the threat. On this occasion the response in the lobbies was not only that it was empty – which had been said in similar circumstances on other occasions – but that the Prime Minister would not have been allowed by his Cabinet to put it into effect. 'We wouldn't have let him get halfway down the Mall,' was a common way of putting it at the time. Though Major was in a weak position at this period vis-à-vis his colleagues, the episode nevertheless demonstrates that, in practice, the Prime Minister is not considered to have the absolute right to determine the date of the next election.

How then did it come to be assumed that he did? The blame is usually attributed to Lloyd George. He called the 1918 election without consulting the Cabinet. There is also the rule that any constitutional innovation, especially one increasing the power of the Prime Minister, can safely be laid at Lloyd George's door. But equal blame should be attached to Sir Ivor Jennings. Perhaps he deserves more of it. For Lloyd George merely called an election. Jennings wrote a textbook.

> Another matter [he wrote] which is now never discussed in Cabinet is the exercise of the prerogative of dissolving Parliament ... No dissolution since 1918 has been brought before the Cabinet ... This is, however, a development since 1918; and if the Prime Minister desires the advice of the Cabinet there is nothing to prevent him from raising the question.[3]

The first two sentences are simply false. They were untrue in the first edition of *Cabinet Government* in 1936, and even more so by the time of the third and final edition in 1959. (Jennings died relatively young at 62 in 1965.) The third sentence is false by implication: for it suggests that, while there would be nothing unconstitutional in a Prime Minister's seeking the Cabinet's advice, none of them (there were nine in 1918-59) actually bothered to do so. This again is untrue. What is true is that since 1918 there has been no rule – in the sense of a generally recognised obligation – that the Prime Minister must consult the Cabinet, still less that the Cabinet must arrive at a collective decision. In practice the decision has usually been made by a small group of senior Ministers. The Cabinet has then been informed. Generally the Cabinet has been given a limited right of dissent, in the sense of: 'Anybody object? That's all right then. We all agree.' Practice, as we shall see, has varied. But, though there are numerous *obiter dicta* to the contrary, there is little doubt that there inheres in the Cabinet a residuary right to overrule the Prime Minister on the date of the election. One of the first of these *dicta* was George Wyndham's. He wrote to A.J. Balfour in 1905 that it rested, as he understood the constitution, with the Prime Minister alone to advise a dissolution. The sole responsibility was his and he must jealously preserve that power in its integrity.[4]

Lord Haldane carries more responsibility. Indeed, the modern doctrine, in its most absolute, Jenningsite form, owes more to Haldane than to Lloyd George. What happened was that, when H.H. Asquith resigned in 1916, George V sent for Bonar Law. He anticipated that, if Law accepted the invitation to form a government, he might do so on condition that a dissolution was granted. The King consulted Haldane, who wrote that the only Minister who could properly give advice as to a dissolution of Parliament was the Prime Minister.[5] But ten years later Asquith would still state that such a question as the dissolution of Parliament was always submitted to the Cabinet for ultimate decision.[6]

As Geoffrey Marshall has put it, the Haldane memorandum to George V unwittingly helped to originate the misunderstanding.[7] What Haldane had been called to advise on was the right of a *potential* Prime Minister such as Law (the politician who in fact became Prime Minister was Lloyd George, not Law) to request or bargain for a dissolution *before* assuming office. A potential incumbent would not be constitutionally entitled to offer advice on anything at all. The Haldane memorandum was not intended to pronounce on the quite different question of the Cabinet's collective rights vis-à-vis the Prime Minister. Neglect of the political circumstances in which the document came to be written led to a misunderstanding of one of the sentences in it.

Shortly afterwards a similar neglect brought about the same misunderstanding by the commentators. This time the words were spoken in the Commons rather than written in a memorandum; their author was not Haldane but Law. Lloyd George, as Prime Minister, wrote to him, as Leader of the Conservative Party and a Cabinet colleague, suggesting that the time had come for a dissolution. Law, for political reasons of his own, wanted Lloyd George to take exclusive responsibility. He said in the House of Commons that nothing was more clearly recognised by our constitutional practice than that those things were not the subject of any written rule but were governed by custom. In his belief there was no custom more clearly defined than that the advice on dissolution which should be given to the Sovereign was a question not for the Cabinet but for the Prime

Minister. John Dillon, the Irish Member, interrupted to say that this was not a recognised practice. He was amazed that the right honourable gentleman should say that it was. He believed that the custom had always been that the advice should be given with the *consent* of the Cabinet.[8]

In 1918 there was certainly no discussion: that was a consequence both of the Prime Minister's personality and of the Cabinet's organisation during the war years.[9] In 1922 there was little more. In 1923, however, Stanley Baldwin's decision to go to the country over protection was widely discussed and much criticised, both inside the Cabinet and outside it, not least by George V. Baldwin's typically skilful – and typically ambiguous – handling of this dissolution illustrates the difficulties of laying down a clear-cut and absolute rule in the manner of Jennings.

The crucial event was, chronologically, the first: Baldwin did not ask for a dissolution but warned the King that he might shortly be asking for one. The Conservative free traders in the Cabinet were 'greatly shaken' when they discovered this on 6 November 1923.[10] Lord Salisbury claimed that the Duke of Devonshire had heard it from 'the highest quarter', presumably the King himself. Salisbury was 'extremely upset'. He asked for help from Philip Lloyd-Graeme (later Cunliffe-Lister, later still Swinton), though he acknowledged that the King could not 'bind the Prime Minister to fix the date of the election'.[11] Salisbury saw Baldwin on the evening of 6 November and on the next day invited several colleagues to his house to consider their attitude. The Duke of Devonshire, Robert Cecil, Edward Wood (later Lord Halifax) and Lord Novar were present. Devonshire disclosed to them that Baldwin had already spoken to the King. They agreed to tender their conclusions to Baldwin in the form of a letter from Wood:

> I think that it is vital that we should give Parliament, and through Parliament the country, an adequate opportunity of examining the question on which they are to be asked to pronounce. If this is not consistent with a December election, I think we should be acting both unwisely and wrongly, and should aggravate the difference of some of our number, if we were to attempt to snatch a verdict, and that, if this is so, the appeal should be deferred. All this in great deference, recognising that fixing these matters is your special perquisite.[12]

At the Cabinet on 9 November, December, January and the spring each found its advocates. According to Lord Curzon, 'the great majority led by me were entirely opposed to a snap election'.[13] But the impression of colleagues was that Baldwin had already made up his mind to dissolve.[14] The final decision was probably made at a meeting attended by Baldwin, Lloyd-Graeme, Sir B. Eyres-Monsell, Leo Amery and Sir Laming Worthington-Evans on 11 November.[15]

On 12 November Baldwin went to York Cottage, Sandringham to ask for a dissolution. The King 'exercised all his influence' to dissuade him from this course. Baldwin remained convinced that an election on the tariff issue 'offered the only way out of his difficulties'. He had, according to the King's note, 'gone too far now' in Baldwin's own estimation. The country expected a dissolution. He would appeal to the country at once, hoped to get the election over by about 6 December and was ready to stand or fall by the result.[16] Lord Curzon wrote to his wife:

> I sent you off a telegram by Marconi to tell you that the thing you most feared is to happen, and that there is to be an immediate dissolution of Parliament, with a general election of December 6 ... [Baldwin] opened the Cabinet this morning by telling us in a sentence that the King had agreed to an immediate dissolution ... I think the Cabinet was profoundly shocked and incensed at the way in which they [sic] have been treated, and at the recklessness with which the government and the country, entirely contrary to the will and wish of either, have been plunged into a general election by the arbitrary fiat of one weak and ignorant man ... Derby is furious, and says Europe is dominated by madmen ... Poincaré and Mussolini – and England is ruled by a damned idiot ... Of course if we win by the same or an enhanced majority, he will be justified ... But if ... we only get a reduced majority, or possibly no majority at all... I think he will then be deposed from the leadership of the party.[17]

As things turned out, the Conservatives got no majority at all; Ramsay MacDonald formed the first Labour government. Baldwin, far from being deposed from the leadership of the party, remained at its head for the next 14 years. He had outfaced his Sovereign, disdained the old Tory grandees and overcome the majority of his Cabinet, who did not want an election. Though he was not exactly young – in November 1923 he was 56 – he was certainly an inexperienced Prime Minister. It was an astonishing political achievement. Whether it established the sole right of the Prime Minister to decide the date of the election may be more doubtful. Asquith, who had no cause to be grateful to Baldwin, certainly did not think so.

This election involved the power of the Prime Minister vis-à-vis not only his colleagues, which has chiefly engaged us up till now, but also his Sovereign, to which we must now turn. It was the latter which Asquith had principally in mind when he addressed a meeting of Liberal MPs at the National Liberal Club on 18 December 1923.

Dissolution of Parliament (he said) was in this country one of the prerogatives of the Crown. It was not a mere feudal survival, but a part, and a useful part, of our constitutional system. It did not mean that the Crown should act arbitrarily and without the advice of responsible Ministers. But it did mean that the Crown was not bound to take the advice of a particular Minister to put its subjects to the 'tumult and turmoil' of a series of general elections so long as it could find other Ministers who were prepared to give contrary advice. The notion that a Ministry which could not command a majority in the House of Commons – a Ministry in a minority of 31 per cent – had the right to demand a dissolution was as subversive of constitutional usage as it was pernicious to the 'general and permanent interest' of the nation at large.[18]

The King soon had the opportunity to put Asquith's principles into practice. In 1924 MacDonald's government was censured over its conduct of the Campbell case. It was supposed to have improperly influenced the withdrawal of a prosecution for sedition against the editor of the *Daily Worker*. Compared to some of the lego-political scandals to which we have become accustomed in the post-war period, especially perhaps since 1980 or thereabouts, it was minor. Asquith delivered one of the speeches which were to bring down the government – though it was also one of the more moderate in tone. On the night of 8-9 October 1924, George V travelled to London from Scotland. MacDonald came to see him on Thursday 9 October 1924 and asked for an immediate dissolution. Reluctantly, the King agreed:

> In granting the Prime Minister's request to dissolve Parliament, I could not help regretting the necessity for doing so, being aware how strongly the country at large deprecates another general election within less than a year and all its attendant dislocations of trade, of the daily business-life of the community and the consequent adverse effect upon the employment of labour, as well as the great expense thereby incurred. I am sorry also that the appeal to the electorate cannot be made upon a more vital issue than that raised this evening in the House of Commons.[19]

The King was criticised, both at the time and later, for granting this dissolution. The years 1918-24 were crucial in the development of British politics. The period 1923-24 marked a turning-point. If the Liberal Party could, under some arrangement, have been given another taste of power, who can tell what the outcome would have been? But Harold Nicolson told us in 1952 that the King had not agreed to the dissolution 'immediately'. He agreed with the 'utmost reluctance' and only after he had ascertained from the leaders of the Conservative and Liberal Parties that they themselves were unable or unwilling to form an administration.[20] The Labour government of 1924 was essentially an unstable structure. Ideas of instability change with years. Jennings asserted in 1959:

> When no party obtains a majority at a general election there are two possibilities only, the formation of a coalition government or the formation of a minority government with opposition support; for another dissolution is not practicable.[21]

Why ever not? There was no difficulty of any kind in 1974. This brings us to what a Prime Minister should do if his or her request to dissolve is refused. Haldane was firm in his memorandum to George V in 1916: the Sovereign, before acting on advice to dissolve, ought to weigh that advice. He might, instead of accepting it, dismiss the Minister who gave it, or receive his resignation. That was the only alternative to taking his advice.[22]

Jennings wrote that Haldane's opinion was 'perhaps too absolute' and that it did not 'necessarily follow' that a Prime Minister who was refused a dissolution would resign.[23] In practice, however, this is what a Prime Minister would do. If, say, in February 1974, the Queen had refused a dissolution to Edward Heath, on the entirely plausible ground that an election would settle nothing, he could have huffed and puffed and said: 'If that is your view, we shall carry on reluctantly.' More probably he would have resigned, when the Queen would have had no alternative but to send for Harold Wilson as Leader of the Opposition. Assuming no division among the Conservatives, the new Labour government would then have been defeated as soon as it met the House of Commons. Wilson could then have asked for a dissolution. If the Queen had refused, she would have had Heath on her hands once again: much better to comply with the request in the first place. B.S. Markesinis is more definite:

> The Crown cannot refuse a dissolution to a majority Prime Minister. The size of the party's majority is irrelevant.[24]

DISSOLUTION IN PRACTICE: THE 1950 DISSOLUTION

The question was much discussed after the 1950 election, the first of our post-war precedents. Four years later, C.R. Attlee was to write:

> It is ... the duty of the Prime Minister to choose the time which, in his view, is the most propitious. In these days the choice is limited. The Budget and the financial year, the local elections and the holiday periods restrict the choice to late autumn, early spring or midsummer. There is always the gamble as to what the weather will be. November and February are notoriously liable to be foggy ... I chose February and was very fortunate in that it turned out to be one of the best months of the year.[25]

Attlee's innocent prose conceals a prolonged and hot dispute among the Labour Ministers of that time. Perhaps the strongest personal factor was Stafford Cripps's desire to go before the Budget. Douglas Jay, then Economic Secretary to the Treasury, told the young James Callaghan that, following the 1949 Devaluation, Cripps was taking attacks on his integrity 'very badly'. He wanted an election in March 1950 'because he refuses to introduce another Budget until he has been fortified by the electorate'.[26] His health was bad, and worsening. He had been wounded by accusations of dishonesty from Churchill and others.[27] Harold Wilson, as President of the Board of Trade, also pressed for an early election; while for Aneurin Bevan and *Tribune* the cause became virtually a campaign, comparable to the one for a Second Front Now. Bevan 'strongly and persistently' pressed the case for October or November 1949 on Attlee. On 30 September 1949 there was a 'special article' in *Tribune*:

> Already civil servants are well-known to be suffering from that peculiar form of suspended animation which afflicts them when a general election is in the offing ... the higher the civil servant, the worse the disease. So many of the top-ranking officials are ingrained with a Tory consciousness that, in the hope or belief in a Tory victory, they recommend action opposed to the spirit of the government.[28]

As early as 19 July 1949, Attlee summoned a group of senior Ministers to discuss the date of the election. Those present included Herbert Morrison, Ernest Bevin, Aneurin Bevan and William Whiteley, the Chief Whip. Stafford Cripps was in Zurich receiving treatment but sent a letter for Attlee to read to the gathering. He wanted an immediate dissolution and an election in the middle of the August holidays. Attlee observed that Cripps was obviously not in good shape. Bevan wanted an election before the end of the year: he was afraid of both a loss of momentum as the legislative programme wound down and the electoral consequences of the next Budget, which he saw as needing to be less popular even than the last one.[29] This was a factor which weighed with Cripps too. As Attlee explained it:

> He thought he would be expected to produce an election Budget, which went against his sense of rectitude. I sympathised with him. It is dangerous to play politics with the Budget. It opens the way to every possible kind of stunt.[30]

With one exception, the senior Ministers present agreed on the need to dissolve before the next Budget, though they were willing to wait until February 1950. The exception was Morrison, who feared that the party machine was not yet up to it and that the country might think the government was 'running away'.[31]

On 12 October 1949 Attlee called a meeting of senior Ministers at No. 10 to discuss the timing of the election. Morrison's view which he had given in the summer had, if anything, hardened: he was for delay. Bevan, Cripps and Dalton were against delay; Wilson, 'half-way against'. On 13 October 1949 Attlee called a meeting of the full Cabinet. It decided against an election before 1950. On the same afternoon the Prime Minister announced that there would be no election in 1949.

The election choice was between February and June 1950. On 7 December 1949 Attlee called another meeting in Downing Street. Apart from Morrison, who (holding the traditional view of the professional Labour organiser about the effect of rain on the moral fibre of the working classes) feared the February weather, all the Ministers present were for that month. Bevin was away ill at Eastbourne, but sent a message saying he was prepared to leave the decision to the meeting, as he was 'no politician'. The Ministers present were Lord Addison, C.R. Attlee, Aneurin Bevan, Stafford Cripps, Hugh Dalton, Herbert Morrison and William Whiteley. Morrison dissenting, they decided the timing of the election of February 1950.[32]

THE 1951 DISSOLUTION

Labour's majority of six caused what in retrospect must appear an extraordinary amount of constitutional head-shaking. There was certainly nothing like it either in 1964 or in October 1974, when the Labour Government won a lower majority, or in February 1974, when it won no majority at all. Sir John Wheeler-Bennett, the King's biographer, noted that the majority was 'so narrow that it would not enable them to proceed nor [*sic*] justify them in trying to proceed'.[33] Winston Churchill was consulted and, in a letter to the King's private secretary, asserted the principle – echoing George V's view of the 1924 dissolution* – that 'a new House of Commons has a right to live if it can and should not be destroyed until some firm issue or situation has arisen to place before the electors'.[34]

A controversy in *The Times* ensued about Attlee's right to demand a dissolution.[35] Lord Simon, a former Lord Chancellor and much else besides, asserted that the Prime Minister had no such right: the situation envisaged was one of the 'rare surviving cases' when 'the Sovereign exercises his own discretion in deciding upon his public action'. The Labour peer Lord Chorley thought that Lord Simon was 'on unsound and dangerous ground'. Fortified by his extensive war-time reading of Victorian political biographies, the young Labour politician Roy Jenkins agreed, pointing out that no request for a dissolution had been refused since the Reform Bill of 1832, and adding that George V appeared 'to have had no hesitation in granting a dissolution', even though 'this involved the country in its third general election within two years'. As we have seen, the King had considerable hesitation: but Nicolson's masterly biography had not appeared at this time. Lord Simon then returned to the battle, basing his argument on Asquith's 1923 speech.† On 2 May 1950 the correspondence was authoritatively and perhaps a little pompously concluded by a writer signing himself 'Senex', which, Wheeler-Bennett informs us, concealed the King's private secretary, Sir Alan Lascelles. He wrote:

> In as far as this matter can be publicly discussed, it can be properly assumed that no wise Sovereign – that is, one who has at heart the true interest of the country, the constitution and the Monarchy – would deny a dissolution to his Prime Minister unless he were satisfied that: (1) the existing Parliament was still vital, viable and capable of doing its job; (2) a general election would be detrimental to the national economy; (3) he could rely on finding another

---

* See above, p. 25.
† See above, p. 21.

Prime Minister who could carry on his government, for a reasonable period, with a working majority in the House of Commons. When Sir Patrick Duncan refused a dissolution to his Prime Minister in South Africa in 1939, all these conditions were satisfied: when Lord Byng did the same in Canada in 1926, they appeared to be, but in the event the third proved illusory.[36]

The King was advised that, though he was constitutionally entitled to refuse a dissolution, the arguments were against doing so.[37] In practice the discussions with Attlee were not so much about the King's theoretical power to refuse a dissolution – which does not seem to have been mentioned at all – as about his worsening health and his projected tour of the Commonwealth (which did not, in the event, take place). On 1 September 1951 the King wrote to Attlee that it would be 'very difficult indeed' for him to go away for five or six months unless it was 'reasonably certain' that political stability would prevail during his absence. On the other hand, it would be disastrous if his visits to three of the self-governing countries of the Commonwealth had to be postponed or interrupted on account of 'political upheavals' at home. It would be a 'great relief' to him if Attlee could now – or even in the next few weeks – give him 'some assurance' that would set his 'mind at rest on this score'.[38]

On 5 September 1951 Attlee replied that he had been giving 'much anxious thought' to a general election. Among factors to which he had given 'particular attention' was the need for avoiding any political crisis while the King was out of the country. He had come to the conclusion that the right course would be to have a dissolution of Parliament in the first week in October. A later date would, he thought, be undesirable, as November was 'seldom a good month from the point of view of the weather'. He would therefore like to make a submission to the King 'in about a fortnight's time' for the prorogation and dissolution of Parliament in the first week of October.[39]

Two weeks later Attlee told the Cabinet that he proposed to call a general election and gave the date. The King's health worsened. He wrote to Attlee that 'so that there is no misunderstanding of recent events by historians in the future', he wanted to put the following on record in his 'secret archives': that when he wrote to Attlee from Balmoral on 1 September urging that a decision should be taken to ensure political stability in the country before he left on his projected Commonwealth tour in January, he had 'no conception' that his physical condition might make it necessary for him to abandon the tour.[40]

Far from having been reluctant to grant a dissolution, as the *Times* correspondence of April-May 1950 had suggested he might be, he had been enthusiastic for the course, in the interests of more stable government during his Commonwealth tour. He was in effect apologising to Attlee for having unwittingly misled him. Attlee later explained in a newspaper interview:

It wasn't a sudden decision. One of the reasons I wanted it was because of
the King. His health was bad and he was going off to Australia. It would have
been unfair to allow a crisis, which might blow up at any time, while he was
out of the country. He would have been worrying all the time whether
something was going to happen.[41]

The royal explanation is not inconsistent with the others that have been
given for the timing of the 1951 election, notably by Attlee himself: the, in
Attlee's word, 'exiguous' majority; the vigorous Conservative opposition
who put down 'prayers' against Orders and kept the House up all night;
the less vigorous Labour Members; above all, the dying Ministers, Bevin
and Cripps.[42] But views among Ministers differed about whether to dissolve or to hang on.

Dalton wrote to Attlee that, if they went to the country in October 1951
– the month he had consistently advocated since May 1951 – Labour might
lose 'a few' seats, enough perhaps to put the Conservatives in with a 'small
majority'. But he thought most of the younger Labour Members, 'who
matter more for the future', would hold their seats. But if Labour hung on
much longer, there would be a 'massacre in the marginals'.[43]

Douglas Jay, on the other hand, thought the 1951 election 'unnecessary
and undesirable'. He put his view strongly to Hugh Gaitskell, saying he
felt it amounted to 'abdication'. To Jay's surprise, Gaitskell was 'not nearly
so strongly convinced' of this, though 'on balance' he tended to agree.
George Brown and Jay went on a deputation to Attlee, but made no
impression.[44]

Herbert Morrison took the same view as he had in 1950. As early as 27
May 1951 Attlee wrote to him saying that he proposed to hold the election
in October 1951. He cited the King's visit to the Commonwealth and
proceeded to whistle to keep up his spirits:

> There is a good prospect of improved meat supplies and a possibility of better
> weather over the holidays. There may be a change in the Korean and Persian
> positions. Something may emerge from the Four Power Talks. In my view
> everything points to having an election in the autumn ... I would like to
> consider with you what other colleagues to bring into consultation.[45]

Morrison suggested a meeting of a few senior Ministers to discuss
timing. Attlee did not respond, though according to Dalton he did talk to
a few colleagues, none of whom disagreed with him about an October
election. In July 1951 Morrison raised the matter with Attlee again,
mentioning the possibility of waiting until 1952: 'As you know, I was
unhappy about the 1950 date as to which Stafford and Nye were wrong. I
don't want us to make another mistake.'[46]

There is no record of any reply from Attlee to Morrison. On 24 June
1951, at an audience with the King, who was concerned about the government's 'unstable position', Attlee had said that he would be asking for a

dissolution in the autumn. On 19 September 1951 he informed a poorly attended Cabinet that he proposed to dissolve. Gaitskell, Morrison and Emanuel Shinwell were at the Ottawa conference. They heard this 'to their dismay'.[47] Attlee informed Morrison of his intention to dissolve shortly before the announcement was made.[48] But this hardly amounted to consultation. It certainly did not prevent Morrison and Shinwell from cabling Attlee urging him to delay any announcement till they could return to discuss the matter. Dalton called it 'a peevish exchange of telegrams across the Atlantic'.[49] Morrison had been kept informed, up to a point: he had not been consulted.

Anyway, he had lost again – though who is to say that he, Jay and a few others were wrong, while the King, Attlee and (according to Dalton) a majority of Ministers were right? Morrison thought that Gaitskell too wanted the election, and that Attlee tended to do what his new Chancellor wanted. Whether he did or not, Gaitskell's view had changed: 'We should be badly beaten, and one hated not to win, and to hand over power to the enemy.'[50] Power was indeed handed over, for 13 years, unnecessarily when judged by the experiences of 1964-6 and 1974-9. The effective decision was taken here by the Prime Minister alone, strongly influenced by the Sovereign.[51]

THE 1955 DISSOLUTION

The timing of the 1955 election was governed by two factors: the desire of Anthony Eden to succeed Winston Churchill and of Conservative Central Office to win the election. The involvement of Central Office in questions of election timing was not new: for example, in October 1928 the Cabinet discussed dissolution twice and arrangements were made for Central Office to give its views.[52] But though in 1955 television was not yet the force it was to become, it is in that election that we can see the first signs of the post-war domination by the party machines. The birds of paradise in Downing Street and the moles in Smith Square a quarter of a mile away seemed to be living separate existences. An increasingly impatient Eden and a growingly obdurate Churchill (marvellously recovered from the stroke which had placed the country in the hands of his son-in-law, Christopher Soames, and R.A. Butler) flitted from luncheon party to the House and then on to a reception and dinner, their doings chronicled by Churchill's indiscreet physician Lord Moran and his factotum Sir John Colville.[53]

On 18 April 1954 Sir Norman Brook, the Secretary of the Cabinet, told Moran that the Conservatives were thinking of a general election in autumn 1955. One thing that was 'definite and fixed' was the Prime Minister's decision that he would not lead the party in another election.[54] Five months later, however, Churchill wrote to Eden making clear that he intended to remain Prime Minister until after an election in 1955:

The dominant fact is that the changes in the rating valuations are said to make it overwhelmingly desirable to have the election before November 1955. It does not seem to me that the brief spell which remains till then gives the best chance to the party or offers a propitious outlook to my successor. Certainly he would court a very heavy responsibility which in fact rests on me. He would have to present in 12 or 13 months the impression of something new and different which would spread the sense of importance. But we must ask ourselves whether this is likely in the prevailing circumstances. It is certain that one-half of the country, instead of judging the new government fairly on its merits, will on the contrary make it their target for electioneering abuse and for unfavourable comparisons. Woolton, whom as party chairman I have consulted, tells me that he has already expressed the opinion that such a procedure would be bad election tactics ... Fag end administrations have not usually been triumphant. I can remember Rosebery after Gladstone and AJB after Salisbury. Both were brushed aside in spite of their ability, experience and charm.[55]

On 8 March 1955 Churchill lunched with Eden. Harold Macmillan, who was also present, recorded in his diary that it seemed settled that Churchill would resign on 5 April. But Sir Roger Makins, the Washington ambassador, nearly spoilt everything by suggesting that President Eisenhower might be prepared to attend a summit. Any mention of summits was calculated to impel Churchill to carry on. He wrote to Eden that this complicated a May election, 'to which I gather you are inclining'. He went on to contrast 'the party politics of a snap election to take advantage of Socialist disunity' with 'a meeting of the Heads of Governments which would give a chance to the world of warding off its mortal peril'. The electorate's response to this contrast 'would not be favourable'. Eden replied crossly that he would not dream of putting party before country. Churchill wrote that he was not accusing him of this, but that his attitude 'would be taken to imply a snap election in May', which would 'rouse a party struggle of intense bitterness'.[56]

On 21 March Moran found Churchill in the Cabinet Room. He showed Moran that now defunct London evening paper the *Star*. A headline – correctly – gave 26 May as the date of the election. Churchill said:

> They are telling me the day I shall have to go. I wonder who gave them the date? I suppose the party. They wanted to fix a date once and for all for the election. The Central Office must have let it out. I don't care.[57]

On 30 March, however, Churchill was discussing the date in Cabinet. Macmillan complained (at any rate, to his diary) about this. It was a matter for the new Prime Minister to decide.[58] On 1 April there was a report in the *Manchester Guardian* that Churchill would not retire until the end of the press strike which was then going on. Churchill said it was 'absurd' – that he would not 'alter the date of the election' because there were 'no papers'.[59] On 3 April he wrote an unposted letter to Eisenhower, saying that the choice of election date was 'one of extraordinary complication' but that 'the decision should be taken by the man whose fortunes are governed by the result'.[60]

On 5 April Churchill resigned and was succeeded by Eden. Three days later he received his first letter from his successor, telling him that the general election was 'likely' to be on 26 May. It was the deterioration in Britain's financial position, Eden explained, which was the 'disagreeable reality' pushing the government towards a May election. He had been tempted to try to show that he could lead 'a good administration' for at least six months before going to the country. But he was increasingly compelled to take account of 'these distasteful economic factors'.[61] These factors, however, went unmentioned in Eden's memoirs. He wrote that the arguments for and against the election were nicely balanced. The country had no love for general elections. If it judged that one was uncalled for, it was likely to be resentful. This feeling would be sharpened if the election was judged to be a snap one – Eden was here reproducing Churchill's argument[*] – intended to 'gain advantage from a certain disarray in the ranks of the opposition'.[62] With the passage of days, the likelihood that the election might be regarded as unwarranted diminished. Public opinion appeared to be more reconciled to it. Eden became convinced that, if the government continued to hold office with such a narrow majority as 17 without an appeal to the country, it would be living in an 'election atmosphere'. This would be 'thoroughly unhealthy'. Accordingly he decided to ask the Queen for a dissolution and the country for a mandate. He had an audience on 15 April 1955 and that night announced the dissolution.[63]

David Carlton, not the friendliest of authors to Eden, writes that this decision 'required a little, but not much, courage'.[64] From Carlton, this must rank as praise indeed. But Eden's own version, true though it may be as far as it goes, is evidently incomplete. It should be supplemented by what he wrote to Churchill on 8 April[†] and by what Sir Norman Brook told Lord Moran on 18 July 1955:

> The party had wanted for some time to go to the country. The real reason why they wanted an election was that the economic situation was as good as it was likely to be. In the autumn it might not be so good. Incidentally, the fact that they came back with a good majority proved they were right. And then when everything was fixed up Ike announced, out of the blue, that he would like to come over.[65] Brook conceded Churchill's view that his resignation, *as distinct from the date of the election*, was not a matter for the Cabinet to decide. However, this time the party knew all about the date, and Anthony could not have given way even if he had wanted to. So Ike was told privately that the Conservative Party had a general election in view. Then when all this was settled, Anthony decided to take a chance and go to the country directly he took over from Winston [italics added].[66]

* See above, p. 256.
† See above.

Brook was certain that this was not merely a trick to force Churchill out. The party genuinely believed it was the right moment to go to the country.

THE 1959 DISSOLUTION

Harold Macmillan faced no comparable difficulties in 1959. Eden was safely out of the way, while no rival was in sight, and Macmillan was toying with thoughts of successors – and, indeed, with the successors themselves. Some of them he invited to lunch at 10 Downing Street on 3 April 1959 specifically to discuss election timing. Those present were R.A. Butler, Lord Hailsham, Lord Poole, Iain Macleod, Edward Heath and Derick Heathcoat Amory. The meeting lasted three hours. Central Office advised, with remarkable exactitude, that an April dissolution would give the Conservatives a majority of 13. Macmillan asked what the effect of the Budget would be, how the Conservatives would stand on 11 June (the proposed date for a general election) and whether they would be better off in October.

He confided to his diary that the chief consideration was the European, or Berlin, crisis. What if there was a summit in August? Would it be better to have a new government by then? But what if it turned out to be a 'Socialist' government or, worst of all, no government at all, with no proper majority. 'What ought I to do, not as party leader but as the Queen's Prime Minister. All these are terribly difficult questions.'[67]

By 18 April he had made up his mind. October was 'the normal, almost conventional date for a Parliament which had been elected more than four years before'. To call a summer election might seem 'almost sharp practice', than which the electorate disliked nothing more.[68] On 22 April the 1922 Committee held its annual luncheon at the Savoy Hotel. Virtually the entire party was there. After discussion with the Chief Whip, Macmillan decided to use the occasion to announce that there would be no spring election in 1959. Among arguments which had weighed with him against either a spring or a summer election was a concern for the Queen's comfort. She had undertaken a 'long and strenuous' tour in Canada. Her pregnancy was announced on 7 August. On 22 August Macmillan wrote to her 'warning her of the probability of my soon asking her to approve a dissolution'.[69]

On 7 September he went to Balmoral and had an audience before dinner. The Queen was 'very gracious'. Macmillan used the occasion to deliver a short constitutional lecture to Her Majesty. The Prime Minister, he explained, had no right to *advise* a dissolution. Certainly the Crown, 'in the long run', had today to accept advice. But the Prime Minister *asked* for a dissolution, which the Crown could agree to or not. This, 'the last great prerogative of the Crown', must be preserved. It might turn out to be 'of vital importance at a time of national crisis'. The Queen formally agreed to his request. The date, according to Macmillan, 'seemed to her well-chosen'. The next day, 8 September, the Cabinet met at seven, and the announcement that Parliament would be dissolved on 18 September, with polling to take place on 8 October, was made an hour later.[70]

THE 1964 DISSOLUTION

In his own memoirs, by contrast, Lord Home was singularly – though typically – uninformative about the 1964 election, which he fought as Sir Alec Douglas-Home. Like the Parliaments of 1974-9, 1987-92 and 1992-7, that of 1959-64 went the whole distance. The reason in 1964, 1979 and 1992 was in all cases the same. There had been a change of Prime Minister: respectively Callaghan for Wilson, Major for Thatcher and Home for Macmillan. After the struggle for the Conservative leadership of October 1963, the possibility of an early election seemed remote. Nevertheless, March 1964 was not finally ruled out till mid-February.[71] The choice then lay between May-June and October. It was the cause of one of the fiercest fights about election timing of modern times.

Home himself was at first inclined towards the early summer, believing that, once the electorate had to confront the possibility of a Labour government, they would not vote Labour. He was supported by the younger members of the Cabinet, notably by Reginald Maudling. As Chancellor, Maudling was also anxious to have a quick decision for his own budgetary purposes. In January 1964 Maudling told James Callaghan that he would prefer the election to be held in the spring to be freer to take any 'necessary corrective action' in the summer.[72] As so often happens, a quick decision was taken to imply a decision that the matter to be decided should come about sooner rather than later. As one of these younger Ministers put it:

> It was always Alec's instinct to go in June, you know. But being the sort of chap he is, he found it impossible to go against his responsible advisers, in this case the organisation men. They simply told us that if we went in June we'd lose. It seemed to me a pretty facile argument. After all, the important point was that we couldn't do any more governing. The delay ossified everything.[73]

However, more experienced Ministers, such as R.A. Butler and Quintin Hogg (into which he had reconverted himself to contest the leadership in the previous year), were on Central Office's side and in favour of waiting till October. So was the former Prime Minister Harold Macmillan, not least because October was thought to be traditionally a good month for the Conservatives. Butler was a particularly strong supporter of October, and made his views clear in Cabinet.[74] Lord Blakenham, the chairman of the party, was assailed with advice. His predecessor at Central Office, Lord Poole, who was widely credited with miraculous powers over elections, was particularly severe both with him and with the Ministers who wanted to go in June:

> A lot of Ministers got unduly influenced by civil servants who told them the

government couldn't be properly carried on. It was bloody silly. If civil servants don't want to do the job, then you sack them and get some others who can. [This was a brisk and inaccurate City man's view of Whitehall in the 1960s. It would not perhaps have been quite so erroneous in the 1980s and 90s.] I made Blakenham bang the table and say he'd walk out if Home had an election in June. People never want advice. They want to be told what to do. That's one of the secrets of life.[75]

In March 1964 Home decided to make an announcement about the election shortly after the Easter recess. On 26 March he consulted most members of the Cabinet in the House of Commons before retiring to Scotland for the Easter recess.[76] On 9 April he announced that he 'intended to carry on the government until the last months of its legal life'.[77] One reason was that Blakenham 'felt that with time we had a chance to win'; while the announcement of the delay 'would steady confidence, for the public media had been carrying on a running speculation which was unsettling to everyone'.[78] The Octobrists had won. They had been almost certainly right to press for delay. For Labour, having earlier been expected to humiliate the Conservatives under the then much-admired leadership of Harold Wilson, won by only four seats.

THE 1966 DISSOLUTION

One of Wilson's characteristics as Prime Minister was to claim – meanwhile taking out his pocket diary to illustrate his point – to have decided a political event months, even years before the time at which he was credited with the decision. The event in question might be an important speech, a Cabinet reshuffle, a general election. The 1966 election was certainly an illustration of Wilson's approach. It was widely believed, then and subsequently, that he held it when he did because Labour won the Hull North by-election on 27 January 1966. He was most anxious to controvert this. The truth, he wrote, was almost precisely the opposite.[79] He had decided on an early election 'quite firmly' before Hull voted. Indeed, had Labour lost, the government would have had to go to the country, as its majority would then have been down to one. If anything, the result was an indication not to have an election, being a vote 'to tell us to get on with the job'.[80]

There is little reason to doubt Wilson's account. His political secretary Marcia Williams (later Lady Falkender) recorded that immediately after Christmas 1965 he had already decided that 'whatever happened' the election would be in March 1966 and that this was 'the best and only possible time'. Winning Hull, 'though marvellous in itself, and indicating that we stood a chance of doing extremely well, was irrelevant to the decision which had already been taken'.[81]

Wilson goes on to tell us that before Hull he decided to consult George Brown as deputy leader and found he had reached the same conclusion.

He then called in James Callaghan, the Chancellor, because it was clear that a March election would be met with the charge that Labour was going to the country to anticipate an unpopular Budget. Callaghan's advice was for a 'neutral Budget'. Weeks after the decision had been taken, when Wilson was trying to drum up interest in the possibility of a March election because he feared apathy, the press would not take it seriously.[82]

However, Wilson's biographer Ben Pimlott points out that he told the press at the very end of February that he had decided on a dissolution 'something like a fortnight ago', which would have been after Hull.[83] In the same month, Wilson told the then head of the International Publishing Corporation, Cecil King, that he was thinking of 24 or 31 March, the latter being the actual date. King promptly and typically passed on the information to Edward Heath, before Wilson had told the Cabinet.[84] But Wilson's statement to King proves nothing about his decision vis-à-vis Hull: it demonstrates only Wilson's (and King's) indiscreet habits.

At all events, on 28 February there was a special meeting of the Cabinet at which, according to Barbara Castle, Wilson 'confirmed' that the election would be on 31 March. 'No one objected.'[85] R.H.S. Crossman wrote that 'we formally decided the election date'.[86] But Wilson decided the election date – at any rate, the election month – at the turn of the year. Subsequently no one influenced (or tried to influence) his decision one way or the other. The election established his reputation as a wonder-working Prime Minister, over the timing of elections, anyway.

THE 1970 DISSOLUTION

Roy Jenkins wrote that Harold Wilson claimed to have pencilled 18 June 1970 into his diary as long ago as 1966.[87] Publicly, Wilson himself was not so ambitious. In his memoirs, he claimed to have 'virtually decided' on Monday 13 April, the day before Jenkins's Budget, that the 1970 election should be held on 18 June.[88] Joe Haines, then Wilson's press adviser, confirms this. The decision, he writes, was taken in the Prime Minister's study at No. 10. In theory the 1966 Parliament could last until the first week of April 1971. But the introduction of decimalisation in February 1971 was held to be so unpopular that the choice was thought to lie between midsummer and autumn 1970.[89]

It is interesting that Haines mentions the unpopularity of decimalisation rather than the possibility of England's doing well in the World Cup of summer 1970. The latter has often been advanced as one of the principal reasons why Wilson went when he did. This, if true, makes a certain amount of sense. What does not make sense is the subsidiary version of the story, which is that Wilson timed the 1966 election because of the World Cup. He cannot have done this, because the election was held in March 1966, whereas England won at Wembley in July. Wilson certainly exploited the occasion in full, appearing unexpectedly on the team's hotel balcony with manager and players. But by this time the election was safely over.

In 1970, by contrast, the election campaign was proceeding as the cup was being contested in Mexico. Wilson would mention 'the lads' in his speeches.[90] It has been said that England's elimination from the contest rebounded on Labour. This may be so. Equally, success in the competition may have been in his mind when he fixed on June. But he does not say so. Nor do the other principal chroniclers of these events, Castle, Crossman, Haines and Jenkins. If the considerations had been important, one would have expected at any rate Wilson and Haines – both of whom were interested in football – to say something about it.[91]

Another factor was Jenkins's virtuous Budget. Both Crossman and Castle attacked him for what they considered to be his moralistic approach. Jenkins replied by pointing out that the government's standing in the opinion polls actually increased after the Budget. Wilson was on Jenkins's side: the Budget's 'moderation' was widely regarded as strengthening support for Labour because of its contrast to the old Conservative pre-election Budgets.[92]

Jenkins told Wilson that no economic developments were likely which would inhibit his freedom over election timing.[93] Peter Shore, the Minister without Portfolio, and Gerald Kaufman, one of Wilson's confidants, were in favour of June. So, 'more reluctantly', was Joe Haines.[94] Marcia Williams said she preferred June 'provided Labour was not going to lose'; otherwise she favoured going on to the 'bitter end'.[95] After the defeat on 18 June Wilson commended Mrs Williams's judgment. Haines commented somewhat ungenerously that she had backed both horses in a two-horse race and that it was easy to be right provided everyone forgot you were also wrong.[96]

The crucial meeting was that of the Management Committee on 29 April. This was the – typically Labourist – name for the Inner Cabinet which Wilson had formally inaugurated But as he could not bear to leave people out, and was certainly alert to the political dangers of so doing, the committee numbered 11, too large to be called an Inner Cabinet. At this meeting Jenkins said he would like more time to think out the economic implications of June and October, as he had only just returned from abroad: 'I must have sounded like Crosland.'[97] He was, however, strongly against going on into 1971. James Callaghan thought Labour would win at any time. Tony Benn was worried about 'certain developments' in the United States.[98] Robert Mellish, the Chief Whip, said that the parliamentary party was evenly divided into three groups, those who were not running again preferring 1971. Fred Peart and Michael Stewart were for June – they tended to follow the Prime Minister's views in all matters – but Denis Healey was doubtful, while only Mrs Castle and Crossman were against June and for October.[99] Crossman thought Wilson had so directed the discussion, from which the Cabinet Secretary, Sir Burke Trend, had been excluded, that the third week of June seemed the obvious choice. He added:

Next day Harold felt entitled to say he had not discussed election prospects with the Cabinet or with any of his ministerial colleagues, though he had in fact spent two hours doing so.[100]

This was different from what had happened in 1966:

> Let me make a note for the record. In the spring of 1966 Harold was deciding election dates absolutely on his own, perhaps consulting a small circle of Marcia, Gerald, Peter, Tony and me, but virtually no one else. Now he sits around with nine of his colleagues at Management Committee prepared, apparently, to see this as a matter for consultation ....[101]

At the next meeting on 14 May, Wilson said: 'I really decided this a month ago.' The Test Match started on 18 June, so an election then would forestall trouble over the South African tour. Orange Day in July and Apprentices' Day in August would not interfere with a June poll. He looked forward to a majority of over 20. 'Everyone agreed? Right: then no one will be able to claim the virtue of hindsight.' Meanwhile the rest of the Cabinet were being kept waiting outside. After 45 minutes they were allowed in. They were told that there was still no decision and that it was important to say also that there had been no discussion.

On 12 May, two days before, Wilson had told the Queen of his 'likely recommendations'. Marcia Williams said it was still not too late to change his mind. He made a 'formal submission' to Her Majesty on 18 May. There was an announcement from No. 10 that evening.[102]

THE FEBRUARY 1974 DISSOLUTION

The timing of the general election of February 1974 was the most puzzling of modern times, not least to its principal participants. The Parliament could have lasted till July 1975. The government had an adequate majority. It was at no stage made clear what the re-elected Conservative government would do with its increased majority, if it managed to obtain one.

These questions perplexed Norman St John-Stevas too. Just before the decision to hold the election was taken, Walter Annenberg, the United States ambassador, gave a dinner party where several Ministers were present. With Margaret Thatcher, St John-Stevas (later Lord St John of Fawsley) had been opposed to an early election, but 'we had come around to accepting its inevitability'. At the dinner he mentioned to Lord Carrington, the chairman of the party, that he had changed his mind. Carrington, who was one of the chief urgers of an election, advised him to tell Edward Heath. The Employment Secretary, William Whitelaw, was also at the dinner. St John-Stevas put to him the question which was never satisfactorily answered: what difference would it make if they did have a general election. After all, they already had a viable working majority. Whitelaw replied sapiently: 'We'll be in a different ball game.'[103]

This reply was, in a sense, slightly surprising. For Whitelaw was, always had been, opposed to the election. He thought the contest was a 'grave risk' to the new Northern Ireland Executive which he had helped create. He had been brought back from Ireland, against his wishes, for the specific purpose of seeking a solution to the miners' dispute. He had been 'swept' into a campaign which he 'dreaded' and he was 'bound to dislike a confrontation from a failure to find a settlement'. In retrospect, he realised that there had been only one choice: to give in to the miners, but to accept the Trades Union Congress's offer of January 1974 to restrain other unions from following their example. His great mistake, he later confessed, was not to oppose 7 February, the date which had originally been urged on Heath, but to surrender over 28 February, the date on which the election was actually held.[104]

Those chiefly responsible for the first of the 1974 elections were Carrington, Jim Prior (his deputy), Douglas Hurd (Heath's political secretary) and William Waldegrave (who had recently arrived at the political office at No. 10 from the Central Policy Review Staff, or the Think Tank). In December 1973 Hurd, Waldegrave and other youthful advisers produced a paper for the Prime Minister. They said that a settlement of the coal dispute on the miners' terms would be in manifest breach of the government's incomes policy and would not be possible. It would destroy its authority; likewise the morale of the Conservative Party 'beyond hope of restoration' within the remaining lifetime of the Parliament. The practical difficulties of holding an election in these circumstances would be great but 'doubtless they could be overcome'. It would be a 'highly charged', even 'violent' election and would be 'impossible to confine to any one issue'. The government campaign would be 'credible' only if it included proposals which would 'bring to an end the industrial action'. Alas, 'it is not easy to see what these would be'.

Despite this regrettable omission, the advisers at No. 10 continued to press their case. The arguments for an election 'fairly early next year' were becoming 'very strong'. On 18 December 1973 Hurd recorded in his Diary:

> Slowly the band wagon for an early general election is beginning to roll – but EH, so far as one can gather, still unconvinced.

Heath was never really convinced, which is why the election took place on 28 February rather than on 7 February, the date those who wanted the election favoured. On Sunday 13 January Heath met party officials at Chequers and seized gratefully on a number of practical difficulties in the way of 7 February. On the same evening a group of senior Ministers divided: Carrington, Prior and the forgotten Chancellor, Anthony Barber, were on one side, Whitelaw and the always pacific Robert Carr on the other. 'A non-decision was taken to have an election.'[105] Carrington believed that on 16 January – the deadline for calling the election on 7 February was 17 January – Heath was prepared to call an election but that Whitelaw took him out to dinner and changed his mind.

On 22 January Heath and his parliamentary private secretary, Tim (later Sir Tim) Kitson, walked into a dinner of the party Whips. Three times a year the Whips dine together away from the House. Once a year the leader joins them. On this occasion Heath asked each to express his view on whether there should be an election. They were not much help to him. Seven were against, seven in favour. But Cecil Parkinson, then a Whip, felt at the time that Heath did not want to call a election at all.[106] Douglas Hurd wrote subsequently as if Heath had not indeed called an election rather than – in Hurd's view – called one on the wrong date:

> Mr Heath, backed by two or three of his wisest colleagues, looked more widely and came to a different view ... The Prime Minister's decision was one which I regretted. But I respected greatly and now respect even more the reasons for which he took that decision.[107]

These reasons were that the opposition was under 'appalling leadership', that he did not believe that a modern Conservative Party should fight an election aimed mainly at the trade unions and that 'truth was great and might still prevail'.[108] But an election was fought, and lost. Perhaps the most striking vignette is provided by that underestimated chronicler, Jim Prior. Late in the afternoon of 17 January he went to see Heath at No. 10. He records this exchange:

> Prior: If it's any consolation, I'd like you to know that all the Labour Ministers were coming up to me in the room to tell me that we have let them off the hook. They're throwing their hats in the air – they haven't been in that kind of mood for weeks.
> Heath: It's all your bloody fault. If you hadn't allowed Central Office to steam this thing up, we would never have got into this position.
> Prior: If you had told us definitely that you were against an election, it wouldn't have been steamed up.[109]

THE OCTOBER 1974 DISSOLUTION

The second election of 1974 proved much less difficult for the Prime Minister. Harold Wilson received a 'discreet assurance' from the Palace that, in the event of a defeat in the House of Commons, his recommendation of a dissolution would be accepted.[110] The Labour government then had no majority. Wilson's view was that Heath knew that Labour could not appeal immediately to the electorate. But equally he knew that an appeal would be made at the earliest opportunity after the summer holidays. In his speech to the TUC at Brighton on 5 September 1974 there was a series of 'anything but oblique' references to the coming general election. Few who heard or read it were in any doubt that there was an odour of dissolution about. On 18 September the expected election was announced.[111] On the same day Barbara Castle recorded in her diary:

Sudden call at short notice to a Cabinet meeting. When I arrived, a little late, Harold was announcing the date of the election: 10 October. Officials had been turned out of the room and we had a discursive chat.[112]

THE 1979 DISSOLUTION

In the period up to this announcement, Harold Wilson does not appear to have consulted the Cabinet at all, certainly not in any formal way. James Callaghan, by contrast, 'led' – his word – a Cabinet discussion on the next election two years before it took place. It was 1977. The Labour government had, with the help of the Liberals under the Lib-Lab Pact, survived a vote of no confidence. Ministers now had plenty of time to consider whether the pact should be renewed or whether they should go for a general election in autumn 1977. He asked particularly for the opinions of those who had been against the pact in the first place. He himself had no doubt that they should carry on. The proceeds from North Sea oil would shortly begin to arrive and Ministers should start thinking about how these were to be used to support the country's economic recovery.[113]

In September 1977 he consulted Tony Benn – never one of his favourite colleagues – about the date when Benn went to see him on some electricity board business. Benn said that it should be 'as late as possible'.[114] In May 1978 he consulted Benn again on the month. Benn said October. 'That's a bit predictable,' Callaghan replied. Benn went on to explain that there was a risk that civil servants would 'abandon' their Ministers if they did not make it clear how long they were staying. Indeed, this was already happening. Callaghan said that he had asked Sir John Hunt, the secretary to the Cabinet, to discuss the matter with the permanent secretaries and had 'warned' him that he would take a 'very serious view' if it was true. In any case, if the polls were going Labour's way, the civil servants would be 'frightened' that the government would be re-elected, 'so they won't want to anger us too much'.[115]

Some time in 1978 Callaghan telephoned the *Daily Mirror* to ask whether an industrial correspondent (who had assisted the Labour Party in the past) would be available to help in an 'imminent' election campaign.[116] At the end of August 1978 he summoned the Cabinet to discuss the timing of the election. From the written record, it appears that there was a definite majority of Ministers who were in favour of the election that autumn.[117] Benn was 'very torn ... I must admit, it is very difficult to give up power before you have to'.[118] Callaghan received advice and opinions from many quarters. Michael Foot came to see him and urged that they should put the idea of an autumn election out of their minds, and concentrate on preparing for the next session. The Chief Whip, Michael Cocks, came separately and also expressed a strong preference for embarking on another session. Cocks said they would have a 'bumpy ride' but believed they could reach the end safely. He reported that the Whips Office had met to discuss the choices and had declared against the autumn.[119]

On 18 August 1978 Callaghan told Denis Healey that he was 'minded to go through the winter if he could survive the vote on the Queen's Speech'. The party organisers in the country and all but two of the Whips preferred delay. Healey warned Callaghan that the growth of output and of living standards would be slower during the winter. Neither of them foresaw the industrial trouble ahead or the defeats over devolution which led to the final adverse vote. What weighed more with Callaghan was the view of the organisers that he could not expect more than another hung Parliament. He was, Healey reported, 'sick of compromises'.[120] In which case, one would surely have expected him to take a risk in the autumn: but no.

Several Cabinet colleagues wrote to Callaghan. More of them were in favour of an appeal to the country, but they conveyed little conviction that Labour could win outright. They based themselves on the prospect of Commons defeats' sapping morale; the damage to the Government if it appeared to be clinging to power; the Prime Minister's personal reputation; the industrial problems in store; and the party's enthusiasm in Scotland.[121]

In early September Callaghan met the General Council of the TUC who had 'convinced themselves' that the election would be held in October. Without revealing his decision against October, he argued the 'alternative case for the spring quite strenuously, but apparently not convincingly'. He met the Cabinet on the morning of Thursday 7 September and informed them of the announcement to be made later in the day, that there would be no election. 'They received the news in a matter of fact way and at once turned to government business.'[122]

The union leaders did not take matters so equably. Callaghan's subtleties had clearly evaded them. They thought they had been deceived. There followed – not necessarily as a consequence, though the union leaders' feeling of betrayal cannot have helped matters – the industrial troubles of 1978-9. In November 1978 the Labour MP George Cunningham secured an amendment providing for a 'hurdle' vote for Scottish devolution. On 1 March 1979 the Welsh rejected devolution massively; the Scots accepted it, but not by the margin required by the Cunningham amendment.

On 14 March 1979 there was an Economic Committee meeting at No. 10. Callaghan concluded that they could not hang on till the summer and – showing a certain amount of prescience – would win or lose a vote of confidence at the end of the month by one or two votes. Surviving on a day-to-day basis was 'just too much'. He had exhibited a similarly despairing attitude at Cabinet on 1 February, saying, according to Benn: 'Someone else can take up the leadership because I am not going on.' On 14 March:

Jim gave the impression that we had to go soon. At least we were talking about it.[123]

The Cabinet decided that the Prime Minister should propose that, since a majority of those voting in Scotland had been in favour of devolution, there should be a 'short interval for reflection'. Defeat in the House followed. On the morning after, Callaghan called the Cabinet together to fix the date of the election. This was complicated by the forthcoming local authority elections and by the first elections of Members to the European Parliament. After Cabinet, Callaghan went immediately to the Palace 'to acquaint the Queen formally of the position and seek a dissolution of Parliament to be followed by a general election on 3 May'.[124]

THE 1983 DISSOLUTION

The 1983 elections followed a smoother path. Much of the preliminary discussion took place at Chequers, the new Conservatives showing a preference for the country house. On 5 January there met Tim Bell and Michael Dobbs (from Saatchis, the advertising agents), Gordon Reece (Margaret Thatcher's public relations adviser), Ian Gow (her parliamentary private secretary), Ronald Millar (her speechwriter), Norman Tebbit and Cecil Parkinson (the only Ministers present, of whom Parkinson was the party chairman). Tebbit had become convinced that, subject to the May local elections results, Mrs Thatcher should call the election in June 1983. October looked a difficult month; while to leave the election till spring 1984 risked leaving the government at the mercy of any unforeseen events with no time to recover. That, at any rate, was Tebbit's opinion. Parkinson agreed with him. However, all Mrs Thatcher's instincts were against an early election. As she said, speaking of herself: 'It would be out of character.'

The subject soon came up after a Sunday lunch at Chequers. As the other guests were leaving, she indicated that Parkinson and Tebbit should remain. At once she brought up the timing of the election, expressing concern at the concentration of expectations on June. Parkinson pointed out the hazards of October. She agreed not to rule out June, subject to the May local government results.[125] The result of the Darlington by-election of 24 March, where the Social Democrats had performed disappointingly, was encouraging enough to the Conservatives to intensify speculation about June. After a discussion, Tebbit and Parkinson agreed that there were only four sensible choices of dates in 1983: 9 June, 23 June, 29 September and 10 November. Tebbit plumped for 9 June.[126]

In April 1983 Mrs Thatcher consulted the Cabinet by summoning small groups. Jim Prior saw her with Nicholas Edwards, Peter Walker and George Younger. He went to the meeting thinking the last thing she would want would be an early election. It was against all her instincts. He was amazed to find that she had virtually decided to go in June. She put all the arguments for an early election, hardly any for October. All the Ministers present favoured the former. A discussion ensued on whether the election should be on 9, 16 or 23 June. The only question was whether she could afford to be away at the economic summit during the campaign. The Ministers thought she could. Prior considered that, if the Social Democrats had prospered at Darlington, thoughts on a June election would have been different.[127]

On 14 April, Sir Geoffrey Howe, the Chancellor, reported to the Cabinet on the work of the group composing the manifesto – a production invariably more written about than read. Election timing was not discussed, but it was clear that June was the favoured choice. In a later meeting with Mrs Thatcher, Tebbit pressed the case for the 9th, despite her commitment to attend the economic summit at Williamsburg during the election period.[128]

But Mrs Thatcher was still not committed to June. On Saturday 7 May the local election results were available. Gow telephoned Tebbit to say that she wanted to see him and Parkinson before the gathering at Chequers on the next day. She wanted to avoid a difficult meeting and for them to set out their case for 9 June beforehand. They arrived at 11.30 a.m. Those present for the main meeting included, in addition to Mrs Thatcher, Parkinson and Tebbit, William Whitelaw, Sir Geoffrey Howe, Michael Jopling, Ferdinand Mount, Ian Gow and David Wolfson. After Parkinson had finished his presentation and answered various detailed questions, Mrs Thatcher held what she liked to call a second reading debate, each person expressing a view. It was clear that all present, with varying degrees of enthusiasm, favoured the 9th. Then the meeting adjourned for lunch with Mrs Thatcher, according to Parkinson, looking 'troubled under pressure'.

After lunch they resumed their discussion, Mrs Thatcher raising various arguments against calling an election, the chief of these that the manifesto was not yet finished. Parkinson pointed out that it could be finished within a couple of hours; whereupon she decided that it should be done. The task completed, Mrs Thatcher was staring into the fire and said: 'Even if I wanted to call an election, the Queen could hardly be available at such short notice.' Gow slipped out and returned to say that he had spoken to Buckingham Palace. The Queen could see Mrs Thatcher at noon next day, Monday 9 May.

On 9 May at 7.00 a.m., Mrs Thatcher asked her principal private secretary, Sir Robin Butler, to arrange an audience with the Queen. It was at 12.25. Ministers were summoned to a special Cabinet at 11.15. Parkinson was asked to go early, at nine. Mrs Thatcher told him she had decided to call the election on 9 June. She was holding a piece of paper written in her own hand and looking like a shopping list: 'the Queen, the Speaker, the Leader of the Opposition ...' – a list of the people she had to inform. She told Parkinson she had written it out at 5.30 that morning, when she had finally taken her decision. To the Cabinet she said that 'after consulting colleagues' she had decided that there would be an election on 9 June. 'Does anyone want to turn that decision over?' No one did.[129]

THE 1987 DISSOLUTION

The decision to hold the 1987 election on 11 June seemed, by contrast, easy and inevitable. As early as July 1986 Norman Tebbit, the party chairman, had given Mrs Thatcher a paper setting out his views on possible dates. In January 1987 she discussed with Tebbit and others further papers which he had sent her about the election. They met at the house of the party treasurer, Alistair McAlpine, to escape detection by the press, which had already started to speculate about election dates. By April 1987 Mrs Thatcher had fixed on June. Chequers was again the location for the final decision; again, it took place three days after the local election results. Having won in May 1979 and June 1983, Mrs Thatcher had become convinced that the early summer was her lucky time of year. Those present at Chequers on 10 May included Nigel Lawson (the Chancellor), William Whitelaw, Sir Geoffrey Howe, Norman Tebbit and Lord Young (who, as Lawson put it, 'had been allotted a somewhat ill-defined role in Central Office once the starting pistol had been fired'). Tebbit presented his analysis, which showed that the Conservatives ought to win a June election quite comfortably. The meeting then discussed dates, and soon settled on 11 June. The Prime Minister's decision, Tebbit wrote, was welcomed by the Cabinet next morning.[130]

THE 1992 DISSOLUTION

John Major could have gone to the country and probably won in December 1990. He could have done the same, with an equal or a greater chance of success, immediately after the Gulf War. He did not do so partly because he considered it would have been wrong to hold an election so soon. He also wanted to have a replacement for the poll tax in position.[131] But some of his backbenchers were growing restive. The favourite date became 7 November 1991, which would enable the Prime Minister to announce the election at the close of his speech to the party conference. The party chairman, Chris Patten, counselled caution, as did the Chancellor, Norman Lamont. There is no doubt, however, that Major took a risk in delaying the election till 1992. There were several Conservatives who thought that, having done so, he ought then to have waited till May, June or even July.

CONCLUSIONS

At the beginning of this chapter, two constitutional problems were stated. They were about the powers of the Prime Minister in relation both to the Sovereign and to his (or her) Cabinet. We do not possess a single modern example of a King or Queen refusing a dissolution. The King was unhappy in 1923 and 1924. His successor was troubled in 1950, but the concern was brought about mostly by meddlesome courtiers and self-appointed (and, usually, self-important) constitutional experts. Neither George VI nor C.R. Attlee lost even part of a night's sleep over any possible refusal of a dissolution.

Nevertheless, both were concerned about what was then thought to be the destabilising size of the government's majority; both wanted to change the parliamentary position. The King's Commonwealth tour (in the event, cancelled) proved crucial to the timing of the 1951 election. The royal prerogative was not used to refuse a dissolution: rather, the royal influence was deployed to secure one. Though this had the most profoundly deleterious consequences for the Labour Party, Attlee was equally in favour of it.

In March-September 1974 everything ran smoothly. Harold Wilson was assured that, if he was defeated in the House, he would be granted a dissolution. But suppose he had asked for a dissolution first, immediately after the election which had produced no clear majority for either major party? If he had been refused one, he would have been entitled to resign, though he would not have been compelled to do so. If the prerogative to refuse a dissolution remains intact, then so also does the power to resign as Prime Minister. It is this power which makes the exercise of the prerogative so risky from the Sovereign's point of view.

However, Edward Heath quite properly remained Prime Minister for a few days after the February 1974 election. If he had asked for a second dissolution, there is little doubt that the Queen would have been entitled to refuse. He would then have had the choice either of continuing as Prime Minister or of resigning. The latter is the course he took, without asking for a dissolution or meeting Parliament.

The second problem is not really a problem. Sir Ivor Jennings is wrong. The dissolution of Parliament regularly comes before Cabinet at, roughly, four-year intervals. But the form in which it is presented varies. James Callaghan believed in consultations but, paradoxically, disregarded the (admittedly weakly-held) view of the majority in the late summer and early autumn of 1978. Both Harold Wilson and Margaret Thatcher relied on groups of half-a-dozen or so and then came to Cabinet challenging reversal, like a boxer inviting a punch from a weaker opponent.

C.R. Attlee consulted more widely in 1950 than in 1951; Wilson more in 1970 than in 1966, though on the former occasion he nevertheless humiliated the Cabinet by exalting the Parliamentary Committee (or Inner Cabinet). Home was in effect consulted by a combination of Central Office apparatchiks and senior Ministers. Heath was forced into an election he did not really want, yet too late from the point of view of those who were urging him on. Until Margaret Thatcher, only Harold Macmillan enjoyed a relatively trouble-free passage to polling day.

It was suggested at the beginning that the reason why Cabinets no longer asked for a dissolution collectively was that, in practice, they had lost the alternative of resigning collectively. But, more and more, elections are being regarded as technical exercises in persuasion, in which the opinions of advertising agents, public relations consultants, opinion pollsters and television experts are considered to be more important than those of departmental Ministers. That is another reason why the Cabinet is content to see itself as an authorising rather than as an initiating body.

Statement by Parliamentary Committee of the Parliamentary Labour Party, 21 January 1957

The Parliamentary Committee of the Parliamentary Labour Party has given further consideration to the constitutional issues arising from the resignation of Sir Anthony Eden as Prime Minister.

When a change of government takes place after a general election no difficulty occurs. It is well understood that the leader of the party which has won a majority is automatically invited by the Crown to form a government.

But, as public discussion has shown, there is still some doubt as to the appropriate constitutional procedure to be pursued when a Prime Minister resigns whilst in office and whilst his government continues to command a majority in the House of Commons.

Each political party must decide its own attitude to this question guided by what appears to be consistent with the spirit of the constitution and with its own internal procedures.

The Parliamentary Committee of the Parliamentary Labour Party therefore feels that it would be proper to declare at this juncture the procedure which it would regard as constitutionally appropriate in such circumstances if a Labour government were in power.

The committee has given careful consideration to the relevant precedents. It has come to the conclusion that the precedent created by Mr Bonar Law in 1922 is the one which offers the best guidance. On that occasion, before accepting the King's invitation to form a government, Mr Bonar Law insisted that the Conservative Party should first elect its leader. This in the view of the Parliamentary Committee, is the precedent most in accord with the spirit of the constitution. It enables the Crown to act in a manner free of all constitutional ambiguity. The committee also feels that this course would be the only one that accords with the democratic organisation of the Parliamentary Labour Party. It therefore considers that, if at any time a Labour Prime Minister resigns or dies while in office and while the government retains its majority in the House of Commons, the appropriate course to follow would be for the Parliamentary Labour Party first to proceed to the election of a new leader who would then be ready to accept the invitation of the Crown to become Prime Minister.

Memorandum by Harold Macmillan to Queen Elizabeth II, 15 October 1963

The choice of a successor to the premiership when a Prime Minister resigns not because of any dispute in the Cabinet or any defeat in the House of Commons but from ill-health, presents a situation that is unusual but not without precedent.

In the present case it is complicated by the fact of there being no accepted heir in the sense that Neville Chamberlain and Anthony Eden were long regarded as the automatic successors to Stanley Baldwin and Sir Winston Churchill when the time came.

In some ways the present situation resembles more that of the resignation of Mr Gladstone in 1894. Then there were many contestants but none outstanding. In the end the choice of Lord Rosebery proved fatal both to the recipient of the honour and to the party which did not recover for more than 10 years.

Under the minute attached I have directed that the Lord Chancellor, the Chief Whips in the Commons and the Lords, and Lord Poole, Chairman of the Conservative Party, should try to get the general opinion of ministers, MPs, peers, and constituency parties.

In view of the complication of the situation all kinds of motives would be operating in the minds of those who answer these questions. Some few (the violent anti-Macmillan rebels) will be content with the success they have had in the assassination of their leader and will not care very much who the successor is. On the whole I would say that they would be for Mr Butler or Mr Maudling — none of them for Lord Hailsham. They are a band that in the end does not amount to more than 15 or 20 at the most. Those who originally in the summer wanted a change to a younger man in order to help the election would presumably either be for Lord Hailsham or for Mr Maudling, since Mr Butler is not so much of a change as all that.

Those who think most of the orderly conduct of government would tend to be for Mr Butler as he is likely to carry on the present policies, which he fully understands, and to give full freedom to the Treasury and to the Foreign Office in carrying out the policies which I initiated, approved and largely directed. It is important for the Crown and for the party that the divergencies of opinion should be analysed while it is possible to do so.

1. Administration: Obviously, members of the Cabinet and those likely to come into direct contact with the future Prime Minister will find it easier to work with Mr Butler. They are afraid that Lord Hailsham would be impulsive, even arrogant, in his handling of their business. This applies to some younger members as well as to the older members of the administration, and is largely due to his habit, when

he is not in the chair, of talking a great deal and sometimes without much reflection.

2. Electioneering: The mass of feeling in favour of Lord Hailsham will be that he will be a better man to fight Wilson, indeed the only one we have. This will be thought to be vital from the point of view of the marginal seats and of the many so-called safe seats now under threat. To some extent this may be countered by those who will argue that Lord Hailsham's recent exhibitions will have caused some dismay and may even cause people to withdraw their support. Experienced politicians will remember that this is often said about leaders. The right wing have nowhere to go except to the right. They are unlikely to vote for Wilson or to abstain to demonstrate their dislike of Lord Hailsham's behaviour. Moreover, the people who dislike his behaviour will be in sympathy with Lord Hailsham's religious views, his churchmanship and so forth. They will merely be shocked at his rather boyish lack of manners. But they will not be shocked by his deviating from strict moral doctrines.

3. Policy: On the surface, and indeed so far as one can see below the surface, there is no great division of policy that is now splitting the Conservative Party. The weakness in the constituencies is not due as in 1905 to a deep division of views on tariff reform and free trade or as in 1945 to the remnants of the terrible disputes that had torn the party before the war — the guilty men and so forth. The difficulty is really due to a certain boredom with material success and apparent inability to harness this to spiritual purposes. But there is no division now as between Europeans and non-Europeans or progressives and reactionaries or free traders and protectionists or pro-nuclear and anti-nuclear, or if these divisions exist they cut across the several groupings and are simply representative of a feeling of difficulty which is shared by everybody on these tremendous problems. So far as there is any direct political difference it may be between dynamism and immobilism. It would be argued by some that Lord Hailsham represents what I was like in my stronger period, I am to a greater extent than people appreciate behind the scenes and would like my successor to be; that Lord Hailsham would press forward with the policies in which I believe, whether they be disarmament, the detente with Russia on one side, or international liquidity etc on the other.

The only other political difference that may emerge is by the strong movement at the end of last week to draft Lord Home unwillingly into the position of leader and Prime Minister. Lord Home is clearly a man who represents the old, governing class at its best and those who take a reasonably impartial view of English history know how good that can be. He is not ambitious in the sense of wanting to scheme for power although not foolish enough to resist honour when it comes to him.

Had he been of another generation he would have been of the Grenadiers and the 1914 heroes. He gives that impression by a curious mixture of great courtesy, and even of yielding to pressure, with underlying rigidity on matters of principle. It is interesting that he has proved himself so much liked by men like President Kennedy and Mr Rusk and Mr Gromyko. This is exactly the quality that the class to which he belongs have at their best because they think about the question under discussion and not about themselves.

It is thinking about themselves that is really the curse of the younger generation — they appear to have no other subject which interests them at all and all their books, poems, dramas and all the rest of it are almost entirely confined to this curious introspective attitude towards life, the result no doubt of two wars and the dying faith. Lord Home is free therefore from many of the difficulties that beset modern people today. But the very fact that he is free from them makes him in my mind at a disadvantage as well as at an advantage because this strange people, tortured by material success and affluence, are seeking release by some teacher who is himself subject to all these pressures and is not ashamed to break the ordinary rules and conventions suitable to more settled intellectual periods. However, the important fact is that Lord Home's candidature has not been set forward on his own merits but has been thought of as a last-minute method of keeping out Mr Butler now that Lord Hailsham has (according to the pundits) put himself out of court by his stupid behaviour in the foyer of the Imperial Hotel at Blackpool.

The Cabinet would be universally for Lord Home obviously, for he is a popular, delightful man and would make an effective chief. He would be the choice of the board if the business is to run quietly, but particularly of a board that did not have to make any difficult appeal to the shareholders and held all the premiums in their pocket.

Next they will prefer Butler because he would not worry them. After that, they would be against Hailsham. With Parliament, the division would be rather different. More anti-Butlers because of his lack of electoral appeal. A good number of pro-Hailshams and a good number of pro-Homes, the former coming chiefly from the Northern and the more threatened constituencies, ie those that can only be won by non-political votes.

Thirdly, the party in the country. Here I think there will be some division. Therefore, we must bear in mind the danger of setting the party in office and in Parliament against the party in the country. All this is familiar to readers of Mommsen and students of the decline of the Roman republic.

References

CHAPTER 1

1. Lord Beaverbrook, *The Decline and Fall of Lloyd George* (1963), 9.

2. See H. Nicolson, *Curzon: the Last Phase* (1934), ch. 3.

3. K.O. Morgan, *Consensus and Disunity* (1979; 2nd edn 1986).

4. See J.M. Keynes, *The Economic Consequences of the Peace* (1919) in *Collected Writings of John Maynard Keynes*, II, 91; R.F. Harrod, *The Life of John Maynard Keynes* (1951; pb edn 1972), 312; R. Skidelsky, *John Maynard Keynes* (2 vols, 1983-92), I, 383; K. Middlemas and J. Barnes, *Baldwin* (1965), 72 n.

5. H. Nicolson, *King George the Fifth* (1952), 370.

6. R. Blake, *The Unknown Prime Minister* (1955), 459.

7. Ibid., 460; Nicolson, *George V*, 370.

8. Royal Archives K 1814: Blake, *Unknown Prime Minister*, 460.

9. Nicolson, *George V*, 370-1.

10. Blake, *Unknown Prime Minister*, 460.

11. Nicolson, *George V*, 371.

12. Ibid., 371; Blake, *Unknown Prime Minister*, 461.

13. P. Goodhart, *The 1922* (1973); S. Ball, 'The 1922 Committee: the Formative Years 1922-45', 9 *Parliamentary History* (1990), 129.

14. For Davidson's political career, see R. Rhodes James, *Memoirs of a Conservative* (1969).

15. Blake, *Unknown Prime Minister*, 521.

16. K. Rose, *King George V*, (1983; pb edn 1984), 267.

17. Ibid., 268; Nicolson, *George V*, 376.

18. Ibid.

19. A.J. Balfour Memorandum: K. Young, *Arthur James Balfour* (1963), 431.

20. Nicolson, *George V*, 376.

21. Balfour Memorandum: Young, *Balfour*, 431.

22. B.E.C. Dugdale, *Arthur James Balfour* (2 vols, 1936), II, 360.

23. W.S. Churchill, 'George Nathaniel Curzon', in *Great Contemporaries* (1937; pb edn 1959), 220 at 234; Blake, *Unknown Prime Minister*, 526. Lord Blake cites Churchill's essay concerning the membership of the Sheringham house party but Churchill does not mention anybody except Balfour.

24. Rose, *George V*, 269.

25. Churchill, *Great Contemporaries*, pb edn, 234.

26. Rose, *George V*, 271.

27. D. Gilmour, *Curzon* (1994), 584.

28. Nicolson, *George V*, 377.

29. N. Chamberlain Diary, 1 June 1923: Rose, *George V*, 272-3.

30. M. Cowling, *The Impact of Labour 1920-4* (1971), 259.

31. Ibid.

32. T. Jones, *Whitehall Diaries* (3 vols, 1969-71), I, 236, cit. Cowling, *Impact of Labour*, 259 n.

33. cf. John Davidson to Randolph S. Churchill: R.S. Churchill, *Lord Derby* (1959), 509.

34. L. Mosley, *Curzon* (1960; Readers Union edn 1961), 265; Blake, *Unknown Prime Minister*, 518.

35. Ibid., 520.

36. Ibid.

37. Ibid., 521.

38. Rhodes James, *Memoirs of a Conservative*, 150-1.

39. Ibid. 155.

40. Churchill, *Derby*, 509.

41. Rhodes James, *Memoirs of a Conservative*, 151.

42. Mosley, *Curzon*, Readers Union edn, 267.

43. Ibid.

44. Blake, *Unknown Prime Minister*, 522.

45. Cowling, *Impact of Labour*, 259.

46. Blake, *Unknown Prime Minister*, 520.

47. Jones, *Whitehall Diary*, I, 235-6.

48. Cowling, *Impact of Labour*, 259.

49. See generally Nicolson, *George V*, 380ff; Rose, *George V*, 324ff.

50. Rhodes James, *Memoirs of a Conserva-*

tive, 184-5; Churchill, *Derby*, 528-9.

51. Derby to Birkenhead, 7 December 1923: Churchill, *Derby*, 541

52. Stamfordham Memorandum, 8 December 1923: ibid., 551.

53. Stamfordham Memorandum, 8 December 1923: ibid., 549.

54. Dawson Diary, 8-10 December 1923: J.E. Wrench, *Geoffrey Dawson and Our Times* (1955), 223.

55. Ibid.

56. Ibid.; Cowling, *Impact of Labour*, 335.

57. Amery Diary, 9 December 1923: Cowling, *Impact of Labour*, 335.

58. Memorandum, 10 December 1923, referring to 9 December: Cowling, *Impact of Labour*, 337.

59. Derby Diary, 10 December 1923: Churchill, *Derby*, 544.

60. Stamfordham Memorandum, 10 December 1923: Churchill, *Derby*, 545.

61. Ibid., 553

62. G.H.L. Le May, *The Victorian Constitution* (1979).

63. Stamfordham Memorandum, 10 December 1923: Churchill, *Derby*, 552.

64. Derby Diary, 11 December 1923: ibid., 547.

65. Stamfordham to Derby, 11 December 1923: ibid., 557.

66. Balfour to Birkenhead, 11 December 1923: ibid., 554.

67. Ibid.

68. Beatrice Webb Diary, 12 December 1923: B. Webb, *Diaries*, ed. N. and J. MacKenzie (4 vols, 1982-5), III, 432.

69. See e.g. R. Douglas, *A History of the Liberal Party 1895-1970* (1971), 175.

70. S. Koss, *Asquith* (1976; pb edn 1985), 264.

71. Earl of Oxford and Asquith, *Memories and Reflections* (2 vols, 1928), II, 209.

72. Ibid.

73. Ibid., 208.

74. D. Marquand, *Ramsay MacDonald* (1977), 298.

75. Asquith to W.M.R. Pringle, 10 January 1924: R. Jenkins, *Asquith* (1964; rev edn 1978), 501.

76. MacDonald Diary, 21 January 1924: Marquand, *MacDonald*, 304.

77. Rose, *George V*, 325.

78. Ibid.

79. Stamfordham Memorandum of meeting with MacDonald: Nicolson, *George V*, 384-5.

80. Ibid.

81. Rhodes James, *Memoirs of a Conservative*, 191.

82. See J.Ll.J. Edwards, *The Law Officers of the Crown* (1964), ch. 11.

83. Rose, *George V*, 335.

84. Ibid.

85. Marquand, *MacDonald*, 374.

86. Ibid., 377.

87. Nicolson, *George V*, 403.

88. Ibid.

89. Ibid., 434.

90. Stamfordham to Sir George Murray, 3 June 1929: ibid.

91. Ibid., 435.

92. Ibid.

93. Ibid.

94. Rose, *George V*, 367.

95. Nicolson, *George V*, 435.

96. Ibid.

97. R. Jenkins, *Baldwin* (1987), 123-4.

98. See P. Devlin, *Taken at the Flood* (1996), 140-1; Jenkins, *Baldwin*, 124-5.

99. N. Chamberlain Diary, 6 July 1931; K. Feiling, *Neville Chamberlain* (1940), 189.

100. P. Williamson, *National Crisis and National Government* (1992), 300.

101. N. Chamberlain to W. Bridgeman, 19 August 1931: Williamson, *National Crisis*, 301.

102. Rhodes James, *Memoirs of a Conservative*, 365.

103. Ibid.

104. Wigram to George V: Nicolson, *George V*, 449.

105. Wigram Memorandum, 22-4 August 1931: Rose, *George V*, 373.

106. MacDonald Diary, 20 August 1931: Marquand, *MacDonald*, 621.

107. MacDonald quoted in C.P. Duff to C. Wigram, 21 August 1931: Williamson, *National Crisis*, 310.

108. Marquand, *MacDonald*, 626.

109. Ibid.

110. N. Chamberlain to his wife, 21 August 1931: N. Chamberlain Diary, 22 August 1931: Williamson, *National Crisis*, 322.

111. N. Chamberlain to his wife and to his sister, 23 August 1931: ibid., 329.

112. N.Chamberlain Diary, 22 August 1931: Feiling, *Chamberlain*, 192.

113. Marquand, *MacDonald*, 629.

114. Ibid.

115. Cabinet 44 (31), 22 August 1931; MacDonald Notes, n.d. but 22 August 1931: Williamson, *National Crisis*, 327.

116. Rhodes James, *Memoirs of a Conservative*, 367.

117. Ibid.

118. Ibid., 368.

119. Ibid.

120. Ibid.

121. MacDonald Diary, 23 August 1931: Marquand, *MacDonald*, 629, 630.

122. MacDonald Diary, 23 August 1931: ibid.

123. Ibid.

124. A.J.P. Taylor (ed), *My Darling Pussy* (1975), 151.

125. Rose, *George V*, 374.

126. Herbert Samuel to Harold Nicolson, 24 February 1949, Nicolson Papers: ibid.

127. Dawson Diary, 23 April 1931: Wrench, *Dawson*, 291.

128. Ibid.

129. Baldwin to his wife, 23 August 1931: Middlemass and Barnes, *Baldwin*, 626; Williamson, *National Crisis*, 337.

130. Cabinet Secretariat: Marquand, MacDonald, 634.

131. Marquand, *MacDonald*, 634; Williamson, *National Crisis*, 339.

132. Cabinet 46 (31): Marquand, *MacDonald*, 635.

133. Nicolson, *George V*, 464.

134. MacDonald Diary, 23 August 1931: Marquand, *MacDonald*, 635-6.

135. Rose, *George V*, 375-6.

136. Chamberlain Diary, 23 August 1931: Feiling, *Chamberlain*, 193.

137. Davidson, Draft Memoirs, 23 August 1931: Rhodes James, *Memoirs of a Conservative*, 370.

138. Rose, *George V*, 376.

139. Davidson, Draft Memoirs, 24 August 1931: Rhodes James, *Memoirs of a Conservative*, 370. Cf. Marquand, *MacDonald*, 636-7.

140. MacDonald Diary, 24 August 1931: Rose, *George V*, 376.

141. Cabinet 47 (31): Marquand, *MacDonald*, 637.

142. Wigram Memorandum, 22-4 August 1931: Rose, *George V*, 376-7.

143. Official Announcement, 24 August 1931: R. Bassett, *Nineteen Thirty-One: Political Crisis* (1958), 167.

144. Viscount Templewood, *Nine Troubled Years* (1954), 22.

145. Rose, *George V*, 378.

146. Marquand, *MacDonald*, 630.

147. Williamson, *National Crisis*, 334.

148. Feiling, *Chamberlain*, 193.

149. Rose, *George V*, 378.

150. Nicolson, *George V*, 460-1.

151. Sir I. Jennings, *Cabinet Government* (3rd edn 1959), 46-7.

152. Cf. Williamson, *National Crisis*, 340.

153. Rose, *George V*, 378.

154. H.J. Laski, *Parliamentary Government in England* (1938), 403.

155. I. Kramnick and B. Sheerman, *Harold Laski* (1993), 299.

156. Rhodes James, *Memoirs of a Conservative*, 406.

157. Marquand, *MacDonald*, 764.

158. Jenkins, *Baldwin*, 136.

159. Feiling, *Chamberlain*, 260.

160. MacDonald Notebook, 1 August 1934: Marquand, *MacDonald*, 761.

161. MacDonald Notebook, 1 October 1934: ibid.

162. MacDonald Notebook, 29 January 1935: ibid., 762.

163. M. Muggeridge, *The Thirties* (1940; new edn 1967), 235.

164. MacDonald Diary, February 1935: Marquand, *MacDonald*, 766.

165. MacDonald Diary, 10 February 1935: ibid., 766-7.

166. Simon Diary, 14 February 1935: Viscount Simon, *Retrospect* (1932), 206.

167. Marquand, *MacDonald*, 769.

168. Jenkins, *Baldwin*, 136.

169. Rose, *George V*, 397.

170. Dawson Diary, 7 June 1935: Wrench, *Dawson*, 324.

171. Rhodes James, *Memoirs of a Conservative*, 418.

172. Ibid., 420; Simon, *Retrospect*, 227; J.W. Wheeler-Bennett, *King George VI* (1958), 318; Churchill, *Second World War*, pb edn, I, 194.

173. Feiling, *Chamberlain*, 292.

174. N. Chamberlain Diary, 25 April 1937: ibid.

175. N. Chamberlain to his sister: ibid., 294.

176. D. Carlton, *Anthony Eden* (1981, pb edn 1986), 161.

177. Channon Diary, 6, 26 September 1939: H. Channon, *Diaries*, ed. R. Rhodes James (1967), 218, 222.

178. Nicolson Diary, 26 September 1939: H. Nicolson, *Diaries* ed. N. Nicolson (3 vols, 1966-8; pb edn 1969-71), 33.

179. Nicolson Diary, 3 October 1939: ibid., 34.

180. Nicolson Diary, 2 November 1939: ibid., 41.

181. Nicolson Diary, 14 December 1939: ibid., 46.

182. Ibid.

183. Channon Diary, 25 April 1940: *Diaries*, 242.

184. Channon Diary, 26 April 1940: ibid., 242-3.

185. Nicolson Diary, 29 April and 1 May 1940: *Diaries*, pb edn, II, 70.

186. Halifax Diary, 3 May 1940: A. Roberts, *The Holy Fox* (1991; pb edn 1992), 194.

187. Channon Diary, 30 April 1940: *Diaries*, 242.

188. Channon Diary, 2 May 1940: ibid., 244.

189. Channon Diary, 3 May 1940: ibid.

190. *Clem Attlee: The Granada Historical Records Interview* (1967), 20.

191. Ibid.

192. Lord Home, *The Way the Wind Blows* (1976), 75.

193. B. Donoughue and G.W. Jones, *Herbert Morrison* (1973), 275.

194. K. Harris, *Attlee* (1982; rev pb edn 1995), 172.

195. Donoughue and Jones, *Morrison*, 271.

196. Butler Papers, diary note, 7 May 1940: A. Howard, *RAB: the Life of R.A. Butler* (1987; pb edn 1988), 93.

197. Wheeler-Bennett, *George VI*, 439-40.

198. Nicolson Diary, 8 May 1940: *Diaries*, pb edn, II, 75.

199. Halifax Papers, 9 May 1946: Roberts, *Holy Fox*, pb edn, 199.

200. Harris, *Attlee*, pb edn, 173.

201. Beaverbrook note: A.J.P. Taylor, *Beaverbrook* (1972; pb edn 1974), 53.

202. Eden Diary, 9 May 1940: R. Rhodes James, *Anthony Eden* (1986; pb edn 1987), 225-6.

203. Earl of Avon, *Memoirs* (3 vols, 1960-5), III, 96-7.

204. Ibid.

205. R.A. Butler, *The Art of the Possible* (1971; pb edn 1973), 85.

206. Halifax Diary, 14 January 1939: Roberts, *Holy Fox*, pb edn, 198.

207. Halifax Diary, 9 May 1940: ibid., 198.

208. Halifax Diary, 9 May 1940: ibid.

209. Feiling, *Chamberlain*, 441.

210. A.J.P. Taylor, *English History 1914-45* (1965), 474.

211. Roberts, *Holy Fox*, pb edn, 198.

212. Cadogan Diary, 9 May 1940: A. Cadogan, *Diaries*, ed. D. Dilks (1971), 280.

213. *Granada Interview*, 21.

214. Ibid.

215. W.S. Churchill, *The Second World War* (6 vols, 1948-54; pb edn 1964), I, 596.

216. Harris, *Attlee*, pb edn, 174.

217. C.R. Attlee, *As It Happened* (1954), 112.

218. *Granada Interview*, 22.

219. Taylor, *English History*, 474.

220. *The Times*, 11 May 1940.

221. Wheeler-Bennett, *George VI*, 422.

222. Blake, 'How Churchill Became Prime Minister' in R. Blake and W.R. Louis (eds), *Churchill* (1993; pb edn 1996), 257.

223. M. Gilbert, *Churchill* (vols III-VII, 1971-88), VI, 300-1; Rhodes James, *Eden*, pb edn, 226; Harris, *Attlee*, pb edn, 175

224. Roberts, *Holy Fox*, pb edn, 207.

225. Taylor, *English History*, 474.

226. *Granada Interview*, 21; Attlee, *As It Happened*, 112; Churchill, *Second World War*, I, 596.

227. Letter from Christopher Meyer, press secretary, to Alan Watkins.

228. Cadogan Diary, 9 May 1940: *Diaries*, 260.

229. Churchill, *Second World War*, I, 597.

230. Margesson to Beaverbrook, 25 May, 1960: Taylor, *Beaverbrook*, pb edn, 531.

231. Halifax Diary 9 May 1940: Roberts, *Holy Fox*, pb edn, 205; Cadogan Diary, 9 May 1940: *Diaries*, 280.

232. Churchill, *Second World War*, I, 597.

233. Roberts, *Holy Fox*, pb edn, 204ff.

234. Churchill, *Second World War*, I, 597-8.

235. Gilbert, *Churchill*, VI, 305.

236. Chamberlain to Beaverbrook, 10 May 1940: Taylor, *Beaverbrook*, pb edn, 532.

237. Gilbert, *Churchill*, VI, 308; Churchill, *Second World War,* I, 597.

238. *The Times*, 11 May 1940.

239. Attlee, *As It Happened*, 112; Harris, *Attlee*, pb edn, 175.

240. War Cabinet 119 of 1940, 10 May 1940: Gilbert, *Churchill*, VI, 312.

241. George VI Diary, 10 May 1940: Wheeler-Bennett, *George VI*, 443-4.

242. Kingsley Wood, 'Question and Answer', Beaverbrook Papers: P. Addison, *Road to 1945* (1975), 162.

CHAPTER 2

1. Attlee, *As It Happened*, 145.

2. Harris, *Attlee*, pb edn, 263.

3. Donoughue and Jones, *Morrison*, 339-40.

4. Harris, *Attlee*, pb edn, 263.

5. George VI Diary, 26 July 1945: Wheeler-Bennett, *George VI*, 636-7.

6. Attlee, *As It Happened*, 196.

7. Harris, *Attlee*, pb edn, 446.

8. *The Times*, 24 April – 2 May 1950, reprinted in G. Wilson, *Cases and Materials on Constitutional and Administrative Law* (1966), 22-6.

9. Wheeler-Bennett, *George VI*, 772.

10. Ibid.

11. Ibid., 796.

12. Gilbert, *Churchill*, VIII, 649.

13. Rhodes James, *Eden*, pb edn, 345.

14. Eden Diary, 23 January 1953: Rhodes James, *Eden*, pb edn, 359.

15. Ibid., 368

16. Ibid.

17. Colville Diary, 19 July 1953: J. Colville, *The Fringes of Power* (1985, 2 vols; pb edn 1986), II, 332.

18. Colville Diary, 31 July – 3 August 1953: ibid., 334-5.

19. Howard, *RAB*, pb edn, 199.

20. J. Margach, *The Abuse of Power* (1978), 84-5.

21. R.A. Butler in BBC Radio Profile, 29 June 1978: Howard, *RAB*, pb edn, 199.

22. Colville Diary, 2 July 1954: *Fringes of Power*, pb edn, II, 364-5.

23. Macmillan Diary, 10 July 1954: A. Horne, *Macmillan* (2 vols, 1988-9), I, 348.

24. Moran Diary, 23 July 1954: Lord Moran, *Winston Churchill: The Struggle for Survival 1940-65* (1966; pb edn 1968), 611.

25. Macmillan Diary, 31 July 1954: Horne, *Macmillan*, I, 353.

26. Moran Diary, 30 July 1954: *Churchill*, pb edn, 616.

27. Moran Diary, 3 August 1954: ibid., 617.

28. Moran Diary, 6 August 1954: ibid., 619.

29. Moran Diary, 16 August 1954: ibid., 621.

30. Moran Diary, 18 August 1954: ibid., 624.

31. Butler to Churchill, 18 August 1954: Howard, *RAB*, pb edn, 209.

32. Moran Diary, 24 August 1954: *Churchill*, pb edn, 624-5.

33. Eden Diary, 27 August 1954: Rhodes James, *Eden*, pb edn, 385.

34. Ibid.

35. Moran Diary, 28 August 1954: *Churchill*, pb edn, 625.

36. Moran Diary, 29 August 1954: ibid., 626.

37. Colville Diary, August 1954: *Fringes of Power*, pb edn, II, 371.

38. Churchill to Eden, September 1954: Rhodes James, *Eden*, pb edn, 386.

39. Eden Diary, 10 September 1954: ibid., 388

40. Macmillan Diary, 2 October 1954: Gilbert, *Churchill*, VIII, 1062.

41. Macmillan to Churchill, 2 October 1954: ibid., 1063.

42. Macmillan Diary, 10 October 1954: ibid., 1065.

43. Moran Diary, 14 October 1954: *Churchill*, pb edn, 636.

44. Moran Diary, 5 December 1954: ibid., 654.

45. Moran Diary, 10 December 1954: ibid., 655.

46. Eden Diary, 21 December 1954: Rhodes James, *Eden*, pb edn, 392.

47. Eden Diary, 22 December 1954: Horne, *Macmillan*, I, 354.

48. Macmillan Diary, 22 December 1954: ibid.

49. Moran Diary, 9 January 1955: *Churchill*, pb edn, 659.

50. Bracken to Beaverbrook, 17 January 1955: Gilbert, *Churchill*, VIII, 1088.

51. Moran Diary, 24 January 1955: *Churchill*, pb edn, 660.

52. Eden Diary, 1 February 1955: Rhodes James, *Eden*, pb edn, 396.

53. Moran Diary, 3 February 1955: *Churchill*, pb edn, 603.

54. Moran Diary, 16 February 1955: ibid., 664.

55. Macmillan Diary, 14 March 1955; Horne, *Macmillan*, I, 354.

56. Moran Diary, 3 March 1955: *Churchill*, pb edn, 671.

57. Macmillan Diary, 14 March 1955: Horne, *Macmillan*, I, 354.

58. Moran Diary, 23 March 1955: *Churchill*, pb edn, 674.

59. Colville Diary, March 1955: *Fringes of Power*, pb edn, II, 376-7.

60. Colville Diary, March-April 1955: *Fringes of Power*, pb edn, II, 377-8.

61. Moran Diary, 1 April 1955: *Churchill*, pb edn, 676.

62. Colville Diary, March-April 1955: *Fringes of Power*, pb edn, II, 378-9.

63. Nicolson Diary, 5 April 1955: ibid., *Diaries*, pb edn, III, 257.

64. Nicolson Diary, 22 May 1952: ibid., 207.

65. Rhodes James, *Eden*, pb edn, 397.

66. Butler, *Art of the Possible*, pb edn, 178-9.

67. Moran Diary, 10 July 1955: *Churchill*, pb edn, 709.

68. Rhodes James, *Eden*, pb edn, 595.

69. Ibid.

70. Howard, *RAB*, 246.

71. Rhodes James, *Eden*, pb edn, 595-6.

72. Ibid., 599.

73. B. Pimlott, *The Queen* (1996), 259.

74. Ibid., 566.

75. Horne, *Macmillan*, I, 458.

76. Howard, *RAB*, 244.

77. Evans to Butler, 14 January 1957: Howard, *RAB*, 245.

78. Earl of Kilmuir, *Political Adventure* (1964), 285.

79. Sir Edward Ford, interview with B. Pimlott: *Queen*, 257.

80. Rhodes James, *Eden*, pb edn, 597, 599.

81. Viscount Stuart of Findhorn, *Within the Fringe* (1967), 179.

82. Kilmuir, *Political Adventure*, 286-7.

83. Howard, *RAB*, 247.

84. R. Blake, 'Anthony Eden' in *DNB 1971-80*, 262 at 271.

85. Private information.

86. Avon Papers, Birmingham University, 11 January 1957: K. Kyle, *Suez* (1991), 533.

87. Avon Papers: Pimlott, *Queen*, 259.

88. Rhodes James, *Eden*, pb edn, 599.

89. A. Montague Browne, *Long Sunset* (1995), 215.

90. Lord Charteris, interview with B. Pimlott: *Queen*, 258.

91. Butler, *Art of the Possible*, pb edn, 197; Rhodes James, *Eden*, pb edn, 600.

92. Butler, *Art of the Possible,* 197.

93. Kilmuir, *Political Adventure*, 285.

94. Interview with Iris Portal on BBC TV 'Reputations', 13 July 1983: Howard, *RAB*, 246.

95. Howard, *RAB*, 246.

96. Rhodes James, *Eden*, pb edn, 598n; Horne, *Macmillan*, I, 460; Howard, *RAB*, 247.

97. Stuart, *Within the Fringe*, 179.

98. Horne, *Macmillan*, I, 459.

99. Kilmuir, *Political Adventure*, 285.

100. R. Blake, *The Conservative Party from Peel to Thatcher* (1970; new pb edn 1985), 278.

101. G. Hutchinson, *Edward Heath* (1970), 86.

102. Nicolson Diary, 10 January 1957: *Diaries*, pb edn, III, 301.

103. Butler, *Art of the Possible*, pb edn, 197.

104. Beaverbrook to Butler, 23 January 1957: Howard, *RAB*, 248.

105. Butler Papers, Diary Note, probably February 1957: ibid., 298.

106. Horne, *Macmillan*, II, 5.

107. The statement is reproduced as Appendix A, and in N. St John-Stevas (ed.), *Collected Works of Walter Bagehot* (15 vols, 1965-86), V, 91 n.

108. Butler, *Art of the Possible*, pb edn, 238.

109. Ibid., 23.

110. H. Macmillan, *Memoirs* (6 vols, 1966-73), VI, 500.

111. Macmillan Diary, 20 September 1963: ibid., 495.

112. Ibid.

113. I. Macleod, 'The Fight for the Tory Leadership', *Spectator*, 17 January 1964.

114. D.R. Thorpe, *Alec Douglas-Home* (1996), 292.

115. Pimlott, *Queen*, 328-9.

116. Macmillan, *Memoirs*, VI, 456.

117. Ibid., 508.

118. Macmillan Diary, 15 October 1963: ibid., 555.

119. Macmillan, *Memoirs*, VI, 496.

120. Macmillan Diary, 11 September 1963: *Memoirs*, VI, 494.

121. Macmillan Diary, 7 October 1963: ibid., 499.

122. Butler Papers: Howard, *RAB*, 308.

123. Macmillan Diary, 15 October 1963: *Memoirs*, VI, 503.

124. Macmillan Diary, 15 October 1963: ibid., 510.

125. Macmillan Diary, 4 October 1963: Horne, *Macmillan*, II, 535-6.

126. T. Benn, *Diaries*, ed. R. Winstone (6 vols, 1987-94; 1 vol pb edn 1996), VI, 418.

127. See Howard, *RAB*, ch. 15.

128. Ibid., 310.

129. Ibid., 310-11; personal knowledge.

130. Butler Papers: Howard, *RAB*, 315.

131. Thorpe, *Douglas-Home*, 274, 276.

132. R.S. Churchill, *The Fight for the Tory Leadership* (1964), 97.

133. Home, *Way the Wind Blows*, 181.

134. Macleod, 'Fight for the Tory Leadership', *Spectator*, 17 January 1964.

135. Thorpe, *Douglas-Home*, 277.

136. Ibid., 278.

137. Macmillan, *Memoirs*, VI, 502.

138. Ibid., 282, 300.

139. Home, *Way the Wind Blows*, 181.

140. Benn, account given to David Butler: *Diaries*, VI, 360.

141. Thorpe, *Douglas-Home*, 269.
142. Macmillan, *Memoirs*, VI, 80.
143. R. Shepherd, *Iain Macleod* (1994), 302.
144. Macmillan Diary, 5 September 1963: Horne, *Macmillan*, II, 531.
145. Ibid.
146. Shepherd, *Macleod*, 302.
147. Macmillan, *Memoirs*, VI, 508-9.
148. Lord Hailsham, *A Sparrow's Flight* (1990), 350; Horne, *Macmillan*, II, 537.
149. Macmillan Diary, 9 October 1963: *Memoirs*, VI, 503.
150. Amery, interview with R. Shepherd: Shepherd, *Macleod*, 309.
151. Howard, *RAB*, 310.
152. Macmillan Diary, 12 October 1963: *Memoirs*, VI, 503, 505.
153. D. Walters, *Not Always with the Pack* (1989), 110 ff.
154. Hailsham, *Sparrow's Flight*, 353-4.
155. Personal knowledge.
156. Home, *Way the Wind Blows*, 182.
157. Ibid., 183.
158. Ibid.
159. Howard, *RAB*, 313.
160. Memorandum by Lord Fanshawe (formerly Anthony Royle, MP), 5 July 1989: Thorpe, *Douglas-Home*, 293.
161. J. Dickie, *The Uncommon Commoner* (1964), 183; Home, *Way the Wind Blows*, 183-4.
162. Goodhart, *1922*, 191.
163. Ibid.
164. Memorandum by Lord Fanshawe, 5 July 1989: Thorpe, *Douglas-Home*, 293.
165. Pimlott, *Queen*, 328-9.
166. *Independent on Sunday,* 1 January 1995; Appendix B.
167. Ibid.
168. Ibid.; Horne, *Macmillan*, II, 556-7.
169. Macmillan, *Memoirs*, VI, 509-10; Churchill, *Fight for the Tory Leadership,* 126.
170. Whitelaw, Bennett and Berkeley, interview with R. Shepherd: *Macleod*, 323-4.
171. Horne, *Macmillan*, II, 559 ff.
172. Ibid., 561-2; I. Gilmour, 'Holding All the Strings', *London Review of Books*, 27 July 1989.
173. Shepherd, *Macleod*, 325ff.
174. Personal knowledge.
175. Macmillan, 'Notes for the Record', 15 October 1963: Horne, *Macmillan*, II, 556.
176. Shepherd, *Macleod*, 333.
177. Macmillan Diary, 18 October 1963: *Memoirs,* VI, 514.
178. Ibid.
179. Churchill, *Fight for the Tory Leader-ship*, 137.
180. Swinton Papers: Pimlott, *Queen*, 329.
181. Horne, *Macmillan*, II, 565.
182. Macmillan Diary, 18 October 1963: *Memoirs*, VI, 515.
183. Ibid.
184. Shepherd, *Macleod,* 331.
185. Macmillan Diary, 18 October 1963: *Memoirs*, VI, 515.
186. Pimlott, *Queen*, 329.
187. Ibid., 333.
188. Thames Television, 'The Day before Yesterday', October 1974: S. Barnes, 'Lord Butler' in *Behind the Image* (1974), 86 at 90-1.
189. Butler Papers, 18 October 1963: Howard, *RAB*, 320.
190. *Spectator*, 17 January 1964. Macleod's article is reprinted in G. Hutchinson, *The Last Edwardian at No. 10* (1980), 123. For a contrary view, see P. Johnson, 'Was the Palace to Blame?', *New Statesman*, 24 January 1964, reprinted in his *Statesmen and Nations* (1971), 88.
191. *Spectator*, 17 January 1964.
192. Pimlott, *Queen*, 334-5.
193. A. Howard and R. West, *The Making of the Prime Minister* (1965), 237.
194. Ibid.
195. H. Wilson, *The Labour Government 1964-70* (1971), 1.
196. Ibid.
197. Home, *Way the Wind Blows*, 215.
198. Wilson, *Labour Government*, 2
199. Ibid.

CHAPTER 3

1. H. Pelling, *A Short History of the Labour Party* (1961, 10th edn 1993), 18, gives the number as 29; D. Butler and G. Butler, *British Political Facts 1900-94*, 7th edn, 214, gives it as 30.
2. MacDonald to Margaret MacDonald, 28 January 1906: Marquand, *MacDonald*, 96.
3. W. Stewart, *J. Keir Hardie* (1921), 236.
4. Pelling, *Short History of the Labour Party*, 3rd edn, 32.
5. Ibid., 20.
6. Stewart, *Hardie*, 227.
7. MacDonald to Glasier, 21 July 1906: K.O. Morgan, *Keir Hardie* (1975; pb edn 1984), 155.
8. Snowden to T.D. Benson: Glasier Diary, 21 July 1906: Morgan, *Keir Hardie*, pb edn, 160.

9. Pelling, *Short History of the Labour Party,* 3rd edn, 20.

10. Morgan, *Hardie,* pb edn, 155.

11. Ibid., 219.

12. MacDonald to Hardie, January 1910: Marquand, *MacDonald,* 120.

13. Barnes to MacDonald, 1 February 1910: ibid.

14. Shackleton to MacDonald, 8 February 1910: ibid., 121.

15. Shackleton to MacDonald, 31 October 1910: ibid.

16. MacDonald Diary, 11 June 1910: ibid., 127.

17. Anderson to MacDonald, 3 August 1910: ibid., 128.

18. Marquand, *MacDonald,* 12.

19. Henderson to MacDonald, 2 January 1911: ibid., 129.

20. Benson to MacDonald, 20 January 1911: ibid., 130.

21. Pelling, *Short History of the Labour Party,* 3rd edn, 20, 32.

22. Marquand, *MacDonald,* 130.

23. *Labour Leader,* 6 February 1911: ibid., 130.

24. *Leicester Pioneer,* 11 February 1911: ibid.

25. Ibid., 136.

26. Ibid., 150.

27. 65 H.C. Deb. 1831, 3 August 1914: ibid., 168.

28. Pelling, *Short History of the Labour Party,* 3rd edn, 36-7

29. MacDonald Diary, 5 August 1914: Marquand, *MacDonald,* 169.

30. MacDonald to Henderson, 23 October 1914: ibid., 178.

31. MacDonald Diary, 18 November 1914: ibid.

32. MacDonald Diary, 10 December 1914: ibid., 179.

33. A.J.P. Taylor, 'Politics in the First World War' in *Politics in Wartime* (1964), 11 at 30-1.

34. The only other Labour member of the Asquith Coalition listed in Butler and Butler, *British Political Facts,* in addition to Henderson is G. Roberts, a Whip.

35. Beatrice Webb Diary, 8 December 1916: *Diaries,* III, 270-1.

36. MacDonald in *Glasgow Forward,* 16 December 1916: Marquand, *MacDonald,* 195.

37. Ibid.

38. Beatrice Webb in May 1918: *Diaries,* III, 282.

39. Beatrice Webb Diary, 14 January 1919: ibid., 330-1.

40. Beatrice Webb Diary, 4 and 7 November 1918: ibid., 316-17.

41. Beatrice Webb Diary, 21 November 1918: ibid., 325; Diary, 17 and 21 November 1918; Pelling, *Short History of the Labour Party,* 3rd edn, 45.

42. Beatrice Webb Diary, 10 January 1919: ibid., 329.

43. Beatrice Webb Diary, 24 September and 1 December 1919: ibid., 348, 352.

44. Pelling, *Short History of the Labour Party,* 3rd edn, 49.

45. Beatrice Webb Diary, 19 June 1921: ibid., 379-80.

46. Beatrice Webb Diary, 10 January 1915: ibid., 329.

47.*New Leader,* 24 November 1922: Marquand, *MacDonald,* 287.

48. *Forward,* 25 November 1922: ibid., 286-7

49. Pelling, *Short History of the Labour Party,* 3rd edn, 68.

50. R. Postgate, *The Life of George Lansbury* (1951), 277.

51. H. Dalton, *Memoirs* (3 vols, 1953-62) I, 277.

52. Beatrice Webb Diary, 28 October 1931: *Diaries,* IV, 263.

53. Postgate, *Lansbury,* 277.

54. Ibid.

55. Beatrice Webb Diary, 28 September 1935: *Diaries,* IV, 358.

56. Harris, *Attlee,* pb edn, 119.

57. Donoughue and Jones, *Morrison,* 235.

58. Harris, *Attlee,* pb edn, 120.

59. B. Pimlott, *Hugh Dalton* (1985; new pb edn 1995), 229-31.

60. Ibid., 231.

61. Dalton Diary, 16 November 1935: cit. Donoughue and Jones, *Morrison,* 238.

62. Harris, *Attlee,* pb edn, 121-2; Donoughue and Jones, *Morrison,* 239.

63. Harris, *Attlee,* pb edn, 122.

64. Beatrice Webb Diary, 27 November 1935: *Diaries,* IV, 366.

CHAPTER 4

1. Pelling, *Short History of the Labour Party,* 3rd edn, 80.

2. L. Hunter, *The Road to Brighton Pier* (1959), 130.

3. Ibid., 123.

4. Ibid., 131.

5. Dalton, *Memoirs,* III, 429.

6. Ibid.

7. Crossman Diary, 6 May 1959: *The Backbench Diaries of Richard Crossman*, ed. J. Morgan (1981), 746.

8. Hunter, *Road to Brighton Pier*, 123.

9. Crossman Diary, 16 March 1955: *Backbench Diaries*, 406.

10. Hunter, *Road to Brighton Pier*, 159.

11. P.M. Williams, *Hugh Gaitskell* (1979), 348.

12. Conversation with Jim Griffiths.

13. Williams, *Gaitskell*, 356.

14. Crossman Diary, 7 October 1955: *Backbench Diaries*, 446.

15. Donoughue and Jones, *Morrison*, 538.

16. Ibid., 536.

17. Dalton Diary, 28 April 1955, quot. *Williams*, Gaitskell, 364.

18. P. Hollis, *Jennie Lee* (1997), 191.

19. E. Shaw, *Discipline and Discord in the Labour Party* (1988), 39-42; M. Foot, *Aneurin Bevan* (2 vols, 1962-73), II, 479; B. Brivati, *Hugh Gaitskell* (1996), 202-13.

20. Williams, *Gaitskell*, 354.

21. *Tribune*, 3 June 1955: quot. Williams, *Gaitskell*, 351.

22. Dalton, *Memoirs*, III, 425; Hunter, *Road to Brighton Pier*, 115.

23. Hunter, *Road to Brighton Pier*, 116.

24. Dalton, *Memoirs*, III, 419-20.

25. Ibid., 422.

26. Dalton Diary, 9 June 1955: *Memoirs*, III, 422.

27. Dalton, *Memoirs*, III, 422.

28. Harris, *Attlee*, pb edn, 535.

29. Foot, *Bevan*, II, 489.

30. Harris, *Attlee*, pb edn, 535.

31. Ibid., 536.

32. Dalton, *Memoirs*, III, 429.

33. *News Chronicle*, 13 September 1955: cit. Hunter, *Road to Brighton Pier*, 134; Harris, *Attlee*, pb edn, 537-8.

34. Crossman Diary, 23 September 1955: *Backbench Diaries*, 441.

35. Williams, *Gaitskell*, 361.

36. H. Cudlipp, *Walking on the Water* (1976), 212.

37. Foot, *Bevan*, II, 495.

38. Ibid., 494.

39. A. Howard, *Crossman* (1990), 197.

40. *Observer*, 16 October 1955: cit. Williams, Gaitskell, 356.

41. Foot, *Bevan*, II, 492.

42. Crossman Diary, 15 October referring to 11 October 1955: *Backbench Diaries*, 448.

43. Dalton, *Memoirs*, III, 426.

44. Williams, *Gaitskell*, 363.

45. Harris, *Attlee*, pb edn, 539.

46. Williams, *Gaitskell*, 363; Hunter, *Road to Brighton Pier*, 144-8.

47. Crossman Diary, 28 October referring to 27 October 1955: *Backbench Diaries*, 448.

48. Hunter, *Road to Brighton Pier*, 159.

49. Harris, *Attlee*, pb edn, 540.

50. Ibid.

51. Williams, *Gaitskell*, 364.

52. Crossman Diary, 4 November referring to 31 October 1955: *Backbench Diaries*, 451.

53. Williams, *Gaitskell*, 363.

54. Dalton Diary, 3 November 1955: cit. Williams, *Gaitskell*, 365.

55. Williams, *Gaitskell*, 365-6.

56. Stuart, *Within the Fringe*, 144.

57. Crossman Diary, 16 November 1955: *Backbench Diaries*, 452-3.

58. Harris, *Attlee*, pb edn, 541.

59. Crossman Diary, 16 December referring to 6 December 1955: *Backbench Diaries*, 455.

60. Harris, *Attlee*, pb edn, 541.

61. Ibid., 541-2; Dalton, *Memoirs*, III, 430.

62. Hunter, *Road to Brighton Pier*, 173-4; Dalton, *Memoirs*, III, 431.

63. Foot, *Bevan*, II, 496.

64. Donoughue and Jones, *Morrison*, 539.

65. Foot, *Bevan*, II, 496.

66. Dalton, *Memoirs*, III, 431.

67. Donoughue and Jones, *Morrison*, 540; D. Smith, *Wilson* (1964), 174-6.

68. Donoughue and Jones, *Morrison*, 539.

69. Hunter, *Road to Brighton Pier*, 135.

70. Crossman Diary, 16 December referring to 8 December 1955: *Backbench Diaries*, 456-7.

71. Howard, *Crossman*, 198.

72. *Daily Mirror*, 10 December 1955.

73. *Observer*, 11 December 1955.

74. Harris, *Attlee*, pb edn, 542.

75. *Tribune*, 16 December 1955.

76. Crossman Diary, 14 May 1959: *Backbench Diaries*, 749.

77. Crossman Diary, 5 July 1959: ibid., 766.

78. Goodman Diary, 4 October 1959: quot. Foot, *Bevan*, II, 627.

79. Foot, *Bevan*, II, 629.

80. D. Jay, *Change and Fortune* (1980), 272.

81. Ibid.

82. Benn Diary, 10 October 1959: *Diaries*, VI, 316-17.

83. H. Massingham in the *Observer*, 15 November 1959: quot. Williams, *Gaitskell*, 544.

84. R. Jenkins, *A Life at the Centre* (1991), 128.

85. Foot, *Bevan*, II, 630.
86. Information from Anthony Howard.
87. Williams, *Gaitskell*, 538.
88. S. Crosland, *Tony Crosland* (1982; pb edn 1983), 92.
89. Information from Lord Jenkins.
90. Jenkins, *Life at the Centre*, 128.
91. Dalton Diary, 11 October 1959: Williams, *Gaitskell*, 538-9.
92. Jenkins, *Life at the Centre*, 129.
93. Dalton Diary, 16 October 1959: quot. B. Pimlott, *Harold Wilson* (1992), 225.
94. Williams, *Gaitskell*, 539.
95. Benn Diary, 11 October 1959: *Diaries*, VI, 317.
96. Jenkins, *Life at the Centre*, 129-30.
97. Benn Diary, 12 October 1959: *Diaries*, VI, 318.
98. Jenkins, *Life at the Centre*, 131.
99. Dalton, *Memoirs*, III, 444; Crosland, *Crosland*, 94.
100. Jay, *Change and Fortune*, 275.
101. Ibid., 275.
102. Crossman Diary, 19 October 1959: *Backbench Diaries*, 791.
103. Hugh Massingham in the *Observer*, 15 November 1959: quot. Williams, *Gaitskell*, 544.
104. Dalton to Gaitskell, 15 November 1959: Williams, *Gaitskell*, 543.
105. Crossman Diary, 25 November 1959: *Backbench Diaries*, 802.
106. Williams, *Gaitskell*, 551.
107. A. Bevan, *In Place of Fear* (1952; new edn 1978), 98-9, 118.
108. Labour Party Conference Report 1959, 83-6.
109. Ibid., 105 ff.
110. B. Levin in the *Spectator*, 4 December 1959.
111. Foot, *Bevan*, II, 651-2
112. Benn Diary, 29 November 1959: *Diaries*, VI, 321.
113. Foot, *Bevan*, II, 651-2.
114. Crossman Diary, 9 December 1959: *Backbench Diaries*, 804.
115. Hetherington Diary, 10 December 1959: quot. Williams, *Gaitskell*, 542.
116. Jenkins, *Life at the Centre*, 132.
117. Benn Diary, 4 January 1960: *Diaries*, VI, 323.
118. Ibid., 20 January 1960: ibid., 324.
119. Crossman Diary, 12 February 1960: *Backbench Diaries*, 812.
120. Benn Diary, 18 February 1960: *Diaries*, VI, 324.
121. Howard, *Crossman*, 224.

122. Driberg to Gaitskell, 14 March 1960: Williams, *Gaitskell*, 568.
123. Benn Diary, 16 March 1960: *Diaries*, VI, 325.
124. Jenkins, *Life at the Centre*, 132.
125. Benn Diary, 16 March 1960: *Diaries*, VI, 326.
126. J. Campbell, *Nye Bevan and the Mirage of British Socialism* (1987), 361.
127. Crossman Diary, 22 March 1960: *Backbench Diaries*, 829.
128. R. Lamb, *The Macmillan Years* (1995), 287.
129. Ibid., 286.
130. Ibid., 287.
131. Macmillan, *Memoirs*, V, 251.
132. R. Neustadt, *Alliance Politics* (1970), 33.
133. Ibid., 32-3.
134. Macmillan Diary, 29 March 1960: *Memoirs*, V, 252.
135. Macmillan to Elizabeth II, 3 April 1960: *Memoirs*, V, 253.
136. Benn Diary, 13 April 1960: *Diaries*, VI, 329.
137. Macmillan, *Memoirs*, V, 253.
138. Crosland to Gaitskell, 4 May 1960: Crosland, *Crosland*, 97.
139. Benn Diary, 5 May 1960: *Diaries*, VI, 329.
140. Crossman Diary, 11 May 1960: *Backbench Diaries*, 844-5.
141. Gaitskell to Williams, 19 May 1960: Williams, *Gaitskell*, 586.
142. Dalton Diary, 12 May 1960: quot. ibid.
143. Dalton to Gaitskell, 30 June 1960: quot. ibid.
144. Benn Diary, 25 May 1960: *Diaries*, VI, 331.
145. Crossman Diary, 20 May 1960, referring to 25 May, *Backbench Diaries*, 853.
146. Macmillan Diary, 25 May 1960: *Memoirs*, V, 254.
147. Lamb, *Macmillan Years*, 287-9
148. Benn Diary, 11 June 1960: *Diaries*, VI, 332.
149. Macmillan Diary, 12 June 1960: *Memoirs*, V, 254.
150. Macmillan, *Memoirs*, V, 255.
151. Gaitskell to Crossman, 13 June 1960: Williams, *Gaitskell*, 589, 591.
152. Lamb, *Macmillan Years*, 290.
153. Gaitskell to E.L. Mallalieu, 23 June 1960: Williams, *Gaitskell*, 598.
154. Lamb, *Macmillan Years*, 291.
155. Benn Diary, 13 July 1960: *Diaries*, VI, 334.

156. Crossman Diary, 30 August 1966: *Backbench Diaries*, 866.

157. Ibid.

158. Crossman Diary, 1 September 1960: *Backbench Diaries*, 871.

159. Crosland to Gaitskell, 1 September 1966: Crosland, *Crosland*, 101.

160. Gaitskell to Crosland, 4 September 1960: ibid., 102.

161. Macmillan, *Memoirs*, V, 255.

162. Benn Diary, 18 September 1960: *Diaries*, VI, 342.

163. Ibid., 20 September.

164. Lamb, *Macmillan Years*, 296-7.

165. Benn Diary, 26 September – 1 October 1960: *Diaries*, VI, 342-6

166. Williams, *Gaitskell*, 610.

167. Benn Diary, 5-8 October 1960: *Diaries*, VI, 348-9

168. Crossman Diary, 13 October 1960: *Backbench Diaries*, 880-1.

169. Information from Lord Greenwood.

170. Crossman Diary, 19 October 1960: ibid., 885.

171. Williams, *Gaitskell*, 624.

172. Smith, *Wilson*, 187.

173. Williams, *Gaitskell*, 625; Pimlott, *Wilson*, 241; Crossman Diary, 20 October 1960: *Backbench Diaries*, 887-92.

174. Pimlott, *Wilson*, 243-4.

175. Crosland to Gaitskell, 21 October 1960: Crosland, *Crosland*, 103.

176. Crossman to Wilson, 21 October 1960: Howard, *Crossman*, 233.

177. Crosland to Gaitskell, 7 November 1960: Crosland, *Crosland*, 103-7.

178. Lamb, *Macmillan Years*, 295.

179. Macmillan Diary, 13 December 1960: *Memoirs*, V, 258.

180. Crosland, *Crosland*, 100.

181. Gaitskell to Crosland, 5 March 1961: *Gaitskell*, 634.

182. Gaitskell to Rodgers, 1 March 1961: ibid.

183. Gaitskell to Williams, n.d. March 1961: Williams, *Gaitskell*, 635.

184. Crossman Diary, 8 March 1961: *Backbench Diaries*, 938.

185. Lamb, *Macmillan Years*, 298.

186. Gaitskell to Watson, 8 June 1961: Williams, *Gaitskell*, 645.

187. *Tribune*, 9 June 1961: quot. Williams, Gaitskell, 648.

188. Dalton, *Memoirs*, III, 445.

189. Personal knowledge.

190. Earl of Longford, *Five Lives* (1964), 242.

191. Williams, *Gaitskell*, 760-1.

192. *Guardian*, 11 January 1963: quot. Howard, *Crossman*, 243.

193. Benn Diary, 18 January 1963: *Diaries*, I, 2.

194. John Harris interview with Ben Pimlott: Pimlott, *Wilson*, 255.

195. P. Paterson, *Tired and Emotional* (1993), 126; A. Roth, *Sir Harold Wilson* (1997), 271; Pimlott, *Wilson*, 256-7; Howard and West, *Making of the Prime Minister*, 19.

196. Lord Wigg, *George Wigg* (1972), 250; Howard, *Crossman*, 244.

197. Pimlott, *Wilson*, 257; Howard, *Crossman*, 244.

198. Wigg, *Wigg*, 257.

199. Crosland, *Crosland*, 11.

200. J. Callaghan, *Time and Chance* (1987), 150.

201. Crossman Diary, 8 February 1963: *Backbench Diaries*, 969.

202. Howard, *Crossman*, 245; Crossman Diary, 8 February 1963: *Backbench Diaries*, 972.

203. Crossman Diary, 7 February 1963: *Backbench Diaries*, 971-2.

204. Ibid., 15-19 February: ibid., 980-1.

205. Wigg, *Wigg*, 258.

206. M. Jones, *Michael Foot* (1994), 394.

207. Benn Diary, 16 March 1976: *Diaries*, III, 535.

208. Ibid., 536.

209. Castle Diary, 16 March 1976: B. Castle, *Diaries* (2 vols, 1980-4; 1 vol pb edn, 1990), II, 691-2.

210. Benn Diary, 17 March 1976: *Diaries*, III, 537-9

211. Crosland, *Crosland*, 315.

212. Ibid.

213. Castle Diary, 18 March 1976: *Diaries*, II, 694

214. Jenkins, *Life at the Centre*, 435.

215. Benn Diary, 22 March 1976: *Diaries*, III, 543.

216. Crosland, *Crosland*, 316.

217. Callaghan, *Time and Chance*, 393.

218. Jenkins, *Life at the Centre*, 436.

219. Crosland, *Crosland*, 313.

220. Benn Diary, 25 March 1976: *Diaries*, III, 544-6.

221. Castle Diary, 25 March 1976: *Castle Diaries*, II, 705.

222. Benn Diary, 30 March 1976: *Diaries*, III, 549.

223. Callaghan, *Time and Chance*, 392.

CHAPTER 5

1. D. Kogan and M. Kogan, *The Battle for the Labour Party* (1982), 14, 22, 27, 33.
2. Benn Diary, 3 October 1978: *Diaries*, IV, 356.
3. Kogan and Kogan, *Battle for the Labour Party*, 62.
4. Jones, *Foot*, 442.
5. Callaghan, *Time and Chance*, 565.
6. D. Owen, *Time to Declare* (1991), 417.
7. Benn Diary, 9 May 1979: *Diaries*, IV, 499-500.
8. Owen, *Time to Declare*, 421.
9. Benn Diary, 27 July, 31 July and 26 August 1979: *Diaries*, IV, 525-8.
10. Kogan and Kogan, *Battle for the Labour Party*, 14-15
11. Ibid., 62-3.
12. Benn Diary, 10-12 September 1979: *Diaries*, IV, 531-4.
13. Ibid., 21-8 September 1975: ibid., 537-40.
14. Benn Diary, 2 October 1979: *Diaries*, IV, 543-5.
15. Owen, *Time to Declare*, 424.
16. Kogan and Kogan, *Battle for the Labour Party*, 14-15, 71-2.
17. Benn Diary, 24 October 1979: *Diaries*, IV, 550-1.
18. Owen, *Time to Declare*, 425.
19. D. Healey, *The Time of my Life* (1989), 473-4.
20. Benn Diary, 31 October, 22 November and 24 December 1979: *Diaries*, IV, 553, 559, 568.
21. Jones, *Foot*, 446.
22. Benn Diary, 17 April and 18 May 1980: *Diaries*, IV, 589, 595.
23. Owen, *Time to Declare*, 440; for the Bishop's Stortford conference, Benn Diary, 13-15 June 1980: *Diaries*, V, pb edn, 5-10.
24. Healey, *Time of My Life*, 474.
25. Owen, *Time to Declare*, 441.
26. Healey, *Time of My Life*, 475.
27. Benn Diary, 6 July 1980: *Diaries*, V, pb edn, 17.
28. Owen, *Time to Declare*, 446.
29. Benn Diary, 21 June-3 July 1980: *Diaries*, V, pb edn, 11-23.
30. Jones, *Foot*, 446.
31. Ibid., 44.
32. Benn Diary, 2 October 1980: *Diaries*, V, pb edn, 34. For the 1980 conference generally see ibid., 1-2 October 1980: ibid., 32-4; Kogan and Kogan, *Battle for the Labour Party*, 78-87; Labour Party Conference Report 1980.
33. Owen, *Time to Declare*, 452.
34. Ibid., 453-6.
35. Kogan and Kogan, *Battle for the Labour Party*, 87.
36. Benn Diary, 6 October 1980: *Diaries*, V, pb edn, 35.
37. Benn Diary, 12 October 1980: *Diaries*, V, pb edn, 36.
38. Jones, *Foot*, 447.
39. Ibid., 450.
40. Jenkins, *All Against the Collar* (1990), 188; I. Mikardo, *Backbencher* (1988), 204: cit. P. Shore, *Leading the Left* (1993), 139.
41. Mikardo, *Backbencher*, 204: cit. Jones, *Foot*, 450.
42. Jones, *Foot*, 452.
43. Ibid., 448.
44. Benn Diary, 22 October 1980: *Diaries*, V, pb edn, 40.
45. Ibid., 28 October 1980; ibid., 42-3; Shore, *Leading the Left*, 138.
46. *Tribune*, 31 October 1980: quot. Jones, *Foot*, 442.
47. Benn Diary, 4 November 1980: *Diaries*, V, pb edn, 44.
48. Benn Diary, 10 November 1980; *Diaries*, V, pb edn, 46.
49. Healey, *Time of My Life*, 477-8.
50. Ibid., 477.
51. Owen, *Time to Declare*, 458.
52. Personal knowledge.
53. Owen, *Time to Declare*, 458.
54. Jones, *Foot*, 453.
55. Benn Diary, 18 November 1980: *Diaries*, V, pb edn, 49.
56. Kogan and Kogan, *Battle for the Labour Party*, 94-7
57. Labour Party Special Conference Report 1981.
58. R. Hattersley, *Who Goes Home?* (1995), 229.
59. Benn Diary, 24 January 1981: *Diaries*, V, pb edn, 69-70
60. Ibid., 18 February 1981: ibid., 91.
61. Ibid., 3 March, 24 March, 13 April and 3 June 1981: ibid., 103, 112, 119, 120 and 135.
62. Kogan and Kogan, *Battle for the Labour Party*, 116.
63. Ibid., 118.
64. Jones, *Foot*, 517.
65. Healey, *Time of My Life*, 445.
66. Ibid., 503.
67. R. Harris, *The Making of Neil Kinnock* (1984), 216. Generally, see ibid., 213-37; Leapman, *Kinnock* (1987), 23-5; Jones, *Foot*, 517-18; Shore, *Leading the Left*, 153-4.

68. Hattersley, *Who Goes Home?* 250.
69. Ibid., 251.
70. Shore, *Leading the Left*, 153.
71. Benn Diary, 12 June 1983: *Diaries*, V, pb edn, 295-8.
72. See A. Watkins, *A Slight Case of Libel* (1990), ch. 2 and *passim*.
73. Hattersley, *Who Goes Home?*, 247; Leapman, *Kinnock*, 25.
74. Jones, *Foot*, 517.
75. Hattersley, *Who Goes Home?*, 250-1.
76. B. Gould, *Goodbye to All That* (1995), 253.
77. J. Sopel, *Tony Blair* (1995), 131.
78. J. Rentoul, *Blair* (1995; rev pb edn 1996), 254-6.
79. A. McSmith, *John Smith* (1993; rev pb edn 1994), 264.
80. Gould, *Goodbye to All That*, 254-6.
81. *Guardian*, 14 April 1992.
82. Ibid.
83. Ibid.
84. *Tribune*, 24 April 1992.
85. Bryan Gould interview with Martin Kettle: *Guardian*, 16 April 1992.
86. *Sunday Times*, 19 April 1992.
87. McSmith, *Smith*, pb edn, 276.
88. 210 H.C.Deb. 1050, 2 July 1992.
89. *Financial Times*, 16 July 1992.
90. *Sunday Times*, 19 April 1992.
91. 104 *Fabian Review*, July 1992.
92. Rentoul, *Blair*, 320-4.
93. Ibid.
94. McSmith, *Smith*, pb edn, 305.
95. *Independent*, 8 June 1993.
96. McSmith, *Smith*, pb edn, 308.
97. *Guardian*, 9 June 1993: quot. Sopel, *Blair*, 161.
98. Sopel, *Blair*, 162-3
99. Rentoul, *Blair*, 329; see also McSmith, *Smith*, pb edn, 305-8.
100. Rentoul, *Blair*, 330.
101. McSmith, *Smith*, pb edn, 309.
102. Rentoul, *Blair*, 335.
103. Ibid., 339.
104. McSmith, *Smith*, pb edn, 311.
105. Rentoul, *Blair*, 382.
106. Ibid., 362.
107. Ibid., 373-5.
108. Sopel, *Blair*, 190-1.
109. Rentoul, *Blair*, 378.
110. Ibid., 379-80.
111. Ibid., 394-8.
112. Personal knowledge.

CHAPTER 6

1. H. Berkeley, *Crossing the Floor* (1972), App. I, 149ff. at 149.
2. Ibid., 149-50.
3. They are collected in H. Berkeley, *The Life and Death of Rochester Sneath* (1974).
4. Berkeley, *Crossing the Floor*, 150.
5. Ibid.
6. Home, *Way the Wind Blows*, 218.
7. Ibid.
8. Berkeley, *Crossing the Floor*, 151ff.
9. G. Hutchinson, *Edward Heath* (1970), 138.
10. The full text is reproduced in Hutchinson, *Heath*, App. III, 222, and in Goodhart, *1922*, 201.
11. Hutchinson, *Heath*, 138.
12. Home, *Way the Wind Blows*, 220. See also Goodhart, *1922*, 203ff.; Hutchinson, *Heath*, 138ff.
13. Thorpe, *Douglas-Home*, 386.
14. J. Campbell, *Edward Heath* (1993), 176.
15. Campbell, *Heath*, 177.
16. Hutchinson, *Heath*, 140.
17. Goodhart, *1922*, 206.
18. Home, *Way the Wind Blows*, 221.
19. Berkeley, *Crossing the Floor*, 98.
20. A. Watkins, 'Iain Macleod' in *Brief Lives* (1982), 97 at 108.
21. Hutchinson, *Heath*, 143-4.
22. Campbell, *Heath*, 654.
23. N. Fisher, *The Tory Leaders* (1977), 147-8: cit. Campbell, *Heath*, 656.
24. Campbell, *Heath*, 655.
25. *The Times*, 22 October 1974: cit. Campbell, *Heath*, 658.
26. Campbell, *Heath*, 657, 659.
27. Fisher, *Tory Leaders*: cit. Campbell, *Heath*, 662 and Campbell, ibid.
28. A. Watkins, *A Conservative Coup* (1991; 2nd pb edn 1992), 174.
29. N. Wapshott and G. Brock, *Thatcher* (1983), 118.
30. Campbell, *Heath*, 664.
31. A. Meyer, *Stand Up and Be Counted* (1990), 56.
32. *The Times*, 10 July 1995.
33. A. Watkins in the *Independent on Sunday*, 13 April 1997.
34. See B. Anderson, 'New Leader, New Voting?', *Spectator*, 17 May 1997.
35. *The Times*, 21 May 1997.
36. Ibid., 22 May 1997.
37. Ibid., 23 May 1997.
38. See generally S. Jenkins, *Accountable to None* (1995; pb edn 1996).

39. *The Times*, 11 June 1997.
40. Ibid., 18 June 1997.
41. Ibid.
42. Ibid., 19 June 1997.
43. Ibid.
44. Ibid.
45. Ibid.

CHAPTER 7

1. Wilson, *Labour Government*, 789-90.
2. Pimlott, *Wilson*, 558.
3. Jenkins, *Life at the Centre*, 303.
4. Pimlott, *Wilson*, 558.
5. Campbell, *Heath*, 284.
6. H. Wilson, *Final Term* (1979), 9.
7. Jenkins, *Life at the Centre*, 367.
8. Wilson, *Final Term*, 9,11.
9. M. Falkender, *Downing Street in Perspective* (1983), 80.
10. Wilson, *Final Term*, 9.
11. Cecil King Diary, 4 March 1974: C. King, *Diaries* (2 vols, 1972-5), II, 349.
12. Campbell, *Heath*, 616; D. Steel, *Against Goliath* (1989), 80.
13. See generally D. Butler, *The Electoral System in Britain 1918-51* (1953).
14. *The Times*, 5 March 1974: quot. Campbell, *Heath*, 616.
15. Jenkins, *Life at the Centre*, 368.
16. Campbell, *Heath*, 616.
17. Wilson, *Final Term*, 10.
18. Falkender, *Downing Street in Perspective*, 82-3.
19. Wilson, *Final Term*, 10.
20. Pimlott, *Wilson*, 647; J. Haines, *The Politics of Power* (1977), 216-18; Falkender, *Downing Street in Perspective*, 168; Healey, *Time of My Life*, 446.
21. See generally K. Burk and A. Cairncross, *Goodbye, Great Britain* (1992).
22. See P. Wright, *Spycatcher* (1987); P. Marnham, *Trail of Havoc* (1987; rev edn 1988), passim.
23. Jenkins, *Life at the Centre*, 297-8.
24. A. Watkins, 'Mr Wilson's Future', *New Statesman*, 21 August 1970.
25. Healey, *Time of My Life*, 446.
26. Wilson, *Final Term*, 227-8.
27. B. Donoughue, *Prime Minister* (1987), 86.
28. Ibid., 11.
29. T. Stuttaford, 'Wilson's Fear of Senility', *The Times*, 25 May 1995.
30. Haines, *Politics of Power*, 9.
31. Ibid., 220.
32. Benn Diary, 22 March 1976: *Diaries*, III, 543.

33. Falkender, *Downing Street in Perspective*, 3.
34. Wilson, *Final Term*, 227-8.
35. Falkender, *Downing Street in Perspective*, 187.
36. Donoughue, *Prime Minister*, 87.
37. Wilson, *Final Term*, 228.
38. Lord Goodman makes no reference to this occasion in his own memoirs, *Tell Them I'm On My Way* (1993).
39. Castle Diary, 21 March 1976: *Diaries*, II, 695.
40. Falkender, *Downing Street in Perspective*, 4-5.
41. Ibid., 229.
42. Healey, *Time of My Life*, 446.
43. Jenkins, *Life at the Centre*, 430.
44. Ibid., 432.
45. Callaghan, *Time and Chance*, 386-7.
46. Haines, *Politics of Power*, 221.
47. Falkender, *Downing Street in Perspective*, 4.
48. Callaghan, *Time and Chance*, 390.
49. Falkender, *Downing Street in Perspective*, 4.
50. Callaghan, *Time and Chance*, 391.
51. Wilson, *Final Term*, 232.
52. Healey, *Time of My Life*, 446.
53. Callaghan, *Time and Chance*, 391.
54. Benn Diary, 16 March 1976: *Diaries*, III, 535.
55. Jenkins, *Life at the Centre*, 434.
56. Castle Diary, 16 March 1976: *Diaries*, II, 689.
57. Castle Diary, 21 March 1976: ibid., 655.
58. Healey, *Time of My Life*, 446.
59. Castle Diary, 16 March 1976: *Diaries*, II, 689-90.
60. Wilson, *Final Term*, 239.
61. Callaghan, *Time and Chance*, 394.
62. Wilson, *Final Term*, 235.
63. Callaghan, *Time and Chance*, 394.
64. M. Thatcher, *The Downing Street Years* (1993), 17.
65. Watkins, *Conservative Coup*, 2nd edn, ch. 2.
66. P. Norton, 'The Conservative Party from Thatcher to Major' in A. King (ed.), *Britain at the Polls 1992* (1992), 29.
67. C. Parkinson, *Right at the Centre* (1992), 4.
68. Thatcher, *Downing Street Years*, 832.
69. Ibid., 690.
70. Ibid., 702. For Lawson's views see his *The View From No 11* (1992), 783-841.
71. Thatcher, *Downing Street Years*, 703.

72. Interview with Simon Jenkins, *The Times*, 29 June 1991. See also Lawson, *View From No 11*, 783ff.

73. Resignation speech, 159 H.C. Deb. 208, 31 October 1989.

74. K. Baker, *The Turbulent Years* (1993), 419.

75. *The Times*, 4 September 1995. The quotation is from a pre-publication extract from B. Connolly, *The Rotten Heart of Europe* (1995).

76. Watkins, *Conservative Coup*, 2nd edn, 213.

77. Thatcher, *Downing Street Years*, 830.

78. Baker, *Turbulent Years*, 376; G. Howe, *Conflict of Loyalty* (1994), 638.

79. Thatcher, *Downing Street Years*, 832.

80. Ibid., 832-3.

81. Howe, *Conflict of Loyalty*, 628, 639.

82. Ibid., 639.

83. Ibid., 643.

84. 178 H.C. Deb. 870, 30 October 1990. The Official Report does not, however, record the 'Hear, hears'.

85. Ibid., 873. The Official Report misprints 'We' for 'He'.

86. Howe, *Conflict of Loyalty*, 844.

87. Thatcher, *Downing Street Years*, 834.

88. Howe, *Conflict of Loyalty*, 646-7.

89. Parkinson, *Right at the Centre*, 19.

90. Baker, *Turbulent Years*, 378.

91. Thatcher, *Downing Street Years*, 833-4.

92. Ibid., 834.

93. Ibid., 835.

94. Baker, *Turbulent Years*, 379.

95. Howe, *Conflict of Loyalty*, 658.

96. Thatcher, *Downing Street Years*, 835.

97. Clark Diary, 4 November 1990: A. Clark, *Diaries* (1993), 342.

98. Baker, *Turbulent Years*, 382.

99. Howe, *Conflict of Loyalty*, 663.

100. Thatcher, *Downing Street Years*, 836.

101. Baker, *Turbulent Years*, 389.

102. Ibid., 659-60.

103. Transcript, *The Thatcher Factor Special*, 103-4; *Independent*, 13 November 1990.

104. Clark Diary, 12 November 1990: *Diaries*, 345.

105. Howe, *Conflict of Loyalty*, 663.

106. Ibid., 664.

107. 180 H.C. Deb. 461, 13 November 1990.

108. Ibid.

109. Ibid.

110. Ibid., 462.

111. Ibid.

112. Ibid., 463.

113. Ibid., 464.

114. Ibid., 465.

115. Baker, *Turbulent Years*, 386.

116. Parkinson, *Right at the Centre*, 24.

117. Baker, *Turbulent Years*, 386.

118. Parkinson, *Right at the Centre*, 24-5.

119. Baker, *Turbulent Years*, 386.

120. Clark Diary, 13 November 1990: *Diaries*, 348.

121. Baker, *Turbulent Years*, 382, 384.

122. Watkins, *Conservative Coup*, 2nd edn, xvi.

123. Thatcher, *Downing Street Years*, 840-1.

124. Baker, *Turbulent Years*, 387.

125. Ibid.

126. Ibid., 388.

127. Thatcher, *Downing Street Years*, 841.

128. Baker, *Turbulent Years*, 392.

129. Ibid., 394.

130. Ibid., 395.

131. Ibid., 395; R. Shepherd, *The Power Brokers* (1991), 24; Watkins, *Conservative Coup*, 2nd edn, xvii, 190-2.

132. Thatcher, *Downing Street Years*, 843.

133. Baker, *Turbulent Years*, 397.

134. Watkins, *Conservative Coup*, 2nd edn, 3.

135. Thatcher, *Downing Street Years*, 844.

136. Benn Diary, 20 November 1990: *Diaries*, V, pb edn, 611.

137. Watkins, *Conservative Coup*, 2nd edn, 4.

138. Baker, *Turbulent Years*, 397.

139. Ibid., 395.

140. Ibid., 396.

141. Clark Diary, 20 November 1990: *Diaries*, 359.

142. Ibid., 359-61.

143. Baker, *Turbulent Years*, 397-9.

144. Ibid., 399.

145. Ibid., 397-8.

146. Thatcher, *Downing Street Years*, 846.

147. Baker, *Turbulent Years*, 440.

148. Thatcher, *Downing Street Years*, 846.

149. Ibid.; Baker, *Turbulent Years*, 403; Watkins, *Conservative Coup*, 2nd edn, 16.

150. Thatcher, *Downing Street Years*, 846.

151. Baker, *Turbulent Years*, 403; Watkins, *Conservative Coup*, 2nd edn, 16.

152. Thatcher, *Downing Street Years*, 846.

153. Ibid., 847-8.

154. Baker, *Turbulent Years*, 400, 402.

155. Thatcher, *Downing Street Years*, 847-8.

156. Watkins, *Conservative Coup*, 2nd edn, 15.

157. Thatcher, *Downing Street Years*, 847-8.

158. Baker, *Turbulent Years*, 401.

159. Thatcher, *Downing Street Years*, 850-1.
160. Ibid.
161. Ibid., 849; Baker, *Turbulent Years*, 402.
162. Ibid.
163. Parkinson, *Right at the Centre*, 1; Thatcher, *Downing Street Years*, 851; Watkins, *Conservative Coup*, 2nd edn, 18.
164. Thatcher, *Downing Street Years*, 851-2.
165. Baker, *Turbulent Years*, 404.
166. Thatcher, *Downing Street Years*, 851-3.
167. Clark Diary, 21 November 1990: *Diaries*, 366.
168. Thatcher, *Downing Street Years*, 853.
169. Baker, *Turbulent Years*, 406.
170. Ibid.; Thatcher, *Downing Street Years*, 854.
171. Ibid., 854-6; Baker, *Turbulent Years*, 408.
172. Ibid.; Watkins, *Conservative Coup*, 24.
173. Thatcher, *Downing Street Years*, 856.
174. Ibid., 856-7; Parkinson, *Right at the Centre*, 2-4; Baker, *Turbulent Years*, 405-11.
175. Thatcher, *Downing Street Years*, 860.
176. Parkinson, *Right at the Centre*, 35.
177. Personal knowledge.
178. Parkinson, *Right at the Centre*, 3-4.
179. See A. Watkins, *A Slight Case of Libel* (1990), *passim*.
180. Personal knowledge.
181. 27 June 1995.
182. *Daily Mail*, 27 June 1995.
183. Redwood statement, 29 June 1995.

CHAPTER 8

1. Le May, *Victorian Constitution, passim*.
2. P. Gordon Walker, *The Cabinet* (1970; rev pb edn 1972), 135.
3. Jennings, *Cabinet Government*, 3rd edn, 239, 419.
4. J.W. Mackail and G. Wyndham, *Life and Letters of George Wyndham* (2 vols, 1925), II, 505, cit. Jennings, *Cabinet Government*, 3rd edn, 417.
5. Nicolson, *George V*, 289.
6. Earl of Oxford and Asquith, *Fifty Years of Parliament* (2 vols, 1926), II, 194.
7. G. Marshall, *Constitutional Conventions* (1984; pb edn 1986), 49-50.
8. 110 H.C. Deb. 2425 (italics inserted).
9. J.P. Mackintosh, *The British Cabinet* (1962; 2nd edn 1968), 361.
10. Cowling, *Impact of Labour*, 314.
11. Ibid.

12. G.M. Young, *Stanley Baldwin* (1952), 66.
13. Lord Curzon to Lady Curzon, 13 November 1923: Lady Curzon, *Reminiscences* (1955), 186-7: quot. B.S. Markesinis, *The Theory and Practice of Dissolution of Parliament* (1972), 77.
14. Young, *Baldwin*, 66.
15. Cowling, *Impact of Labour*, 315.
16. Nicolson, *George V*, 379-80.
17. Lord Curzon to Lady Curzon, 13 November 1923: ibid.
18. *The Times*, 19 December 1923: reproduced in Markesinis, *Dissolution*, 87.
19. Nicolson, *George V*, 380.
20. Ibid., 400 n. 1. Nicolson mistakenly writes 'Labour' instead of 'Liberal'. See Rose, *George V*, 336.
21. Jennings, *Cabinet Government*, 3rd edn, 30-1.
22. Nicolson, *George V*, 289.
23. Jennings, *Cabinet Government*, 3rd edn, 289.
24. Markesinis, *Dissolution*, 120.
25. Attlee, *As It Happened*, 193.
26. Callaghan's note at the time: Callaghan, *Time and Chance*, 98, 99.
27. Dalton, *Memoirs*, III, 337-8.
28. Foot, *Bevan*, II, 275; Dalton, *Diaries*, 461: cit. Pimlott, *Wilson*, 149.
29. Donoughue and Jones, *Morrison*, 448-9.
30. F. Williams, *A Prime Minister Remembers* (1961), 227-8.
31. Donoughue and Jones, *Morrison*, 448-9.
32. Donoughue and Jones, *Morrison*, 448-9; Pimlott, *Dalton*, 573; Harris, *Attlee*, pb edn, 438-441.
33. Wheeler-Bennett, *George VI*, 771.
34. Ibid., 772.
35. The letters, spanning the period 24 April – 2 May 1950, are usefully reproduced in Jennings, *Cabinet Government,* 3rd edn, Appendix, and in Wilson, *Cases and Materials on Constitutional and Administrative Law*, 21-6.
36. *The Times*, 2 May 1950.
37. Marshall, *Constitutional Conventions*, 215.
38. Harris, *Attlee*, 486.
39. Ibid.
40. Ibid., 487.
41. Interview with Frank Barber, *News Chronicle*, 20 April 1959: quot. Foot, *Bevan*, II, 349.
42. Attlee, *As It Happened*, 206-7; *Granada Interview*, 47

43. Dalton, *Memoirs*, III, 376-7, Pimlott, *Dalton*, 605.

44. Jay, *Change and Fortune*, 209-10.

45. Harris, *Attlee*, 485.

46. Ibid., 486; Donoughue and Jones, *Morrison*, 501-2.

47. Williams, *Gaitskell*, 283.

48. Donoughue and Jones, *Morrison*, 501-2.

49. Dalton, *Diaries*, 19 September 1951: quot. Donoughue and Jones, *Morrison*, 502.

50. Williams, *Gaitskell*, 283.

51. See Wheeler-Bennett, *George VI*, 790-4.

52. P.R.O. Cab 23/58 and 23/59, 1 and 10 October 1928: cit. Markesinis, *Dissolution*, 107.

53. While Sir John Colville is highly informative about the resignation of Churchill in *The Fringes of Power*, Lord Moran has more information about the timing of the election.

54. Moran Diary, 1 April 1954: cit. Gilbert, *Churchill*, VIII, 965.

55. Churchill to Eden, 24 August 1954: ibid., 1050-1.

56. Ibid., 1102-4.

57. Moran, *Churchill*, 673

58. Macmillan Diary, 30 March 1955: quot. Gilbert, *Churchill*, VIII, 1105.

59. Moran, *Churchill*, 673

60. Gilbert, *Churchill*, VIII, 1118.

61. Ibid., 1126.

62. Avon, *Memoirs*, I, 270.

63. Ibid., 272.

64. Carlton, *Eden*, pb edn, 371-2.

65. Moran, *Churchill*, 708-9.

66. Ibid.

67. Macmillan Diary, 3 April 1959: quot. Macmillan, *Memoirs*, IV, 744.

68. Ibid., 745.

69. Ibid., 746.

70. Ibid., 750; see also Horne, *Macmillan*, II, 145ff.

71. D. Butler and A. King, *The British General Election of 1964* (1965), 80-1.

72. Callaghan, *Time and Chance*, 154.

73. Howard and West, *Making of the Prime Minister*, 134-5.

74. Howard, *RAB*, 331.

75. Howard and West, *Making of the Prime Minister*, 135.

76. Butler and King, *Election of 1964*, 81.

77. Home, *Way the Wind Blows*, 212.

78. Ibid.

79. Wilson, *Labour Government*, 159.

80. Ibid.

81. M. Williams, *Inside Number 10* (1972; pb edn 1973), 78.

82. Wilson, *Labour Government*, 201.

83. *The Times*, 1 March 1966: cit. Pimlott, *Wilson*, 396.

84. Cecil King Diary, 27 February 1966: *Diaries*, I, 59; Pimlott,*Wilson*, 396.

85. Barbara Castle Diary: *Diaries*, I, 109.

86. Crossman Diary, 28 February 1966: *Diaries*, I, 464.

87. Jenkins, *Life at the Centre*, 297.

88. Wilson, *Labour Government*, 778.

89. Haines, *Politics of Power*, 170.

90. Personal knowledge.

91. There is a peripheral reference in the Crossman Diary, 29 April 1970: *Diaries*, III, 904.

92. Wilson, *Labour Government*, 775.

93. Jenkins, *Life at the Centre*, 296-7.

94. Haines, *Politics of Power*, 170.

95. Ibid.

96. Ibid.

97. Jenkins, *Life at the Centre*, 296; Castle Diary, 29 April 1970: *Diaries*, I, 792-3.

98. Ibid.

99. Ibid.; and Crossman Diary, 29 April 1970: *Diaries*, III, 904-5.

100. Ibid.

101. Ibid.

102. Wilson, *Labour Government*, 781; Castle Diary, 14 May 1970: *Diaries*, I, 799; Crossman Diary, 14 May 1970: *Diaries*, III, 920-1; Williams, *Inside Number 10*, 333; Pimlott, *Wilson*, 554.

103. N. St John-Stevas, *The Two Cities* (1984), 69-70.

104. W. Whitelaw, *The Whitelaw Memoirs* (1989; pb edn, 1990), 155, 169-70; *Sunday Times*, 7 May 1989: quot. Campbell, *Heath*, 587.

105. S. Fay and H. Young, *The Fall of Heath* (1976), 26: quot. Campbell, *Heath*, 585.

106. Parkinson, *Right at the Centre*, 122.

107. D. Hurd, *An End to Promises* (1979), 130; see also 118-30.

108. Ibid., 130.

109. J. Prior, *A Balance of Power* (1986), 92.

110. Ben Pimlott, interview with Joe Haines: Pimlott, *Wilson*, 624.

111. Wilson, *Final Term*, 37, 44, 49.

112. Castle Diary, 18 September 1974: *Diaries*, II, 185.

113. Callaghan, *Time and Chance*, 462-3.

114. Benn Diary, 13 September 1977: *Diaries*, IV, 214.

115. Ibid., 303-4, 23 May 1978.

116. Donoughue, *Prime Minister*, 164.

117. Ibid., 160.

118. Benn Diary, 2 September 1978: *Diaries*, IV, 332-3.

119. Callaghan, *Time and Chance*, 514.

120. Healey, *Time of My Life*, 461-2.

121. Callaghan, *Time and Chance*, 515.

122. Ibid., 517.

123. Benn Diary, 1 February 1979, 14 March 1979: *Diaries*, IV, 431, 472.

124. Callaghan, *Time and Chance*, 561, 563.

125. N. Tebbit, *Upwardly Mobile* (1988; pb edn 1989), 252-3.

126. Ibid., 255

127. Prior, *Balance of Power*, 149.

128. Tebbit, *Upwardly Mobile*, 256.

129. Thatcher, *Downing Street Years*, 288-9; Parkinson, *Right at the Centre*, 223-4; Tebbit, *Upwardly Mobile*, 256-9.

130. Thatcher, *Downing Street Years*, 569, 574-5; Tebbit, *Upwardly Mobile*, 331; Lawson, *View from No. 11*, 694-5; Whitelaw, *Memoirs*, 349.

131. *Election Call*, BBC1 and Radio 4, 8 April 1992.

Select Bibliography

Addison, P., *The Road to 1945* (1975)

Alexander, A. and Watkins, A., *The Making of the Prime Minister 1970* (1970)

Anderson, B., 'New Leader, New Voting?', *Spectator*, 17 May 1997

Attlee, C.R., *As It Happened* (1954)

—— *Clem Attlee: the Granada Historical Records Interview* (1967)

Avon, Earl of, *Memoirs* (3 vols, 1960-5)

Bagehot, W., *The English Constitution* (1867, World's Classics edn 1928) and in *Collected Works* ed N. St John-Stevas, V (1974). See also Crossman, R.H.S.

Baker, K., *The Turbulent Years: My Life in Politics* (1993)

Ball, S., 'The 1922 Committee: the Formative Years 1922-45', 9 *Parliamentary History* (1990)

—— and Seldon, A. (eds), *The Heath Government 1970-4* (1996)

Barber, J., *The Prime Minister Since 1945* (1991)

Barnes, S., *Behind the Image* (1974). See also Crosland, S.

Bassett, R., *Nineteen Thirty-One: Political Crisis* (1958)

Beaverbrook, Lord, *The Decline and Fall of Lloyd George* (1963)

Benn, T., *Diaries* ed R. Winstone (6 vols 1987-94, 1 vol pb edn 1996)

Berkeley, H., *Crossing the Floor* (1972)

Bevan, A., *In Place of Fear* (1952, new edn 1978)

Blake, R., *The Unknown Prime Minister: the Life and Times of Andrew Bonar Law 1858-1923* (1955)

—— *The Conservative Party from Peel to Major* (1970, 3rd edn 1997)

—— 'Anthony Eden' in *Dictionary of National Biography 1971-80* (1986)

—— and Louis, W.R. (eds), *Churchill* (1993, pb edn 1996)

Bogdanor, V., *The Monarchy and the Consitution* (1995)

Brazier, R., *Constitutional Practice* (1988, pb edn 1994)

—— *Ministers of the Crown* (1997)

Brivati, B., *Hugh Gaitskell* (1996)

Burk, K. and Cairncross, A., *Goodbye, Great Britain: the 1976 IMF Crisis* (1992)

Butler, D.E., *The Electoral System in Britain 1918-51* (1953)

—— *British General Elections since 1945* (1989)

—— and King, A., *The British General Election of 1964* (1965)

—— and Butler, G., *British Political Facts* (1963, 7th edn 1994)

Butler, R.A., *The Art of the Possible* (1971, pb edn 1973)

—— *The Art of Memory* (1982)

Cadogan, A., *Diaries 1938-45* ed. D. Dilks (1971)

Callaghan, J., *Time and Chance* (1987)

Campbell, J., *Nye Bevan and the Mirage of British Socialism* (1987)

—— *Edward Heath* (1993)

Carlton, D., *Anthony Eden* (1981, pb edn 1986)

Castle, B., *Diaries* (2 vols 1980-4, 1 vol pb edn 1990)

Channon, H., *Diaries* ed R. Rhodes James (1967)

Churchill, R.S., *Lord Derby: King of Lancashire* (1959)

—— *The Fight for the Tory Leadership* (1964)

—— *Winston S. Churchill* (I-II 1966-7)

Churchill, W.S., *Great Contemporaries* (1937, pb edn 1959)

—— *The Second World War* (6 vols 1948-54)

Clark, A., *Diaries* (1993)

Colville, J., *The Fringes of Power* (1985, 2 vol pb edn 1986)

Connolly, B., *The Rotten Heart of Europe: the Dirty War for Europe's Money* (1995)

Cowling, M., *The Impact of Labour 1920-4* (1971)

Crosland, S., *Tony Crosland* (1982, pb edn 1983)

—— *Looking Out, Looking In* (1987). See also Barnes, S.

Crossman, R.H.S., *Cabinet Diaries* ed J. Morgan (3 vols 1975-7); ed A. Howard (1 vol 1979)

—— *Backbench Diaries* ed J. Morgan (1981)

—— Introduction to W. Bagehot, *The English Constitution* (Fontana pb edn 1963)

Cudlipp, H., *Walking on the Water* (1976)

Curzon, Lady, *Reminiscences* (1955)

Dalton, H., *Memoirs* (3 vols 1953-62)

—— *Diaries* ed B. Pimlott (2 vols 1986-7)

de Smith, S.A. and Brazier, R., *Constitutional and Administrative Law* (1971, 7th edn 1994)

Devlin, P., *Taken at the Flood* (1996)

Dickie, J., *The Uncommon Commoner: a Study of Sir Alec Douglas-Home* (1964)

Donoughue, B., *Prime Minister* (1987)

—— and Jones, G.W., *Herbert Morrison: Portrait of a Politician* (1973)

Douglas, R., *A History of the Liberal Party 1895-1970* (1971)

Dugdale, B.E.C., *Arthur James Balfour* (2 vols 1936)

Edwards, J.Ll.J., *The Law Officers of the Crown* (1964)

Falkender, M., *Downing Street in Perspective* (1983). See also Williams, M.

Fay, S. and Young, H., *The Fall of Heath* (1976)

Feiling, K., *Neville Chamberlain* (1940)

Fisher, N., *Iain Macleod* (1973)

—— *The Tory Leaders* (1977)

Foot, M., *Aneurin Bevan* (2 vols 1962-73)

Gaitskell, H., *Diary 1945-56* ed P.M. Williams (1983)

Gilbert, M., *Winston S. Churchill* (III-VIII 1971-88)

Gilmour, D., *Curzon* (1994)

Gilmour, I., *The Body Politic* (1969)

—— *Dancing with Dogma: Britain under Thatcherism* (1992)

—— 'Holding All the Strings', *London Review of Books*, 27 July 1989

Goodhart, P., *The 1922* (1973)

Gordon Walker, P., *The Cabinet* (1970, rev pb edn 1972)

Gould, B., *Goodbye to All That* (1995)

Griffith, J.A.G., *The Politics of the Judiciary* (1977, 5th edn 1997)

—— 'A Pilgrim's Progress', 22 *Journal of Law and Society* (1995)

—— and Ryle, M., *Parliament* (1989)

Hailsham, Lord, *A Sparrow's Flight* (1990)

Haines, J., *The Politics of Power* (1977)

Harris, K., *Attlee* (1982, rev pb edn 1995)

Harris, R., *The Making of Neil Kinnock* (1984)

—— *Good and Faithful Servant: the Unauthorised Biography of Bernard Ingham* (1990)

Harrod, R.F., *The Life of John Maynard Keynes* (1951, pb edn 1972)

Hattersley, R., *Who Goes Home?* (1995)

Healey, D., *The Time of My Life* (1989)

Hennessy, P., *Cabinet* (1986)

—— *The Hidden Wiring: Unearthing the British Constitution* (1995)

—— *Muddling Through: Power, Politics and the Quality of Government in Postwar Britain* (1996)

—— 'Her Majesty's Puzzle: Politics, the Monarchy and the Constitution' (Johnian Society Lecture 1997)

Heuston, R.F.V., *Lives of the Lord Chancellors* (2 vols 1964-87)

Hollis, P., *Jennie Lee: a Life* (1997)

Home, Lord, *The Way the Wind Blows* (1976)

Horne, A., *Macmillan* (2 vols 1988-9)

Howard, A., *RAB: the Life of R.A. Butler* (1987, pb edn 1988)

—— *Crossman: the Pursuit of Power* (1990)

—— and West, R., *The Making of the Prime Minister* (1965)

Howe, G., *Conflict of Loyalty* (1994)

Hunter, L., *The Road to Brighton Pier* (1959)

Hurd, D., *An End to Promises* (1979)

Hutchinson, G., *Edward Heath* (1970)

—— *The Last Edwardian at No. 10* (1980)

Jay, D., *Change and Fortune: a Political Record* (1980)

Jenkins, C., *All Against the Collar* (1990)

Jenkins, R., *Asquith* (1964, rev edn 1978)

—— *Baldwin* (1987)

—— *A Life at the Centre* (1991)

Jenkins, S., *Accountable to None: the Tory Nationalisation of Britain* (1995, pb edn 1996)

Jennings, I., *The Law and the Constitution* (1933, 5th edn 1959)

—— *Cabinet Government* (1936, 3rd edn 1959)

—— *Parliament* (1939, 2nd edn 1961)

—— *The Queen's Government* (1954)

Johnson, P., 'Was the Palace to Blame?', *New Statesman*, 24 January 1964, in *Statesmen and Nations* (1971)

Jones, M., *Michael Foot* (1994)

Jones, T., *Whitehall Diaries* (3 vols 1969-71)

Keynes, J.M., *The Economic Consequences of the Peace* (1919) and in *Collected Works*, II (1971)

Kilmuir, Earl of, *Political Adventure* (1964)

King, A. (ed), *Britain at the Polls 1992* (1992)

King, C.H., *Diaries* (2 vols 1972-5)

Kogan, D. and Kogan, M., *The Battle for the Labour Party* (1982)

Koss, S., *Asquith* (1976, pb edn 1985)

Kramnick, I. and Sheerman, B., *Harold Laski: a Life on the Left* (1993)

Kyle, K., *Suez* (1991)

Lamb, R., *The Macmillan Years: the Emerging Truth* (1995)

Laski, H.J., *Parliamentary Government in England* (1938)

Lawson, N., *The View from No. 11* (1992)

Leapman, M., *Kinnock* (1987)

Le May, G.H.L., *The Victorian Constitution* (1979)

Longford, Earl of, *Five Lives* (1964)

Mackail, J.W. and Wyndham, G., *Life and Letters of George Wyndham* (2 vols 1925)

Mackintosh, J.P., *The British Cabinet* (1962, 2nd edn 1968)

Macleod, I., 'The Tory Leadership', *Spectator*, 17 January 1964

Macmillan, H., *Memoirs* (6 vols 1966-73)

McSmith, A., *John Smith: a Life 1938-94* (1993, rev pb edn 1994)

Margach, J., *The Abuse of Power* (1978)

Markesinis, B.S., *The Theory and Practice of Dissolution of Parliament* (1972)

Marnham, P., *Trail of Havoc: in the Steps of Lord Lucan* (1987, rev edn 1988)

Marquand, D., *Ramsay MacDonald* (1977)

Marshall, G., *Constitutional Conventions* (1984, pb edn 1986)

—— and Moodie, G.C., *Some Problems of the Constitution* (1959, 4th pb edn 1967)

Meyer, A., *Stand Up and Be Counted* (1990)
Middlemass, K. and Barnes, J., *Baldwin* (1969)
Mikardo, I., *Backbencher* (1988)
Montague Browne, A., *Long Sunset* (1995)
Moran, Lord, *Winston Churchill: the Struggle for Survival 1940-65* (1966, pb edn 1968)
Morgan, K.O., *Keir Hardie: Radical and Socialist* (1975, pb edn 1984)
—— *Consensus and Disunity: the Lloyd George Coalition Government 1918-22* (1979)
—— *Callaghan: a Life* (1997)
Mosley, L., *Curzon* (1960, Readers Union edn 1961)
Mount, F., *The British Constitution Now: Recovery or Decline?* (1992)
Muggeridge, M., *The Thirties* (1940, new edn 1967)
Nicolson, H., *Curzon: the Last Phase* (1934)
—— *King George the Fifth: His Life and Reign* (1952)
—— *Diaries and Letters* ed N. Nicolson (3 vols 1966-8, pb edn 1969-71)
Neustadt, R., *Alliance Politics* (1970)
Owen, D., *Time to Declare* (1991)
Oxford and Asquith, Earl of, *Fifty Years of Parliament* (2 vols 1926)
—— *Memories and Reflections* (2 vols 1928)
Parkinson, C., *Right at the Centre* (1992)
Paterson, P., *Tired and Emotional: the Life of Lord George-Brown* (1993)
Pelling, H., *A Short History of the Labour Party* (1961, 10th edn 1993)
—— *Origins of the Labour Party* (1954)
Pimlott, B., *Hugh Dalton* (1985, new pb edn 1995)
—— *Harold Wilson* (1992)
—— *The Queen: a Biography of Elizabeth II* (1996)
Postgate, R., *The Life of George Lansbury* (1951)
Prior, J., *A Balance of Power* (1986)
Rentoul, J., *Tony Blair* (1995, rev pb edn 1996)
Rhodes James, R., *Memoirs of a Conservative: J.C.C. Davidson's Memoirs and Papers 1910-37* (1969)
—— *Anthony Eden* (1986, pb edn 1987)
Riddell, P., *The Thatcher Era* (1983, rev edn 1991)
—— *Honest Opportunism: the Rise of the Career Politician* (1993)
Roberts, A., *The Holy Fox: a Life of Lord Halifax* (1991, pb edn 1992)
—— *Eminent Churchillians* (1994)
Rose, K., *King George V* (1983, pb edn 1984)
Roth, A., *Sir Harold Wilson: Yorkshire Walter Mitty* (1977)
St John-Stevas, N., *The Two Cities* (1984)
Shaw, E., *Discipline and Discord in the Labour Party* (1988)
Shepherd, R., *The Power Brokers* (1991)
—— *Iain Macleod* (1994)
—— *Enoch Powell* (1996)
Shore, P., *Leading the Left* (1993)
Simon, Viscount, *Retrospect* (1952)
Skidelsky, R., *John Maynard Keynes* (2 vols 1983-92)
Smith, D., *Harold Wilson: a Critical Biography* (1964)
Sopel, J., *Tony Blair: the Moderniser* (1995)
Steel, D., *Against Goliath* (1989)
Stewart, W., *J. Keir Hardie* (1921)
Stuart of Findhorn, Viscount, *Within the Fringe* (1967)
Taylor, A.J.P., *English History 1914-45* (1965)
—— *Beaverbrook* (1972, pb edn 1974)
—— (ed), *My Darling Pussy: the Letters of Lloyd George and Frances Stevenson* (1975)
—— 'Politics in the First World War' in *Politics in Wartime and Other Essays* (1964)

Tebbit, N., *Upwardly Mobile* (1988, pb edn 1989)
Templewood, Viscount, *Nine Troubled Years* (1954)
Thatcher, M., *The Downing Street Years* (1993)
Thorpe, D.R., *Selwyn Lloyd* (1989)
—— *Alec Douglas-Home* (1996)
Walters, D., *Not Always with the Pack* (1989)
Wapshott, N. and Brock, G., *Thatcher* (1983)
Watkins, A., *The Liberal Dilemma* (1966)
—— *Brief Lives: with Some Memoirs* (1982)
—— *A Slight Case of Libel: Meacher v Trelford and Others* (1990)
—— *A Conservative Coup: the Fall of Margaret Thatcher* (1991, 2nd pb edn 1992)
Webb, B., *Diaries* ed N. and J. MacKenzie (4 vols 1982-5)
Wheeler-Bennett, J.W., *King George VI: His Life and Reign* (1958)
Whitelaw, W., *The Whitelaw Memoirs* (1989, pb edn 1990)
Wigg, Lord, *George Wigg* (1972)
Williams, F., *A Prime Minister Remembers* (1961)
Williams, M., *Inside Number 10* (1972, pb edn 1975). See also Falkender, M.
Williams, P.M., *Hugh Gaitskell* (1979)
Williamson, P., *National Crisis and National Government* (1992)
Wilson, G., *Cases and Materials on Constitutional and Administrative Law* (1966)
Wilson, H., *The Labour Government 1964-70* (1971)
—— *Final Term: the Labour Government 1974-6* (1979)
Wrench, J.E., *Geoffrey Dawson and Our Times* (1955)
Wright, P., *Spycatcher* (1987)
Young, G.M., *Stanley Baldwin* (1952)
Young, K., *Arthur James Balfour* (1963)

Index